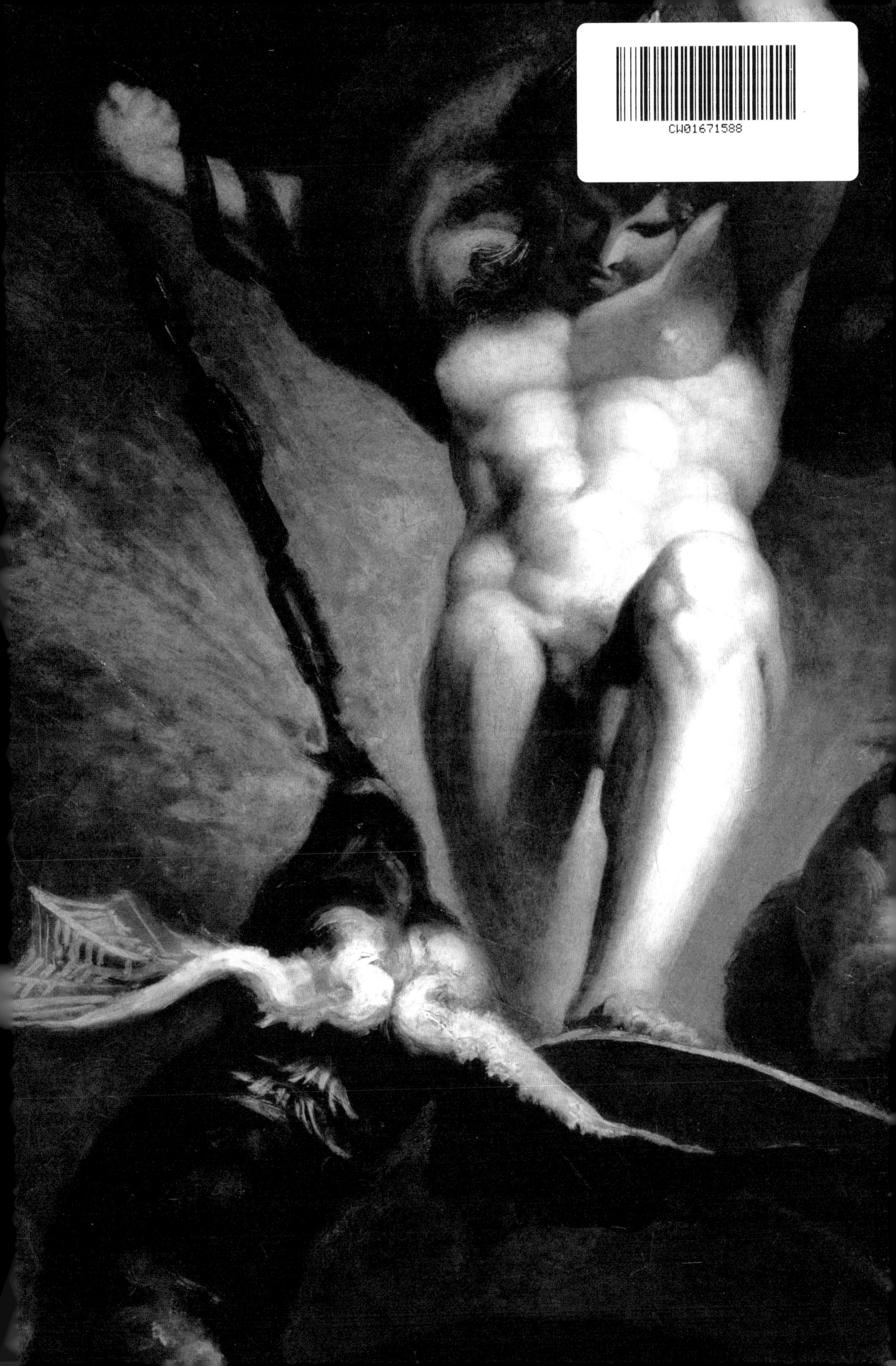

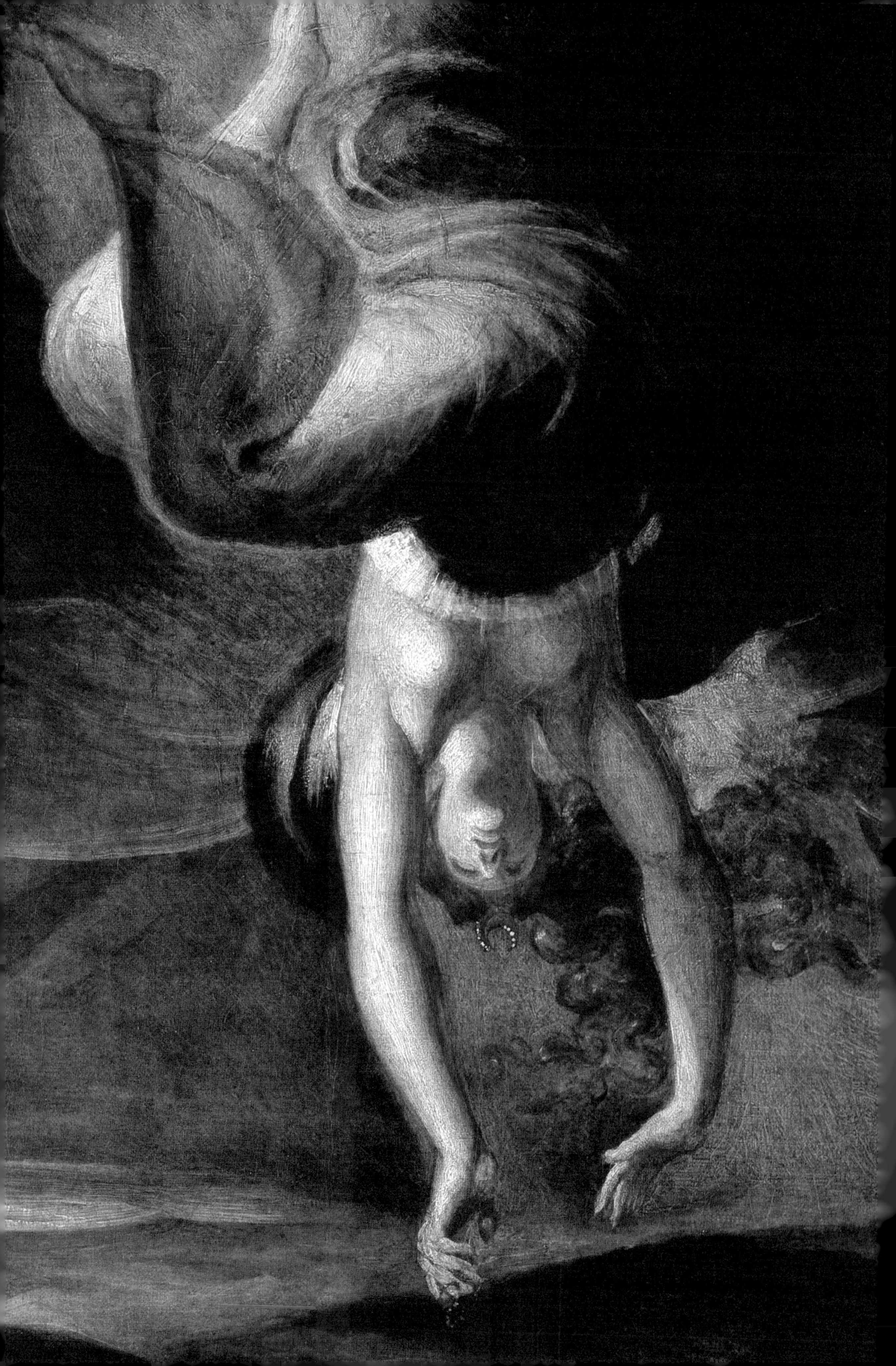

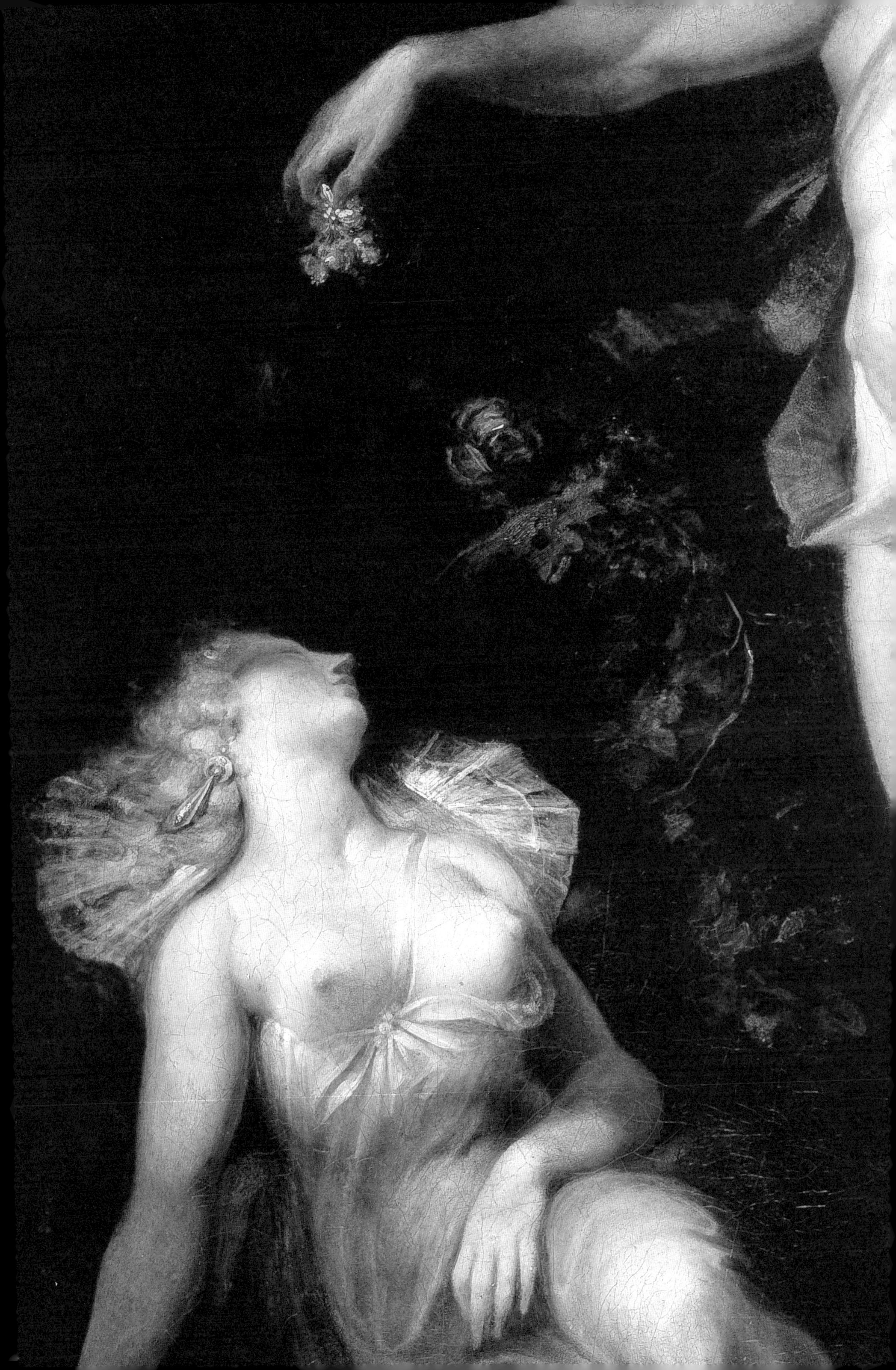

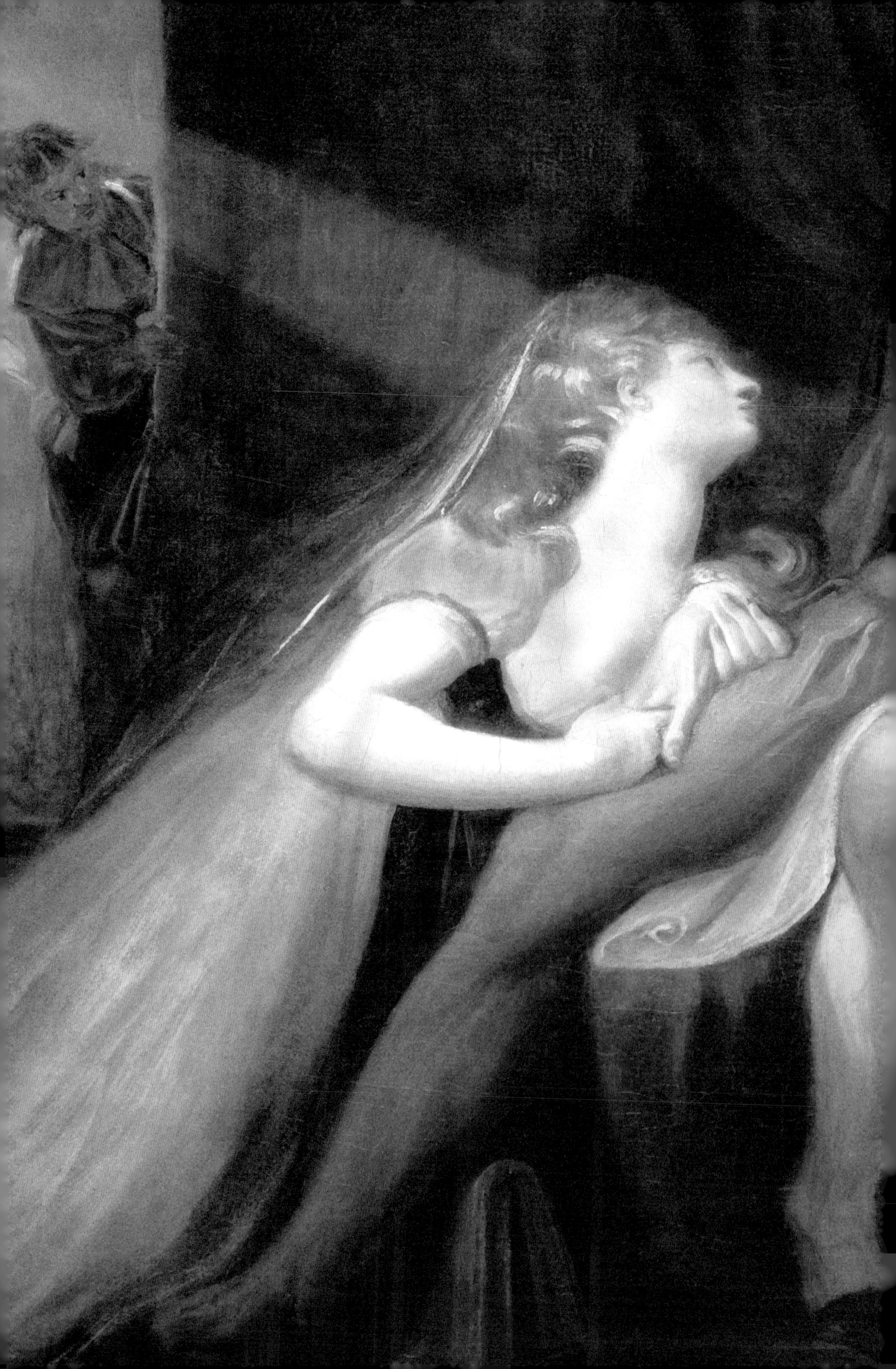

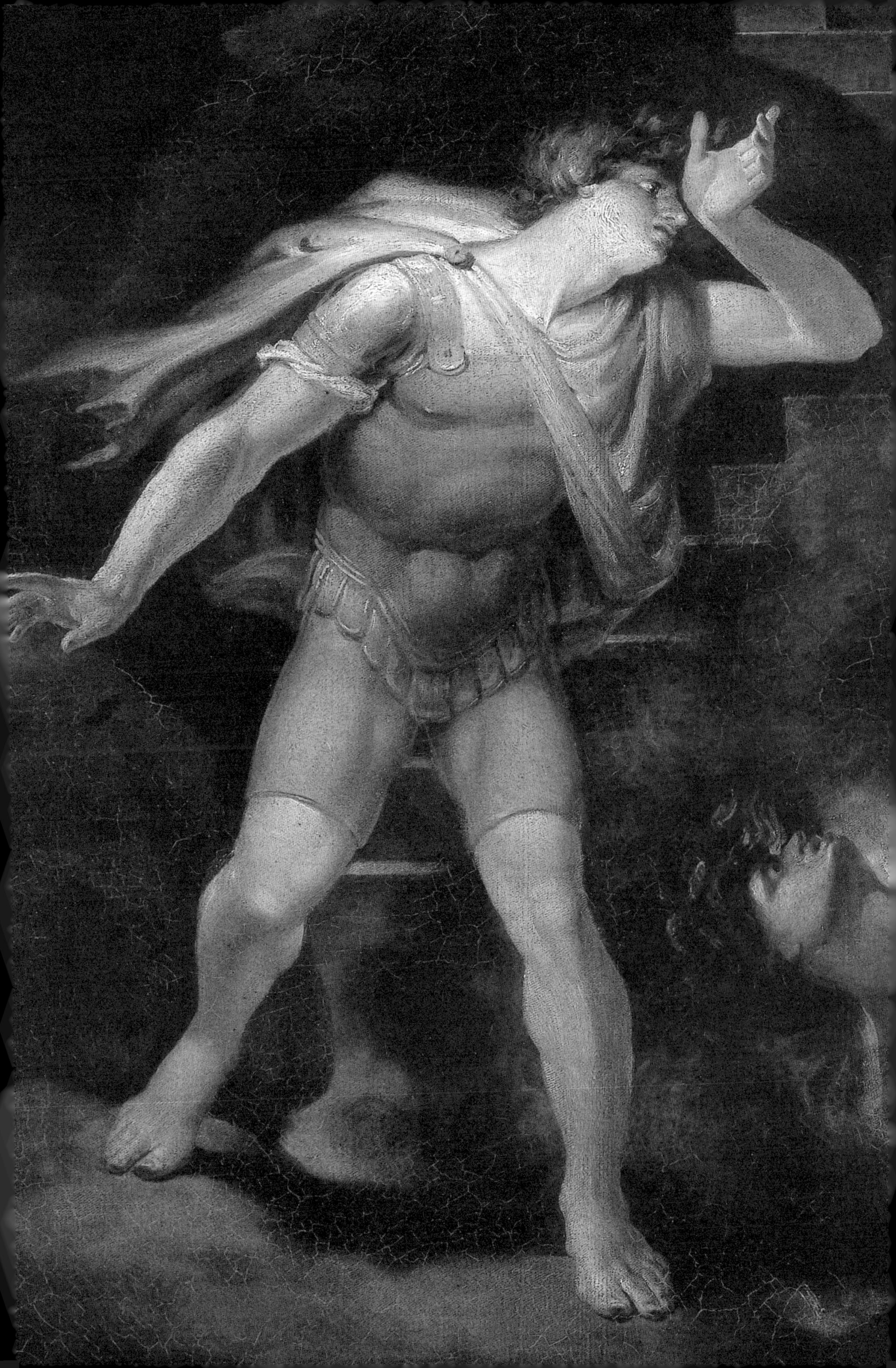

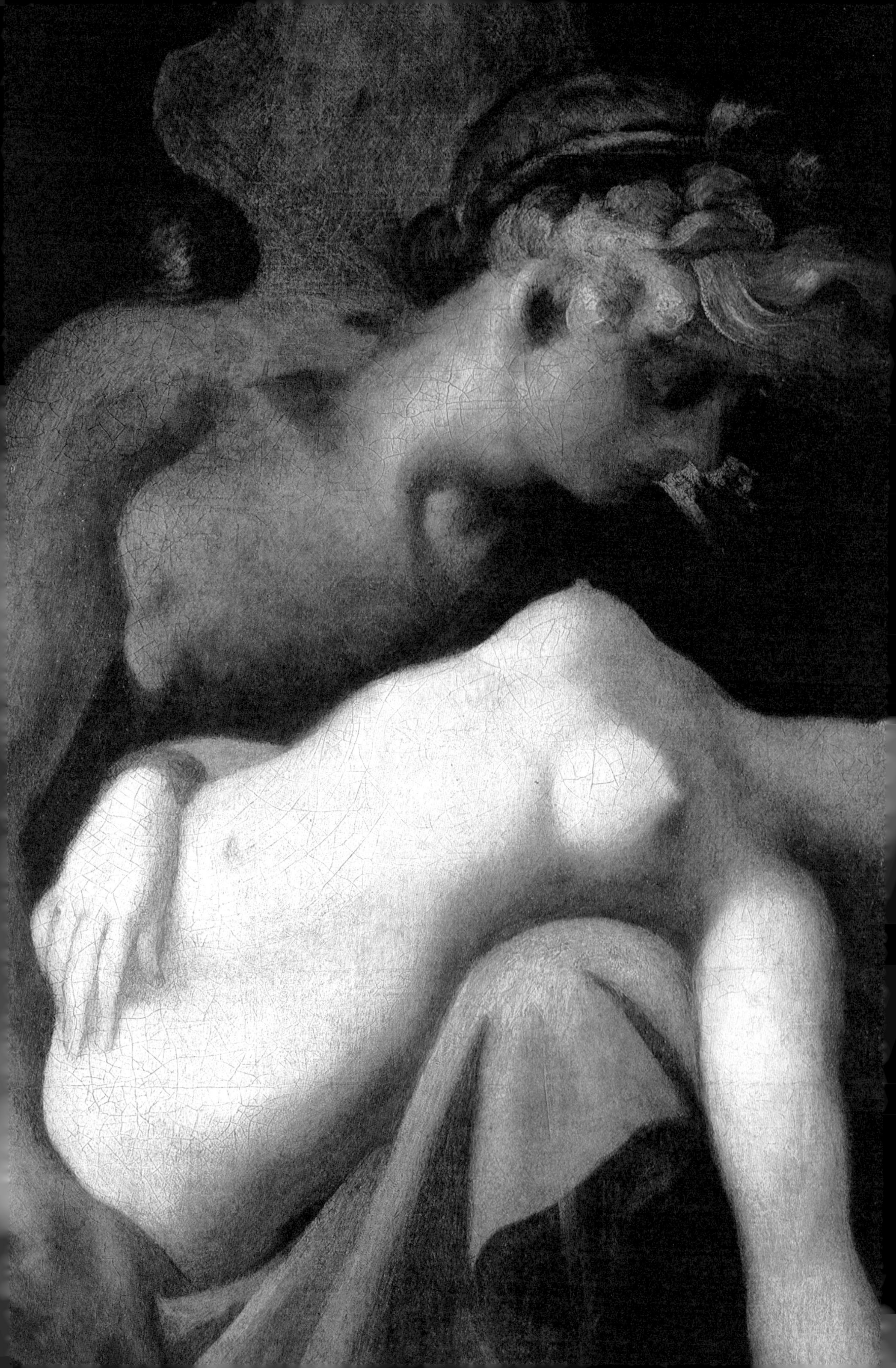

Fuseli
Drama and Theatre

Kunstmuseum Basel

Fuseli
Drama and Theatre

Edited by Eva Reifert with Claudia Blank
With contributions by Beate Hochholdinger-Reiterer, Alexander Honold, Thom Luz, Caroline Rae and Eva Reifert

PRESTEL
Munich · London · New York

Preface and Acknowledgments

Henry Fuseli (Johann Heinrich Füssli) is in many respects an artist of transitions and transgressions. Geographically speaking, his biography links his Swiss origins with his adopted country, England; art-historically speaking he stands on the threshold between Classicism and Romanticism; and, finally, his oeuvre develops from a close dialogue between literature and visual art. The renown of the artist, who polarized opinion during his lifetime and acquired the nickname of 'the wild Swiss' in London, was founded on the scandal-provoking picture *The Nightmare* (Detroit Institute of Arts), which triggered both horror and fascination in the public when it was first exhibited at London's Royal Academy in 1782.

Basel has a long tradition of engaging with the work of this self-taught artist, who cared little for artistic conventions and instead gave free reign to his imagination. Our exhibition, with its focus on the worlds of literature and theatre, encourages immersion in forms of visual storytelling, as well as close attention to Fuseli's painterly staging strategies in relation to the contemporary theatre. Both of these aspects provide an ideal context for those Fuseli paintings in our collections that are based on literary themes, ranging from Shakespeare to William Cowper.

No special exhibition can manage without the support and trust of its lenders, be they private individuals or institutions. First and foremost we would like to express our immense gratitude to Kunsthaus Zürich, in particular to Christoph Becker and Philippe Büttner, who supported our project with goodwill and expertise from the start. Without the numerous, generously granted loans from the collection of the Kunsthaus Zürich this exhibition would not have been possible. We also owe a big thank-you to our colleagues at the Goethe-Museum Frankfurt, in particular for the very helpful support of its director, Mareike Hennig. We sincerely thank Martin Myrone of the Tate and Mark Evans of the Victoria and Albert Museum, both London, for their collegial advice and assistance as well as for important loans. We also wish to express our heartfelt thanks to the Folger Shakespeare Library in Washington for important works in the exhibition, as well as the Kunst Museum Winterthur, the Kunstmuseum Luzern and the Museum zu Allerheiligen in Schaffhausen for their contributions.

On the private side, the dedicated commitment of Ulla Dreyfus-Best deserves a particular mention; our gratitude is also due to the Stiftung für Kunst, Kultur und Geschichte. Furthermore, we express our sincere thanks for all the other loans from private and public collections in Europe, the USA and Australia.

Petra Maisak, the former head of the Goethe-Museum in Frankfurt who is acknowledged as one of the foremost experts in the field of Fuseli studies, Franziska Lentzsch, who organised the last great retrospective of the artist's work in Switzerland, and Andreas Beyer of the University of Basel were sources of inspiring conversation and advice during the preparation of the exhibition. The early appreciation of Fuseli in Basel by Paul Ganz was greatly illuminated by the information contributed by Conrad Ulrich, Zurich, to the Fuseli Society, for which we express our thanks. In particular, however, I wish to thank my colleague Eva Reifert, curator of Nineteenth-Century and Modern Art at the Kunstmuseum Basel, for her clear vision and unwavering commitment.

This catalogue brings together perspectives from different disciplines. My sincere thanks go to the authors Beate Hochholdinger-Reiterer, Alexander Honold, Caroline Rae and Thom Luz who, with Eva Reifert, were ready to look beyond their respective disciplinary boundaries. In the curatorial field, the project was ably supported by Claudia Blank. Many thanks to our colleagues from the Old Masters department, Bodo Brinkmann and Gabriel Dette, who also contributed to the catalogue. In the context of preparing this exhibition, we were able to undertake a comprehensive analysis of the Fuseli paintings in our collection. For this research in the field of conservation I would like to thank our conservators Werner Müller and Sophie Eichner. For the careful design of this catalogue we thank Büro 146 in Zurich. We thank the team at the Prestel publishing house, Anja Besserer, Katharina Haderer and Cilly Klotz, for their careful coordination. For the printing of this book we are grateful for the support of the Berta Hess-Cohn Stiftung, Basel.

Without the financial support of the Sulger Stiftung, the Isaac Dreyfus-Bernheim Stiftung and the Foundation for the Kunstmuseum Basel we would not have been able to realize this exhibition.

Josef Helfenstein,
Director

Lenders

Aarau, Aargauer Kunsthaus
The Art Institute of Chicago
Dallas Museum of Art
Staatliche Kunstsammlungen Dresden
Frankfurt am Main, Frankfurter Goethe-Museum
Hamburger Kunsthalle
Staatliche Kunsthalle Karlsruhe
Liverpool, Walker Art Gallery
London, King's College
London, Tate
London, Victoria and Albert Museum
Kunstmuseum Luzern
Lytham St Annes Art Collection, Fylde Borough Council
Mamiano Traversetolo, Fondazione Magnani Rocca
Melbourne, National Gallery of Victoria
New Haven, Yale Center for British Art
New Haven, Yale University Art Gallery
New York, The Metropolitan Museum of Art
Paris, Musée du Louvre
Schaffhausen, Museum zu Allerheiligen
Staatsgalerie Stuttgart
Stratford-upon-Avon, Royal Shakespeare Company
Washington, D. C., Folger Shakespeare Library
Kunst Museum Winterthur
Winterthur, Stiftung für Kunst, Kultur und Geschichte
Kunsthaus Zürich
Kunstsammlung des Kantons Zürich
Städtische Kunstsammlung Zürich
together with private collectors who prefer
to remain anonymous

Sponsors

The exhibition was generously supported by:
Sulger Stiftung
Isaac Dreyfus-Bernheim Stiftung
Foundation for the Kunstmuseum Basel
The catalogue was printed with the support of
the Berta Hess-Cohn Stiftung, Basel.

Fuseli. Drama and Theatre
Eva Reifert

In 1934, Paul Ganz, the former conservator of the Kunstmuseum Basel, wrote to the physician and Fuseli enthusiast Konrad Ulrich in Zurich: 'We need to establish a small well-funded club whose objective it will be to secure for the greatest of Swiss masters the renown he deserves.'[1] Three years later, the two men and several associates founded the Fuseli Society, whose mission was 'to elevate the art of the father of Romanticism Henry Fuseli, which languishes in obscurity, to the station commensurate with its true value'. They acquired some of Fuseli's paintings, brought them to Switzerland and sent them to exhibitions to spread the word about him. Their activities showed some success: by 1945, the public had been able to see the artist's works not only in Zurich and Basel, but also in Paris, Frankfurt and Geneva.[2]

Fuseli's popularity has risen considerably in the intervening decades, thanks in no small part to his spellbinding depictions of ghosts and dream scenes – who doesn't know *The Nightmare*? They have earned the artist the reputation of an early exponent of 'Gothic Art'. It was not until 2005 that a retrospective at the Kunsthaus Zürich – which now holds the single most important collection of Fuseli's works on paper and canvas – outlined the context in which his art emerged by presenting drawings from his years in Rome and portraying the London art scene of his time.[3] Building on this more comprehensive understanding of his oeuvre, we can now organize the presentation in Basel around a twofold focus: on the one hand, *Drama and Theatre* examines a core question and mainspring of Fuseli's art, the role of great literature as a key source of inspiration;[4] on the other hand, this thematic orientation lay behind the decision to centre the show on the artist's paintings, leaving aside his works on paper.

A cursory survey of Fuseli's paintings reveals how little interest the imitation of nature and classical ideals held for him: their most salient quality – muscular heroes whose anatomy he bent at will in his quest for exalted gestures, scenes illuminated by hard lighting and yet suffused with an impenetrable dark mystery – is that they are immediately recognizable. The subjects, however, are the fancies of an extraordinarily well-read intellectual's mind. Instead of painting what he saw or submitting to the constraints of what might be possible in reality, Fuseli tapped into his imagination and mined world literature for a rich variety of extreme emotions.

Dedicated sections of our exhibition accordingly explore the inspiration he found in ancient and medieval legends, more recent and contemporary literature, the tragedies and comedies of Shakespeare and Milton's verse epic *Paradise Lost.* A special section gauges the extent to which his compositions are informed by narrative patterns even when he did not draw on an identifiable literary source.

Fuseli's firm belief in the primacy of the imagination and the enthusiasm for the theatre sparked in him by the encounter with Shakespeare's dramas in particular are two central pillars of his conception of art. To shed more light on these aspects, we venture outside the confines of art history and hand the floor to historians of literature and the theatre. Alexander Honold traces the formative influence of the poetological ideas of Johann Jakob Bodmer and Johann Jakob Breitinger, Fuseli's teachers in Zurich, on his understanding of art. Beate Hochholdinger-Reiterer reconstructs the beginnings of the artist's interest in Shakespeare's works and pinpoints the developments in the London theatre scene from the 1760s onward that allowed the dramatic arts to become a key influence on Fuseli's art. In this sense, *Drama and Theatre* spotlights the dramas, tragedies, comedies, legends and poems that Fuseli came to know through performances or that fired up that avid reader's imagination. Yet the exhibition's theme may also be taken adjectivally, identifying the hallmarks of his art – the 'dramatic' and 'theatrical' qualities of the narrative painting whose conception and execution bespeak the artist's fervent embrace of the spectacular.

Given the focus of our presentation, the opportunity to bring in practitioners of contemporary theatre was too good to pass up. Thom Luz, the resident director at Theater Basel, created a production that responds to Fuseli's atmospheric and often enigmatic works; he offers his reflections on this creative dialogue in an artist's statement in these pages. Caroline Rae examines the possibility that Fuseli's dramatic chiaroscuro may have been heightened by gradual alterations of the colour characteristics of his paints and conservation measures.

The exhibition's focus on the themes of literature and theatre is reflected in the concentration on the more dramatic medium of Fuseli's artistic production, his painterly translations of those themes. Fuseli had first made a name for himself with drawings: works in pen, brush and pencil enhanced with washes.[5] Encouraged by Joshua Reynolds, he had taken up oil painting during his stay in Rome. After returning to England in 1779, it was as a painter that he made a splash in the burgeoning London art market and on the city's exhibition scene. As he sought to translate the drama of his literary themes into formidable visual art, painting – with its stately-to-monumental formats and distinctive representative character – was the natural choice of medium. Our exhibition, which is devoted to Fuseli's star turn on the art stage, accordingly reserves the limelight for his paintings. Like the artist himself, it has one central goal: to be anything but boring.

1 Paul Ganz in a letter to Konrad Ulrich, 4 October 1934, private archive of his son, Dr. Conrad Ulrich, Zurich.

2 See Berger 2016, p. 191. In 1938, the association had six members, who had jointly acquired twenty-seven paintings by Fuseli.

3 The project was directed by Franziska Lentzsch; see exh. cat. Zurich 2005.

4 This aspect is so central that Gert Schiff used it to organize the catalogue raisonné of the artist's work he compiled; see Schiff 1973.

5 Fuseli's graphic oeuvre has been the subject of several dedicated exhibitions, including, most recently, *Shockingly Mad. Henry Fuseli and the Art of Drawing*, which was on view at the Art Institute of Chicago in 2017–18.

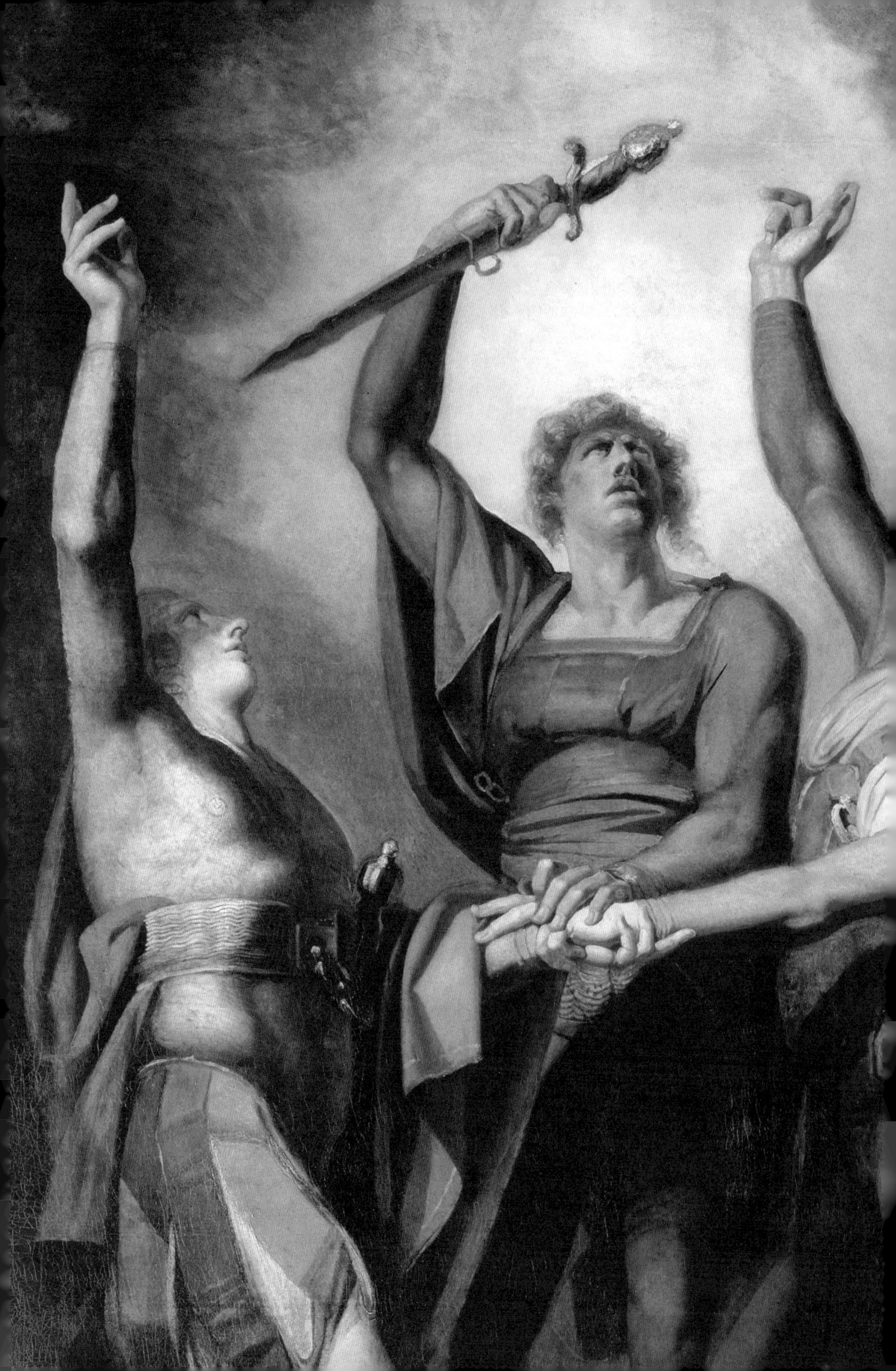

Henry Fuseli:
Great Literature, Sublime Paintings

Eva Reifert

In November 1786, John Boydell, one of Great Britain's most successful publishers of fine art prints, hosts a company of well-known artists and prominent art connoisseurs. The evening's conversation spawns an idea that promises to breathe new life into the genre of British history painting and British visual art as a whole. A splendid new building erected for the purpose is to house a permanent exhibition of paintings commissioned from the country's most outstanding artists. The projected gallery's great unifying theme, the company agrees, can only be found in the works of the writer who, over the past several decades, has increasingly come to be regarded as the embodiment of England's autochthonous culture as distinct from, say, French-dominated Classicism: William Shakespeare. The roster of artists to be entrusted with this most British of missions includes Henry Fuseli, a native of Switzerland formerly known as Johann Heinrich Füssli, who has only recently settled in London.[1]

Around the same time, the widely esteemed poet William Cowper, who has recently brought out his magnum opus, the six-volume poem *The Task*, decides to produce a complete translation of Homer's *Iliad*. To drum up support for the project from his publisher, Joseph Johnson, he has sent him a sample, and he is irritated when Johnson returns it with comments and a note: a friend, he writes, has entered a few observations in the manuscript itself.[2] Yet Cowper's annoyance melts away as he recognizes the 'taste, judgement and learning' that speak from the annotations. Without knowing the name of the critical intellect who has reviewed his translation from the Greek, he replies that he accepts 'the strictures of your friend, and will submit my translation to them with all my heart'.[3] An unlikely alliance is struck between the great poet and a 'foreigner, who has raised himself to high rank in the arduous profession of a painter', as Cowper's biographer describes Fuseli.[4]

It was hardly obvious that Henry Fuseli, who had been back in London since 1779 after spending almost a decade in Rome, would be among the British artists recruited by Boydell to create paintings for his Shakespeare Gallery; or that he would advise the preeminent living English poet on his translation of Homer. Fuseli is reported to have traced his exceptional erudition to his mother's schooling, which he recalled frequently and fondly.[5] He had, moreover, grown up surrounded by learned and independent minds: his father, a painter and art writer in Zurich, had exchanged letters and struck up friendships with many fellow artists and intellectuals of his time, such as Friedrich Gottlieb Klopstock, Johann Joachim Winckelmann, Salomon Gessner and Christoph Martin Wieland. Fuseli's biographer John Knowles fleshes out the picture of his childhood with anecdotal elements such as his early zealous interest in entomology. In Zurich, he attended the Collegium Carolinum, where he became close to his schoolmates Johann Caspar Lavater and the brothers Jacob and Felix Hess. His teachers Johann Jakob Bodmer and Johann Jakob Breitinger, two philologists of the first rank, introduced him to the ideas of *Empfindsamkeit* and *Sturm und Drang.* Perhaps more importantly, they instilled in him a philosophy that, while recognizing the primacy of reason, the key tenet of the Enlightenment, also acknowledged the role sense perception and imagination had to play as aesthetic principles in their own right. Fuseli's fascination with Shakespeare and Milton, with Dante, Jean-Jacques Rousseau and the recently rediscovered *Nibelungenlied* likewise dated back to his studies in Zurich. He effortlessly learned English, French and Italian – in no small part, as Knowles avers, because he wanted to read the great authors in the original languages – and improved his knowledge of Latin and Greek when, in keeping with his father's wishes, he took up theology at university. Fuseli and his friend Lavater took orders in 1761.

That a parson from Zurich eventually wound up in London was the consequence of an imbroglio in which he and his friends became entangled after they jointly penned a pamphlet denouncing a corrupt magistrate.[6] Fuseli left his native city in 1763 and, in the company of the theologian Johann Georg Sulzer, reached Berlin, where his illustrations of Shakespeare's *Macbeth* and *King Lear* appear to have won the plaudits of the British ambassador to the Prussian court.[7] Plans were made to dispatch Fuseli to London as a literary envoy between Switzerland and Germany on the one hand and England on the other.[8] When the ambassador travelled to the British capital in 1764, Fuseli went with him.

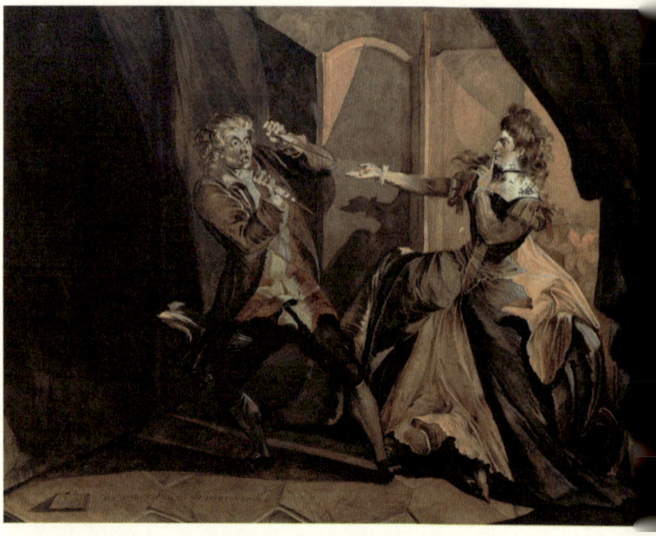

Fig. 1: Henry Fuseli, *Garrick and Mrs. Pritchard as Macbeth and Lady after the Murder of King Duncan*, 1768, pen and watercolour with white highlights, 32.3 × 39.4 cm
Kunsthaus Zürich (Schiff 341)

In London, Fuseli initially seemed destined for a career in literary circles. He wrote poetry and criticism, translated Winckelmann into English and composed his *Remarks on the Writings and Conduct of J. J. Rousseau* (1767).[9] He was introduced to the influential publisher Joseph Johnson, who would later put him in touch with the poet William Cowper, as related above. Yet he also worked on his visual art and moreover discovered the theatre, as is illustrated by the drawing *Garrick and Mrs. Pritchard as Macbeth and Lady after the Murder of King Duncan* (fig. 1), created after a performance in 1766 in which the famous thespians David Garrick and Hannah Pritchard evidently left him deeply impressed.[10] Finally, when Joshua Reynolds, already one of the country's foremost painters, encouraged him to pursue a career as an artist after all, Fuseli set out for Rome in 1770. For the next eight years, he lived in the Italian capital, examining – through the prism of his subjective preferences and interests – the works of the ancient as well as more recent masters, delving once again into the study of Greek[11] and devoting more and more time to oil painting. Meanwhile, he deliberately rejected any association with academic institutions as well as the practice of painting after nature. However refined and subtle his taste in literature might be, for his visual art, he chose to model his depictions of heroes on a quite conventional prototype, the sculpture of one of the *Horse Tamers* on the Quirinal (fig. 2). The exalted heroic figure bristling with dynamic energy that emerges in Fuseli's works of this time would be characteristic of his art for the rest of his life; he would remain faithful, too, to his unwavering belief in artistic genius and the power of the imagination. Michelangelo before all others became the role model he strove to emulate, but the art of the Mannerists and the pathos of the late Baroque likewise left a discernible imprint in his oeuvre. As the principal figure in an international circle of artists whose aspiration was nothing less than to revitalize European art by

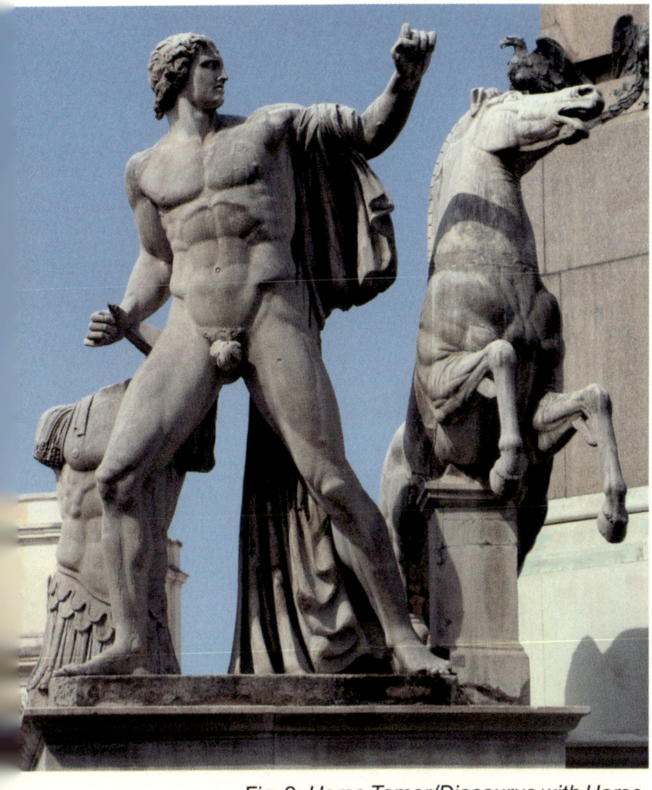

Fig. 2: *Horse Tamer/Dioscurus with Horse*,
Roman copy after Greek model, height 560 cm
Rome, Piazza del Quirinale

introducing sublime and heroic themes, Fuseli abandoned Winckelmann's noble simplicity and quiet grandeur in favour of dramatic intensity and pointed emphasis.[12]

Far from being drowned out by this profusion of novel sources of inspiration, his fascination with Shakespeare synthesised with his admiration of Michelangelo: sketches for a temple dedicated to Shakespeare's memory (fig. 3) are recognizably patterned on the Sistine Chapel. The skill with which Fuseli moulded his artistic identity, in the eyes, too, of the outside world, is evident, for example, in the letters Johann Gottfried Herder sent to his mentor Johann Georg Hamann from Rome: the artist, he wrote, was a 'genius sweeping one along like a torrent, an idolater of Shakesp[eare] and now Shakesp[earean] painter'; elsewhere he described Fuseli as a 'painter of character' and 'young Michelangelo of the Germans'.[13]

Shortly after his return to London, the newly established Royal Academy solicited works for its first exhibition, to be held at the recently completed Somerset House. Fuseli submitted a monumental oil painting: a scene from Milton's *Paradise Lost* (cat. 50). After several earlier drawings, the work was unmistakable evidence that the great British writer's verse epic had engaged his pictorial imagination. Each new work he contributed to the Royal Academy's expositions over the following years signalled his ferocious determination to generate buzz about himself and his art in the British capital. On one occasion, he challenged Reynolds, by now the president of the Academy, with an act of open rivalry. Aware that Reynolds would submit a *Death of Dido*, Fuseli painted his own version of the ancient theme. His calculation proved correct: not only were the works of the newcomer without academic training (cat. 12) and the Academy's president (fig. 4) facing each other in the gallery, the reviewers also drew comparisons between them.[14] Besides the ancient subject from Virgil's *Aeneid*, Fuseli showed his *Queen Katherine's Dream*, a scene from Shakespeare that had never been translated into painting (cat. 39). The following year, in 1782, he presented his *The Nightmare* (fig. 5; see cat. 69). Although

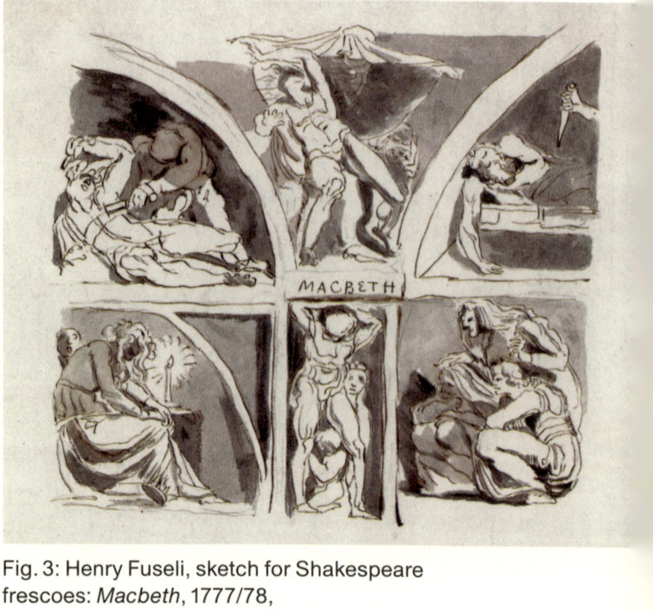

Fig. 3: Henry Fuseli, sketch for Shakespeare frescoes: *Macbeth*, 1777/78,
pen and ink drawing, washed, 27.3 × 19.6 cm
London, British Museum (Schiff 476)

the contemporary response to this daring composition with its lugubrious eroticism was evenly divided between enthusiasm and outrage,[15] the picture imprinted itself so indelibly on the collective memory that it came to lead a life of its own quite detached from the artist who created it: as an emblem of the dark flipside of the Enlightenment and the seed of Romanticism, the sphere of the irrational, where dream blends into manic delusion.[16]

Boydell's Shakespeare Gallery and Fuseli's Milton Gallery

At the time John Boydell came up with his idea for a Shakespeare Gallery, the young Royal Academy's stated objective was to develop and foster a specifically British art; British history painting, in particular, was to be cultivated as the island nation's distinctive answer to Classicism, where the French held hegemony, and a second key genre on a par with portraiture.[17] Meanwhile, the Shakespeare revival promoted with great energy by the famous actor David Garrick had borne fruit – 'The Bard' was generally accepted as the national author.[18] It followed that paintings on Shakespearean themes informed by the generic conventions of history painting promised to be a positively ideal fulfilment of the ambition to bring an autochthonous and patriotic art into being.

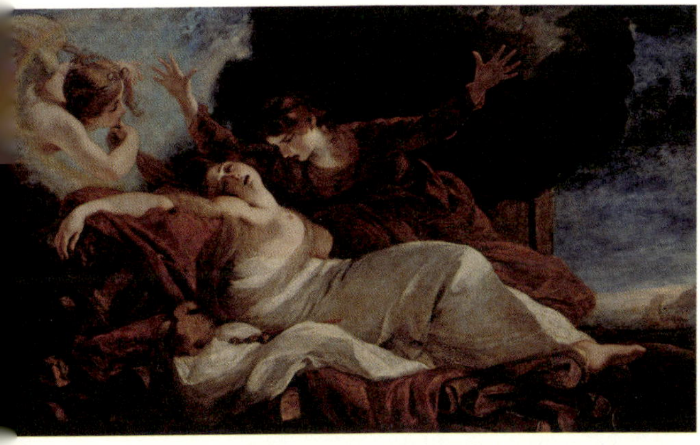

Fig. 4: Joshua Reynolds, *The Death of Dido*, c. 1775–81, oil on canvas, 147.5 × 239.2 cm
London, Royal Collection Trust

So if, by 1786, when Boydell held his dinner party, Fuseli's name was on the list of artists who were thought capable of nurturing a genuinely British painting with British themes, it was

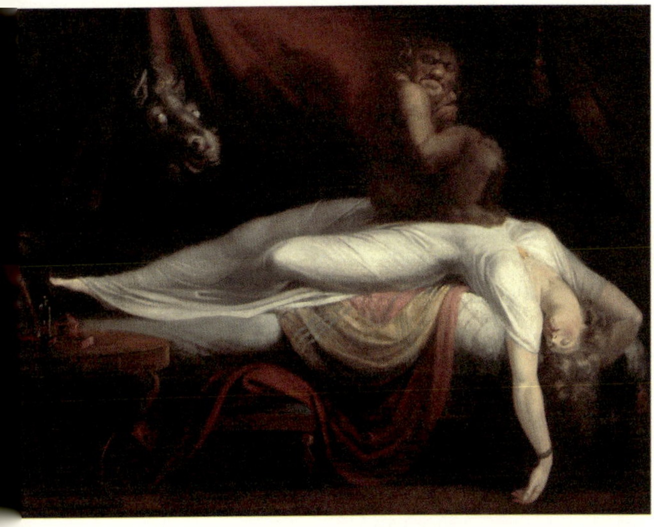

Fig. 5: Henry Fuseli, *The Nightmare*, 1781, oil on canvas, 101.6 × 126.7 cm
Detroit Institute of Arts (Schiff 757)

because he had recommended himself for the mission in several respects. In the annual expositions, he had established himself as a creator of history paintings based on ancient subjects as well as episodes from Shakespeare and Milton. He took Reynolds's emphasis on 'great style', 'genius' and 'taste'[19] – the Academy president's cautious modernization of the classical artistic ideal – and subjected it to a radical reinterpretation in line with the eccentric style he had devised in Rome, in which academic rules, technical precision, the imitation of nature and anatomical accuracy no longer counted for much. His art was more geared toward the spectacular and sensational; in his painterly practice as in his personal bearing, he groomed the public image of an original genius.[20] With works such as *The Three Witches* (cat. 43) Fuseli had moreover secured a monopoly of sorts over depictions of the supernatural,[21] making him an obvious fit for Boydell's aspiration to compile a gallery that would match Shakespeare's originality, creativity and ingenuity; he had built a reputation, one might say, as the 'Shakespeare of canvas'.[22] Boydell commissioned him to compose one painting each based on *King Lear, Henry IV, Hamlet, The Tempest, Henry V* and *Macbeth*, and three after *A Midsummer Night's Dream*, a comparatively sizable contribution to the venture.[23]

The idea of the literature gallery soon attracted imitators; one, Thomas Macklin, acted with such celerity that his Gallery of Poets, for which Fuseli painted a *Prince Arthur and the Fairy Queen* (cat. 16), opened its doors in 1788, a year before Boydell's own exposition. The Irish Shakespeare Gallery that the publisher and bookseller James Woodmason sought to establish in Dublin in 1793 and then in London the following year likewise boasted contributions by Fuseli, including two scenes from *Macbeth* (fig. 6; cat. 44).[24]

By this time, Fuseli had already resolved to dedicate a gallery composed entirely of his own work to his idol John Milton.[25] In keeping with the

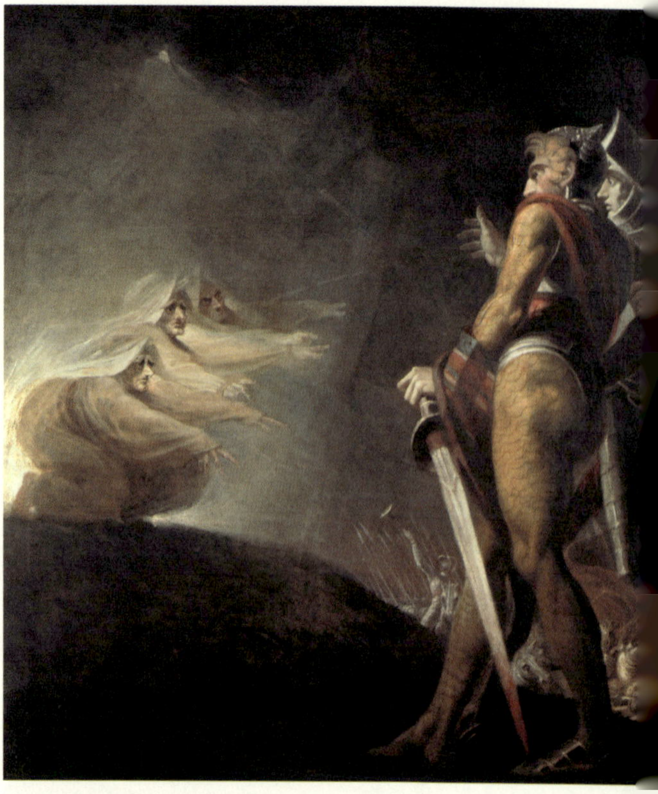

Fig. 6: Henry Fuseli, *The Three Witches Appearing to Macbeth and Banquo*, 1793/94, oil on canvas, 168 × 135 cm
Petworth House, National Trust (Schiff 880)

commercial model pioneered by the other literary galleries, in which the exhibition of paintings was from the outset intended to go hand in hand with their dissemination in the form of printed reproductions, he initially made plans with Johnson and Cowper for a richly illustrated book to accompany the presentation.[26] This scheme fell through when the symptoms of Cowper's mental illness worsened. Fuseli nonetheless plunged himself into the work; though vexed by persistent financial difficulties, he devoted almost a decade to grappling with Milton's life and oeuvre. His identification with the great writer, who, in his thinking, embodied the type of the artist-creator together with Michelangelo, went so far that he described the Milton Gallery as 'a monument of myself'.[27]

Literature and the stage as sources of inspiration

The ancient subjects Fuseli treated[28] were commonplaces of his profession; the literary galleries and his study of Milton, Edmund Spenser, Cowper and Shakespeare, on the other hand, were part of a phenomenon in Great Britain in the latter half of the eighteenth century that grew out of a concurrence of the literary and visual tastes of the time. Paintings after literary sources – primarily from the English canon – occupied an increasingly prominent place in public expositions such as those mounted by the Royal Academy, considerably enlarging the thematic spectrum of traditional history painting. This tendency revived an idea known by the Horatian formula *ut pictura poesis* and introduced into the English-language discourse by John Dryden and Alexander Pope: the notion of a kinship between painting and literature grounded in the understanding that pictures were silent poems and poetry was painting translated into words.[29] Meanwhile, the public was already familiar with visual art directly inspired by the stage: the first theatrical portraits and depictions of selected scenes had preceded the literary painting by roughly a century and continued to be popular genres in Fuseli's time – in no small part because, in David Garrick, Sarah Siddons and her brother John Philip Kemble, the theatrical world had produced stars who made obvious sitters for portraits. Both domains, literature and the theatre, make their presence felt in Fuseli's works – the composition *The Dispute between Hotspur, Glendower, Mortimer and Worcester about the Division of England*, for example, interweaves the interlocution scene with a (double) portrait of John Philip Kemble (fig. 7), while the Shakespeare-inspired *Henry V Reveals the Conspiracy of Cambridge, Scroop and Grey* (cat. 40) looks like a classic history painting.

Following Lessing, Fuseli conceived of literature and the theatre as time-based media in which action unfolded successively; by contrast, he argued, the painting's essential elements were its spatial extension and the energy contained in the moment it rendered – an instant 'big with the past, and pregnant with the future'.[30] Most of his paintings accordingly adapt his sources of inspiration by distilling climactic moments and turning-points that reflect the action in condensed form. In other works, however, his themes are so obscure that even an attentive reader is not likely to recall the particular passages on which they are based; see, for instance, the literary similes from Milton's *Paradise Lost* (cat. 6, 51, 52). On the whole, then, Fuseli's engagement with literature takes place in a peculiar intermediate realm between sensationalism and hermeticism. Decoding his references can be a challenge even with familiar sources such as *Romeo and Juliet* (see cat. 46, 47). This aspect so dismayed one reviewer of Fuseli's Milton Gallery that he suggested that the painter produced solely for academic viewers and did not care if most beholders were put off by his choice of subjects.[31]

Contemporary reports on Fuseli are almost as effusive on his enormous literary erudition as on his eccentric comportment.[32] His student Benjamin Robert Haydon, for instance, offers a vivid account of how Fuseli, busily daubing paint onto a canvas, would 'all of a sudden ... burst out with a quotation

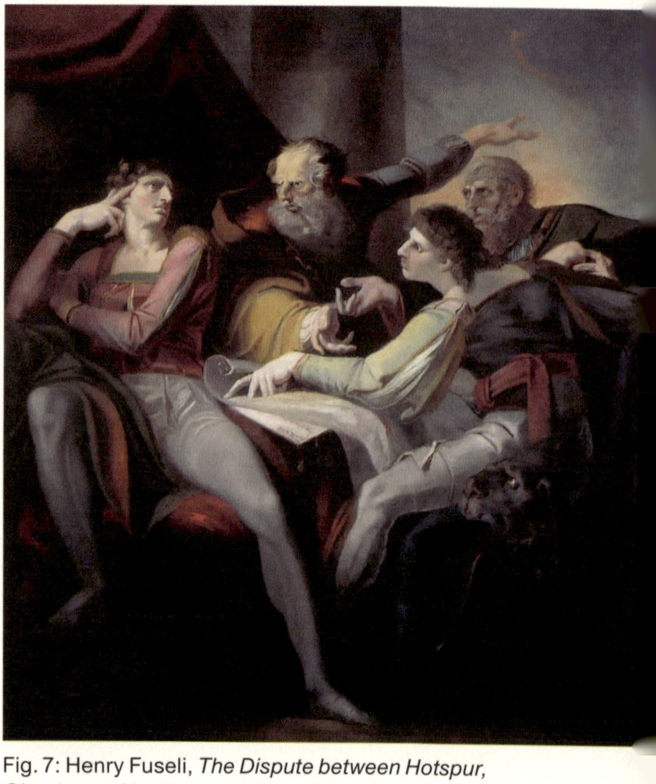

Fig. 7: Henry Fuseli, *The Dispute between Hotspur, Glendower, Mortimer and Worcester about the Division of England*, 1784, oil on canvas, 211 × 180 cm
Birmingham Museums and Art Gallery (Schiff 723)

from Homer, Tasso, Dante, Ovid, Virgil, or perhaps the Niebelungen [sic], and thunder round to me with "Paint dat!"'.[33] If the banker Thomas Coutts, who had supported the artist financially since his time in Rome, is to be believed, Fuseli was able to recite any passage from Shakespeare at will;[34] Cowper, meanwhile, praised his exquisite taste in literature.[35] He seems to have embodied the Reynoldian ideal of the artist possessed of a comprehensive literary education.

A maximum of expression for the epic sublime and the supernatural

Epic plots such as *Paradise Lost, Macbeth, Hamlet, King Lear* and those of Nordic mythology held a magical allure for Fuseli: they were grand – his word was 'sublime', a key term in eighteenth-century aesthetics – dramatic or imbued with maximum pathos, vaulting the artistic imagination into regions far beyond visible reality. The action of *Paradise Lost*, for example, plays out between Heaven and Hell; Satan's threat to God's creation is followed by the Fall of Man and the first couple's expulsion from Paradise. Although few authors could hope to rival Homer in Fuseli's eyes, he did count Book II of *Paradise Lost* as well as the first three acts of *Hamlet* among the unmatched triumphs of human genius.[36] The pictorial invention, he believed, needed to find its point of departure among the themes of such great poetry and tradition, which he subdivided into the categories of the epic sublime, the dramatic and the historic. 'The first', Fuseli wrote, 'astonishes, the second moves, the third informs.'[37] So the latter category of history painting, whose foremost objectives are instruction and moral edification, is complemented by two others: the dramatic, which is enriched by character and pathos, and the epic sublime, which imparts general ideas and universal maxims.[38]

The grand or sublime is a central motif throughout the lectures he gave as professor of painting between 1801 and 1805 – an appointment for which he had recommended himself with his Milton Gallery. It transcends the categories of the dramatic and historic by virtue of its superior degree of abstraction and, Fuseli believed, provides the most suitable material for both literature and painting. What is unusual about his use of the term, however, is that the sublime in his sense may also refer to shocking themes and emotional extremes such as, most strikingly, 'terror'.[39] In other words, it encompasses all subjects that are charged with sufficient emotional intensity to touch the spectators' hearts and move them – lofty and exalted subjects as well as others energized by opaque and morally questionable forces like those that are unmistakably at work in *Macbeth* and *Paradise Lost*. It is no coincidence that Satan, under Fuseli's brush, metamorphoses into a youthful hero and symbol of artistic creation;[40] in *Macbeth*, too, it is the inscrutable darkness at the character's heart that appeals to him. In his telling, the murderous general who seizes the kingship is a superb figure, 'a character too great to be daunted by an extraordinary event'.[41]

Although Fuseli was familiar with the aesthetic and poetological debates of the time, the sublime ultimately manifests itself in his painterly practice in the guise of a single-minded embrace of dramatic staging.[42] The dramatic and sublime do more than instruct and edify, they powerfully touch the beholder's emotions. To convey these subjects in the work of art and move and astonish the viewer, then, the painter must pull out all the stops of intensified expression. The depiction of great and universal themes with a revelatory quality has no room for the mundane or the sort of lowly detail associated with ordinary life. Fuseli instead harnesses the means of simplicity, symbolism and typification as visual equivalents for the generic and overarching character of the sublime. In keeping with his maxim that '[t]he copious is seldom grand',[43] his scenes usually feature a drastically reduced set of characters and are defined by extreme light-dark contrasts. His urge to present heroes and virgins in archetypal psychological states and place them in immediately recognizable emotional constellations frequently results in faces that recall the period's treatises on physiognomy and schematic classifications of the emotions.[44] The tragic hero suddenly flinching from his own actions or the expression of unnameable horror that seizes Lady Macbeth may be echoes of conventional poses on the stage; what they are without doubt is theatrical.[45] In the conflict between human anatomy and exalted gesture that often stretches Fuseli's bodies to the breaking point, it is inevitably the will to artistic expression that prevails: see, for instance, *Thor Battering the Midgard Serpent* (cat. 13).

In his depictions of supernatural phenomena, too, Fuseli routinely overstepped the bounds of lowly reality and the classical canon with evident relish; hence his art's reputation as a textbook example of proto-Romantic 'Gothic Art'.[46] The many versions of the 'Weird Sisters' from *Macbeth* (cat. 42–44), Undine (cat. 30) or the Miltonian theme of Sin pursued by Death – who, in the painting, veils himself in menacing dark clouds (fig. 8) – beckoned as opportunities to prove his ingeniousness: the preternatural glow that surrounds the 'Fire King' (cat. 31) and the nocturnal demon galloping toward the beholder (cat. 52) cannot fail to thrill.

As Cowper made progress on his translation of Homer, Fuseli once upbraided him for taking too many liberties with the original,[47] but his own work reveals that he hardly thought of himself as a faithful translator of his literary sources. His oeuvre includes veritable illustrations such as the commissioned pictures based on Wieland's *Oberon* (cat. 19–26), but in his representative paintings, Fuseli gave free rein to his imagination, a key aspect of his public brand as an eccentric artist.[48] He portrayed King Lear as an older man bursting with vigour rather than a feeble dotard (fig. 9),[49] and his fascination with entomology, detailed knowledge of English folk beliefs and ironic distance from the superstitions of his contemporaries are palpable in his elaboration on the realm of Shakespearean faeries.[50] In some instances, these idiosyncratic interpretations seem to grow primarily out of a probing psychological scrutiny of the object. In his rendering of

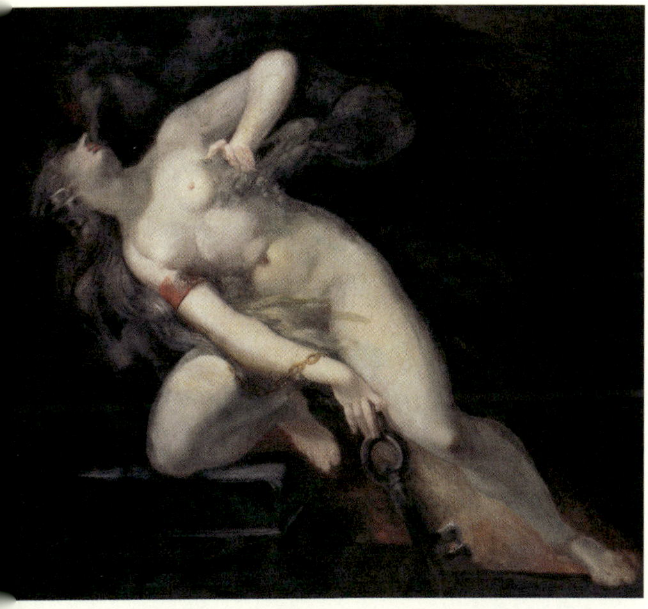

Fig. 8: Henry Fuseli, *Sin Pursued by Death*, 1794–96, oil on canvas, 119 × 132 cm
Kunsthaus Zürich (Schiff 892)

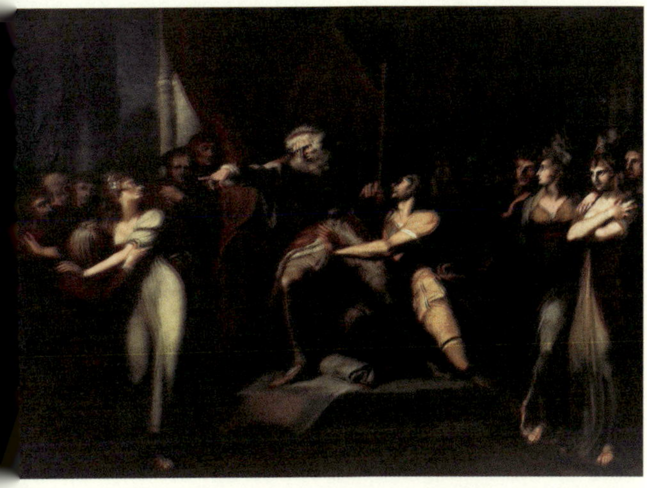

Fig. 9: Henry Fuseli, *King Lear Admonishing Cordelia*, c. 1784–90, oil on canvas, 267.3 × 364.5 cm
Toronto, Art Gallery of Ontario (Schiff 739)

Macbeth's vision of the armed head, for example, he lends the apparition the king's own features (cat. 44), remarking that nothing could be more sinister than an encounter with oneself.[51] Fuseli's determination to retain his own voice is even more salient in his engagement with the revered oeuvre of Milton: defying the tradition of visual art based on *Paradise Lost*, he portrays Satan as the hero and true protagonist; the above-mentioned selection of literary similes as points of departure for paintings likewise reveals a shift of emphasis. Fuseli did not interpret the text so much as use it as a source of stimuli that animated his creative visual imagination and invention.[52]

Beyond the literary painting

In 1791 – Fuseli had just begun work on his Milton project – he outlined his rich repertoire in a letter to his friend and patron William Roscoe, claiming that he had treated or at least thought through almost every interesting subject from Homer to Shakespeare. More en passant, the letter also mentions scenes and characters of his own devising such as 'Ezelin' and 'Belisane'.[53] The legend of Ezzelin Bracciaferro, a Count of Ravenna who, upon returning from a Crusade, kills his putatively or actually unfaithful wife, is a plot Fuseli had contrived in the early 1770s and rendered in at least three paintings (fig. 10).[54] In the case of *Percival Delivering Belisane from the Enchantment of Urma* (cat. 67), he initially referred inquisitive beholders to a source they were unable to identify because it was actually a fiction;[55] the same letter of 1791 reveals that this, too, was a story he had made up from whole cloth.[56] Such freewheeling mythopoeic invention – which Fuseli pioneered in the domain of visual art – turned the genesis of the literary painting on its head. Instead of distilling a key moment from an existing narrative and translating it into painting, his conceits appear to have been born of his urge to express a particular constellation of excessive emotions and his desire for the one explosive instant,

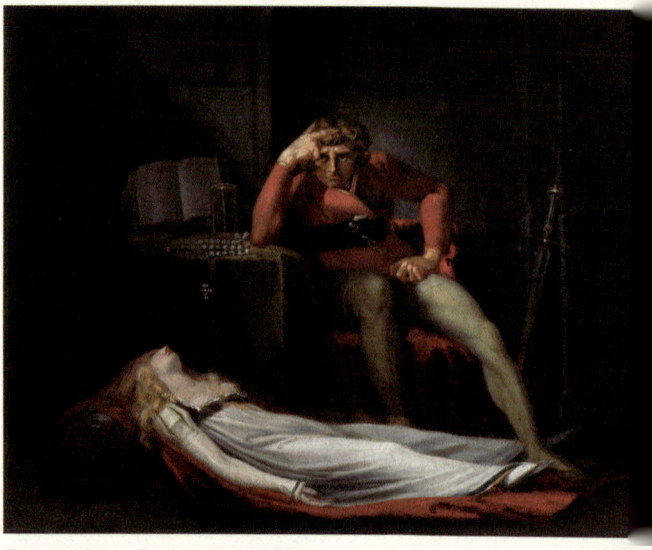

Fig. 10: Henry Fuseli, *Count Ezzelin Bracciaferro Musing over the Body of His Wife Meduna, Slain by Him for Her Infidelity during his Absence in the Holy Land*,
c. 1780, oil on canvas, 49 × 61 cm
London, Sir John Soane's Museum (Schiff 360)

and then he came up with narratives to underpin them.[57] This, too, is a phenomenon in Fuseli's oeuvre that is perhaps best understood as the result of his quest for maximum dramatic intensity. What he described as 'Philosophical Ideas made intuitive' or 'Sentiment personified'[58] was the spark that ignited his exuberant imagination. Everything that moved him and with which he was determined to move the beholder manifests itself in these narrative concoctions – in the supernatural and unfathomable, in evil and delusion, in sinful seduction and virtuous innocence. The means of representation are the same as in his literary adaptations – what is striking is the degree of abstraction implicit in this approach.

One final genre in which Fuseli ventured beyond the literary painting proper in order to depict the creative process and artistic act of conception are his portraits of authors such as Milton, Shakespeare and Cowper – meta-literary paintings, as it were. For Shakespeare, he resorted to the visual trope of the great man in infancy, showing the future dramatist as a baby between allegories of tragedy and comedy (cat. 64). In Milton's case, meanwhile, his identification with the great writer – who, like himself, struggled to make a living and achieve recognition – spawned five paintings based on episodes in his subject's life (cat. 59–63).

In the new century, after Fuseli was appointed professor of painting and, in 1804, elected the Royal Academy's Keeper, he undertook to illustrate a posthumous edition of the poetry of Cowper, who had died in 1800.[59] In *The Poet's Vision* (cat. 65), the painting to be reproduced for the tome's frontispiece, the poet, translator of Homer and admirer of Milton is asleep; a volume of the *Iliad* – the book that sealed the painter's and the writer's bond over their shared enthusiasm for Homer – rests open in his hand. The muse hovering above Cowper is another 'Philosophical Idea made intuitive', an allegory of what was perhaps the mainspring of Fuseli's work throughout his long life: the inspired imagination.

1 See Dias 2013, p. 7.
2 See King 1983, p. 470.
3 'I am delighted with taste, judgement, and learning that discover themselves in the strictures of your friend, and will submit my translation to them with all my heart.' Cowper 1981, p. 468.
4 See Hayley 1835, p. 583.
5 See Cunningham 1859, p. 223.
6 Fuseli, Lavater and Felix Hess had circulated the pamphlet anonymously but revealed their identities during the official inquest it prompted. It then seemed advisable for them to leave Zurich for a while.
7 See Cunningham 1859, p. 226.
8 See Knowles 1831, vol. 1, p. 27.
9 Fuseli first conceived the idea of a collected edition of his 'odes' as early as the mid-1760s, but many of his poems were not published until after his death; see Guthke 1972/73, p. 418. On Fuseli's translations of Winckelmann, see Schiff 1973, vol. 1, p. 52. For the *Remarks on Rousseau*, Fuseli's response to the controversy between the Genevan philosopher and David Hume, see Mason 1951, pp. 121–22.
10 Franziska Lentzsch touches on Fuseli's enthusiasm for the theatre and the inspiration he found there in the catalogue

accompanying the Zurich exhibition; Lentzsch 2005, pp. 201–11; and see Beate Hochholdinger-Reiterer's contribution to the present volume, pp. 59–76.
11 See Knowles 1831, vol. 1, p. 54.
12 On Fuseli's influence on the artists in Rome, see exh. cat. New Haven 1979; see also Solkin 2016, p. 169.
13 See Herder 1889, pp. 85, 90.
14 On this episode see Myrone 2001, pp. 84–85.
15 See Frayling 2006, pp. 9–20.
16 The Goethe-Museum in Frankfurt dedicated an exhibition to this work, its context and its cultural afterlife; exh. cat. Frankfurt am Main 2017.
17 On the Royal Academy's exhibitions, see Solkin 2001.
18 The phenomenon is discussed in Beate Hochholdinger-Reiterer's contribution to the present volume, p. 65.
19 Reynolds (1770) 1975, p. 43.
20 For an analysis of how the contemporary exhibition practice, in which paintings were presented closely spaced, the emergence of a public art audience and the concurrent development of art criticism prompted artists to vie for public attention, see, e. g., Solkin 2015, pp. 179–80. For a discussion that places Fuseli in the context of the idea of genius and the pursuit of originality, see Pressly 2008.
21 See Dias 2013, p. 130.
22 As Rosie Dias notes, several contemporary reviews of Boydell's gallery drew parallels between Fuseli and Shakespeare; ibid., p. 136. The phrase 'Shakespeare of canvas' appears in Cunningham 1859, p. 281.
23 The gallery opened with an initial stock of thirty-four works by eighteen artists; by the following year, it had grown to twice that size. In 1805, when it was wound down, it encompassed 167 works by thirty-three artists working in widely different styles. Boydell's Shakespeare Gallery is also discussed at length in Sillars 2006.
24 See the introduction to the 'Shakespeare' section in this volume, p. 119.
25 See the introduction to the 'Milton' section in this volume, p. 141.
26 For the original subscription model, in which Fuseli would have designed the illustrations accompanying a text edited and annotated by Cowper, as well as the publisher Francis Isaac Du Roveray's book project, see Hattendorff 1997, p. 83.
27 Fuseli in a letter to Roscoe, 21 June 1795, in: Fuseli 1982, p. 135. On Fuseli's identification with Milton, see Schiff 1963, pp. 29–30; for the parallels Fuseli drew between Michelangelo and Milton and the idea of the artist as creator, see Hattendorff 1997, p. 95.
28 See the introduction to the section 'Classical Antiquity and the Middle Ages' in the present volume, p. 81.
29 *Ut pictura poesis* means 'As is painting, so is poetry'. For a discussion see Lee 1967. The standard work on the interrelation between literature and painting in Great Britain is Altick 1985.
30 That is Fuseli's characterization of this fleeting moment, which corresponds to similar constructs in theatre and literary theory (see the contributions to the present volume by Alexander Honold, pp. 37–57, esp. p. 41, and Beate Hochholdinger-Reiterer, p. 75). In his theoretical remarks on the subject in the third of his academy lectures, Fuseli refers to Lessing's *Laocoön*; see Knowles 1831, vol. 2, pp. 134, 160. See also Fuseli's aphorism no. 239, in: Knowles 1831, vol. 3, p. 149.
31 Dallaway 1800, p. 524.
32 John Knowles, for example, concludes his biography of Fuseli with an extensive account of his personality; Knowles 1831, vol. 1, pp. 350–70.
33 Haydon 1853, vol. 1, p. 33.
34 Farington 1978–98, vol. 9, p. 3407 (entry dated 24 February 1809).
35 Hayley 1835, p. 583.
36 Knowles 1831, vol. 1, p. 358.
37 Aphorism no. 36, in: Knowles 1831, vol. 3, p. 74.

38 For a discussion of the sublime in Fuseli's oeuvre in the context of the contemporary aesthetic and poetological theory, see Frommert 1996.

39 In a review of Thomas Hickey's *History of Painting and Sculpture* signed 'R. R.', Fuseli singles out 'terrour' as a 'chief ingredient of the Sublime', echoing the philosophical aesthetics of Edmund Burke: 'Terrour [...] composes in all instances, and in the utmost extent of the word, fit material for both [the painter and the poet].' Fuseli 1792, p. 165.

40 On the shifting signification of the figure of Satan, see Hattendorff 1997, p. 96.

41 See Fuseli's anonymous review of Boydell's Shakespeare Gallery; Fuseli 1789, p. 111.

42 Martin Myrone has characterized this lack of conceptual precision in the use of the term as a general phenomenon of the period; Christian Frommert, meanwhile, has charted the exact place of Fuseli's understanding of the sublime in the context of the contemporary philosophy; Myrone 2001, p. 80.

43 Aphorism no. 56, in: Knowles 1831, vol. 3, p. 81.

44 See aphorism no. 162, ibid., p. 126: 'He who aims at the sublime, consults the classes assigned to character by physiognomy, not its anatomy of individuals.' Fuseli illustrated selected sections of his friend Lavater's *Physiognomische Fragmente* and later translated the work into English. See also Herrmann 1994, pp. 20–21.

45 See Bindman 2010, p. 82 as well as Beate Hochholdinger-Reiterer's contribution to the present volume, pp. 73–74.

46 On the role of Fuseli's oeuvre in 'Gothic horror and fantasy' as an important phenomenon of the late eighteenth century, see Myrone 2006a.

47 '[D]oes the Translator imagine he improves upon his original, by confining himself in a vague manner to the general sense of passages [...] without the least attention to their detail?' Fuseli, qtd. in King 1983, p. 473.

48 See the introduction to the section on 'Recent and Contemporary Literature' in the present volume, on Fuseli's *Oberon* illustrations, p. 103.

49 Fuseli's interpretation of Lear diverged sharply from contemporary conceptions of the character. Ludwig Tieck, for one, was so vexed by it that he speculated that Fuseli did not actually know the play. See Schiff 1973, vol. 1, pp. 143–44.

50 For an analysis of the faerie realm of *A Midsummer Night's Dream* and Fuseli's 'excessive imagination', see ibid., p. 151.

51 Knowles quotes Fuseli with the following argument: 'What, I would ask, would be a greater object of terror to you, if, some night on going home, you were to find yourself sitting at your own table, either writing, reading, or otherwise employed? would not this make a powerful impression on your mind?' Knowles 1831, vol. 1, p. 190.

52 As Hattendorff notes, the paintings Fuseli created for his Milton Gallery show the influence of Lessing's *Laocoön* on his thinking. See Hattendorff 1997, pp. 93–94; his friendship with Blake also contributed to his allegorical interpretation of *Paradise Lost*. See Hall 1985, pp. 58–63 for an account of their friendship.

53 Fuseli in a letter to Roscoe, 22 October 1791; in: Fuseli 1982, p. 74.

54 The earliest drawing based on this theme dates from the early 1770s (Schiff 416). Gert Schiff counts three paintings; Schiff 1973, vol. 1, pp. 98–99.

55 See ibid., p. 138.

56 See ibid., p. 139.

57 See the introduction to the section on 'Pictures of Authors, Free Inventions' in the present volume, p. 159.

58 '[...] but Such Situations as I have myself Combined Such as Ezelin, Belisane &c; Philosophical Ideas made intuitive or Sentiment personified, suit in my opinion, Small Canvases eminently ...'; Fuseli, letter to Roscoe, 22 October 1791, in: Fuseli 1982, p. 74.

59 See the introduction to the section on 'Recent and Contemporary Literature' in the present volume, on Fuseli's Cowper illustrations, p. 103.

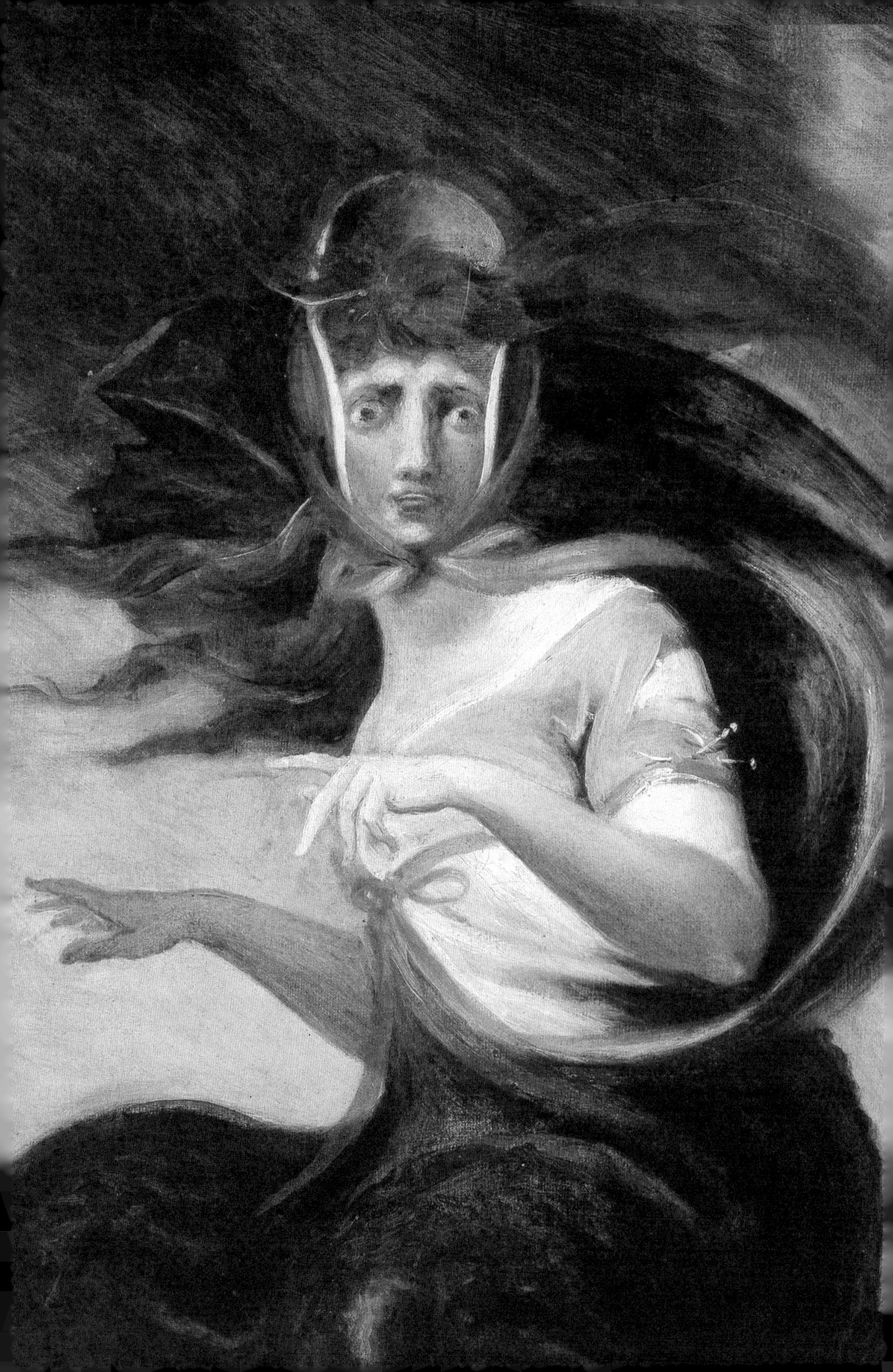

Action, Setting, Momentum: Henry Fuseli and Literature

Alexander Honold

A mediator between art forms and cultures

In his work the Swiss-born artist Johann Heinrich Füssli, who in England was known as Henry Fuseli, casts a sharp light on extreme psychological states. The dynamism of unremitting conflicts between opposing forces dominates the emphatically dramatic *mises en scène* of his drawings and paintings. Fuseli employs a wide-ranging repertory of figures to address the interaction between violence and desire, the interplay of numbing fear and muscle-bound heroism, the battle of the sexes and the dichotomy between the mind and the senses. Few other oeuvres have drawn so extensively on literature for their subject matter. Fuseli did not paint or draw 'from nature', but derived his motifs from his knowledge of major works of world literature. He devoted long and intensive study to these verbal models, which he valued as documents; yet in translating this basic material into images he absorbed it fully into his unmistakable affective visual rhetoric.

The main figures in Fuseli's literary subjects generally engage in emphatically physical activity in a state of intense excitement, as they battle, for example, against hostile natural elements or the unspeakable horrors of a dream. He presents extreme emotions, such as rage, triumph, terror and grief, and he evokes elemental realms of water, darkness and momentous borderline situations in the life of the soul. The figures acting out the subject gesture energetically, their state of immense psychological tension expressed by tortuous, elongated or contorted poses that harbour an element of instability because they have been adopted on the spur of the moment. They mostly form part of compositions based on contrast, with bold diagonals or oppositions of light and dark used to site the figures within bipolar fields of tension filled with an almost palpable electric charge that seems to pass to the viewer.

As embodied in the figures, action and suffering do not constitute semantic opposites, but unite to form a single expressive pictorial form. Neither do destiny and the individual moment appear as antitheses, since the representation usually focuses on a particularly fruitful point in time that encapsulates a narrative momentum, pointing to future developments in the situation depicted. Fuseli approaches his subjects in terms of the stage, inspired by his intensive engagement with the theatre and its gestures.[1] Even when drawing on purely textual sources, he condenses complex narratives into intensely vibrant single scenes. Fuseli's pictorial imagery can therefore be said to have adopted the poetological aesthetic model of the 'pregnant moment', as described by Lessing in his *Laocoön* and developed by Goethe.[2] From the third decade of his life Fuseli moved between languages and cultures with remarkable ease.[3] In addition, his personal circumstances equipped him with the wherewithal to become a closely observant and multi-talented mediator between various arts. Writers and literary scholars were the principal influence on him in his youth and during his years as a student in Zurich. The pastoral poet Salomon Gessner was his godfather, and the theologian and physiognomist Johann Caspar Lavater his friend and companion. Johann Jakob Bodmer and Johann Jakob Breitinger, both writers and professors of literature in Zurich, instructed him in ancient Greek and Latin and in the history of literature.

Fuseli's education and training did not lack for unexpected developments, constellations and encounters.[4] Hence the balance of his interests did not really tip in favour of the visual arts until he returned from Rome. Even then, his reading and his knowledge of literature continued to play a major part in his career. His preferred motifs and figures came from the works of Shakespeare, Homer, Dante and Milton, for example, or from medieval German epic poems and Romantic fairy tales. Apart from Shakespeare's plays, his sources were for the most part purely textual, as opposed to theatrical. With narrative content detached from concrete realisation in another form, he was able to give it special, individual and meaningful emphasis. The situations presented thus obey exclusively artistic dictates, the imagination engaging with the literary model to generate a free, atmospherically appropriate interpretation of scenes suggested by the text, but not necessarily described in it.

The artist's adaptations of literary sources pursue an ideal of extreme condensation of form and content.

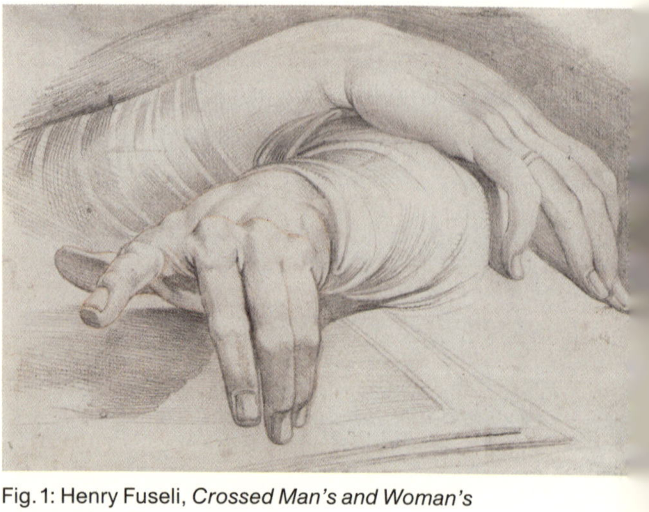

Fig. 1: Henry Fuseli, *Crossed Man's and Woman's Hand*, 1775–79, pencil and red chalk on paper, 17.2 × 23.5 cm
Winterthur, Stiftung Oskar Reinhart (Schiff 507)

Against the background of the aesthetic distinctions established by Lessing in *Laocoön*, the tension Fuseli sets up between immobility and movement can be understood as the deliberate espousal of an aesthetic of momentum or the unstable moment. This genuinely theatrical aesthetic of the 'pregnant moment', developed by Fuseli principally in his London period, had been preceded by stages in his artistic formation dominated by the historical approach to aesthetics propagated by his mentors, Bodmer and Breitinger. The rehabilitation of the visual imagination[5] undertaken by these men in their critical writings and their activities as teachers and editors can be seen as the root of Fuseli's mediation between literature and art.

Johann Jakob Bodmer and Johann Jakob Breitinger: Fuseli's aesthetic mentors

Fuseli spent his years as a student in Zurich in the intellectual circle of Bodmer and Breitinger. Both of them played a distinctive part in the debates generated by the new philosophical discipline of aesthetics in the first third of the eighteenth century.[6] Alexander Gottlieb Baumgarten, in his principal work, *Aesthetica*, which began publication in 1750, and in his other writings, stressed the importance of sensory perception as an independent epistemological mode in contrast to reasoning founded in intellectual notions. In the literary Enlightenment, too, engagement with the processing and manipulation of sense impressions acquired ever greater significance. Discussion of the rules and criteria governing beauty and accomplishment in the arts increasingly came to encompass the whole issue of the sensory and imaginative faculties as anthropological givens.

Bodmer and Breitinger taught at the Collegium Carolinum in Zurich, the former as professor of Helvetian History, the latter as professor of Hebrew and, later, Ancient Greek Literature, Logic and Rhetoric. In their teaching and publications they both opposed the prescriptive poetics of the writer and literary theorist Johann Christoph Gottsched, which held sway in Germany.[7] Gottsched summarised his rationalist poetics in the compendium *Critische*

Dichtkunst (1729; 4th edition, 1751), which ranks as the paradigmatic formulation of prescriptive Enlightenment poetics. It is nothing less than a manual for composing and judging works of literature in accordance with strictly rational laws governing definitions, genres and forms.

Bodmer and Breitinger, too, adduced rational grounds for defining poetic possibilities and genres, yet they emphasised the importance of factors not necessarily susceptible to rational control, not least the novel, the wonderful, the unlikely and the repulsive. Breitinger's *Critische Dichtkunst*, published in 1740, deliberately provided an alternative to Gottsched's narrowly circumscribed poetics by attaching far greater value to the imagination. Breitinger takes as his point of departure the concept of mimesis, introduced by Aristotle in his *Poetics*, which describes the purpose of all the arts as imitation or, to put it in Enlightenment terms, as the imitation of nature. With Breitinger, as with Bodmer, mimesis functions as a kind of corrective to dogmatic directives based on established conventions and authorities and includes an emancipatory element that seems almost to anticipate Jean-Jacques Rousseau.

'The world is an academy and Man a pupil', Bodmer and Breitinger state in their *Von dem Einfluß und Gebrauche Der Einbildungs-Krafft* (1727).[8] Breitinger's *Critische Dichtkunst* also invokes this implicitly anti-academic view of nature as an educational agent: 'Nature is the wise master whose school these artists attend; it presents them with numberless excellent archetypes for admiration and imitation, by means of which they can explore the possibilities of their art and put it to the test.'[9] Art thus consists in combining the study of nature with a 'second creation', a notion echoing Shaftesbury's description of the artist as a 'second maker'.[10] And further: 'Just as the painter can take as material for imitation everything that vision's sensory instruments can make intelligible and present by means of light and colour, so it is within the capacity of the poet-as-painter to depict everything from life and nature that can be imitated by means of words and figures of speech in a sensory, palpable and emphatic way and be impressed on the imagination, which is the eye of the soul.'[11] Hence Breitinger, like Bodmer, interpreted the close bond between poetic composition and visual art – a bond that in the Enlightenment continued to dominate aesthetic discourse in terms of Horace's *ut pictura poesis* (as is painting, so is poetry) – not as the heterologous determination of verbal forms of expression by their visual counterparts, but as a phenomenon involving differences between the two arts in the pursuit of their shared goal of imitating nature.

In Bodmer's and Breitinger's poetological writings the concept of imagination came to play a key role in establishing poetry's place as a medium within the *paragone*. In their jointly published journal *Die Discourse der Mahlern* (1721–23) the two men had already emphasised imagination as the quality that 'distinguishes the good poet from the common singer' (meaning a simple versifier), because 'rich and transformative poetry ... takes its life and character from the imagination alone'.[12] Here Bodmer and Breitinger use the Latin-derived term 'imagination', but in their subsequent writings they preferred the German compound noun 'Einbildungs-Krafft' (imaginative power or force) to characterise the aesthetic faculty as an epistemological mode supplementing sensory apperception.

Sensory knowledge provides strong and vivid impressions of the world of objects, yet the sensations these arouse have an impact on the disposition only for as long as 'an object is present and perceptible'. 'Vision', of vital importance in the interaction between the senses, is affected especially strongly by this limitation because, as Bodmer and Breitinger argue, 'we spend half our lives in the darkness of the night' and would therefore be forced to discard 'the best part of our knowledge every evening when the light disappears'[13] if we were not able to call on a faculty that complements the senses – the imagination.

According to Bodmer and Breitinger, the wisdom of the Divine Father equipped humanity with the capacity to preserve images of the external world presented via the senses by exercising our inherent mental and emotional powers and to imitate and refashion those images. 'Hence he granted the soul

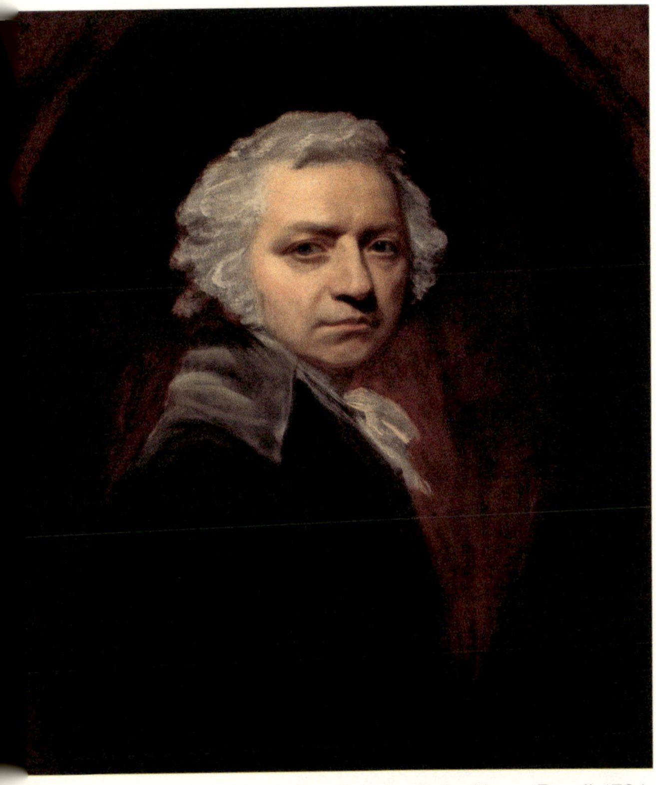

Fig. 2: John Opie, *Henry Fuseli*, 1794, oil on canvas, 76.2 × 63.5 cm London, National Portrait Gallery

the special power of being able to take up, reproduce and awaken at will the notions and emotions received from the senses, even in the absence or extreme remoteness of the objects. We call this power of the soul the *imagination*, and its benefit is that things from the past that have vanished from our senses can still stand before us and affect us no less strongly than they did before.'[14] Bodmer and Breitinger's position on the close link between poetic and visual creation has sometimes been interpreted vis-à-vis the paragone as advocating a normative stylistic primacy of depiction and description for poetry, but the passage just quoted makes it quite clear that they viewed the link as consisting in the power of creating and recreating images of impressions received via sensory perception, a procedure expressed in the verbal proximity between 'image' and 'imagination'.

In making their plea in favour of the imagination, Bodmer and Breitinger had to address the objection that its products are mostly empty – and perhaps even dangerous – illusions and phantasms that cannot be placed on a level with sensory knowledge, let alone be said to match the concepts of reason. In their *Discourse der Mahlern* the two authors state that 'we delight in descriptions and depictions of vice, wickedness and ugliness, of the terrifying and the sad, as long as they are natural'.[15] They thus permitted artists and writers much greater creative freedom than was possible within the dictates of classical doctrine, which defined 'decorum' (*bienséance*) and 'verisimilitude' (*vraisemblance*) clearly and rigidly. It was this opening up of restrictive classical aesthetics that enabled Bodmer and Breitinger to become Fuseli's prime mentors (fig. 3).

The two philologists' ideas on poetry and art differed in three basic ways from the prescriptive poetics of a Gottsched. First, they were far more liberal in their assessment of the suitability and legitimacy of the genres used by poets. Secondly, they showed a marked interest in the vividness, or intensity, of the emotions aroused by aesthetic imitation. Finally, they openly rehabilitated aesthetic values that lay outside the conventions of the ethically based aesthetics advanced by Gottsched and his followers in terms of reason. The shift in discussion of aesthetic effects from the primacy of didactic applicability to that of emotional affectivity had consequences for poetry in that it influenced choice of subject matter to a not inconsiderable degree.

Breitinger proposed that poetry and art should concentrate not on didactic functions, but first and foremost on the elaboration of sense impressions, since these were most likely to set in motion the feelings of the reader or viewer. He focused here on the key concept of motion in the affective sense, hitherto defined in coherent conceptual terms, and skilfully distinguished it rhetorically from the contrasting affective notion of boredom: 'people endure more burdens from a life without feelings than from feelings themselves. Just as they find boredom more burdensome than uncertainty, so they prefer the pleasure of being moved to the pleasure of being instructed.'[16] Further factors governing choice of subject and the artistic means appropriate to it then emerge for Breitinger virtually of their own accord, from inner necessity. There could be no doubt that 'materials best suited to arouse and capture the emotions [are] of a stronger and surer effect than the presentation of the dead works of nature'.[17]

Breitinger therefore rates the representation of human beings engaged in action higher than the depiction of landscapes, if not for reasons of dignity, then with regard to the greater range of possible affective qualities. Among action-based subjects those have the 'strongest effect', he asserts, 'that arouse the fiercest, most vehement and most repulsive emotions, such as fear, horror and pity'. Making visible such emotional states is neither reprehensible nor harmful, 'because the art of imitation cleanses these passions ... of any real repulsiveness, which is why tragedy attracts more strongly than comedy'.[18] By invoking the imperative of sensory-based emotion in *Critische Dichtkunst*, and by viewing 'pleasure in being moved' as integral to the human condition, Breitinger enabled 'delight' in the products of artistic imagination to be located and legitimised at an elementary anthropological level.

Bodmer and Breitinger's rehabilitation of the wonderful[19] gives an idea of the dynamism that could be generated by their re-evaluations and redefinitions in the

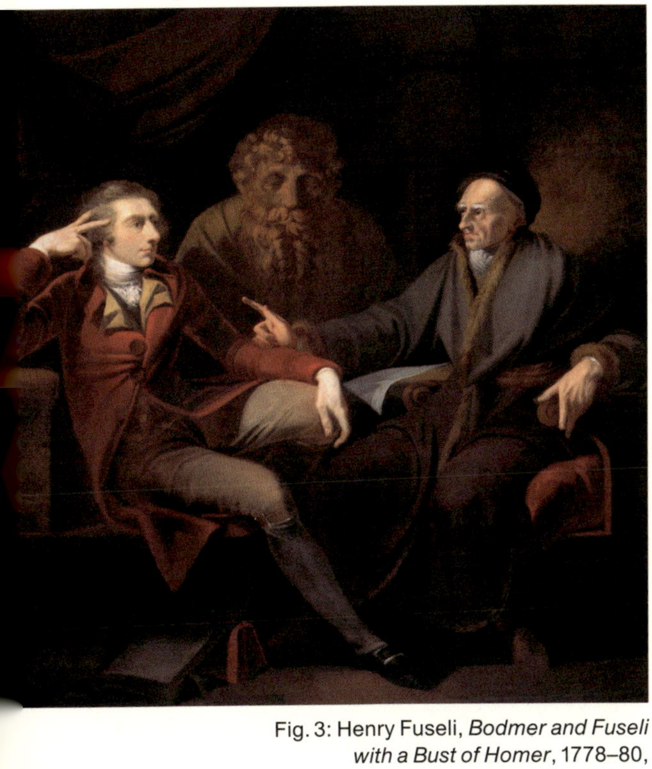

Fig. 3: Henry Fuseli, *Bodmer and Fuseli with a Bust of Homer*, 1778–80, oil on canvas, 163 × 150 cm Kunsthaus Zürich (Schiff 366)

fields of poetics and art theory because it unlocked the door to a conception of both empirical and artistically rendered reality widened to include supernatural and figurative phenomena. Breitinger, moreover, judged 'allegorical beings' and poetry's approach to 'metaphors and other flowery forms of speech' more mildly than Gottsched.[20] On the one hand, Breitinger highlights the epistemological differences between his own times and earlier ages and cultural epochs, in which the forces of nature and social circumstances had presented themselves to thinking individuals in real terms as personifications of a kind that later periods could view only as allegories. On the other, he treats verbal exploitation of such figurations as part of a creative freedom that permits the real to be over- or under-reached in regard to its ontological categories.[21]

It is easy to see why Breitinger attached great importance to the mythical and allegorical components of poetic creative freedom, for they engendered the broader realm necessary for an updated reception of antique, medieval and popular literature. Without a 'tolerance of allegory' justified in these semiotic cultural terms, every form of mythological representation – for example, the epic poetry of Homer, Sophocles, Virgil and Ovid – would come into irreconcilable conflict with the dictates of verisimilitude, as would the religiously grounded poetry of Dante and Milton. The foundation in nature-based mimesis, the conceptual strengthening of the imagination and motion, and the re-evaluation of the wonderful thus interacted argumentationally in a way that encouraged the expansion both of the historical literary canon and of contemporary artistic options, now freed from restrictive norms, in the direction of a universal literary perspective *avant la lettre*. That perspective would range from Homer, via Dante, Shakespeare and Milton, to English fairy tales, the Germanic medieval *Nibelungenlied* and other anti- or non-classical material, such as the Romantic figure of Undine (an excellent example of a natural element rendered more vivid by personification, as outlined by Breitinger).

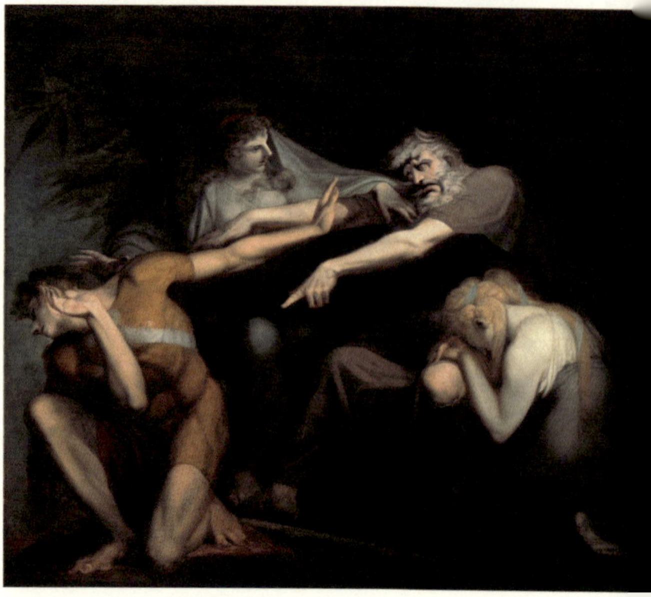

Fig. 4: Henry Fuseli, *Oedipus Cursing His Son Polynices*, 1786,
oil on canvas, 149.8 × 165.4 cm
Washington, D. C., National Gallery of Art (not in Schiff)

By describing both the sensory activation of the imagination when liberated from restrictive didactic requirements and the affective goal of intensified motion of the soul as not only permissible, but also particularly promising avenues of artistic development, Breitinger and Bodmer made an inestimable contribution to the actual emancipation of aesthetic creativity (and its theoretical examination) from heteronomous rules and predetermined functions, be they of an ethically didactic, a behaviourally moral, a religious, a political or whatever other kind. Both philologists, but especially Bodmer, publicised their views in the shape of translations, editions and commentaries and, in doing so, almost single-handedly opened up an international arena of reception and dissemination for the German-speaking world. Underlining the seriousness and consistency of their endeavours, this enlarged the scope of the results.

Bodmer's and Breitinger's activities as literary critics and editors soon proved at least as stimulating as their writings on aesthetic and poetological issues. Bodmer's translation of Milton's *Paradise Lost*, titled *Johann Miltons Verlust des Paradieses*, first appeared in 1732. Followed by five further, revised editions and complemented by a 'defence' of the poem, *Vertheidigung des Gedichtes Joh. Miltons von dem verlohrnen Paradies* (1740), this was not the first German translation of the work, but the version that played a decisive part in its acceptance in the German-speaking world. Henceforth Milton's tale of Paradise, Hell and the inevitable Fall of Man would form part of German literature's frame of reference. In publishing Minnesang poems from the *Manessische Liederhandschrift* (1748) and editions both of Wolfram von Eschenbach's *Parzival* and the *Nibelungenlied*, Bodmer aimed principally to expand the temporal scope of the standard cultural repertoire and to establish an uninterrupted chain of documented literary history. By promoting the work of Milton, Shakespeare and Alexander Pope, on the other hand, he sought to draw attention to major achievements in the English language and in English literature. Opening up fresh perspectives on the world of Mediterranean antiquity, the German Middle Ages and English literature of recent centuries, Bodmer und Breitinger exerted a crucial influence on the budding artist Fuseli, an influence that extended far beyond his years as a student in Zurich and proved to be enormously productive.[22]

Scenes from Milton's *Paradise Lost*

At the end of the 1770s, following a brief intermezzo in Zurich on his way back to England from Rome, Fuseli decided to settle for good in London and establish himself as an artist there. *Satan Starting from the Touch of Ithuriel's Spear* (1779) belonged among the first brilliant samples of his ability (cat. 51). The group of figures in this painting depicts one of those transformatory situations characteristic of Milton's narrative. Satan, the great adversary who had fallen from grace and been driven from God's Heaven, has risen from the deepest depths of his damnation and stolen up on the first humans on the earth that God has created for them. Aiming to infect them with the poison of temptation, he approaches Eve in the form of a toad and whispers unfounded assertions in her ear so as to pollute her joy in her innocent love and make her susceptible to sin. Warned of his presence, the guardian angels Ithuriel and Zephon search the garden of Eden for the intruder in the evening and find him engaged in this role of diabolic prompter 'close at the eare of Eve', as described towards the end of Book IV:

> Squat like a Toad, close at the eare of *Eve*;
> Assaying by his Devilish art to reach
> The Organs of her Fancie, and with them forge
> Illusions as he list, Phantasms and Dreams,
> Or if, inspiring venom, he might taint
> Th' animal spirits that from pure blood arise
> Like gentle breaths from Rivers pure, thence raise
> At least distemperd, discontented thoughts,
> Vaine hopes, vaine aimes, inordinate desires
> Blown up with high conceits ingendring pride.
> (*Paradise Lost*, IV, 1062–1075).[23]

The corrupter's mission is clear, his strategy devious. For if Satan succeeds in instilling in Adam and Eve the negative sentiments the poet describes and in leading them astray with false hopes and harmful desires, they will lose forever the inner harmony established by untroubled happiness and God-fearing piety and will therefore have to forsake the timelessness of Paradise. If the stratagem of tempting woman triumphs here, at Eve's ear, then, Satan reasons, evil would no longer be simply a metaphysical principle forming part of the foundations of divine order, but would infiltrate irreversibly the new divine experiment of life on earth and become a determining factor in actions there.

The diabolic protagonist has positioned himself to attain this goal, but has not yet begun his murmuring work of temptation. By listing the forms taken by illusions, phantasms and dreams uniformly, one after the other, Milton underlines the sensuous force of such inner images and, at the same time, relativises the differences between them. They are all fruits of the imagination, whether cultivated consciously and actively, developed involuntarily in dreams or formed pathologically by an overactive mind. Milton's interest in Eve and Satan, and that of his follower Fuseli, focuses in this scene first of all, then, on the products of the aesthetic principle that systematically subverts the borders between mental and sensory activity and, through the work of Bodmer and Breitinger at the latest, had become the main focus of poetological debate: it is the uncontrollable wilfulness of the imagination that the tempter seeks to stir up in Eve – at this point still in vain.[24]

The guardian angel, immediately recognising the satanic intruder despite his disguise, intervenes literally at the last minute in this first encounter of Eve with the corrupter (IV, 810–819). Timely discovery of the interloper thwarts his cunning and the bold action of the guardian repulses an indirect assault on the divine order of Paradise. This aversion of evil will not be final, and the here-and-now of this particular moment plays a decisive part in Milton's depiction of the scene. It resembles the spark that ignites the fuse of a powder keg and sets in motion the flame that eventually leads to detonation (fig. 5). The powerful scene, permeated by the opposing forces of the combating figures, leaves the result of the duel between Satan and Ithuriel, and the further course of the narrative, hanging in the balance. Yet the programmatic title, *Paradise Lost*, makes it obvious to the viewer of the painting, and to the reader of Milton's poem, which path events can be expected to take.

In Milton's final scene the archangel Michael takes 'Our lingring Parents' by the hand 'and to th' Eastern Gate / Led them direct, and down the Cliff as fast / To the subjected Plaine'. From there the banished pair cast a wistful glance back at Paradise aglow in the morning sun (suggested by a bubble of light behind the guardian angel in Fuseli's painting), 'so late thir happie seat' and its gates now closed to them forever (XII, 780–790; see cat. 57).

Milton was better suited than any other poet of his age to embody the power of inner vision nourished by the imagination because by 1654 he was completely blind. In combination with his epic *chef-d'œuvre*, this qualified him in the eyes of his admirers to be seen as the incarnation of a *poeta vates* (soothsayer poet) reminiscent of Homer. Milton himself suggests this bold comparison when he has the bard or narrator of his poem address some great poets and prophets of classical antiquity, including 'Maeonides' (that is, Homer) and 'Tiresias', as 'equal'd with me in Fate' and follows this with the *cri de cœur* 'were I equal'd with them in renown' (III, 44–47). A passionate advocate of the Puritans' cause in their ultimately unsuccessful republican revolt, Milton was in 1649 appointed Secretary for Foreign Tongues by the Council of State and continued to hold political office even when struck by blindness, but became *persona non grata* at the Restoration. With the onset of blindness he became dependent on outside help in producing all his writings. In connection with the literary work of his late period his daughters, in particular, were accustomed to read to him and to take down verses from dictation.

Fuseli's depiction of this multi-media association of the spoken word of an elderly father with the writing hand of a youthful daughter in *Milton Dictating to his Daughter* calls to mind the original conception of poetry, embodied in the word *dictare*, as a form of literary production in which verbal inspiration and its material documentation were physically and personally distinct (cat. 63).[25]

In his painting of this type of collaboration, which resembles a scene from a chamber play, Fuseli links interdependent aspects of the poetic working process notionally by separating them visually. The composition suggests that Milton's daughter, brightly illuminated as she stands at a

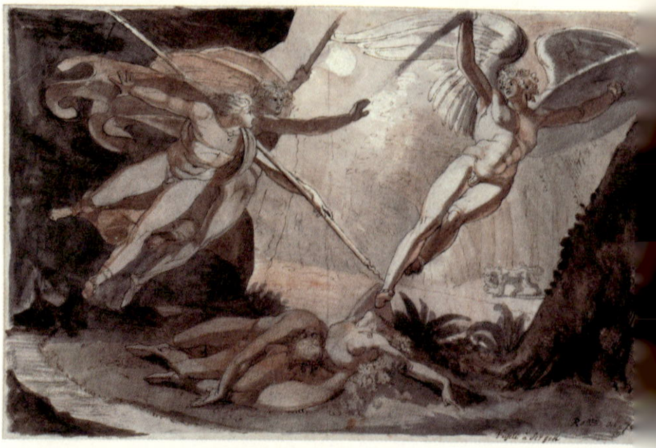

Fig. 5: Henry Fuseli, *Satan Starting at the Touch of Ithuriel's Spear*, 1776,
ink and brown wash on paper, 27.1 × 39.3 cm
Stockholm, Nationalmuseum (Schiff 482)

lectern to the left of centre, is writing down in the book in front of her words being uttered by the poet, seated in shadow on the right. A second female figure – presumably another of Milton's daughters – sits embroidering on the far left, behind and beyond the scribe. In 'choreographic' terms, the arrangement defines the standing figure of the writing woman as the chief person in the narrative.

Approached diagrammatically, then, the image establishes a hierarchy that privileges the figure who is in possession of the writing utensils and the skills associated with them. An alternative reading, however, would see the sequence of figures as a logical reflection of the chronology of literary production, in which the father's speech and the left-hand daughter's embroidery represent the extremes of the process. In this view, dictated words shape the literary idea in the moment of its emanation, while the making of a woven fabric – a texture – grants the orally articulated words enduring form as a book or other printed matter. Between the two, and linking them, stands the material activity of transcription.

If inspired poetry, initially and principally, entails words transmitted orally by a narrator or bard, its origins, according to the teachings of classical antiquity, must be imagined as female, taking the form of the muses, spring nymphs and fairies who breathe energy and ideas into the poet's mind. As Friedrich A. Kittler has stressed, the instruments of literary socialisation in the Age of Education, beginning in the eighteenth century, were also female – the mothers who imparted and passed on language.[26] Woman's role as an essential agent of literacy is addressed in several paintings by Fuseli, including *Milton when a Boy, Instructed by his Mother* and *Milton when a Youth* (cats 59, 60). In conception, both pictures show themselves to be biographical pre-echoes of the daughter-dominated household maintained by the poet in old age, when he depended on female assistance. The unknown beauty benignly devoted to the boy stretched out before her is an auspicious dream image that the writer would later not be able see with open eyes and, for that very reason, points to his future destiny as a poet–seer. The idea of Milton being repeatedly guided by allegorically idealised female figures may well have engendered in Fuseli a special fascination for the English poet's personality and biography.

The battle of the sexes, dream apparitions and the magical moment

For Fuseli harmony and disharmony between the sexes was just as much a basic fact of nature as the opposition between fluid and solid or the contrasting interplay of light and dark. A further – and particularly fertile – polarity existed in the conflict between manifestations of the physical world and the various spirits of nature and figures of legend that played such a significant part in popular lore and individual dream visions.

Literary sources proved especially fruitful for Fuseli when they contained situations involving or actually describing acts of imagination, as in Milton's account of Eve's dream. A second-degree narrative opens up whenever a single character is dreaming or several people bring about an evocation of supernatural beings through a joint ritual. That type of narrative goes hand in hand with increased activity of the imagination, valued so highly by Fuseli and his poetological mentors.

The dream visions and dream figures that haunt the souls of the protagonists in Fuseli's work, revealing the real motives behind their actions (and usually the cost as well), do so within a clearly defined performative framework, established, in the manner of an actual staging, by the setting. In this way, the artist can make visible the workings of the imagination reflexively, echoing their own means and forms. The heroically active body, a constant pictorial trope in Fuseli's work ever since his years in Rome, was increasingly abetted in his images by facial expressions suggestive of mental activity.[27]

Formal clarity and transformative energy are the two forces working against each other in Fuseli's imaginarium devoted to natural elements and the battle of the sexes. The latter, virtually omnipresent in the artist's work around 1800, came more and more to bear traits of conflict and interaction between the former, with tense bodies and flowing robes, along with solid forms and supple lines, developing into the basic dramaturgical components of his imagery.

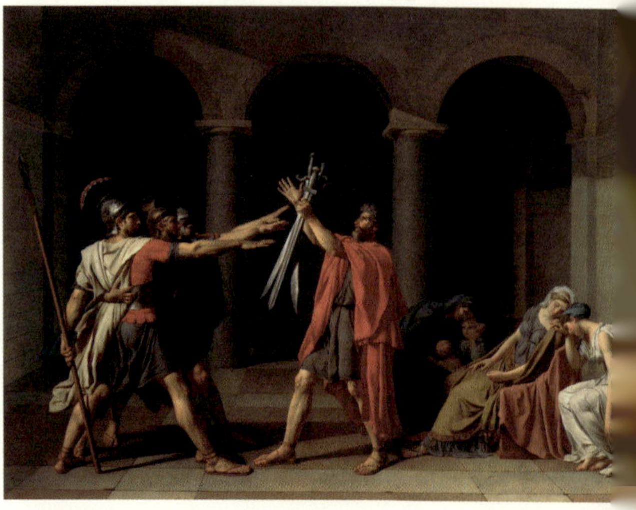

Fig. 6: Jacques-Louis David, *The Oath of the Horatii*, 1784, oil on canvas, 330 × 425 cm Paris, Musée du Louvre

Groupings of figures in rows, a configuration often used by Fuseli, have a particularly compelling effect in his work and are semantically charged in very different ways in a wide range of contexts. The groups generally consist of three figures, most notably the witches from Shakespeare's *Macbeth* and the Danube water-sprites from the *Nibelungenlied* (cats 43, 44, 14), but also the figures in the central scene of the political mythology surrounding the origins of the Swiss Confederacy. As Jacques-Louis David, the painter of the French Revolution, was to do later in *The Oath of the Horatii* (fig. 6), Fuseli comes remarkably close in *The Oath on the Rütli* to the archaic, ritual dimension of this grouping (cat. 15). The subject is the solemn act sealing the union of the three original cantons, known together as the Waldstätte. Its visual realisation takes the form of a performative 'choreography' in which the formation adopted by the figures embodies their triune will.

A study for painting (fig. 7) shows the legendary act marking the foundation of the Swiss state. In accordance with the formula *e tribus unum* (out of three, one) the three warrior heroes – here still depicted *all'antica* – join their left hands while raising their right arms heavenwards in swearing the vow and calling on divine aid. The geometrically elaborated arrangement of the figures and the almost dancing poses invest the group with a lightness rather unusual in Fuseli's work, but the historical significance of the legendary event weighs all the more heavily for that.

The appearance of the trio of witches before Macbeth and Banquo in Shakespeare's drama (I, 3) is a *locus classicus* of Fuseli's art (cat. 42). In the play the scene establishes the salient part performed in the story by the supernatural and elemental dimension of the spirit world. By joining together in a circle as they dance ('dancing in a ring'; Macbeth, I, 3), the 'weird sisters' instantly activate the

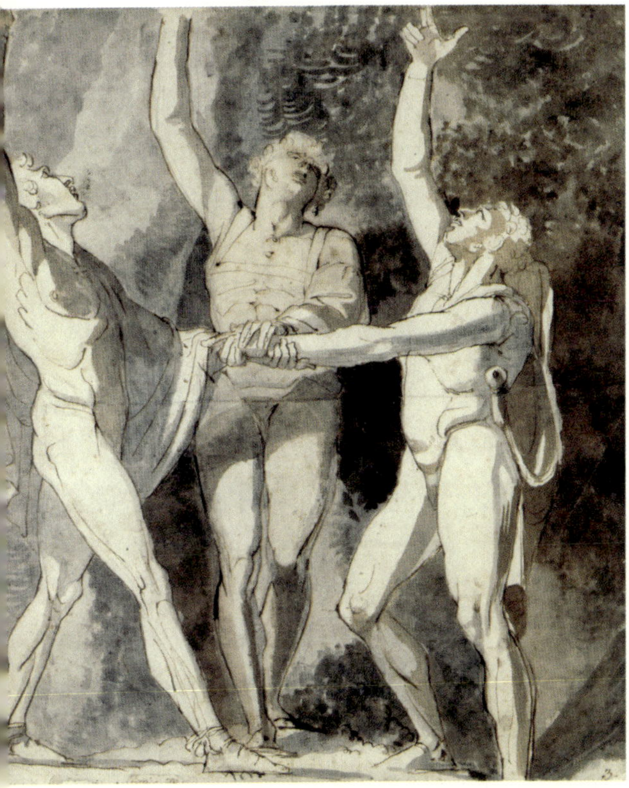

Fig. 7: Henry Fuseli, Study for *The Oath on the Rütli*, 1779, pen and brown ink over pencil on paper, 41.4 × 34.5 cm
Zurich, Kunsthaus Zürich (Schiff 412)

magic of which they speak. They look both backwards and forwards in time, recalling and admonishing, and, by suggesting that they possess structurally superior knowledge, set in motion the tragic dynamism of entrapment fundamental to the plot, contributing to the uncertainty of the play's main characters without forestalling their fatal actions. The witches are an especially rewarding motif for visualising the drama's narrative in pictorial terms because their appearances address the fateful course of the drama as a whole and condense its overall temporal context into fleeting manifestations of its momentum.

Hagen and the Nymphs of the Danube, showing how three water-sprites attempt to prevent Hagen from continuing his journey by crossing the river, exhibits a similar pictorial structure (cat. 14). The confrontation between a male hero mounted on a horse and three female nature spirits across from him articulates sharply the opposition between the sexes and interprets it as the expression of a disruption of natural relations, giving the scene by the river an uncanny twist. Though ominous in character, the warnings voiced by the nixies are not enough to stop the knight in his path or make him change his mind, but as a narrative prolepsis they anticipate symbolically the catastrophic ending of the tale and thus expand the moment depicted to encompass the fateful dimension of the future.[28]

In Fuseli's images involving encounters between the sexes the men, usually depicted naked, display prominently flexed muscles, while the women often adopt elegant poses redolent of total control of the body beneath drapery falling loosely in flowing lines. This can be seen in the figures of Kriemhild and Hagen in the scene from the cycle of *Nibelungenlied* paintings in which

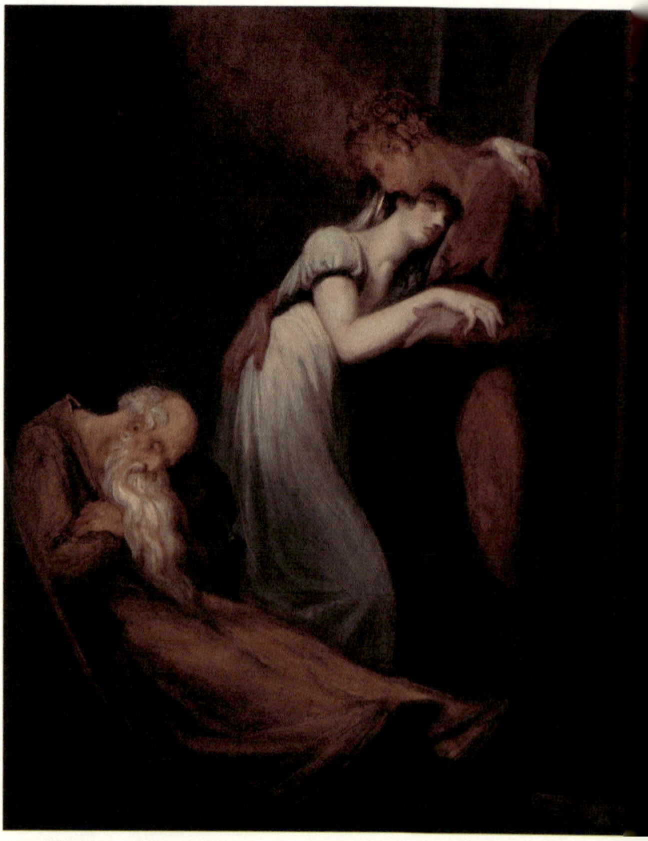

Fig. 8: Henry Fuseli, *Huon and Amanda with the Dead Alfonso*, 1804–05, oil on canvas, 60 × 44 cm
Dallas, The Nona and Richard Barrett 2013 Trust (Schiff 1788)

Siegfried's widow demonstratively presents half of Gunther's severed, mask-like head to her husband's murderer, who shifts nervously on his chain. The folds of Kriemhild's robe reveal a light, almost dance-like twist in her pose, which signals to the viewer the cold-heartedness and premeditation with which the heroine intends to implement the vengeful strategy that will change the course of events.

Fuseli's heroes are pure physique. Raking light frequently accentuates the muscles and tendons of their naked bodies, granting them a plasticity reminiscent of the sculptor's art. The bodies of the artist's female figures are exposed far less often and they mostly bear thin, light robes that might be said to evoke an allegorical dimension. In contrast to the emphatically physical existence of his male warriors, Fuseli's women therefore tend to represent metaphysical aspects and abstract principles.

Similar observations can be made with regard to Fuseli's renderings of scenes from the epic poem *Oberon* by Christoph Martin Wieland and the fairy tale concerning the water-sprite Undine by Friedrich de la Motte Fouqué (fig. 8, cats 19–26, 30). In these the artist again applied an all-embracing visual vocabulary to specific subjects and narrative contexts. Here, too, the painter and draughtsman extracted from the literary sources those features that permitted their inclusion in an arena of opposing forces and, in doing so, presented an almost universal *theatrum mundi* of times, cultures and elements.

1 See the essay by Beate Hochholdinger-Reiterer in the present volume, pp. 59–76.
2 Wolf 2002.
'Fuseli is the forerunner of those many artists and writers exiled in the twentieth century who, like Kandinsky, Picasso und Joyce ..., never became entirely at home in their host countries and perhaps drew their revolutionary force from that fate.' Schiff 1974, p. 9.
4 See the essay by Eva Reifert in the present volume, pp. 19–35.
5 Klemm 2005, p. 88.
6 Bender 1973.
7 Martus 2015, pp. 504–15. Gottsched collaborated with the theatrical couple Johann and Caroline Neuber in playing a major part in the reformation of drama in Germany along early Enlightenment lines. Invoking the example of French classical tragedy and its art of sublime declamation, the reformers rejected popular, improvisatory forms of theatre. Bauer and Wertheimer 1983.
8 Bodmer and Breitinger (1727) 1980, p. 29.
9 Breitinger (1740) 1980, p. 83.
10 Later in *Critische Dichtkunst* (ibid., p. 140) Breitinger defines 'poetry' as the 'imitation of Creation' and a 'species of Creation'.
11 Ibid., p. 84.
12 Bodmer and Breitinger (1721–23) 1980, p. 3.
13 Bodmer and Breitinger (1727) 1980, pp. 30–31.
14 Ibid., p. 32.
15 Bodmer and Breitinger (1721–23) 1980, p. 12.
16 Breitinger (1740) 1980, p. 106.
17 Ibid., p. 107.
18 Ibid.
19 Ibid., pp. 135–60: 'Von dem Wunderbaren und dem Wahrscheinlichen'.
20 Ibid., p. 153.
21 For Breitinger, it was the business and prerogative of the poet to 'create entirely new beings through the power of his imagination and either to present things that are not beings as actual persons ... and skilfully make them take on all manner of reasonable actions and opinions, or to raise those beings that are already real to the level of a higher nature by granting opinions and thoughts to lifeless creations, as when he attributes thoughts and speech to forests, landscapes and all other inanimate beings, or lends animals more wit and reason than they have in their sphere'. Ibid., p. 145.
22 Stähli 2009.
23 Milton 1796, p. 160.
24 Though here instantly deflected, Satan's powers of temptation will prove to be a persistent and consequential threat. In Book V Eve tells her companion that during the previous night a dream 'of offence and trouble' had implanted in her the tempter's malignant suggestion that she could unhesitatingly taste the forbidden fruit of the Tree of Knowledge (*Paradise Lost*, V, 39–120).
25 Gärtner 2006, esp. p. 68.
26 Kittler 1991, pp. 15–16.
27 For Fuseli's development of Lavater's physiognomics, see Vogel 2001, pp. 88–94.
28 Honold 2009.

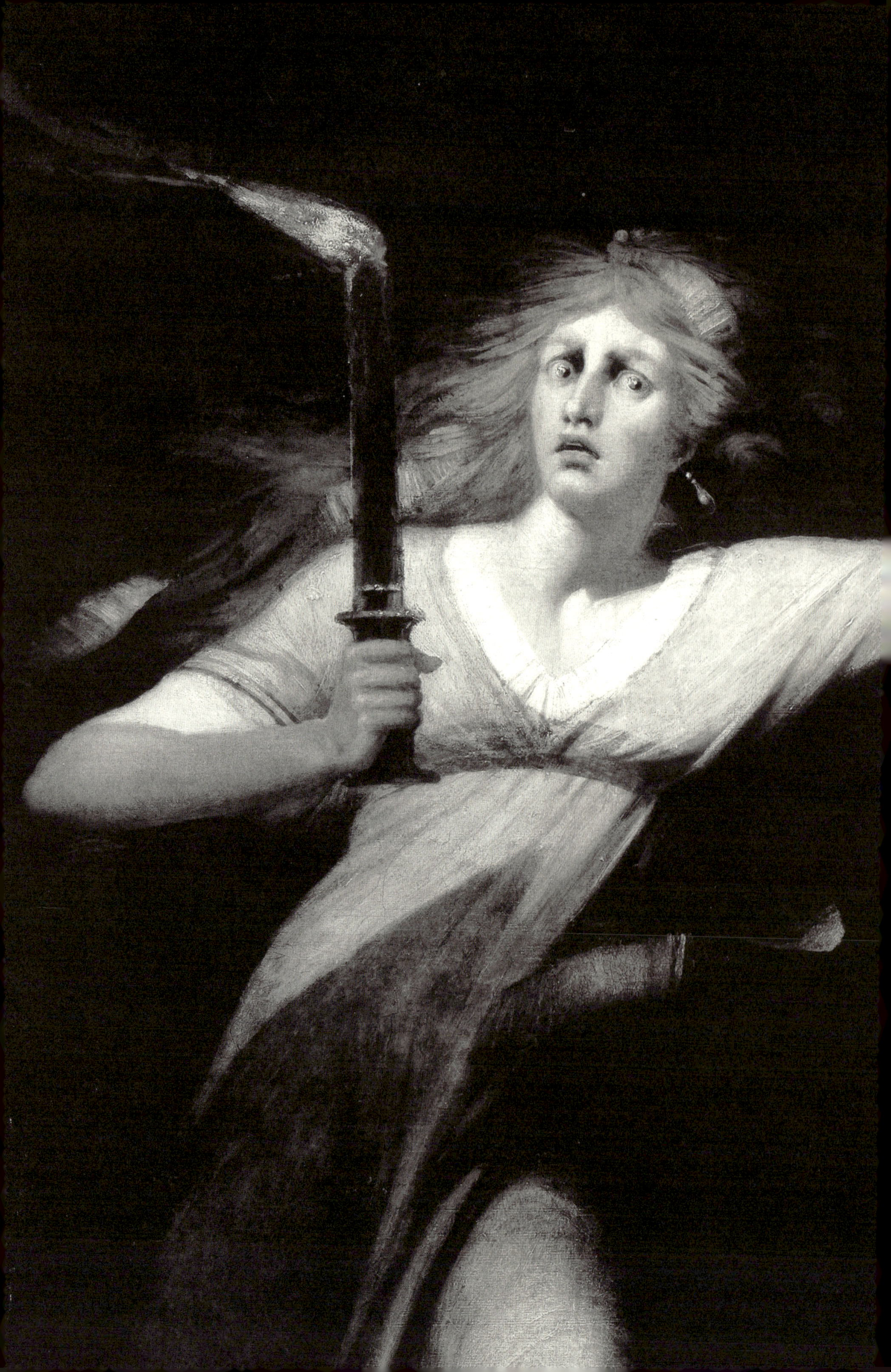

‘Shakespeare’s Painter’: Henry Fuseli and the London Stage

Beate Hochholdinger-Reiterer

‘Shakespear’, according to an article Gotthold Ephraim Lessing and Christlob Mylius penned for their newly launched theatre journal *Beyträge zur Historie und Aufnahme des Theaters* (1750), belonged to a host of poets ‘scarce known in these parts save perhaps by name’.[1] In the mid-eighteenth century, the plays of the English playwright William Shakespeare were still unfamiliar on the German-speaking stage; where they were known, it was only as heavily abridged and edited adaptations designed to meet the requirements of touring companies, and advertised – if at all – under the name of the adapter. The dearth of practicable translations for the theatre aside, what intellectual circles most lacked was an understanding of the specificity of Shakespeare’s playwriting – a lack attributable to the predominance of the French Classicist ideal, with its leanings towards a normative poetics, as advocated by Johann Christoph Gottsched, professor of literature in Leipzig.

In Zurich, however, the philologists Johann Jakob Breitinger and Johann Jakob Bodmer propagated a concept of art that was completely antithetical to the doctrine of the Leipzig School. In the opinion of Breitinger and Bodmer, art and literature did not have to be confined to the imitation of nature but could also draw from the imagination, just as they could give shape to the fantastic – assuming its possibility – as opposed to the probable alone.[2] Rather than emulating French Classicism, Bodmer and Breitinger aligned themselves with English Sensualism, publishing *Die Discourse der Mahlern* (1721–23), a journal modelled on Joseph Addison’s moralistic weekly *The Spectator*, and winning international acclaim for their ambitious aesthetic and literary theories of art. Bodmer made a name for himself as a patron of the arts, facilitating cross-cultural understanding with translations of works by John Milton and Homer, the publication of forgotten medieval texts and as co-founder of the publishing house of Orell & Compagnie (1734). As teachers at the Collegium Carolinum in Zurich, Bodmer and Breitinger had a formative influence on numerous emerging talents, among them Henry Fuseli und Johann Caspar Lavater.

According to his biographer John Knowles, Fuseli had a command of several languages from an early age – including English, which was uncommon at the time: this enabled him to read

Shakespeare, whose work he would be engaged with throughout his life, in the original.[3] Allegedly, Fuseli even attempted a translation of *Macbeth* when still a student. We can assume that Fuseli saw his first performances of Shakespeare's plays in London. Whether he ever attended a professional theatrical performance in Zurich is still unknown. In a city which was exceedingly hostile towards the theatre until the nineteenth century, Fuseli would have had only one opportunity to see a professional theatre company there. During his youth there was a sensational guest performance in Zurich by one of the most renowned German touring companies: the famous Ackermann company which, seeking refuge in Switzerland from the ravages of the Seven Years' War, stayed in the city for a total of five weeks between 1757 and 1760. Obtaining a concession to perform in Zurich remains one of the greatest achievements of the company's actor-manager Konrad Ernst Ackermann – given that until then, save for one exception, no public performances had been given in Zurich for more than 130 years. The presence of the Ackermann company is recorded as having been 'a cultural and social event of unprecedented magnitude'.[4] The company gave twenty-one performances in Zurich, all of which, judging by the proceeds, were sell-outs. The best actresses and female dancers of the company received invitations from patrician families to instruct their daughters in graceful comportment and taste in fashion. Such recognition is particularly remarkable considering that, at the time, the reputation of touring theatre companies in the entire German-speaking area was deplorable. The theatre reformists of the Enlightenment era accordingly endeavoured to advance the social revaluation of actors and actresses. A particular admirer of the Ackermann company was Christoph Martin Wieland, who lived in Switzerland between 1752 and 1760 at the invitation of the Bodmer family. Impressed by the Ackermann company's performances, Wieland swiftly completed his domestic tragedy *Lady Johanna Gray*, which was premiered by the company in Winterthur in 1758.

Shortly after his return to Biberach, Wieland began translating twenty-two of Shakespeare's plays into German; these were issued by Bodmer's publishing house from 1762 onwards. Despite occasionally meeting with harsh criticism, Wieland's translations proved essential for the gradual adoption of Shakespeare's plays on the German stage. Even Fuseli was dismissive of Wieland's translations of Shakespeare, as a letter to Bodmer written in 1766 shows: 'I wished Wieland's Swabian flame might have consumed him ere he laid unholy hand on Shakespeare.'[5] It was only in the course of the gradual emancipation from the French Classicist ideal of dramatic literature that a shift in the reception of plays occurred in the mid-eighteenth century: rather than performances acting as catalysts for literary and scholarly debate, it was the theoretical discussions about Shakespeare which spurred the inclusion of his plays in the repertoire, winning them widespread acclaim during the 1770s in the so-called *Sturm und Drang* movement.[6] Just as in England, Shakespeare's plays were presented in German-speaking areas mainly in the form of heavily edited adaptions. The reasons for this were primarily of a practical nature, although reservations concerning the content of the plays were also voiced: written for the Elizabethan theatre, the plays' rapid changes of scene and setting were considered impossible to perform in the eighteenth century due to the continental development of the proscenium stage and its cumbersome perspective scenery.

By the second half of the eighteenth century, Shakespeare's plays were already part of the literary canon of his native country, making 'The Bard' a key figure in the formation of England's self-image: 'Shakespeare came to represent ... a way for England to forge its identity by celebrating its national hero, whether in criticism, in performance, or in popular culture. The eighteenth century created Shakespeare as a national export for England, but the nation was similarly served by its icon, who helped England develop its understanding of itself.'[7]

In contrast to the dominant French culture and literature and their Classicist poetics, Shakespeare became a symbol for 'the vigorous independence of the English, their resistance to political and literary absolutism'[8] which the political conflicts between England and France in the colonies and during the Seven Years' War only compounded.

The state of the theatre in London

The protracted theatre closures of 1642 to 1660 marked a significant caesura in London's vibrant theatre scene. Following King Charles I's declaration of war against Parliament, and exacerbated by the Puritans' animosity towards the theatre, Parliament issued a decree ordering the closure of all theatres in order to maintain public order. During this time, many English troupes migrated to mainland Europe in a search for new sources of income, thereby contributing to the further development of the touring company system there.

When England's theatres reopened under Charles II in 1660, it became necessary to fall back on printed plays which had been popular before the closures – the plays of Shakespeare and Ben Jonson, for example. However, only adaptations of the originals were being performed, not so much for reasons of content but because new plays and adaptations attracted more attention and theatre architecture had changed.[9] From 1660 on, new theatre venues were being built which combined elements of the English Renaissance stage with the principle of the modern proscenium stage as developed on the continent. The thrust stage, which consisted of a platform extending far into the audience (the apron), was used as the main performance area and helped maintain close proximity between the actors and the audience. Scenery flats and stage machinery were stored backstage, unconcealed. While in the English Renaissance theatre the standing area known as the pit was thronged with so-called groundlings – the impecunious audience that could not afford the more expensive seats in the galleries – the slanted auditorium floor of the new buildings was fitted with seats. The pit was surrounded by galleries which were partitioned into boxes, with the royal box located at the centre, directly opposite the stage. Until well into the eighteenth century, it was also customary for nobility to be seated on the stage itself, primarily in order to flaunt their status (fig. 1).

One significant innovation in comparison with the conventions of English Renaissance theatre consisted in the appearance, for the

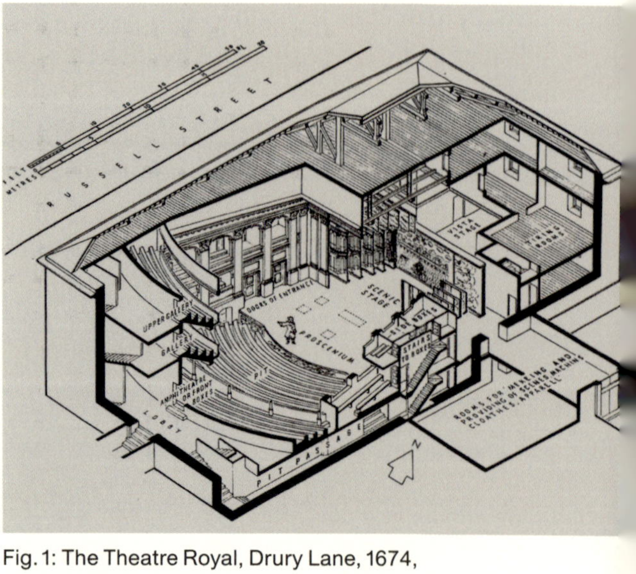

Fig. 1: The Theatre Royal, Drury Lane, 1674, constructed by Christopher Wren, scale reconstruction by R. Leacroft

first time, of actresses. While records show professional actresses to have been members of continental Commedia-dell'Arte companies since the sixteenth century, it was only during the Restoration that women first appeared on English stages. Until the theatre closures, all female roles in Shakespeare's plays had been performed by boy-actors.

Shakespeare's increasing popularity from the late 1730s on is attributable to a number of factors: the price war between the publishers Tonson and Walker led to cheap editions of individual plays being put on the market, which made access to Shakespeare's work easier; in 1737, the Licensing Act was passed in order to maintain control and censorship over the theatres; and all plays for performance were required to be submitted for vetting to the Lord Chamberlain, the most senior officer of the Royal Household. The new laws also restricted the previously profitable business of theatre licensing. London was to have no more than two theatres licensed to give dramatic performances (patent theatres). The resulting monopoly of London's two main stages – the Theatre Royal, Drury Lane, which was home to the King's Players, and the Lincoln's Inn Fields Theatre where the Duke's Players performed until 1732, when their licence passed to the Theatre Royal, Covent Garden – was only broken in 1843 with the Theatre Regulation Act. Censorship of the stage continued in Great Britain until 1968. Non-licensed theatres proved resourceful in their attempts to circumvent the strict regulations, for instance by advertising a concert as the main event and declaring the ensuing comedy as an encore performance, or by performing melodramas and light entertainment which, because of their high percentage of music, would not be considered dramatic theatre.

Following the Licensing Act, managing directors of patent theatres progressively fell back on Shakespeare's plays which, having already been performed, were no longer subject to censorship. Also, women played a crucial part in the Shakespeare-renaissance of the eighteenth century. 1738 saw the foundation of the Shakespeare Ladies Club, which was dedicated to promoting the dramatist's work. Its members addressed theatre directors directly and campaigned for the increased inclusion of Shakespeare's plays in the repertoire, thereby initiating a rediscovery of his history plays. With their interpretations of Shakespeare's female roles, famous actresses of the time including Catherine 'Kitty' Clive and Hannah Pritchard also left an indelible mark on following generations.

Shakespeare became the most performed playwright over the course of the eighteenth century and had a profound influence on other authors and different literary genres.[10] In 1741, a memorial statue to him was erected in Poets' Corner in Westminster Abbey. Shakespeare's portrait and representations of his fictional characters became the subject matter of painting and sculpture and were used to decorate upper class homes. In addition, his birthplace of Stratford-upon-Avon developed into a place of 'Shakespeare-veneration', the 'locus of biographical myth-making'.[11]

Theatrical experiences in London

When, at the suggestion of Bodmer and his student Johann Georg Sulzer, Fuseli moved to London in 1764 to act as a cultural go-between, he was already familiar with Shakespeare's works, having been able to read them in English due to his knowledge of languages. Yet it was only in London that he was able to witness live performances of Shakespeare's plays, with David Garrick in the lead, no less, the most popular Shakespearean actor in Europe at the time. In a lengthy letter to Salomon Dälliker written in November 1765, Fuseli expresses his desire to share two things with his friends in London: '... the theatre and the picture exhibition. Garrick, Cibber, Powell, Yates; Lear and Alicia, Orestes and Hermione!'[12] In the same letter, Fuseli remarks wryly: 'Since I came to England, German literature has been dead to me.'[13]

According to his biographer John Knowles, Fuseli realised that theatre was the best school at which to perfect his English, while it was

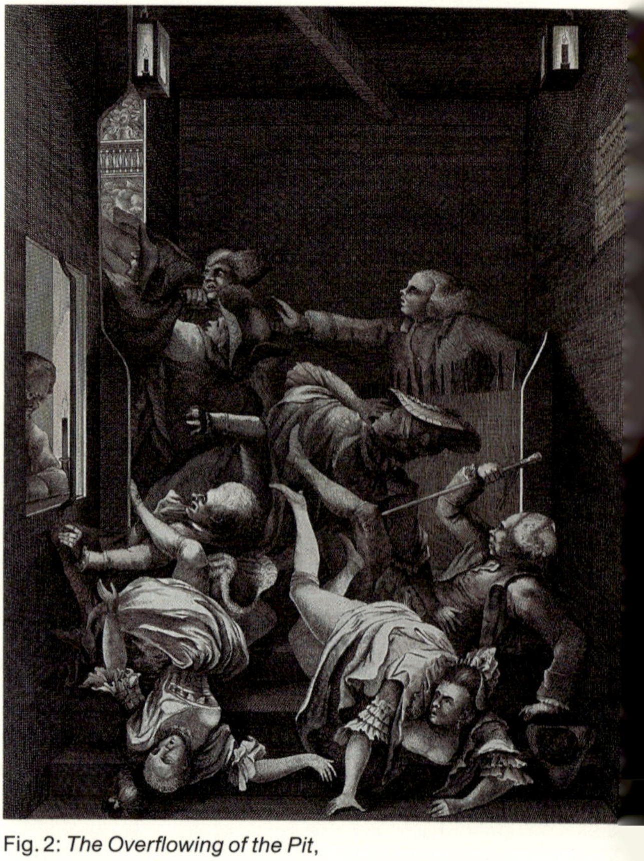

Fig. 2: *The Overflowing of the Pit*,
engraving after the painting of Samuel Hieronymus Grimm, 1771, 35 × 25.6 cm
London, British Museum

Garrick's magnificent art which taught him to imitate the passions. Fuseli missed no opportunity to see Garrick play and was always to be found in the front row, even when this involved unpleasantness.[14] When Fuseli became an ardent theatregoer in London, the convention of numbering auditorium seats had not yet taken hold. So while performances usually began at 6pm, audiences would jostle for position in front of the theatre gates hours in advance in order to, literally, fight for good seats (fig. 2).

Stimulated by his early experience of the theatre, Fuseli made two sketches on paper depicting David Garrick and Hannah Pritchard as Macbeth and Lady Macbeth (fig. 1, p. 22), and Garrick in the role of Richard III (fig. 3). In comparison with many other of Fuseli's Shakespearean images, these sketches are closest to contemporaneous stage practice. For these compositions, the artist chose emotionally charged moments in which Garrick's mimetic and interpretive ability must have been readily apparent.

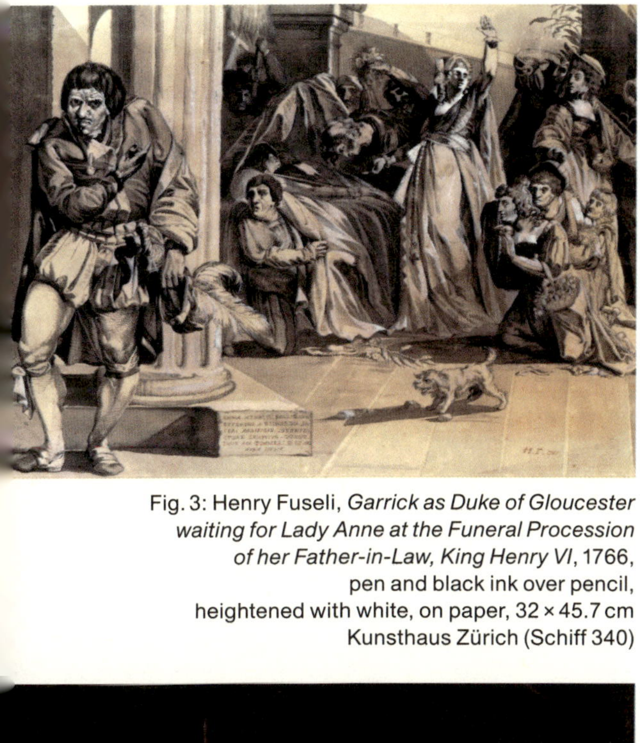

Fig. 3: Henry Fuseli, *Garrick as Duke of Gloucester waiting for Lady Anne at the Funeral Procession of her Father-in-Law, King Henry VI*, 1766, pen and black ink over pencil, heightened with white, on paper, 32 × 45.7 cm Kunsthaus Zürich (Schiff 340)

Unlike the oil painting of 1812 (fig. 4), which seems stylized and abstract, Pritchard and Garrick are depicted in clothing customary for the contemporaneous stage. A framing curtain and a folding screen can be seen in the background, indicating a theatrical scene. The focal point, however, is Macbeth's expression of horror at the murder of King Duncan by his own hand – a hand which still grips the bloody murder weapon, while Lady Macbeth already endeavours to cover up the crime.

For his representation of Garrick as Richard III,

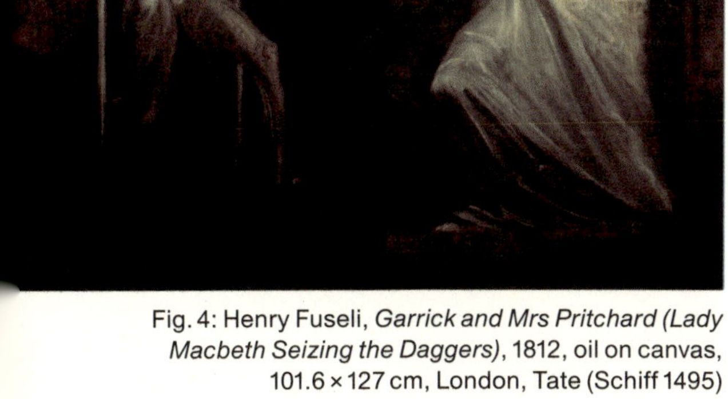

Fig. 4: Henry Fuseli, *Garrick and Mrs Pritchard (Lady Macbeth Seizing the Daggers)*, 1812, oil on canvas, 101.6 × 127 cm, London, Tate (Schiff 1495)

Fuseli drew on one of the most brazen seduction scenes of dramatic literature: the Duke of Gloucester, later to become King Richard III, woos Lady Anne beside the coffin of her father-in-law, whom the selfsame Duke had murdered. The pen and ink drawing depicts the moment just before the misbegotten Duke and the funeral train cross paths.

Fuseli's representations of Garrick were made during the time when so-called theatrical portraits were on the rise, a genre which emerged in the mid-eighteenth century primarily for financial reasons, as it benefitted both painters and the portrayed. 'The market for theatrical images seemed to grow spontaneously with the consolidation of the patent theatres, the increasing visibility of British art through the medium of the Royal Academy and more advanced and appropriate printing techniques.'[15]

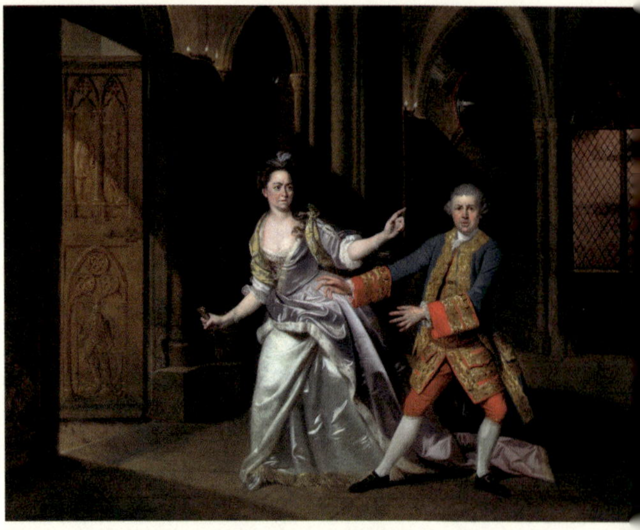

Fig. 5: Johan Zoffany, *Garrick and Mrs. Pritchard in 'Macbeth'*, 1768, oil on canvas, 102 × 127.5 cm
London, Garrick Club

By association, the popularity of actors such as David Garrick rubbed off on the artists that portrayed them, just as theatrical portraits were able to enhance the fame of actors and actresses. During the second half of the eighteenth century, the public was less interested in the plays performed than in the actors themselves, both as artists and private individuals. Francis Hayman, Benjamin Wilson, Johan Zoffany and Joshua Reynolds were among the best-known theatrical portraitists of the time. Theatrical portraits,

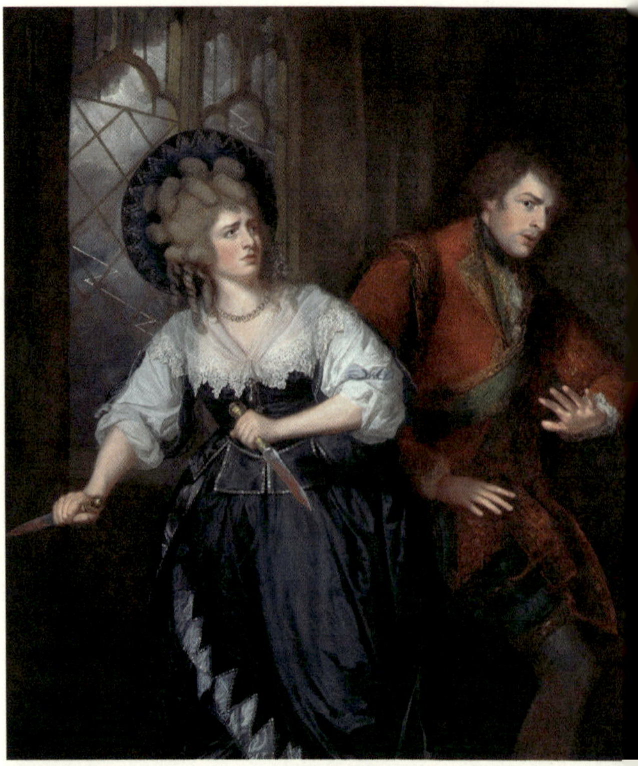

Fig. 6: Thomas Beach, *John Philip Kemble und Sarah Siddons in 'Macbeth'*, 1786, oil on canvas, 179 × 152.4 cm
London, Garrick Club

which for the most part depict actors in leading roles, enjoyed great popularity in the form of paintings, engravings or book illustrations.[16] They are, however, only of limited use to historians as visual sources of theatrical practice on the contemporaneous London stage, even though the actors presumably wore stage costumes and struck characteristic poses and expressions when being portrayed (figs. 5 and 6).

Fuseli's Shakespearean images defy all attempts to attribute documentary value to them. Only rarely are direct connections between actors and the characters depicted made by name. His composition of a sleepwalking Lady Macbeth, for instance, is rather enigmatic (cat. 45). Might the eminent actress Sarah Siddons, who dominated London's theatre scene from the 1780s with her brother, John Philip Kemble, have served as a model for this painting of 1783, although she demonstrably played the part in London for the first time in 1785? Even those pictures which seem to have been inspired by Fuseli's actual theatre experiences are nonetheless drawn from his imagination and can therefore, at best, only be interpreted phenomenologically. From a phenomenological perspective, the perception and experience of a performance are the starting points for the process of reflection. From this perspective, it is interesting to note which elements of a performance were chosen during the process of perception – which is always selective – and thus considered relevant by the spectator. The theatre historian Allardyce Nicoll succinctly remarks on the significance of images drawn from the imagination: 'they reveal what eighteenth-century audiences *thought* they saw.'[17]

Unlike the stages of the English Renaissance, the new theatre edifices of the Restoration period were equipped with curtains which concealed the stage during the prologue, though changes of scene and setting continued to be carried out with the curtains drawn aside. Only during the second half of the eighteenth century did the painted act drop become a staple in the production of theatrical illusion, enabling scene changes as well as exits and entrances to be carried out hidden from view.

Fuseli's representation of Cordelia's death in *King Lear* is framed by a curtain which seems to indicate a theatrical scene (cat. 41). Here, as with all of his compositions which reference Shakespeare's plays, no specific theatre event can be inferred from the representation because Fuseli never considered himself a chronicler of theatre.

During his time in London, adaptations of *King Lear* were being performed which dispensed with the deaths of Cordelia and Lear. In the original, the third and last scene of the fifth act is set in the British camp near Dover. Towards the end of the scene, Lear enters holding the dead Cordelia in his arms. The red-brown curtain drawn by Fuseli might be construed as representing either a tent or a theatre curtain, though the latter would have been green, according to Nicoll.[18] If Fuseli chose to represent a curtain, then presumably only as a symbol of the theatre or a stage action, like the use of masks to symbolise theatrical situations, irrespective of whether or not masks were actually being used on stage in the relevant era.

The lighting equipment available in mainland Europe at the time was comparatively more sophisticated than that in London during the Restoration, where the stage was lit with candles and oil lamps until fitted with gas lights in the 1820s. The modernisation and improvement of lighting systems in London began only in 1765, after David Garrick had familiarised himself with continental standards during his tour of Europe. The conspicuous contrasts between light and dark in Fuseli's Shakespearean images may have been inspired by his visits to the theatre inasmuch as stages could only be unevenly lit prior to the electrification of the theatres. The downstage area was usually brighter due to the footlights which illuminated the actors from below. Additional light emanated from candles in candle holders mounted on the side walls. At Drury Lane, Garrick did away with the chandelier hanging over the stage and in all probability fitted reflectors to various light sources, thereby increasing overall brightness and making novel lighting effects possible. During his acting career at Drury Lane – of which he became managing co-director in 1747, partnered by James Lacy – lighting costs multiplied, which we can assume was because he had his sights set on a more ideal stage lighting. Indeed, his specific style of acting, characterised as it was by nuanced gestures and facial expressions, positively demanded the best possible visibility. Yet despite technical improvements with respect to lighting, London's stages remained only poorly lit.

Fuseli's consistently sombre Shakespearean paintings, with their striking contrasts and the occasional highlighting of brighter passages, may have been inspired by his visits to the theatre, even to the point of imaginatively transcending them (see cat. 38, 47). His paintings seem to anticipate the experiments in lighting design which became technically possible only after the electrification of theatres in the 1880s.

David Garrick's acting art

When David Garrick made his first appearance as a professional performer in London in 1741, Shakespeare's plays already formed an indisputable part of the repertoire. For his London debut at Goodman's Fields Theatre, Garrick made the shrewd tactical decision to play the lead in Colley Cibber's adaptation of *Richard III*. Because Goodman's Fields did not possess a licence, the performance officially took place only as an addition to an evening concert. Garrick, who was announced merely as 'a GENTLEMAN, (Who never appear'd on any Stage;)'[19], thus remained anonymous for his London debut. However, this first appearance of the self-taught Garrick, who had previously worked as an amateur actor, met with resounding success as it introduced the London audience to an entirely new concept of acting. Instead of adhering to the French ideal of a rhetorical style characterised by artificial grandiloquence and statuesque posturing, Garrick adopted a realist approach hitherto unknown on the London stage, the success of which ushered in a radical reorientation of theatrical practice even on the European continent.[20] During his tenure as managing co-director at Drury Lane, Garrick, who was not only an actor but also a dramatist and adapter, set about rediscovering the 'original versions' of Shakespeare's works for the stage. However, although Garrick drew on early editions of Shakespeare's plays for his numerous adaptations, he nevertheless made substantial textual alterations in order to increase their effectiveness in front of an eighteenth-century audience. For his version of *Hamlet* for instance, Garrick cut all the comic elements, such as the character of Osric or the churchyard-scene, in order to underscore the tragic action. His *Romeo and Juliet*, on the other hand, included an additional scene in which the pair of lovers exchange dying words, which was primarily designed to intensify the pathos of the performance. Garrick fervently cultivated his image as 'Shakespeare's trustee'[21] by erecting a temple in honour of the playwright in the garden of his villa, as well as by the planning and realisation of the *Shakespeare Jubilee* at Stratford-upon-Avon in 1769, which also marked the beginning of the discovery of Shakespeare's birthplace as a tourist destination (fig. 7).[22]

The acting style brought to perfection by Garrick was lauded by his contemporaries for its 'naturalness'. What distinguished it was its attention to character development, the use of nuanced facial expressions and gestures, the use of diction closer to everyday speech rather than the bombastic artificiality common to actors at the time, its psychological verisimilitude and a 'corporeal eloquence' on a par with the dramatic text. With this style, Garrick created 'the illusion of a homogeneous character which concealed the ontological difference between the real actor and the fictional role'.[23] The preference for realistic acting ushered in by Garrick during the mid-eighteenth century also contributed to the development and establishment of an illusionist, text-based theatre. This form of theatre monopolised the most prestigious European stages until well into the twentieth century.

With regard to the theatre, 'nature' and 'realism' must always be considered relational terms and historicised accordingly. In the course of the eighteenth century, the concept of nature went through a profound change. During the early Enlightenment, the term was strongly influenced by the rationalist systems theory of Christian Wolff, whose student, Gottsched, later transferred it to the field of

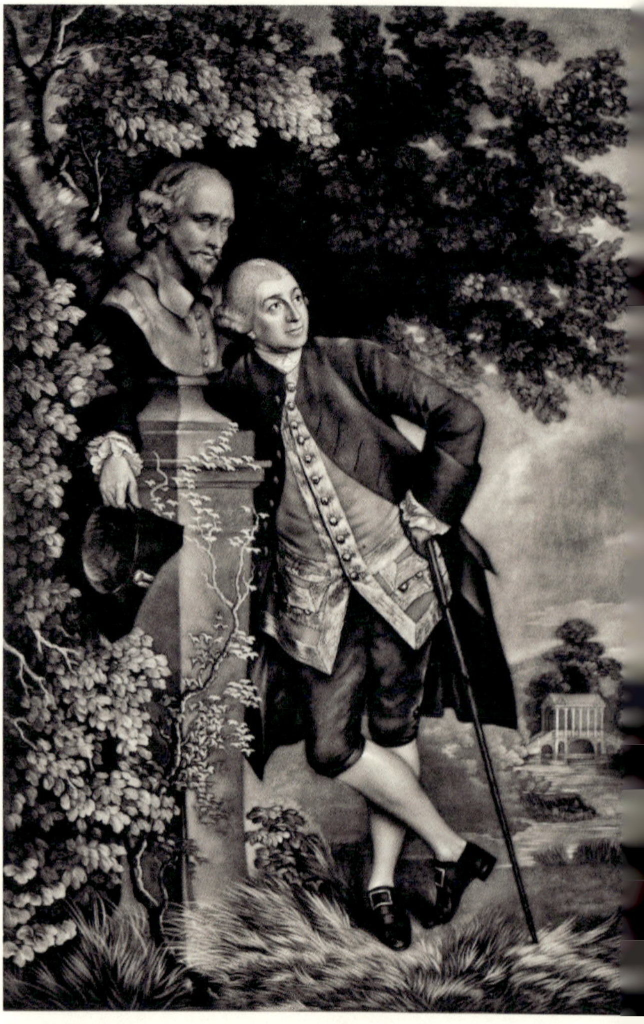

Fig. 7: *David Garrick Leaning on a Bust of Shakespeare*, Mezzotint, 1769, 61.6 × 38.5 cm
After a portrait by Thomas Gainsborough, London, Garrick Club

literature. Wolff and Gottsched sought to incorporate poetics into a rational, self-consistent and systematic theory of art in which subjective judgement no longer possessed any validity, only empirically deducible norms. 'Nature' became a thoroughly rationalised category comparable to 'reason'.[24] A substantial shift concerning this rationalist concept of nature took place during the mid-eighteenth century. Influenced by currents of English Sensualism, which considered sensory perception as constituting the basis of all knowledge, the rationalist concept of nature was gradually superseded by an empiricist one. It was precisely these shifts concerning the concept of nature which affected the 'new' realist style of acting, based as it was on the considerably more comprehensive observation of human action.

Surviving eyewitness accounts of Garrick's character representations attempt to capture and explain his acting style and its effects. One of the most vivid of these accounts – which proved highly influential especially in the German-speaking area – was that written by Georg Christoph Lichtenberg, a scholar from Göttingen, and cited in *Lichtenberg's Visits to England* (German 1775; English 1938). For the duration of Lichtenberg's stay, Garrick, who was then nearing the end of his career, was the undisputed star of the London stage. In disregard of any mention of a character's age within a text, Garrick – as was accepted practice at the time – continued to play the leads for which he had won most renown, like Hamlet and Macbeth, until his retirement in 1776. Lichtenberg's meticulous description of Garrick's reaction to the appearance of Hamlet's father's ghost subsequently became the template for the Hamlet-representations of German actors Friedrich Ludwig Schröder and Johann Franz Hieronymus Brockmann.

Hamlet, wearing a black costume, enters to await the ghost. He is accompanied by Horatio and Marcellus, both of whom are in uniform: 'Hamlet has folded his arms under his cloak and pulled his hat down over his eyes; it is a cold night and just twelve o'clock; the theatre is darkened, and the whole audience of some thousands are as quiet, and their faces as motionless, as though they were painted on the walls of the theatre; even from the farthest end of the playhouse one could hear a pin drop.'[25] Horatio is the one to discover the ghost, who 'has already appeared and stands motionless, before anyone is aware of him'.[26] At this moment, Hamlet is downstage with his back towards the audience. At Horatio's signal, Hamlet turns suddenly towards the auditorium 'and at the same moment staggers back two or three paces with his knees giving way under him; his hat falls to the ground and both his arms, especially the left, are stretched out nearly to their full length, with the hands as high as his head, the right arm more bent and the hand lower, and the fingers apart; his mouth is open: thus he stands rooted to the spot, with legs apart, but no loss of dignity, supported by his friends, who are better acquainted with the apparition and fear lest he should collapse. His whole demeanour is so expressive of terror that it made my flesh creep even before he began to speak. The almost terror-struck silence of the audience, which preceded this appearance and filled one with a sense of insecurity, probably did much to enhance this effect.'[27]

In many accounts, Garrick's style of acting is repeatedly described as being able to enthral the audience without uttering a single word, by means of his masterful body language alone. Rather than the appearance of the ghost itself, it was Hamlet's reaction towards it which most affected the audience. Garrick's virtuosity stirred the audience to identify with the character.

In his travel accounts – which of course are not entirely free of anecdotal exaggeration – the diplomat Helfrich Peter Sturz gives a description of one of Garrick's scenes in *Macbeth*: 'When, with an expression of satanic resolve to commit murder, he imagines seeing a dagger and, with a grip as if reaching for a crown, he grasps at its hilt, a stranger in my box, who, not knowing one word of English, had understood nothing of the plot, fell unconscious of fright.'[28]

In Fuseli's painting *Gertrude, Hamlet and the Ghost of Hamlet's Father* (cat. 48) as well as in his watercolour *Garrick and Mrs. Pritchard as Macbeth and Lady after the Murder of King Duncan* (fig. 1, p. 22), the focus is on the artistic realisation of terror which is communicated by means of facial and bodily expression.[29] In this they are similar to Garrick's representations of the same emotion. By means of external signs of the body, both the theatre audience and the beholder of Fuseli's art were supposed to be able to identify the psychological state of the protagonists.

From the second half of the eighteenth century, dramaturgy and performance turned their attention towards the characters of the play, their behaviour, motivation and psychological disposition. In one of his lectures, Fuseli emphasized that this interest in the fictional characters was a distinguishing feature of Shakespeare's art and that the dramatic action was merely a means of showcasing them.[30]

The visualisation of interiority and of the hidden subconscious became the mainspring of realist acting. Actors were soon considered 'experts of the soul'[31] capable of making the psychological visible through their bodies for an attentive audience to decipher. Audiences of the eighteenth century seemed most keen to experience emotional thrill or excitation as well as an externalisation of feeling and emotions – an aspect which resonates through Fuseli's work in his penchant for the spectacular.[32] The theatre's potential to elicit such experiences from historical subjects resulted in a literal theatre craze in the second half of the century – a craze which Fuseli, accustomed to Zurich's animosity towards theatre, clearly could not escape. Just as Lichtenberg tried to approximate Garrick's acting by giving detailed descriptions of especially vivid scenes, so did Fuseli choose the most memorable moments for his Shakespearean images.

Versed in the art of theatre, Shakespeare wrote tailor-made texts for specific ensembles which lent themselves well to stagings – which is also the reason why his plays do not include extensive stage directions. The stage action appropriate to any scene could only be deduced from the written dialogue. In the fourth scene of the first act, for instance, Hamlet commands his companions to release him so that he can follow his father's ghost. Lichtenberg describes Garrick's rendition of this scene in the following way: 'The ghost beckons to him. You see him free himself from his friends, who are warning him not to follow it and holding him back; his eyes remain fixed on the ghost, even as he speaks to his companions.'[33] Fuseli made an illustration of this scene years after Garrick had already retired from acting, and yet his composition seems to capture precisely what Lichtenberg described (fig. 8).

Fuseli's preference for the supernatural, for apparitions, witches and fairies as motifs for his Shakespearean images, is conspicuous (cat. 42, 43, 46; fig. 8).[34] And while his representations of phantasmagorical horror may have been inspired by

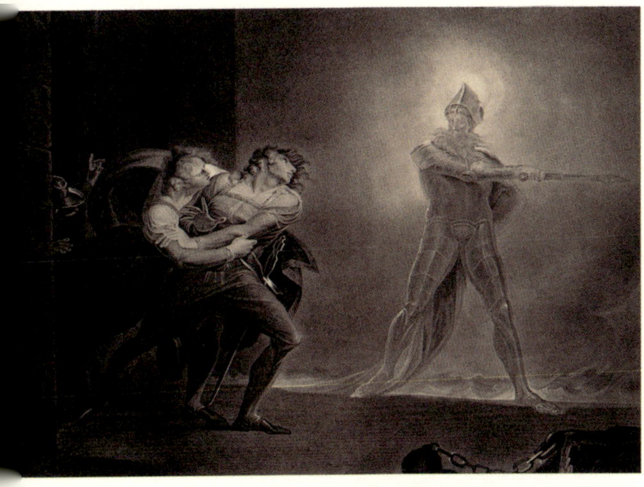

Fig. 8: *Hamlet, Horatio, Marcellus and the Ghost*, 1796, stipple engraving by Robert Thew after Henry Fuseli, 44.3 x 59.9 cm Kunsthaus Zürich (Schiff 731)

contemporary theatre, those of Shakespeare's *A Midsummer Night's Dream* eliminate all such reminiscences (cats 32–36). Fuseli devoted himself to the first scene of the fourth act of *Macbeth*, in which the king visits the Weird Sisters, a number of times (cat. 44). According to Knowles, Fuseli laboured to add to the scene what he thought the poetry lacked. Knowles cites the artist as saying: 'To say nothing of the general arrangement of my picture, which in composition is altogether triangular, (and the triangle is a mystical figure,) I have endeavoured to shew a colossal head rising out of the abyss, and that head Macbeth's likeness. What, I would ask, would be a greater object of terror to you, if, some night on going home, you were to find yourself sitting at your own table, either writing, reading, or otherwise employed? would not this make a powerful impression on your mind?'[35]

Fuseli's lifelong study of Shakespeare's work makes him 'one of the most rigorous and distinguished authorities on Shakespeare during his time'.[36] Even as early as 1773, Lavater, in a letter to Herder, almost prophetically characterised Fuseli, who was then resident in Rome, as 'Shakespeare's painter .... He does not draw portraits but all his traits are true and yet caricature.'[37]

1 Lessing 1985–2003., vol. 1, pp. 728–29. Transl. Marcel Behn.
2 See Alexander Honold's essay in the present volume, pp. 37–57.
3 See Eva Reifert's essay in the present volume, pp. 19–35.
4 Eichhorn 1965, p. 44.
5 Letter from Fuseli to Bodmer, 7.2.1766, in Füssli 1942, pp. 120–26, see p. 123. Transl. Marcel Behn.
6 See Häublein 2005; Paulin 2007.
7 Ritchie/Sabor 2012, p. 8.
8 Schabert 2009, p. 610. Transl. Marcel Behn.
9 See Ritchie/Sabor 2012, p. 4.
10 See ibid., p. 6.
11 Schabert 2009, p. 611. Transl. Marcel Behn.
12 Letter from Fuseli to Dälliker, 12, 13, 14, 15.11.1765, in: Füssli 1942, pp. 101–16, see p. 110. Transl. Marcel Behn.
13 Ibid., p. 111. Transl. Marcel Behn.
14 See Knowles 1831, vol. 1, p. 39.
15 West 1991, p. 31.
16 See ibid.
17 Nicoll 1980, p. 111 (emphasis in original).
18 See ibid., pp. 100, 102.
19 Playbill, qtd. in ibid., p. 1.
20 See Hochholdinger-Reiterer 2014.
21 Roselt 2014, p. 130. Transl. Marcel Behn.
22 See Schabert 2009, p. 124; Stochholm 1964.
23 Roselt 2014, p. 131. Transl. Marcel Behn.
24 See Siegrist 1984.
25 Georg Christoph Lichtenberg, 'Lichtenberg's Visits to England as Described in His Letters and Diaries', trans. and ed. Margaret L. Mare and W. H. Quarrell, Oxford 1938, qtd. in 'Gothic Documents. A Sourcebook 1700–1820', ed. E. J. Clery and Robert Miles, Manchester 2000, p. 107.
26 Ibid., pp. 107–08.
27 Ibid.
28 Sturz 1779, p. 12. Transl. Marcel Behn.
29 See Vogel 2001.
30 See Knowles 1831, vol. 2, pp. 195–96.
31 Ruppert 1995, p. 70. Transl. Marcel Behn.
32 See ibid., pp. 80–90.
33 Georg Christoph Lichtenberg, 'Lichtenberg's Visits to England as Described in His Letters and Diaries', trans. and ed. Margaret L. Mare and W. H. Quarrell, Oxford 1938, qtd. in 'Gothic Documents. A Sourcebook 1700–1820', ed. E. J. Clery and Robert Miles, Manchester 2000, p. 108.
34 See Becker 2005.
35 Knowles 1831, vol. 1, pp. 189–90.
36 Mason 1964, p. 85.
37 Letter from Lavater to Herder, 4.11.1773, trans. in: Petra Maisak, 'Henry Fuseli – "Shakespeare's Painter"', http://shakespeare-gesellschaft.de/en/publications/boydell-catalogue/petra-maisak.html

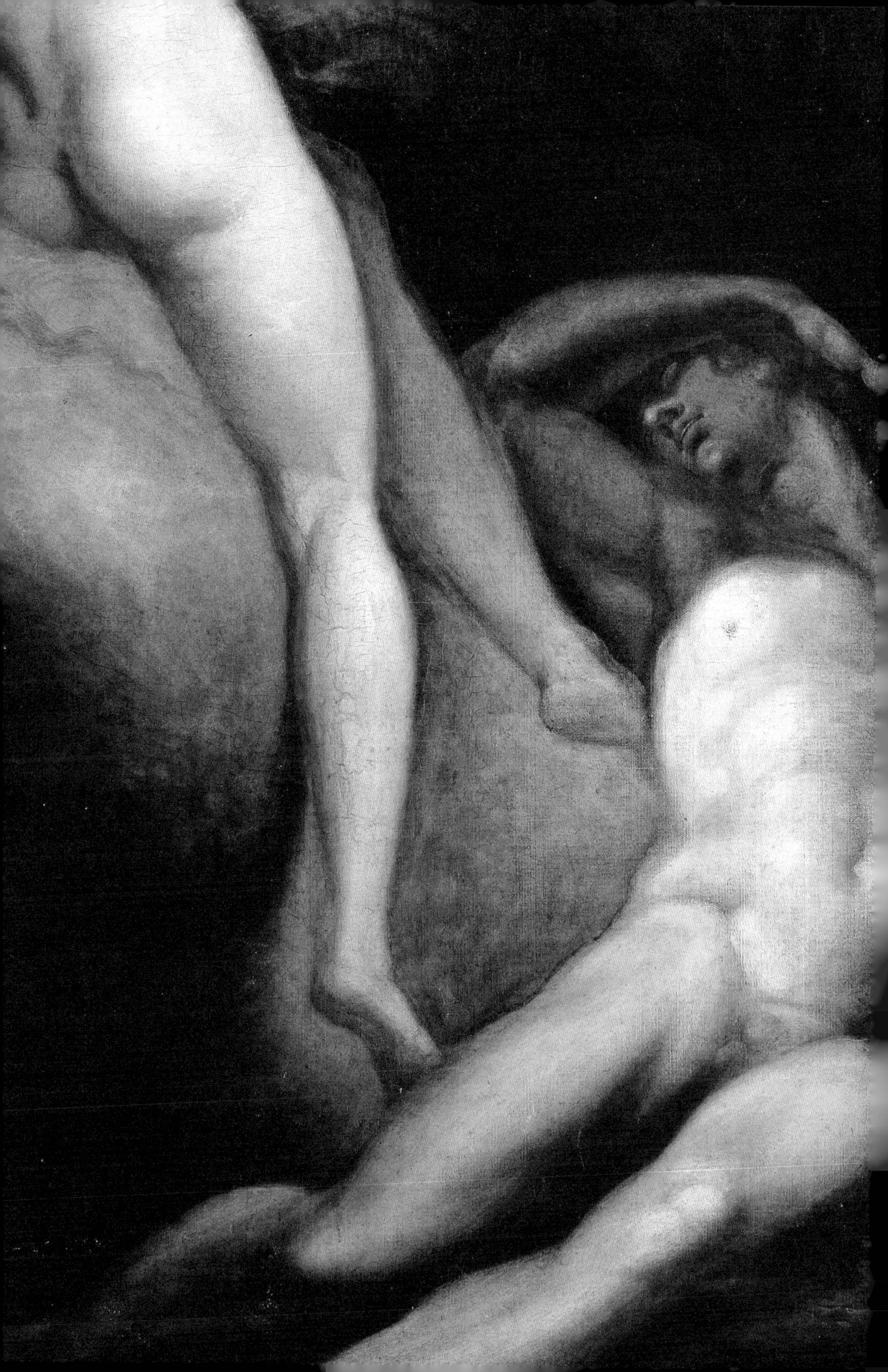

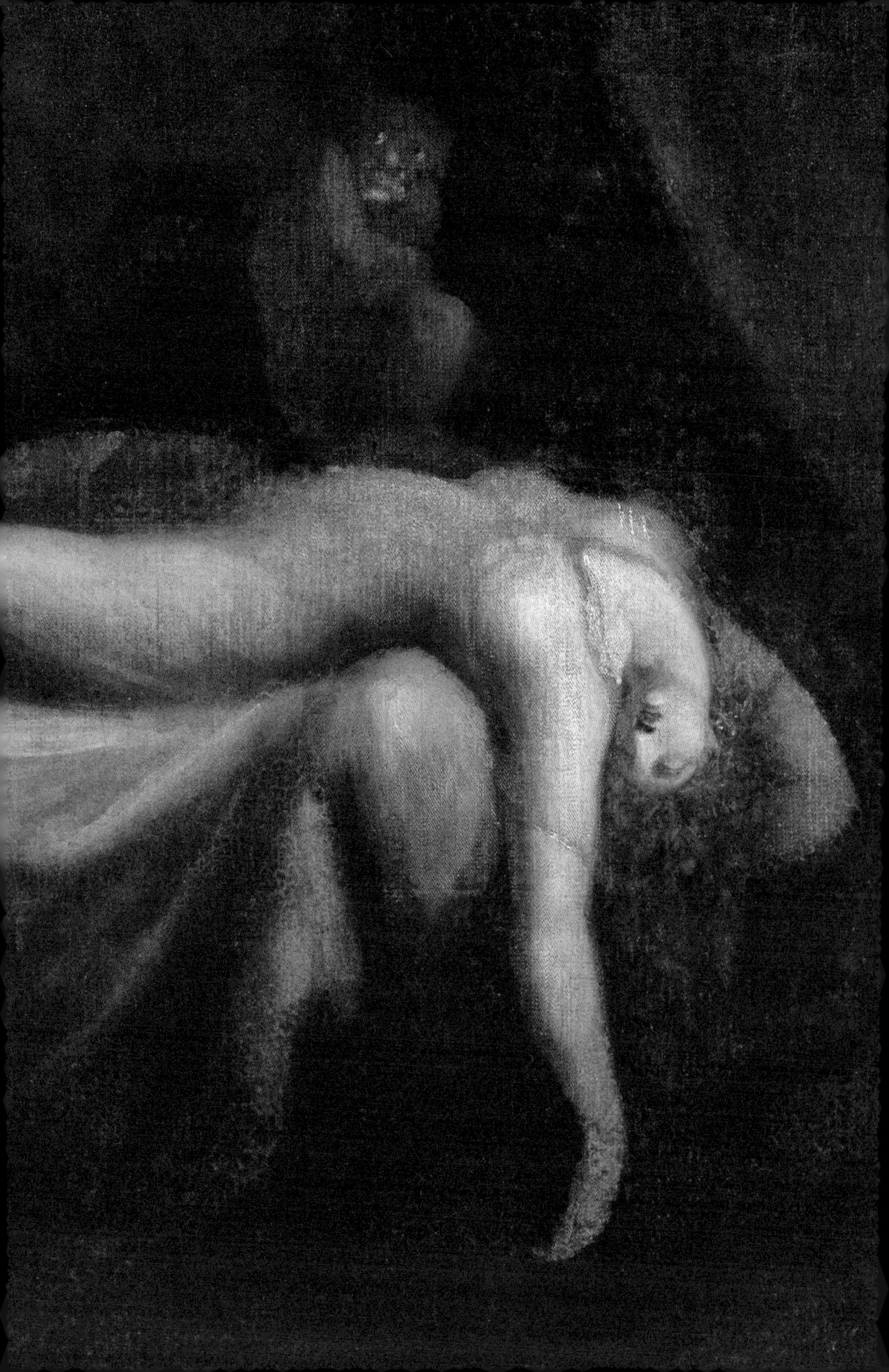

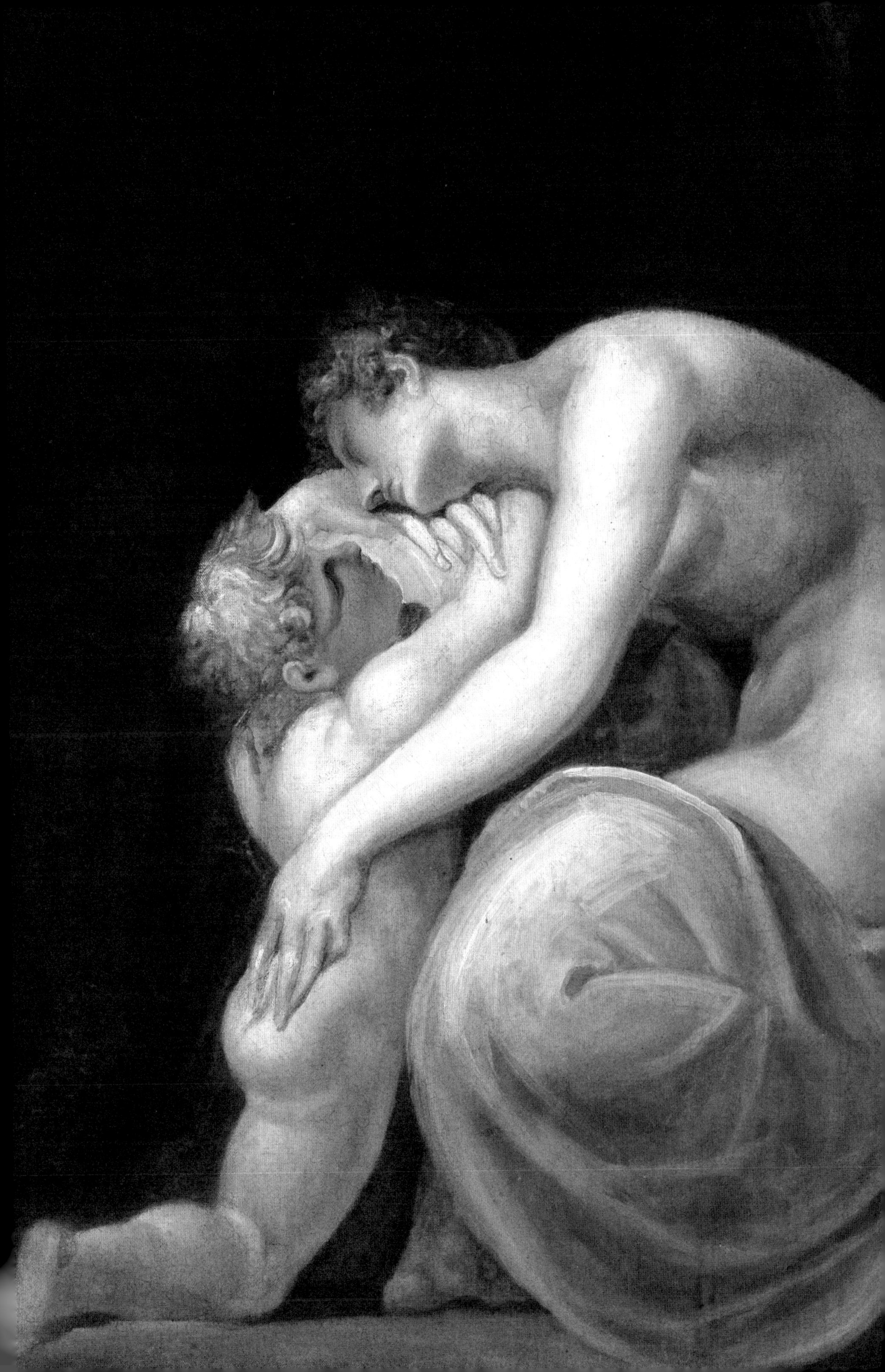

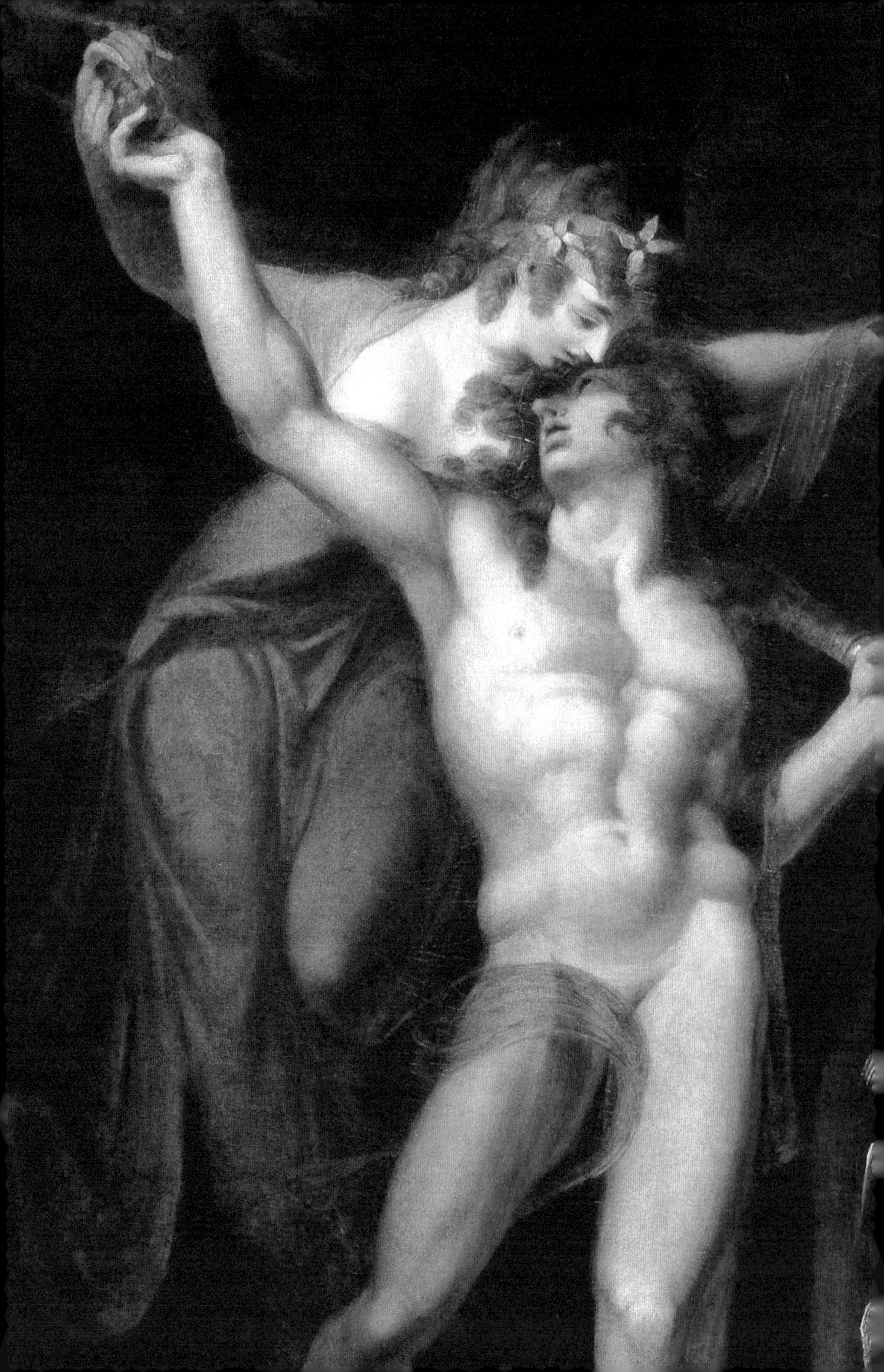

Classical Antiquity and the Middle Ages

In 1799 Henry Fuseli inaugurated his contribution to the fashion for 'poets' galleries' in Britain – a temporary exhibition of work based on the writings of his revered Milton (see 'Milton', pp. 141–43). It featured two literary subjects significantly older than British seventeenth-century poetry: the twelfth painting in the gallery depicted *Odysseus between Scylla and Charybdis* (cat. 6), an episode from Homer's *Odyssey*, while the thirty-fourth showed Kriemhild plotting vengeance over the sword of the murdered Siegfried, a scene from the *Nibelungenlied*. Why did he include these? The justification in both cases was slim. Milton devoted no more than three lines to Odysseus' adventure, which is one of two parallels from classical mythology he cites in order to underline the dynamism of the rising figure of Satan, and Fuseli even passes over in silence the other comparison, with the Argonauts, in the quotation from Milton he used to caption his painting.[1] Still flimsier is the pretext provided by Milton's poem *Il Penseroso* for invoking the *Nibelungenlied*, for the passage in question mentions only bards in general who sing the praises of great deeds in solemn and serious tones.[2]

The use of a motif from the *Odyssey* that for Milton represented no more than an almost random allusion must be seen first and foremost as evidence of the enormous influence that classical subject matter had exerted for centuries on the arts in the West. Fuseli had perfected his Ancient Greek and Latin as a budding theologian at the Collegium Carolinum in Zurich, where he was a valued student of two philologists of European standing: Johann Jakob Bodmer and Johann Jakob Breitinger. Bodmer, who had translated works by both Homer and Milton, encouraged Fuseli in his enthusiasm for English literature. Yet when the almost forty-year-old artist came to paint a large picture of himself conversing learnedly with his teacher and mentor, a canvas that is both a double portrait and a declaration of intent, it was Homer and Homer alone who, in the shape of a larger than life-size stone guest, gravely watched over the two intellectuals' deliberations.[3] The Classicist in Fuseli lived on. Later, for example, in London, he complied with a request by the publisher Joseph Johnson to revise translations of Homer's epic poems made by William Cowper, a poet whose work he admired and illustrated.[4]

A shift in perceptions of Homer's work occurred in the eighteenth century, encouraged by a gain in currency of the notion of the 'noble savage' advanced by Michel de Montaigne and by the belief propagated by Jean-Jacques Rousseau and others that humanity had existed in a state of nature prior to being corrupted by civilisation.[5] The classical legacy was no longer viewed exclusively in normative terms, as the epitome of rationality and sublimity, but increasingly as a manifestation of the savage, primeval and archaic. Fuseli reflects this move towards the irrational both in his powerful and striking interpretations of the standard scenes from classical mythology and in his depictions of surprising, out-of-the-way subjects that lay outside the iconographical canon.

Longing for a primordial and unspoilt existence, before and beyond urbanisation, could avail itself of two further focuses. In Switzerland the early Confederates were glorified as almost superhuman mountain-dwellers endowed with outstanding health, virtue and resilience by a largely natural living environment. The Zurich physician Johann Jakob Scheuchzer had helped to pioneer such attitudes with his reports on scientific expeditions in the Alps, one of which, *Itinera alpina tria*, had been published in London in 1708.

Bodmer eagerly took up the subject, but shifted the emphasis from topography and natural history to literature and history. Bodmer promoted a second projection surface for yearnings after pre-urban life by maintaining that medieval poetry had blossomed during the Hohenstaufen era. At first, he was unable to name any relevant texts, but these turned up in due course. In 1746, for instance, he borrowed the *Grosse Heidelberger Liederhandschrift* from Paris, published excerpts from the manuscript and, to his great patriotic delight, was able to connect its genesis with the patrician Manesse family of Zurich. Yet he still lacked an epic poem capable, as it were, of competing on equal terms with Homer. The discovery in 1755 of a copy of the *Nibelungenlied* therefore came as a godsend – so much so that he initially disowned its real finder, his friend Jacob Hermann Obereit, and claimed the 'breakthrough' for himself.

Contemporaries were soon lauding the heroic Nibelung tale as the 'German *Iliad*' (Johann von Müller). Bodmer's pupil Fuseli was as much inspired by this idea as his teacher.[6] Receiving the latter's publication of excerpts from the manuscript in 1769, he immediately accorded the *Nibelungenlied* second place in the pantheon, 'directly after Homer'.[7] Over the years his appreciation of the work increased to the point where, in two poems of his own, he asserted that 'Der Dichter der Schwesterrache' ('The Poet of The Sister's Revenge', the title of one of the poems) put Homer in the shade and he called 'Sivrit [Siegfried] a better Achilleus'.[8]

This trial of strength between the *Nibelungenlied* and classical antiquity informed Fuseli's idiosyncratic treatment of the German poem, which verges on the thoroughly bizarre. Nudity *all'antica* dominates, and only occasionally is there evidence of *convenevolezza*, the notion developed over centuries of artistic practice and theory that costumes and settings should be historically apposite.[9] Fuseli was not the only one to subvert this principle, however: Goethe, for example, also questioned its validity.[10]

Fuseli sometimes used Greek letters when writing German inscriptions on his *Nibelungenlied* drawings,[11] instinctively letting himself be guided even in such details by the paradigm of Homer. Ultimately, too, his manner of narrating episodes from the *Völkerwanderung* (Migration Period), Swiss history and Norse mythology is always the same and does not differ from his approach to classical themes. In each case the subject matter mutates into a projection surface for artistic concepts and, sometimes, for obsessions. BB

1 Schiff 1963, pp. 60, 145.
2 Ibid., p. 155.
3 See p. 45, fig. 3: Henry Fuseli, *The Artist in Conversation with Johann Jakob Bodmer*, 1778–81, oil on canvas, 163 × 150 cm, Kunsthaus Zürich (Schiff 366); see Gonon 2007.
4 Schiff 1973, vol. 1, p. 125; see King 1983.
5 Debrunner 1996, pp. 45, 82–83 et passim.
6 Ibid., p. 90.
7 Letter from Fuseli to Lavater, London, 23 July 1769; qtd. in Füssli 1942, p. 146.
8 Füssli 1973, p. 97.
9 Haussherr 1984.
10 Ibid., pp. 45–47.
11 Schiff 1000, 1380, 1381, 1386, 1534.

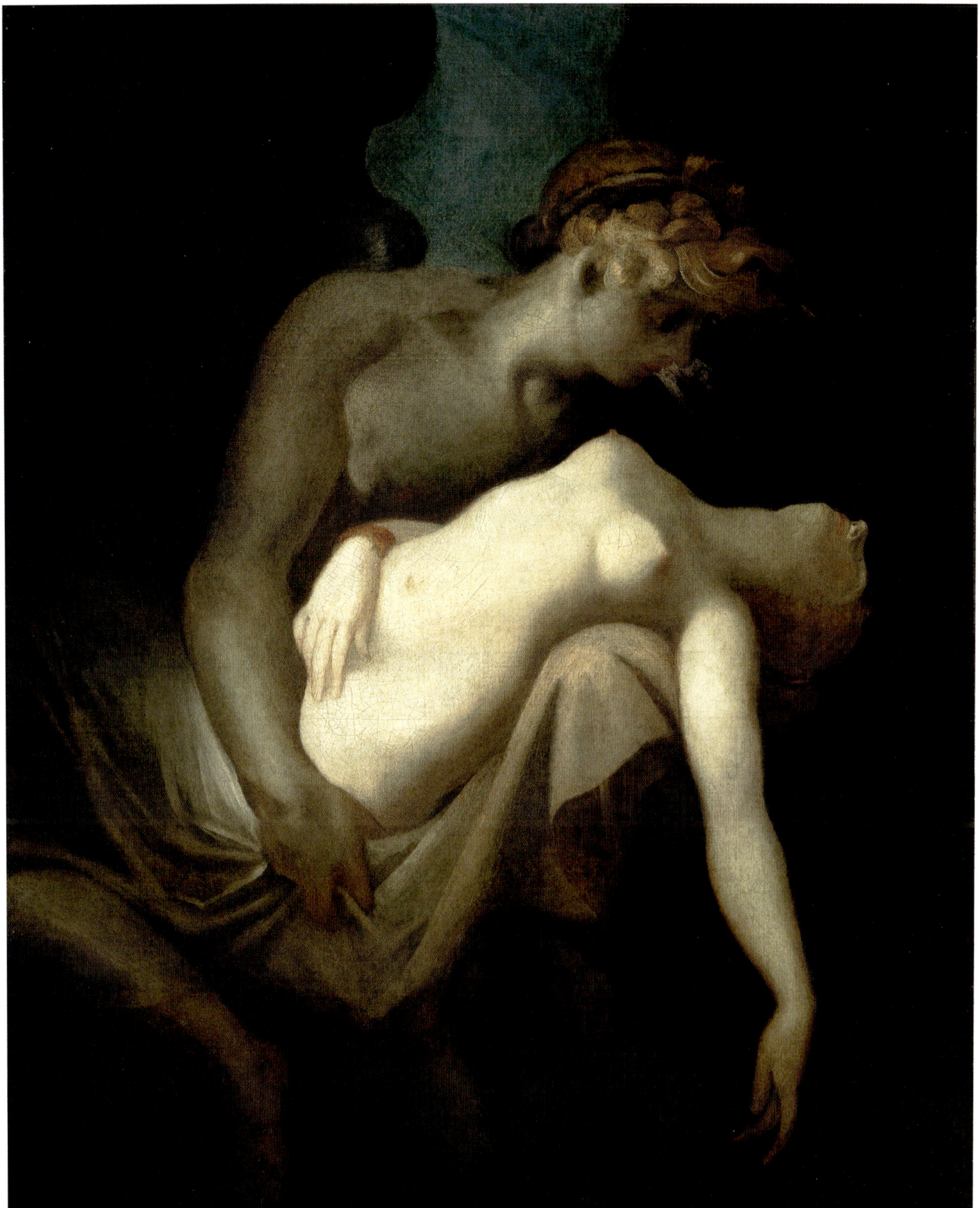

Cat. 1 *Amor and Psyche*, c. 1810

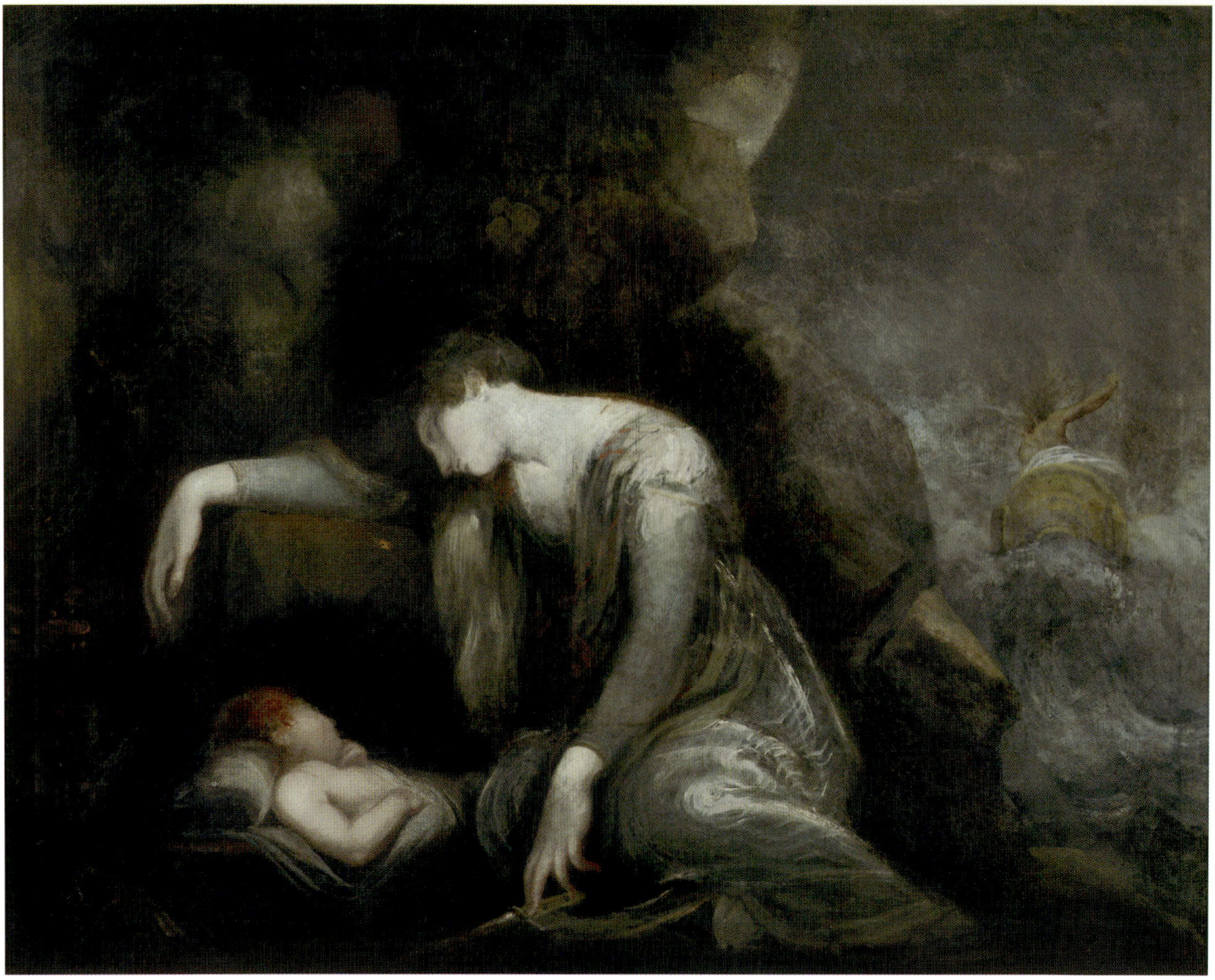

Cat. 2 *Danaë and Perseus on Seriphos (?)*,
c. 1785–90

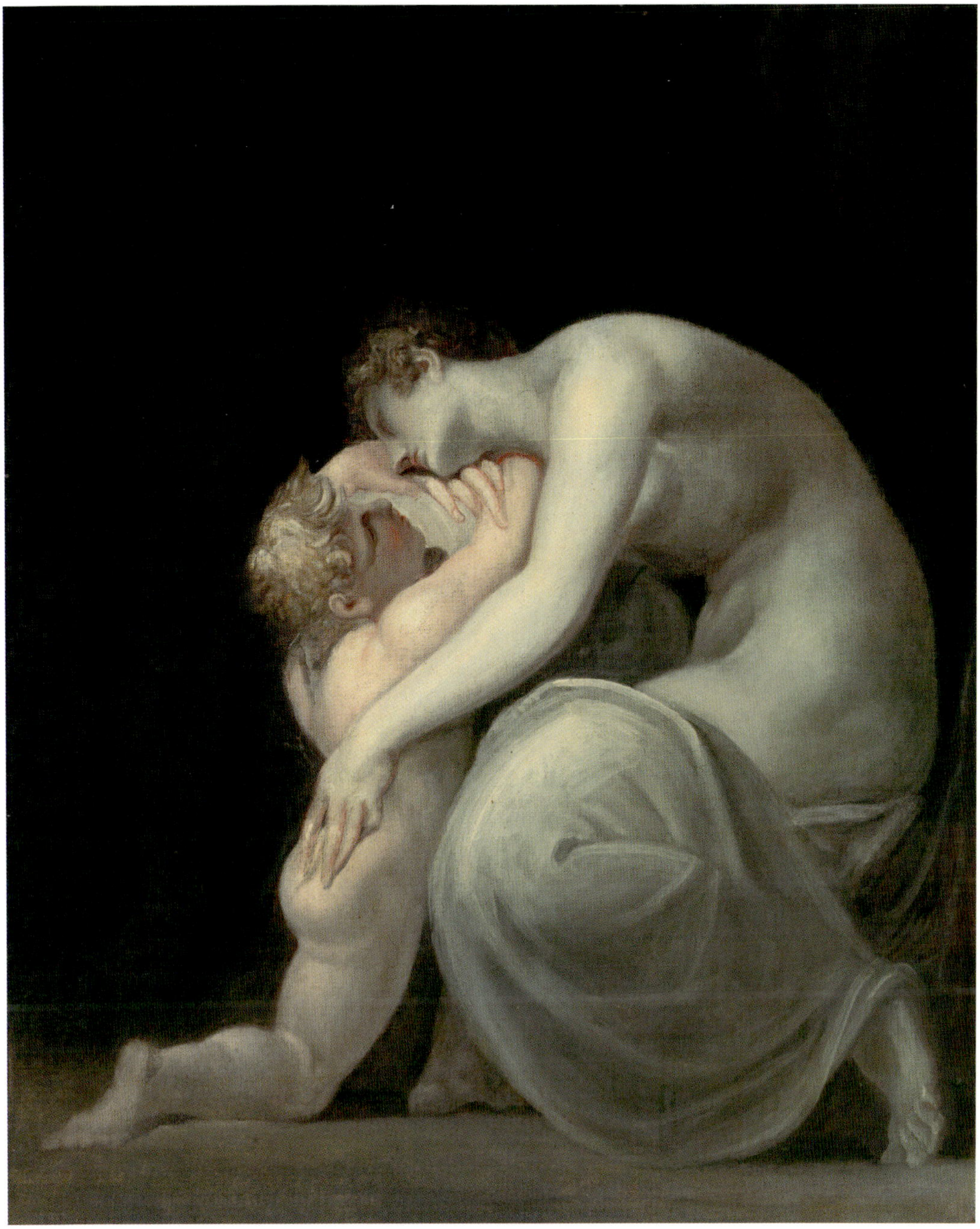

Cat. 3 *Tekemessa and Eurysakes*,
c. 1800–10

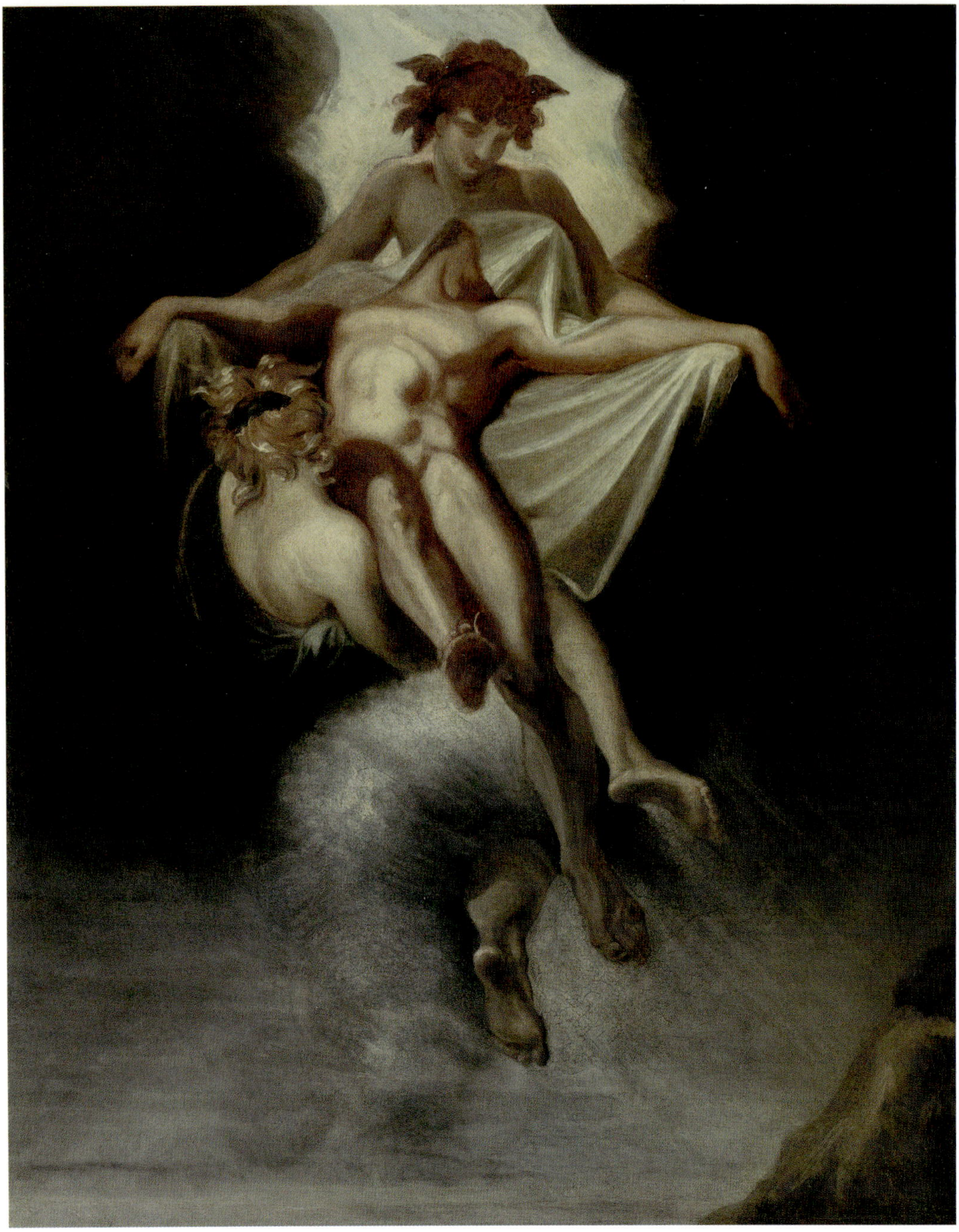

Cat. 4 *Sleep and Death Bear the Body of Sarpedon Away to Lycia*, 1803

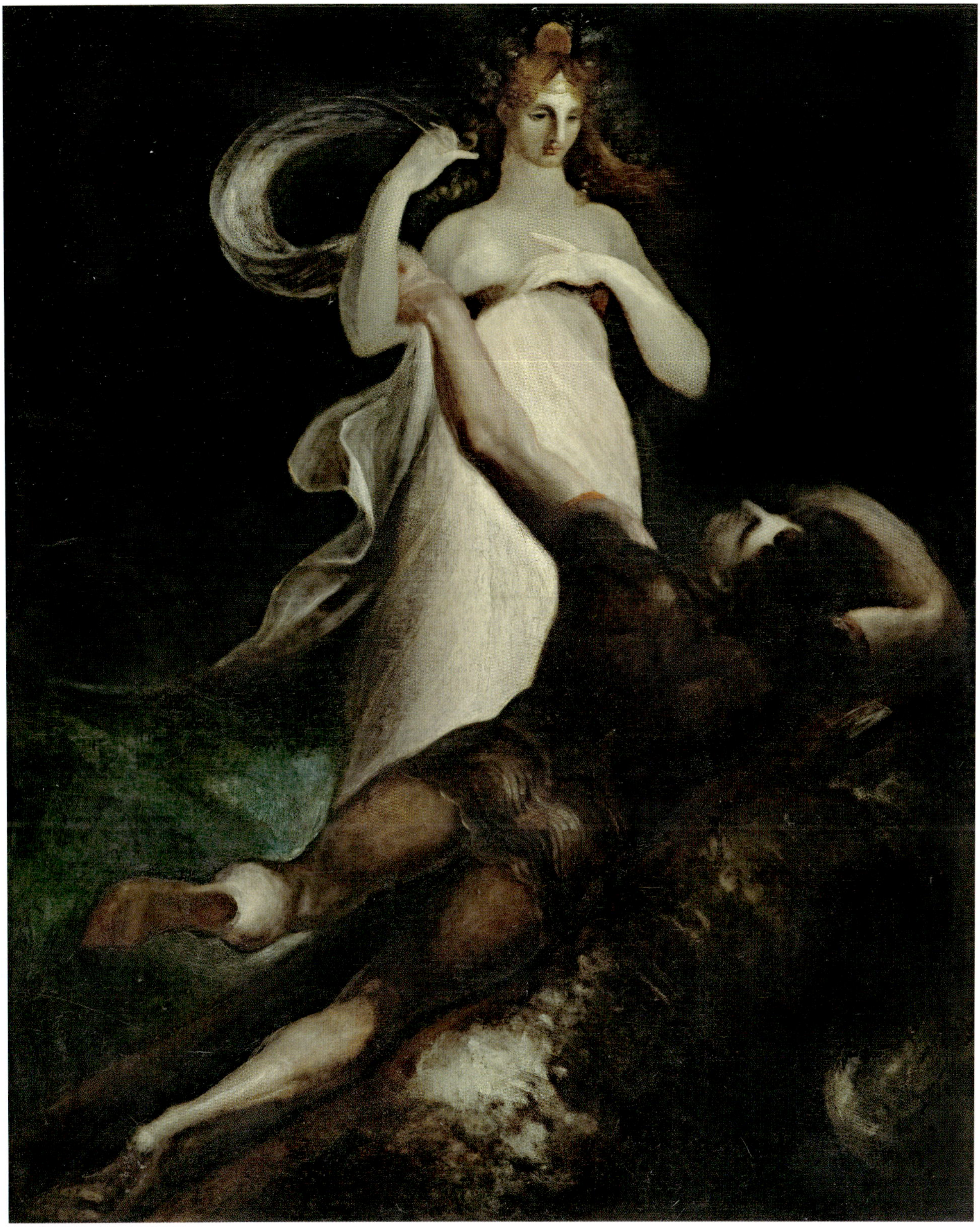

Cat. 5 *Odysseus, on the Raft, Receives the Sacred Veil from Ino–Leucothea*, c. 1805–10

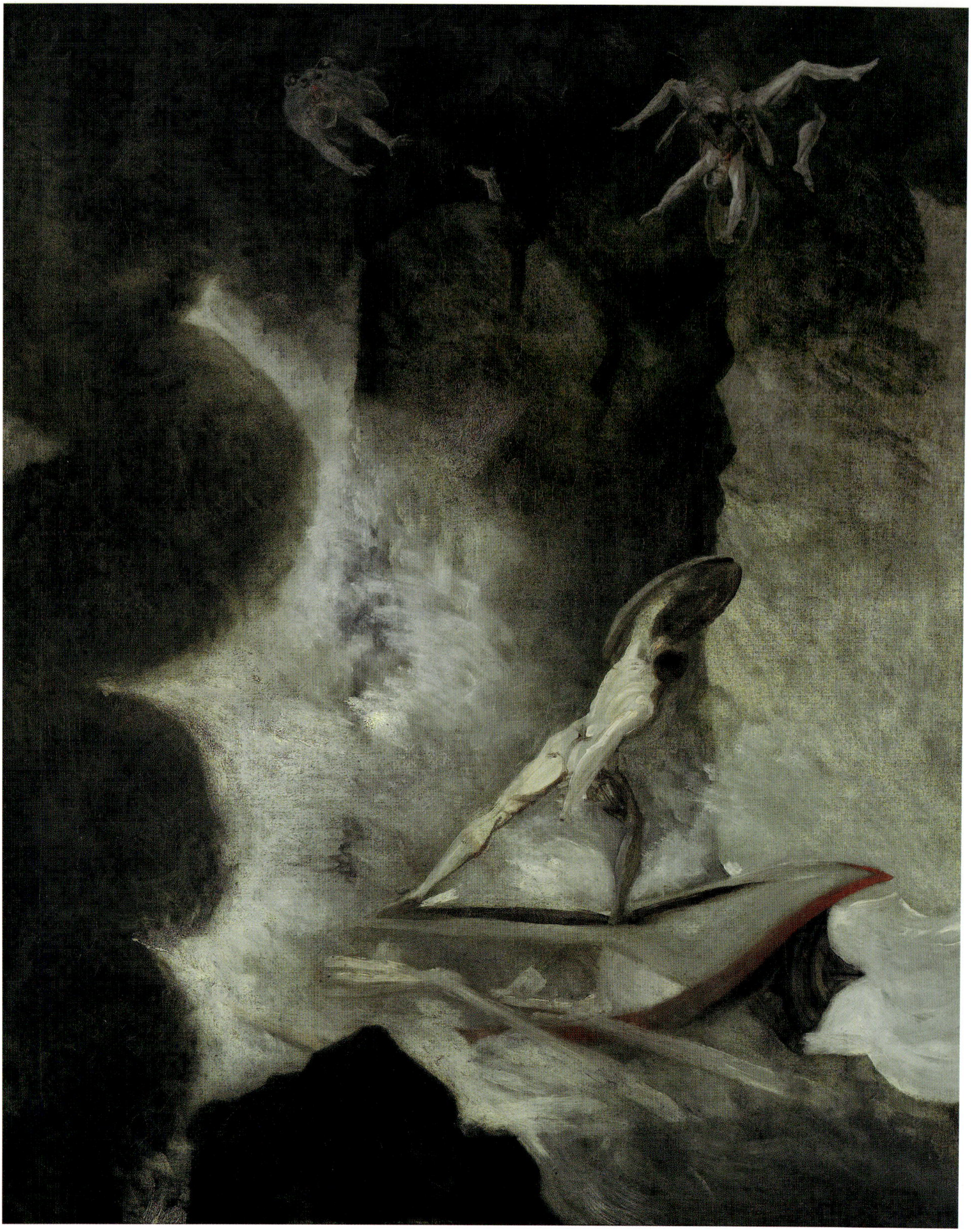

Cat. 6 *Odysseus between Scylla and Charybdis*, c. 1794–96

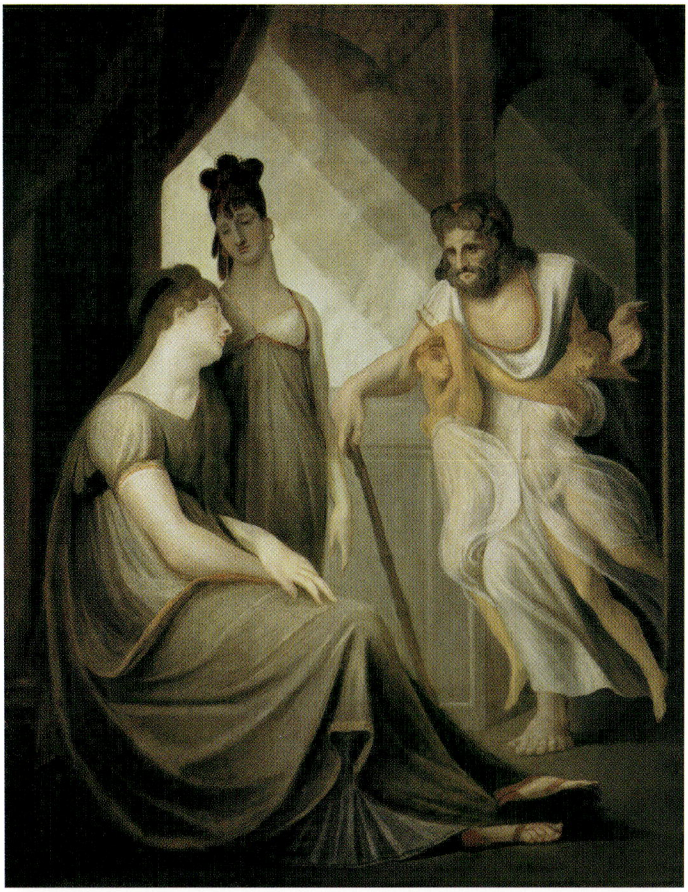

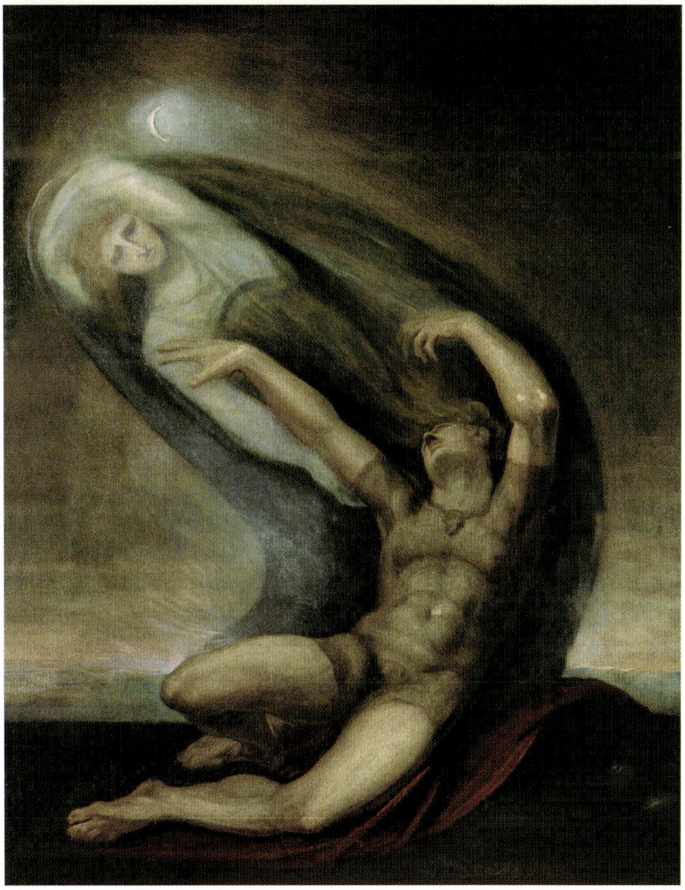

Cat. 7 *Thetis Asks Hephaestus to Provide Achilles with Armour*, 1803

Cat. 8 *Achilles Grasping at the Shade of Patroclus*, 1803

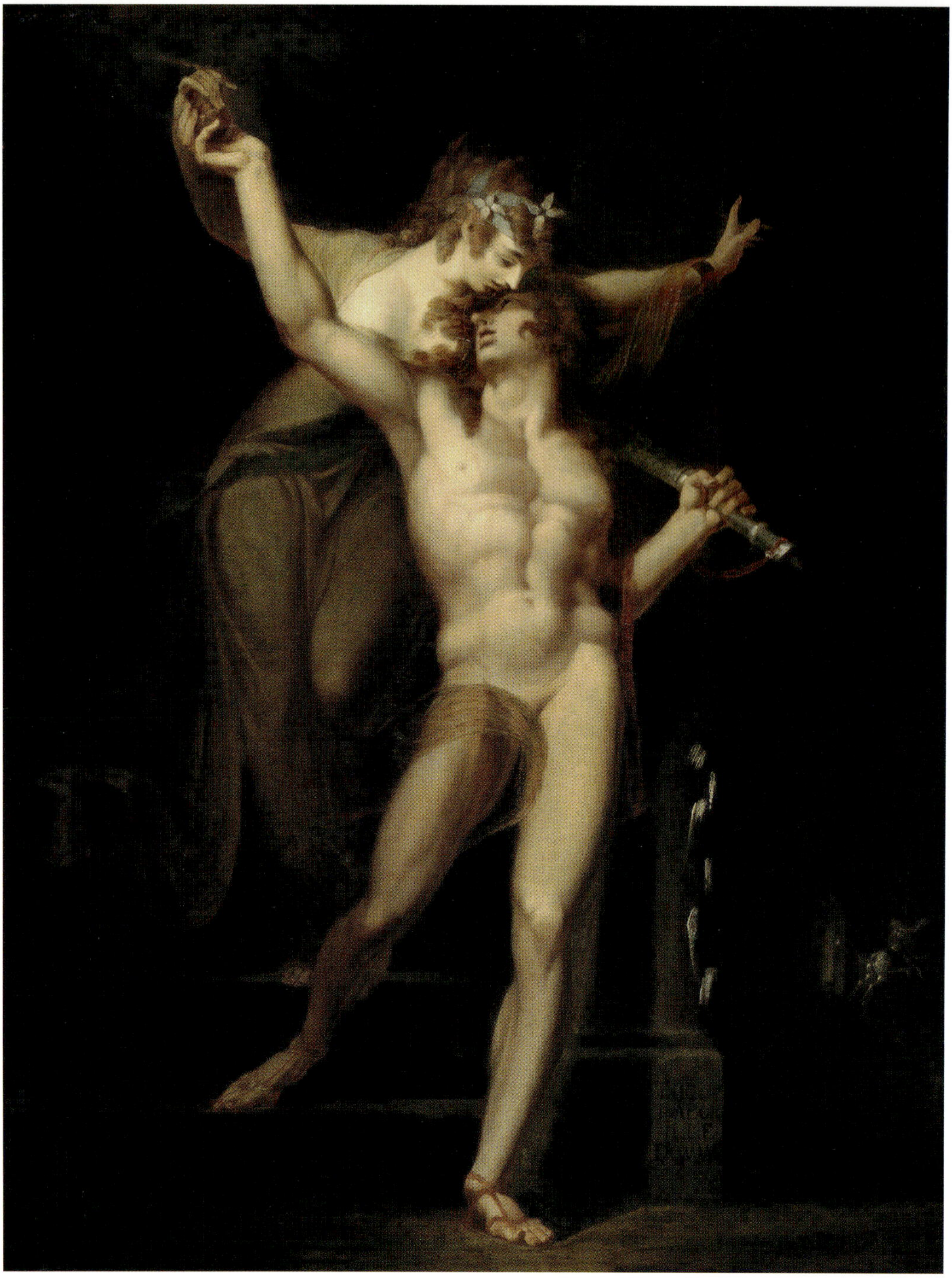

Cat. 9 *Theseus and Ariadne*, 1788

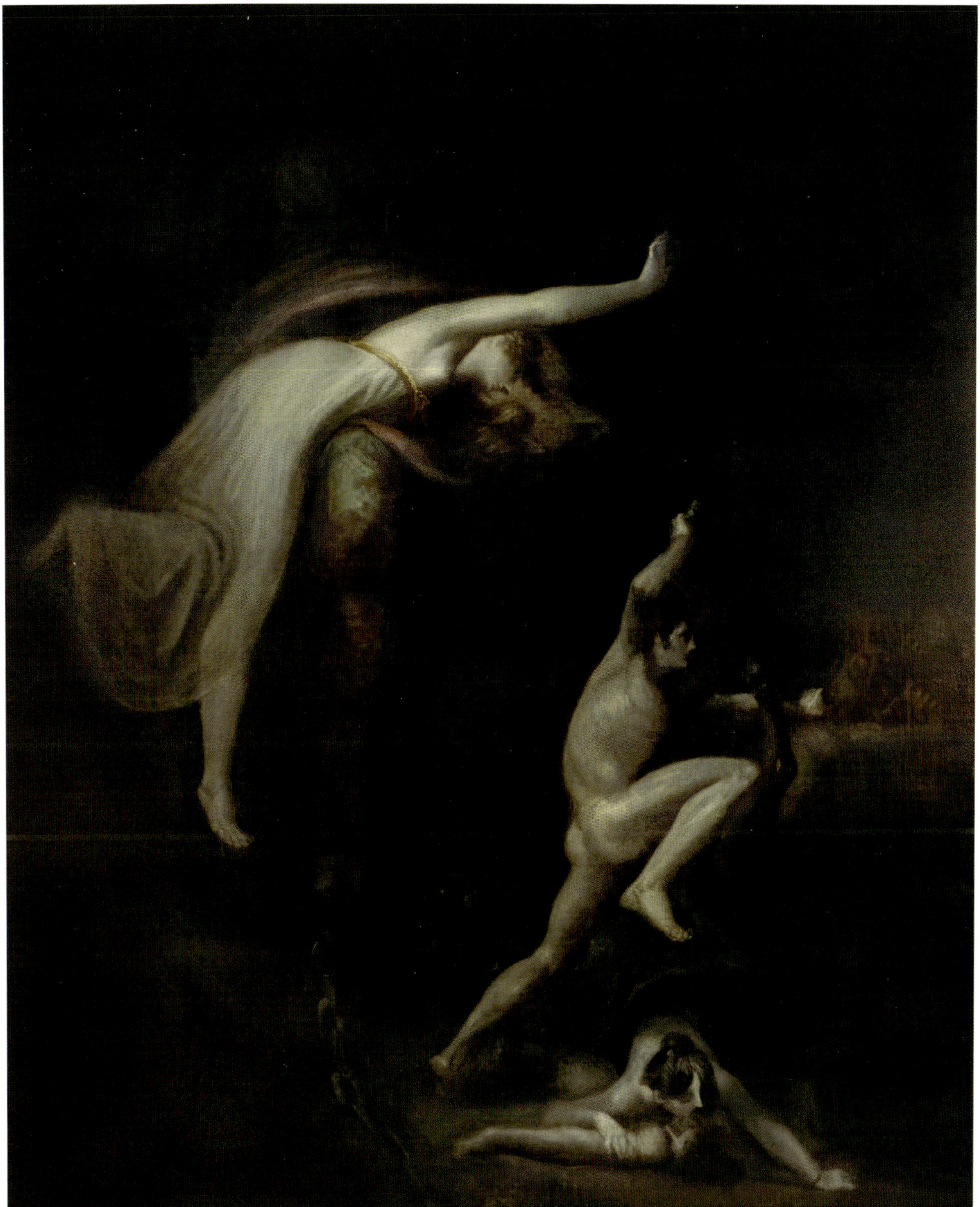

Cat. 10 *Ariadne Watches Theseus Fighting the Minotaur*, c. 1815–20

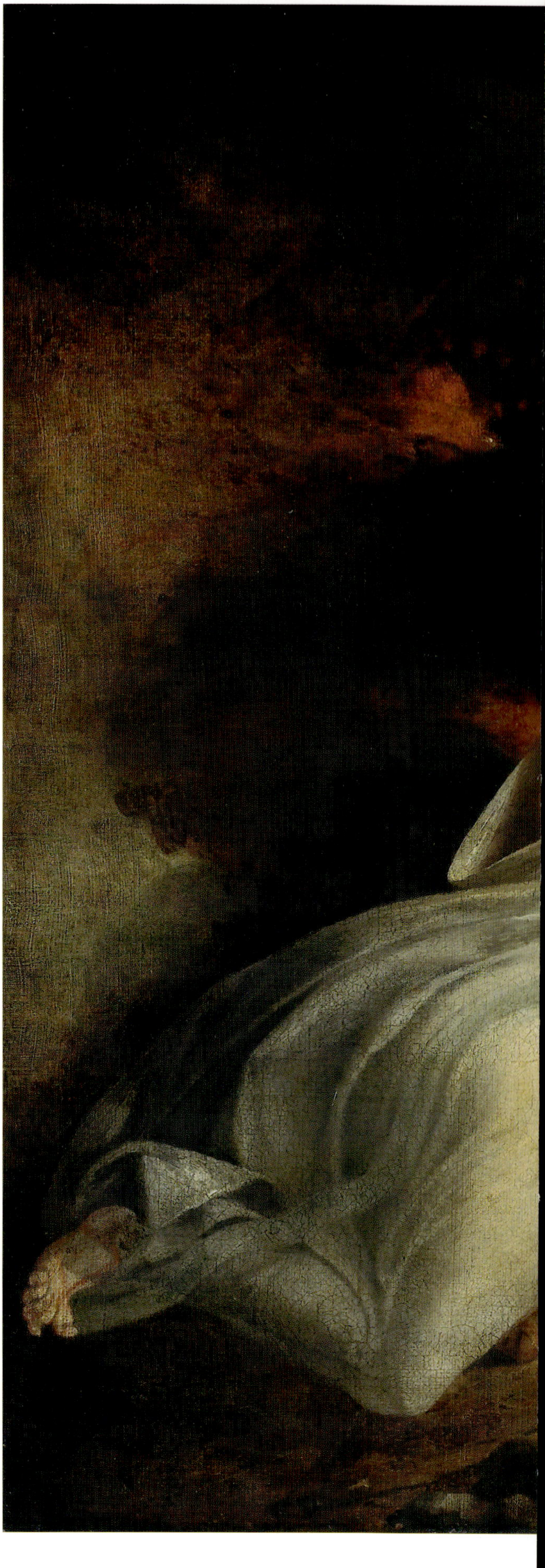

Cat. 11 *The Death of Oedipus*, 1783–84

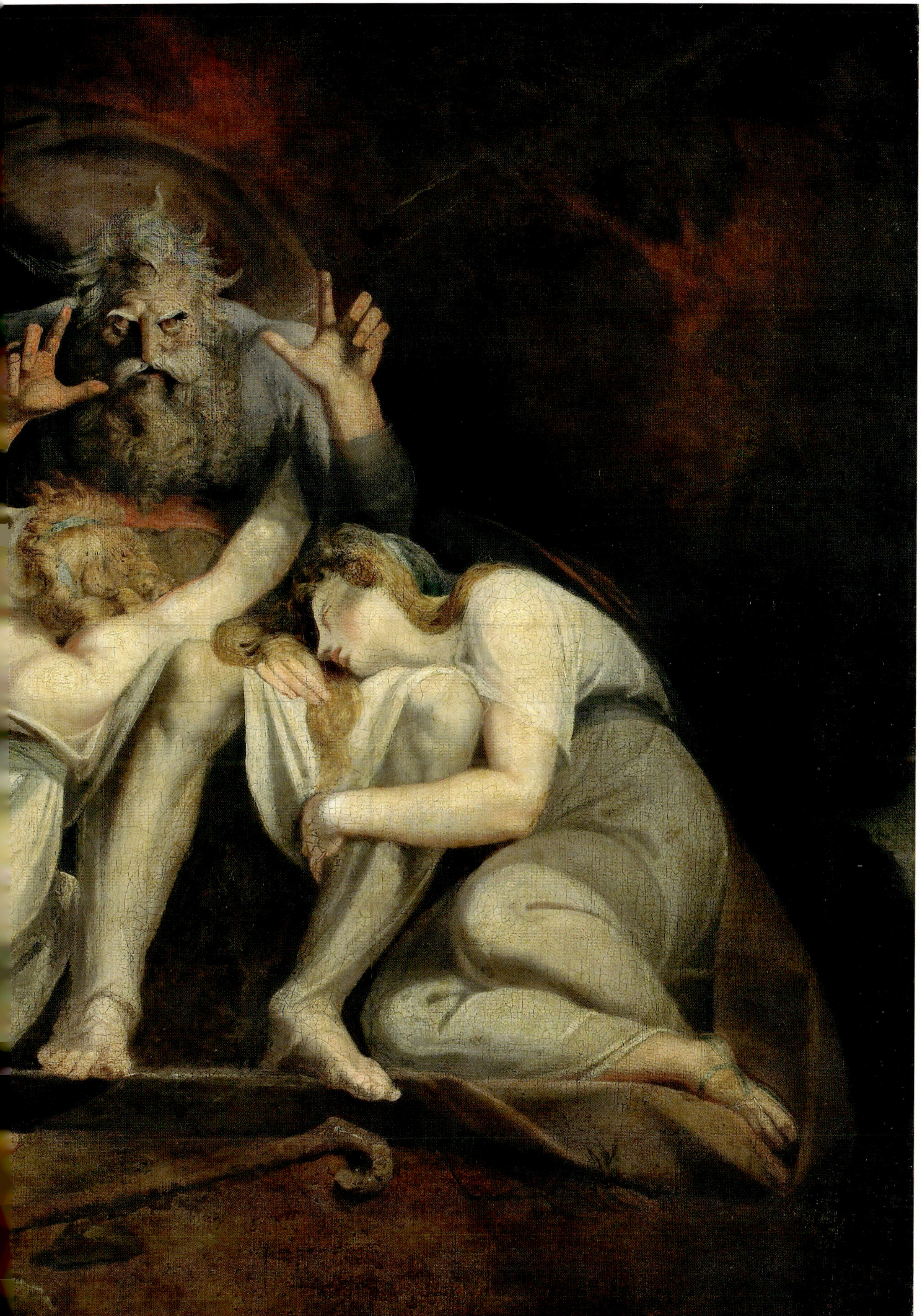

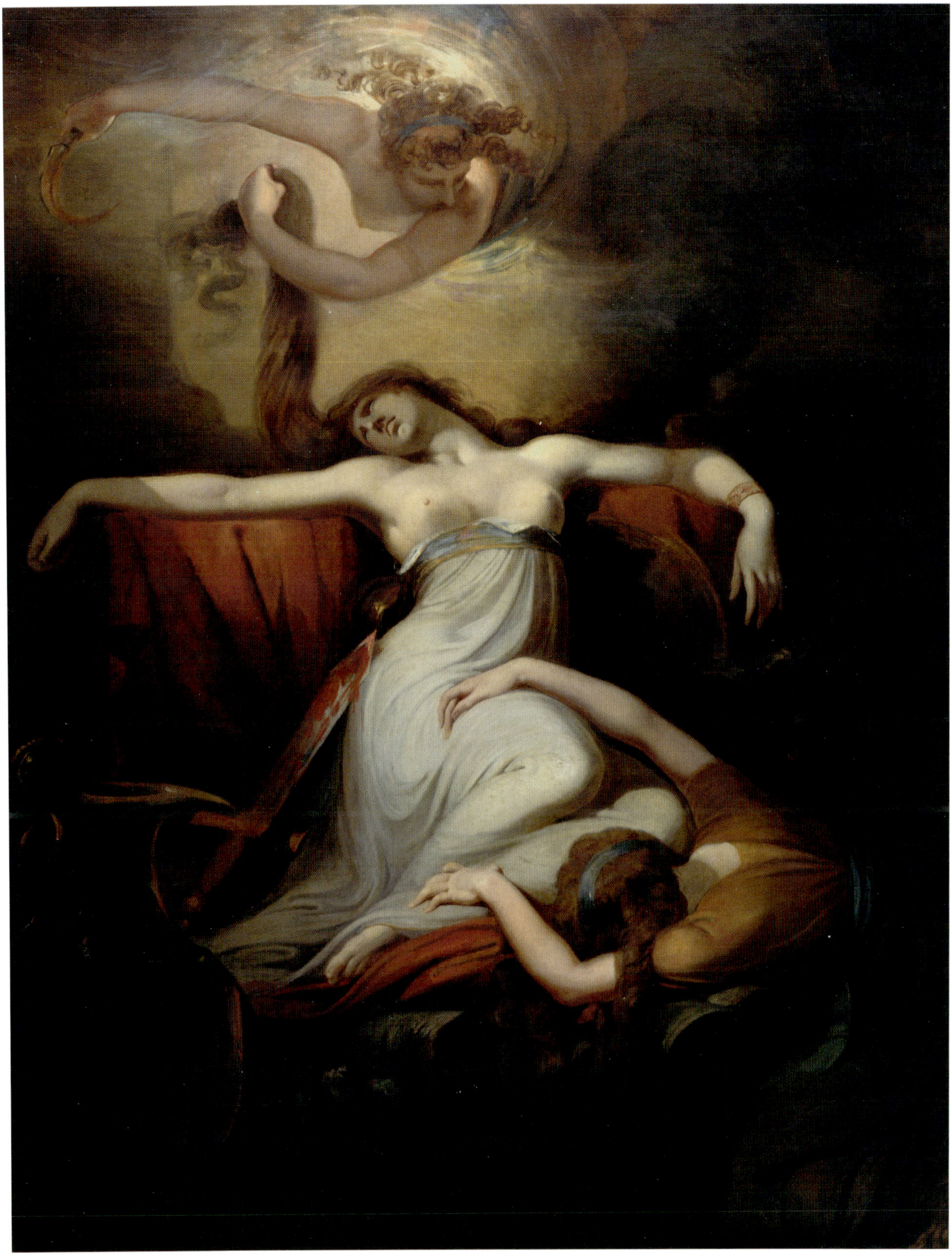

Cat. 12 *Dido*, 1781

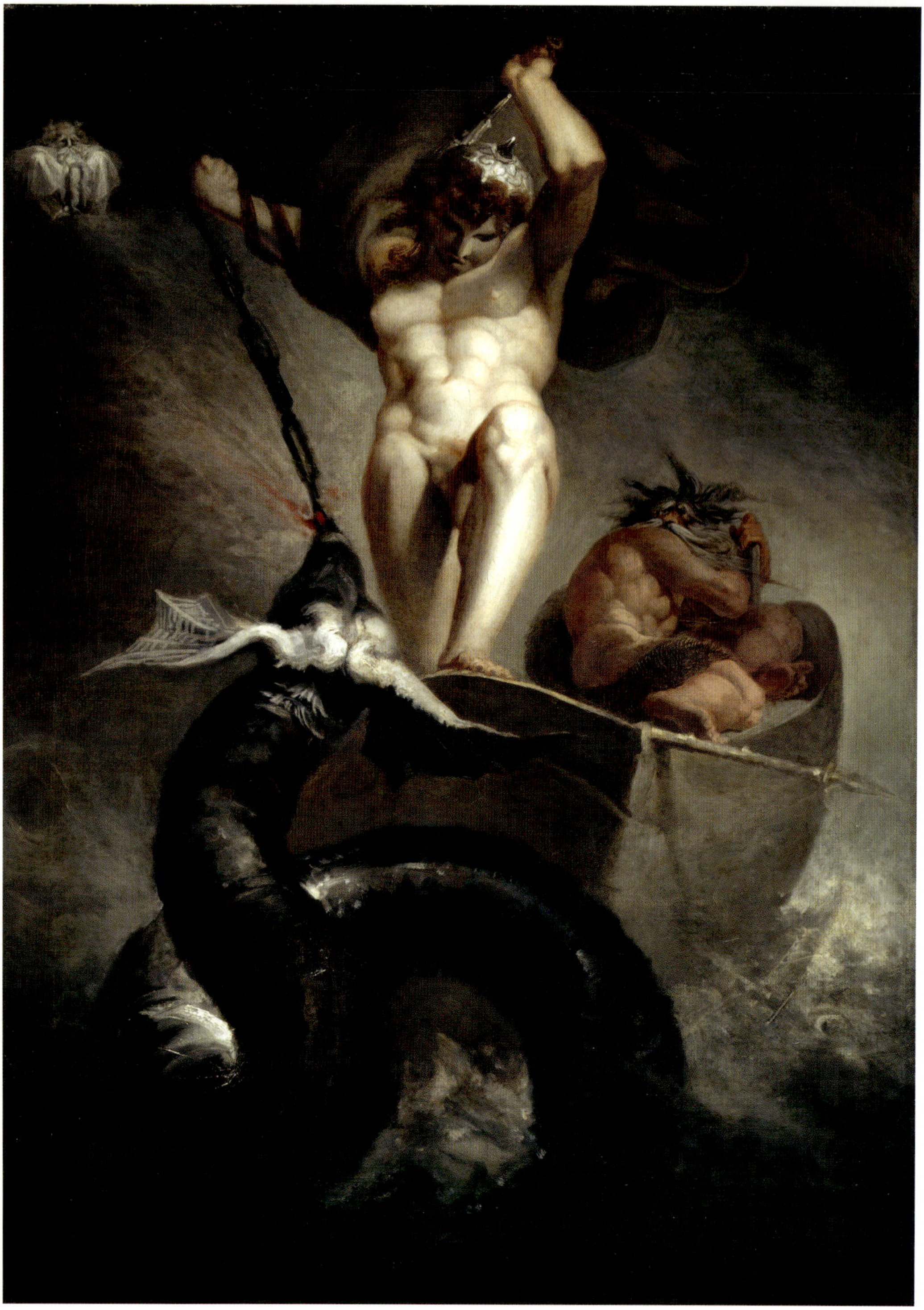

Cat. 13 *Thor Battering the Midgard Serpent*, 1790

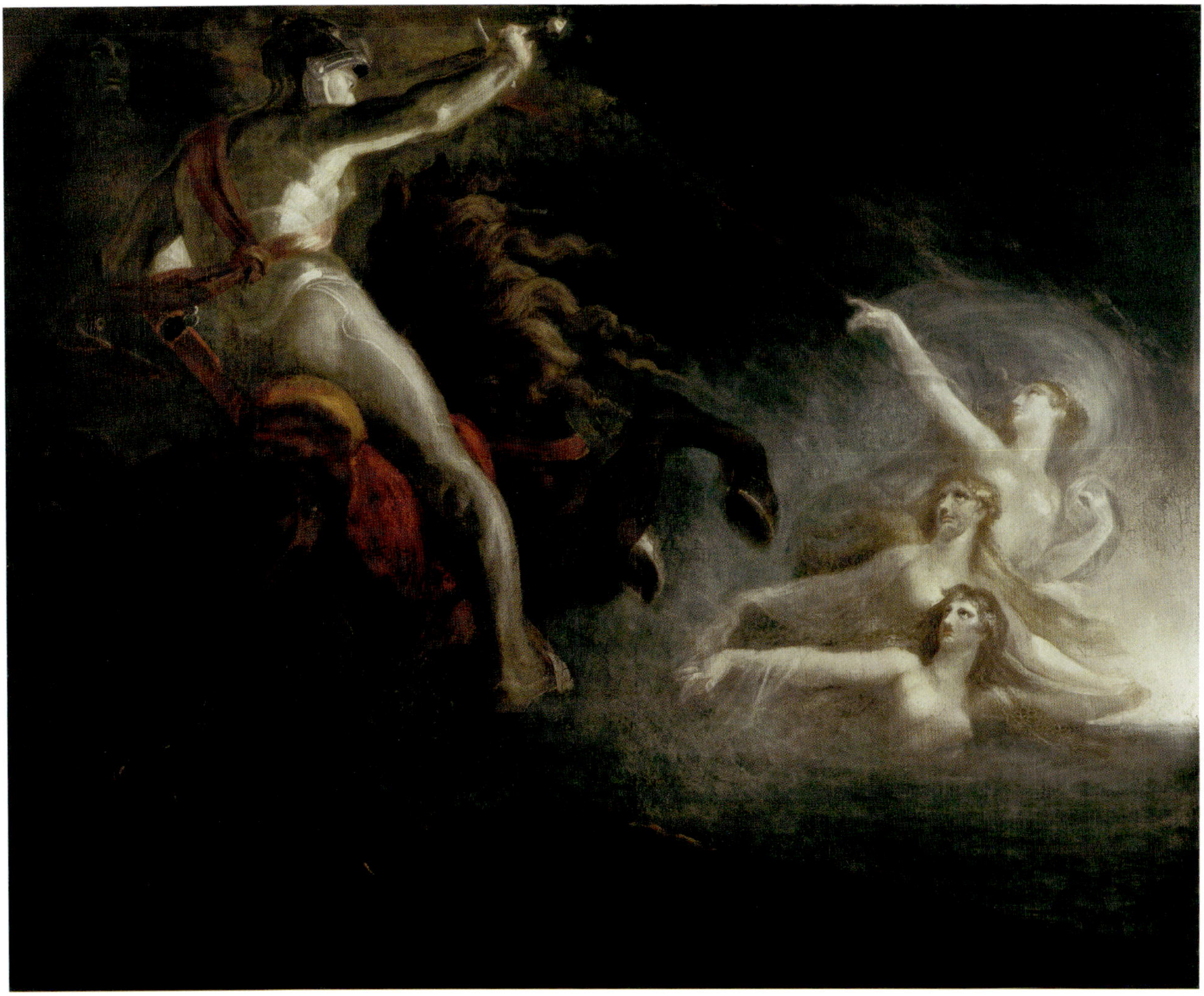

Cat. 14 *Hagen and the Nymphs of the Danube*, c. 1800–15

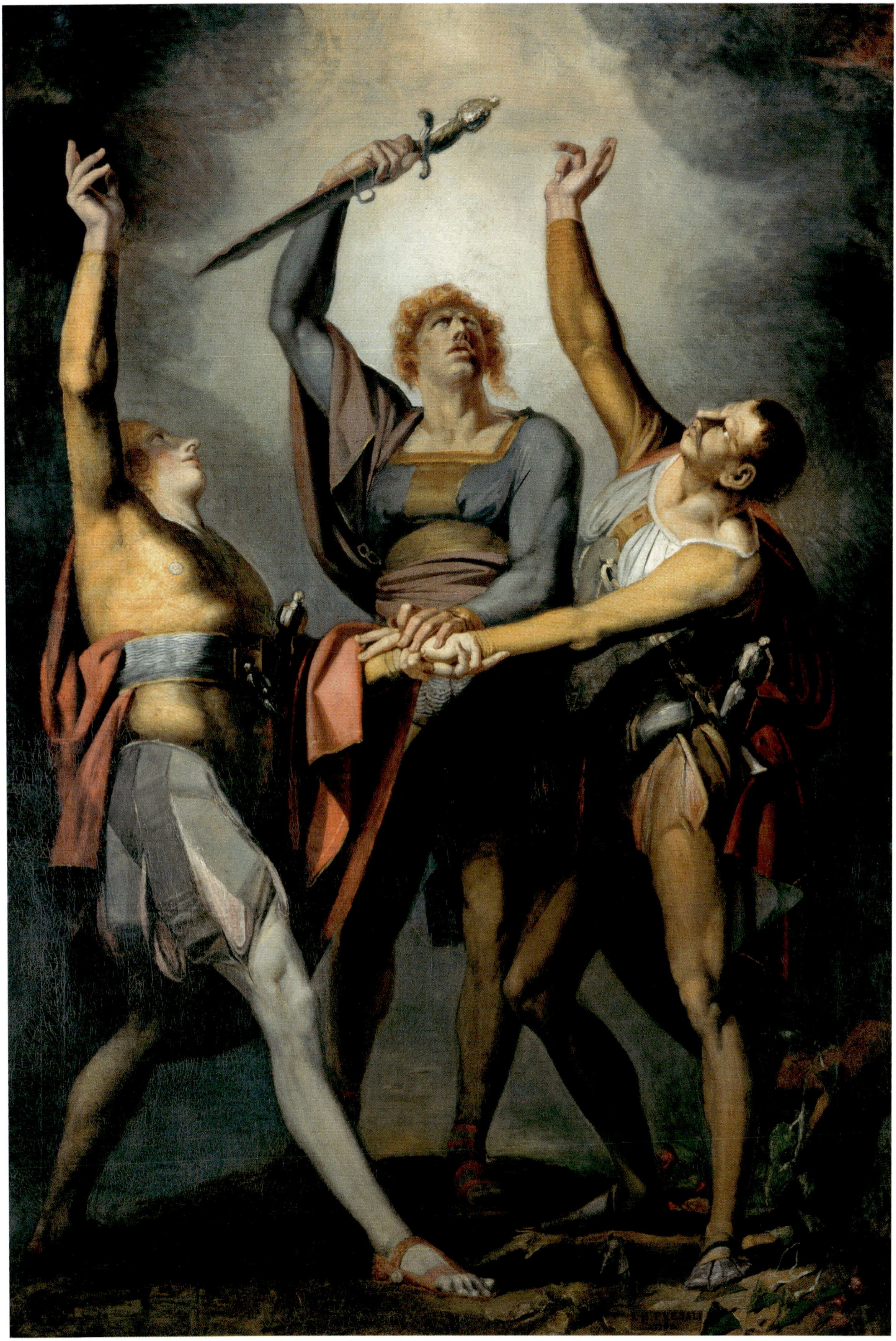

Cat. 15 *The Oath on the Rütli*, 1779–81

Recent and Contemporary Literature

It would be odd if a painter who had enjoyed extensive philological schooling in the circle of Johann Caspar Lavater and Johann Jakob Bodmer, who had become acquainted with the poetry of Friedrich Gottlieb Klopstock at an early age and who was himself active as a writer and translator[1] had not engaged with the literature of his own day in addition to that of such major authors of the past as Homer, Shakespeare and Milton. More recent literature may not have prompted Fuseli to produce a body of work comparable in size and significance to that which he devoted to the two leading lights of English literature,[2] yet it, too, clearly stimulated his creative imagination to the full. The authors involved in his activity in this field, which was mostly the result of commissions for book illustrations, ranged in time from the Scot James Thomson to the Prussian Friedrich de la Motte Fouqué. Thomson's *Seasons* (cat. 18), first published in full in 1730 and influenced by Milton, was highly esteemed by the next generation, the Romantics, for its intensely imaginative descriptions of the sublimity and terror of nature,[3] while de la Motte Fouqué's fairy-tale novella *Undine* (cat. 30) achieved widespread popularity throughout Europe soon after its publication in 1811 and appeared in English translation in 1818.[4]

The circumstances surrounding Fuseli's works relating to contemporary texts are sometimes obscure. That applies, for instance, to '*The Fire King*', an early horror poem by Walter Scott less than typical of the artist's literary tastes (cat. 32). Personal involvement informed other examples included here. Fuseli never met the English poet and translator William Cowper, but for a number of years helped to revise his new English versions of Homer's *Iliad* and *Odyssey*.[5] Moreover, Cowper was to have written the commentary in a de luxe edition of Milton's work, the abandonment of which led the artist to set up his Milton Gallery (see 'Milton', pp. 141–43).[6] Fuseli also valued the poet's own work, once saying in conversation that he thought him 'the best of all the Poets of his [Cowper's] period'.[7] It is therefore scarcely surprising that the artist contributed several images to an edition of Cowper's poems published posthumously in 1807 (cats 27–29). These included not only illustrations to *The Task* (1785), generally considered Cowper's masterpiece, in which the poet paints a picture of country life as the idyllic antithesis of the perceived decadence of urban existence,[8] but also the frontispiece, titled *The Poet's Vision*, which is nothing short of a monument in Cowper's honour (cat. 65).

The German writer Christoph Martin Wieland and his *Oberon* were already familiar to Fuseli when he received a commission for twelve illustrations to a translation by William Sotheby of Wieland's epic poem, published by Cadell & Davies in 1805 (see cats 19–26).[9] The paths of the author and artist had crossed in Zurich. Wieland lived there from 1752 to 1759, at the same time as Fuseli, and belonged to Bodmer's inner circle, even staying in his house for a time. Again like Fuseli, it was in Zurich that Wieland became acquainted with the work of Milton and, above all, Shakespeare, many of whose plays he would later translate into German. In the pietistic world of Zurich – and elsewhere – Wieland soon came to be regarded as 'immoral', which inevitably led to a break with Bodmer and Lavater.[10] Probably for the same reason, Fuseli's recorded comments on the author are almost all ironically derogatory.[11] Yet *Oberon* would seem to have been made for him. With its various borrowings, from the thirteenth-century *Histoire de Huon de Bordeaux*, *The Canterbury Tales* by Geoffrey Chaucer, Shakespeare's *A Midsummer Night's Dream* and other sources,[12] it offered not only heroic deeds, dramatic conflicts and fairy-tale beings, but also irony and frank eroticism, all of which found their way into the illustrations. A comment made by Fuseli in a letter to William Roscoe indicates how well he knew the original text.[13] He refers to 'Sotheby's ex-Wielanded Oberon',[14] and Sotheby's English version was indeed more of a recreation than a straightforward translation: it replaced Wieland's eight-line units with the nine-line stanzas familiar to English readers, for instance, and it eliminated no less than sixty-one stanzas, among them those that have been called 'the most immoral' and the most salacious since Chaucer.[15] The artist's *Oberon* cycle testifies to the appeal the poem held for him and, after finishing it, he remarked in the same letter to Roscoe that, despite modest financial rewards, 'I was for the most part amused by my task' – adding that he intended to repeat some of the compositions on a larger scale in order to achieve the effect envisaged:[16] an indication of the value he attached to these images. GD

1 See, for example, Tomory 1974, pp. 9–12, and the introduction by Eva Reifert in the present volume, pp. 19–35.
2 Fuseli's illustrations to Lavater's *Physiognomische Fragmente* – twenty-four for the French edition, twenty-seven for the English – do not belong in the present context and are therefore left out of account here. For them, see Weinglass 1994, pp. 34–46, 96–114.
3 Richetti 2017, pp. 84–89.
4 Schiff 1973, vol. 1, p. 380.
5 Ibid., p. 125.
6 Stuttgart 1997, p. 12.
7 Joseph Farington, diary entry of 28 May 1803, in: Farington 1923, vol. 2, p. 103.
8 Matthews 2011, pp. 110–40.
9 For a detailed account of Wieland's critical history in Britain, see Yuill 1985.
10 Described in detail in Mielsch 1994, pp. 10–47.
11 For Fuseli's relations with Wieland, see Schiff 1973, vol. 1, pp. 324–27.
12 For Wieland's sources, see Heinz 2008, pp. 227–28, and Yuill 1985, pp. 136–38.
13 His library contained several works by Wieland, including an edition of *Oberon*: Fuseli 1982, pp. 584–95, nos. 145, 146.
14 Letter of 1 Feb. 1805 from Fuseli to Roscoe; qtd. in Fuseli 1982, p. 312.
15 Yuill 1985, pp. 132–33.
16 Letter of 1 Feb. 1805 from Fuseli to Roscoe; qtd. in Fuseli 1982, p. 312.

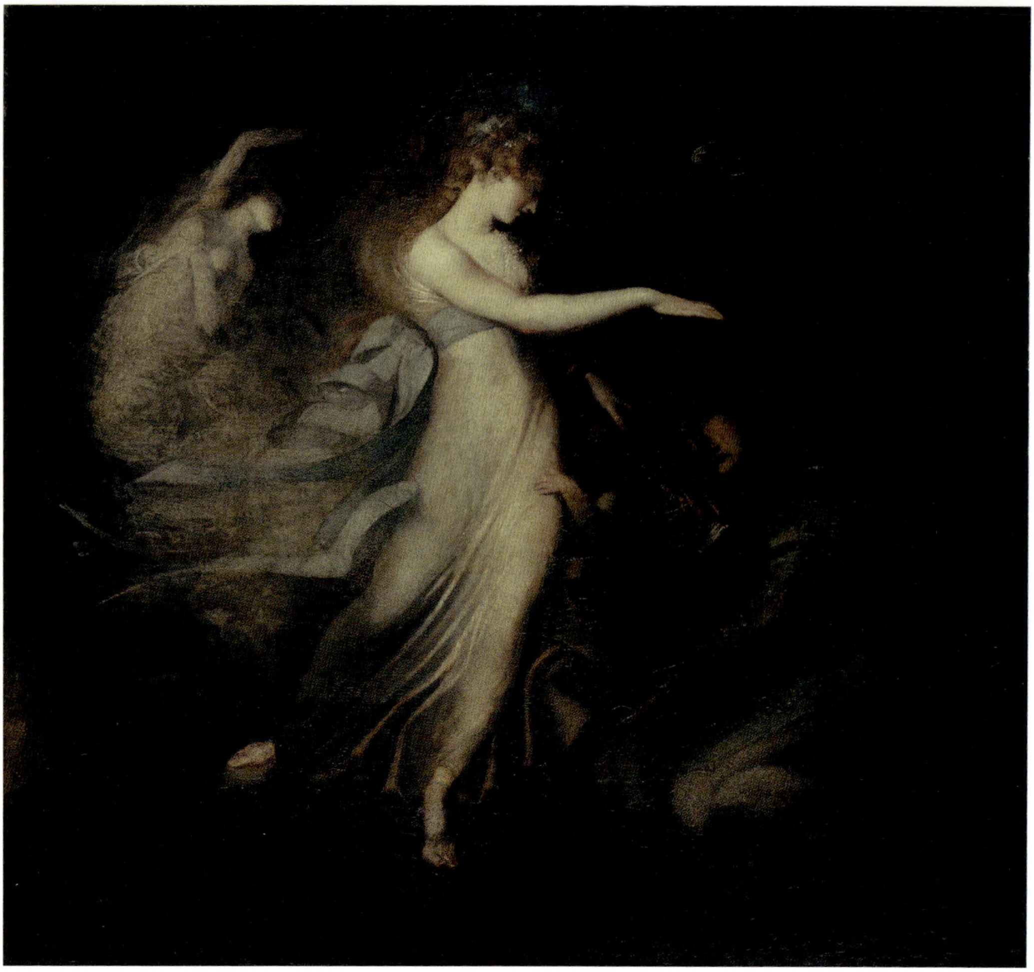

Cat. 16 *Prince Arthur and the Fairy Queen*, 1785–88

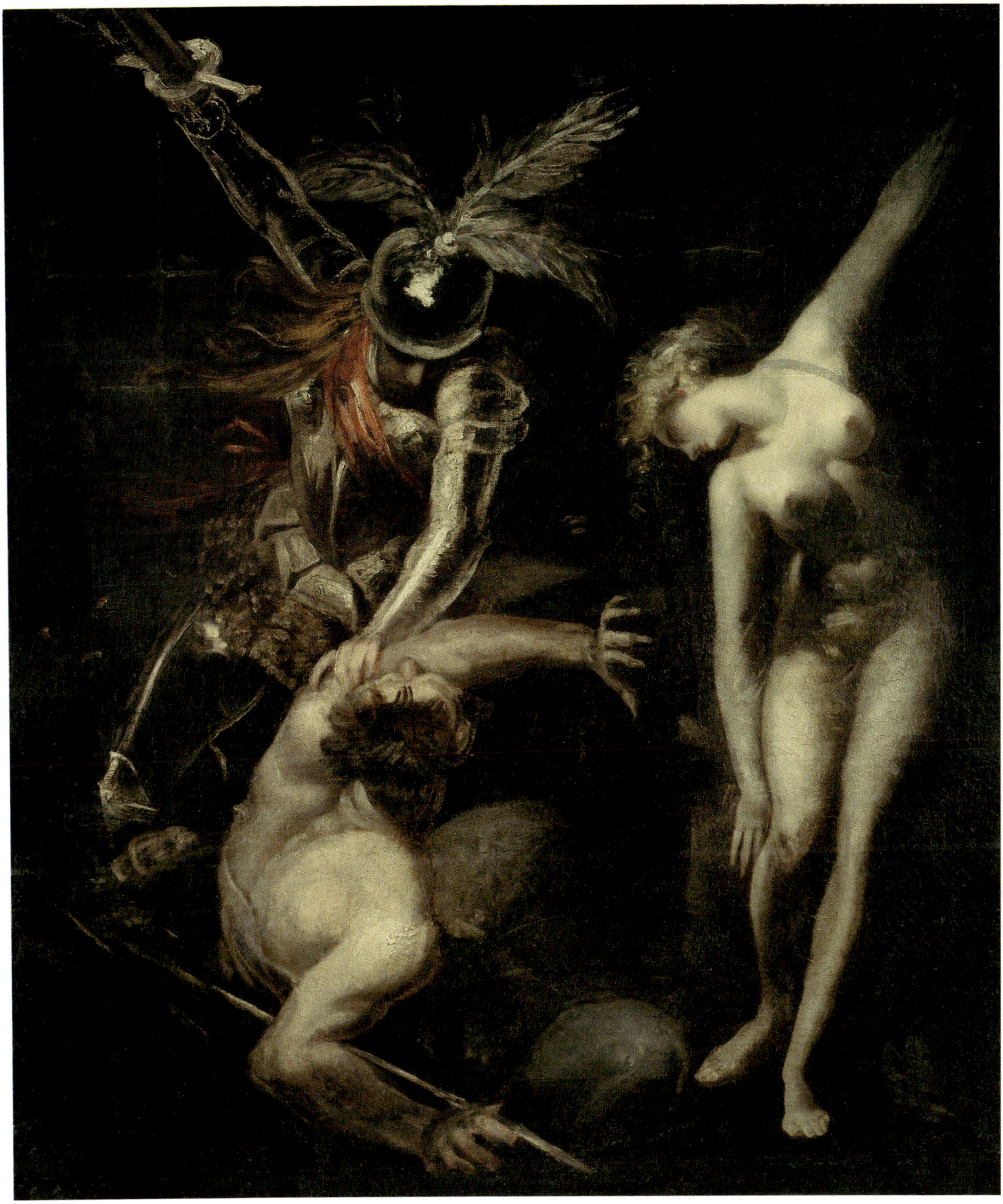

Cat. 17 *Britomart Freeing Amoretta from the Spell of Busirane*, 1824

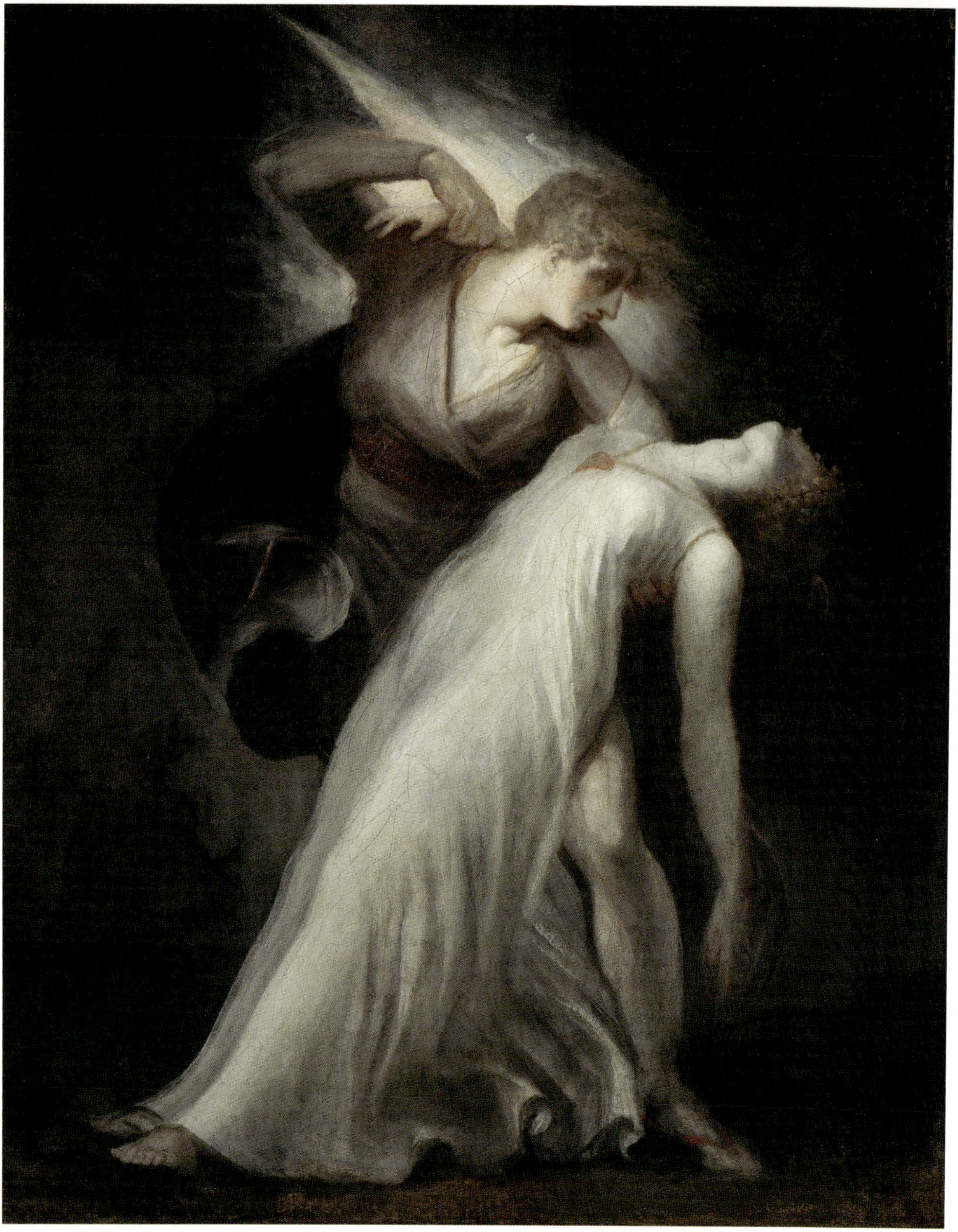

Cat. 18 *Celadon and Amelia*, 1801

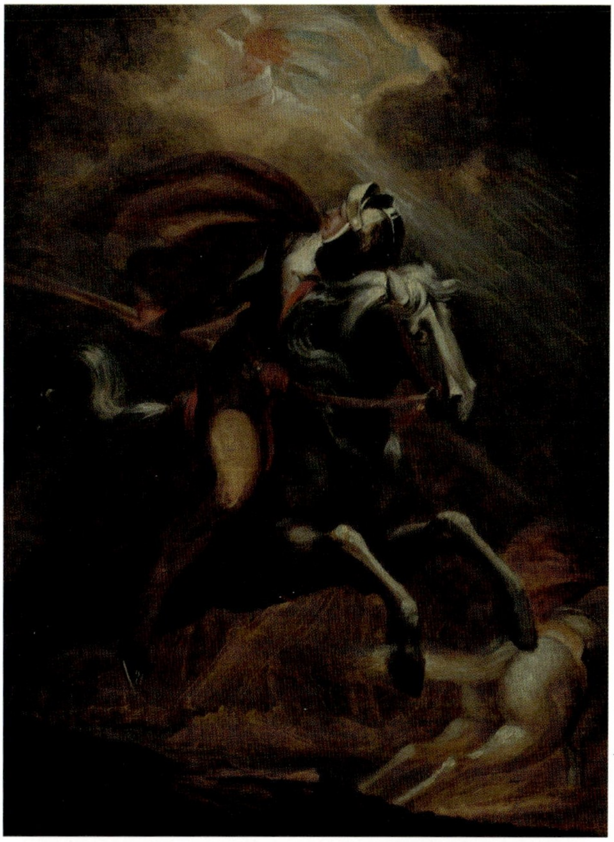

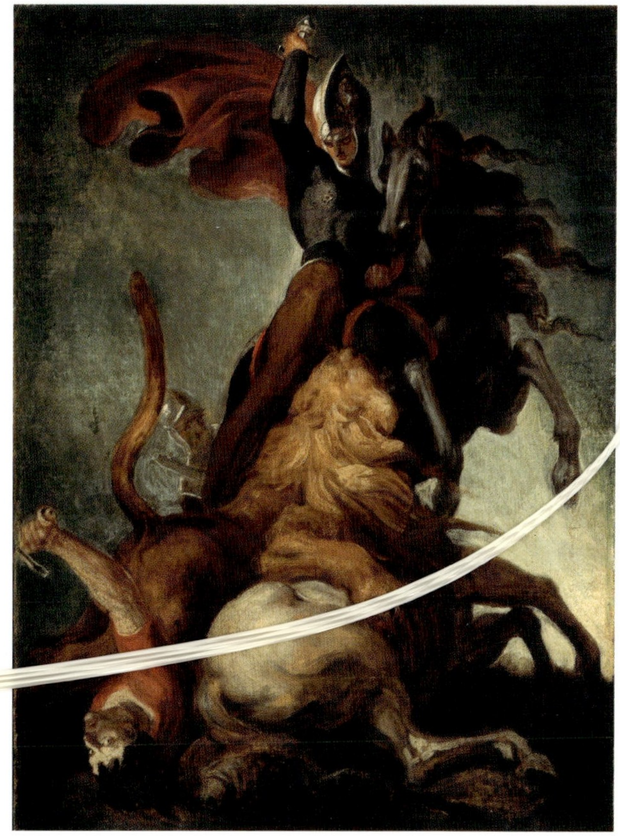

Cat. 19 *Sherasmin and Huon Fleeing from Oberon*, 1804–05

Cat. 20 *Huon Freeing Babekan from the Lion*, 1804–05

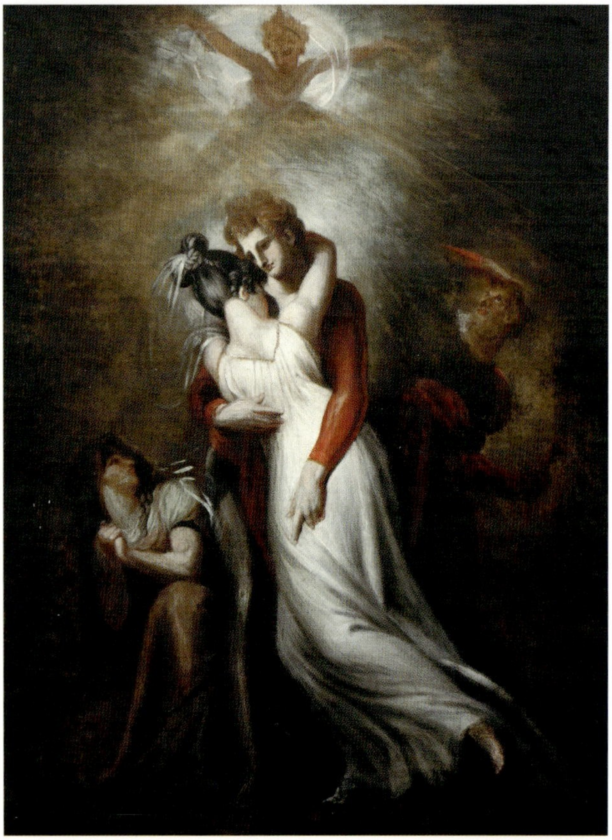

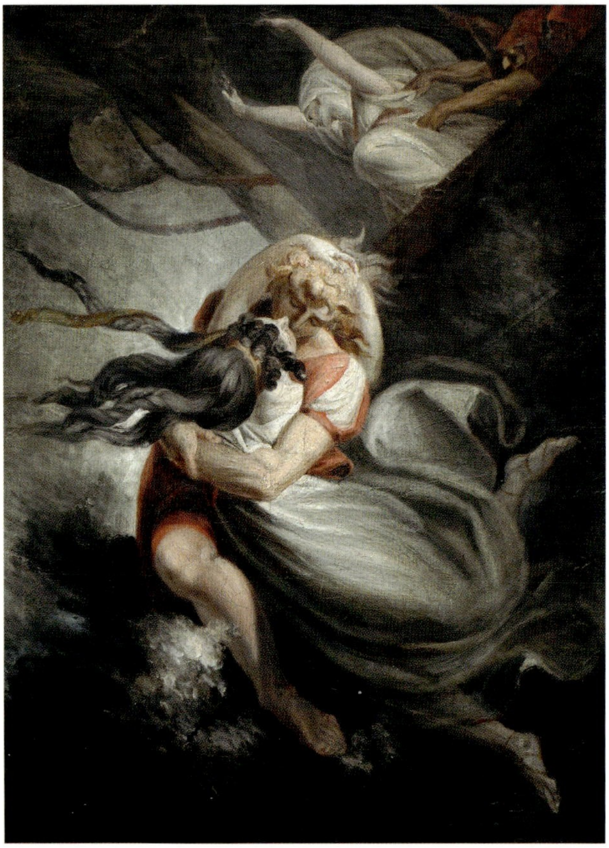

Cat. 21 *Huon and Rezia United, with Fatme, Sherasmin and Oberon*, 1804–05

Cat. 22 *Amanda/Rezia Plunges into the Sea with Huon, while Fatme is Held Back*, 1804–05

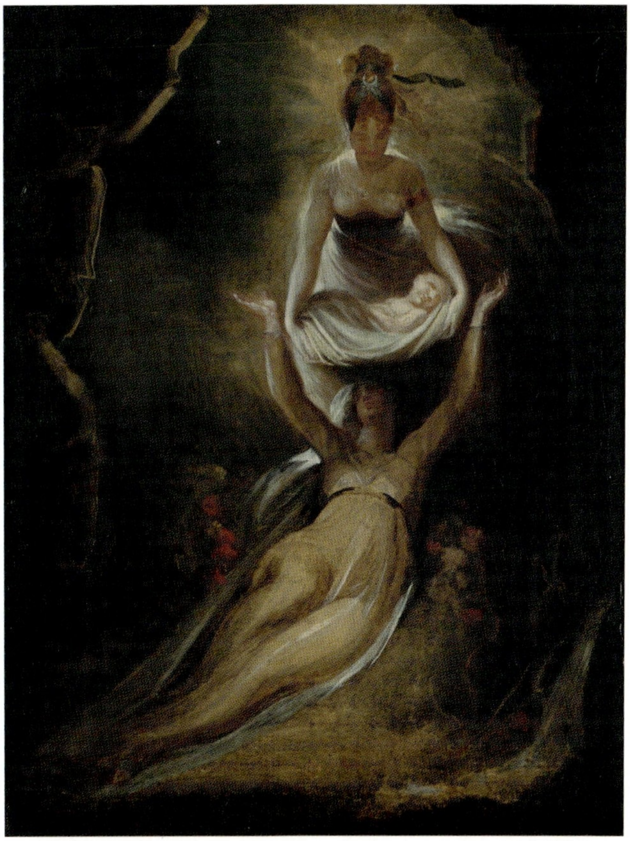

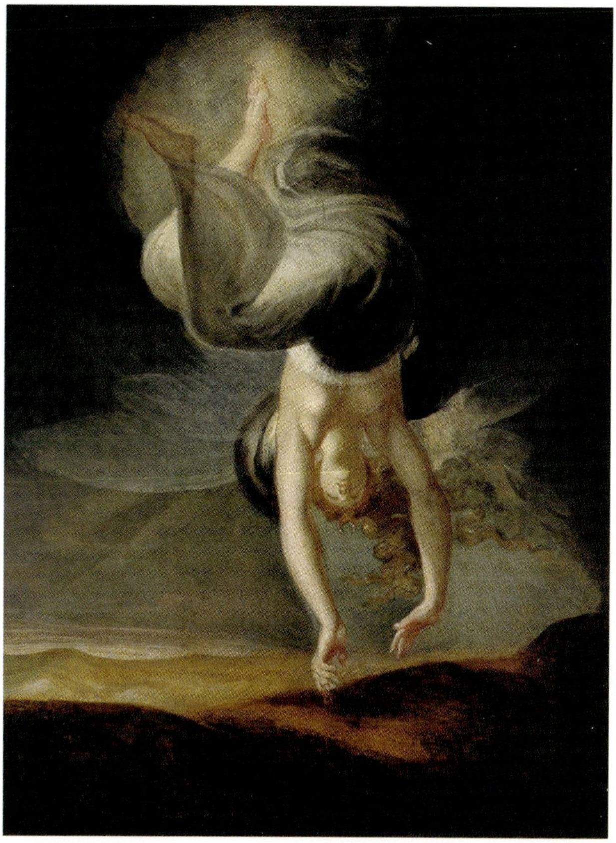

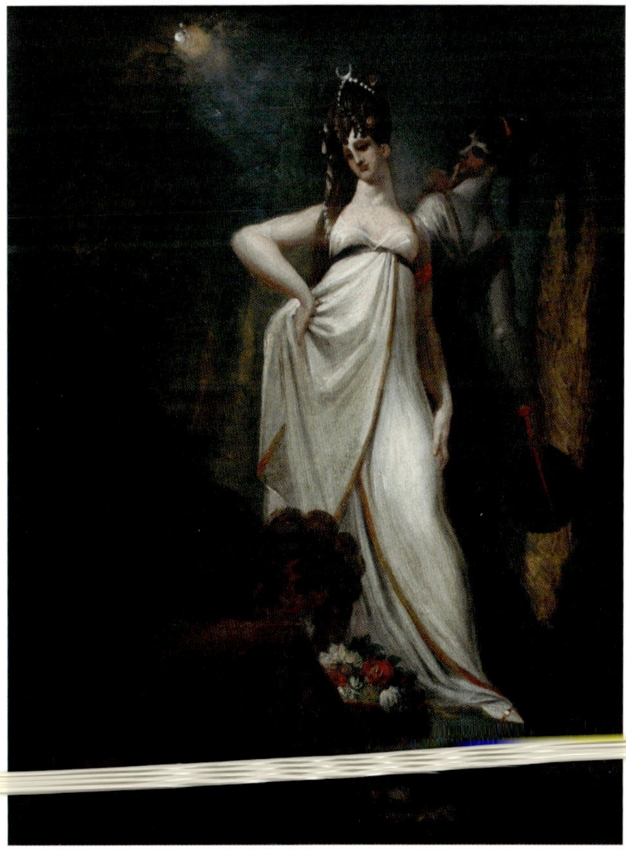

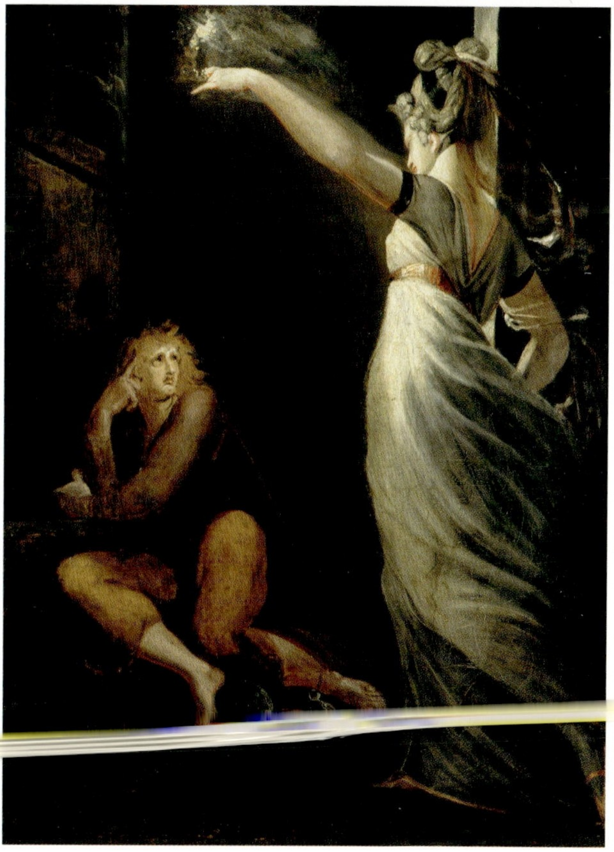

Cat. 23 *Titania Shows Amanda her Son, Born in the Grotto*, 1804–05

Cat. 24 *Titania Finds the Magic Ring on the Shore*, 1804–05

Cat. 25 *Huon, Disguised as a Gardener, Meets Sultana Almansaris Accompanied by Nadine*, 1804–05

Cat. 26 *Almansaris Visits Huon in Prison*, 1804–05

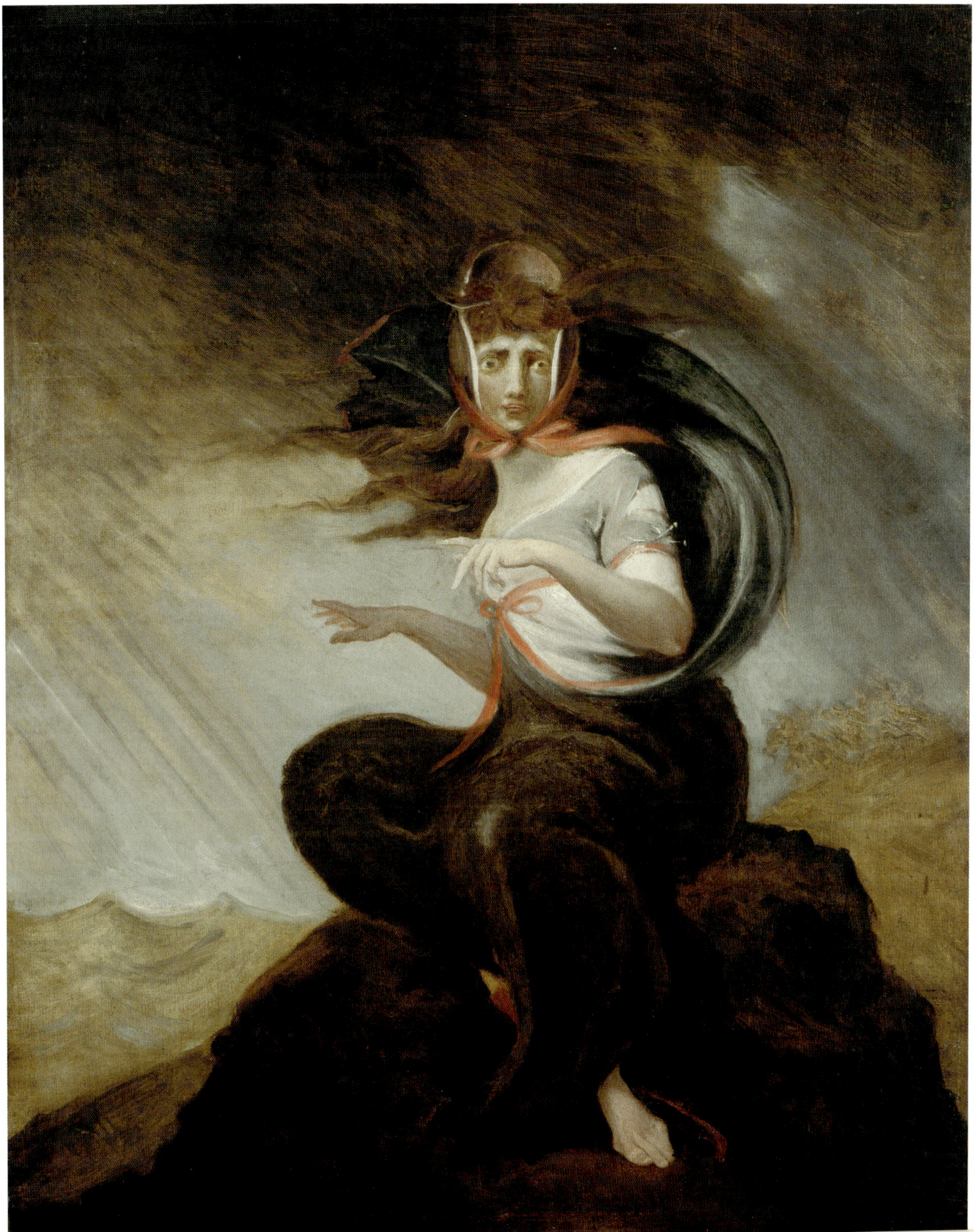

Cat. 27 *Mad Kate*, 1806–07

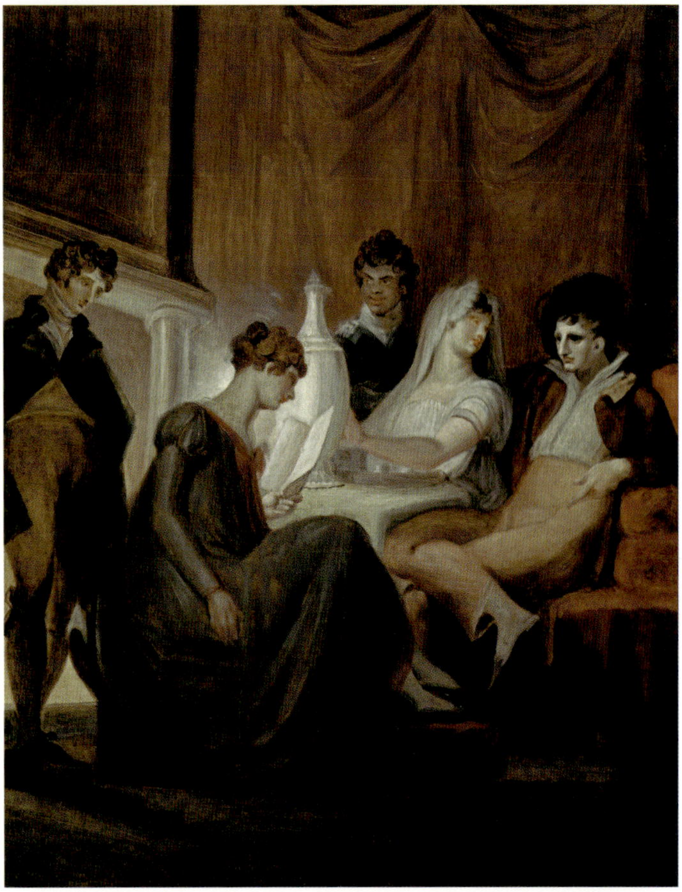

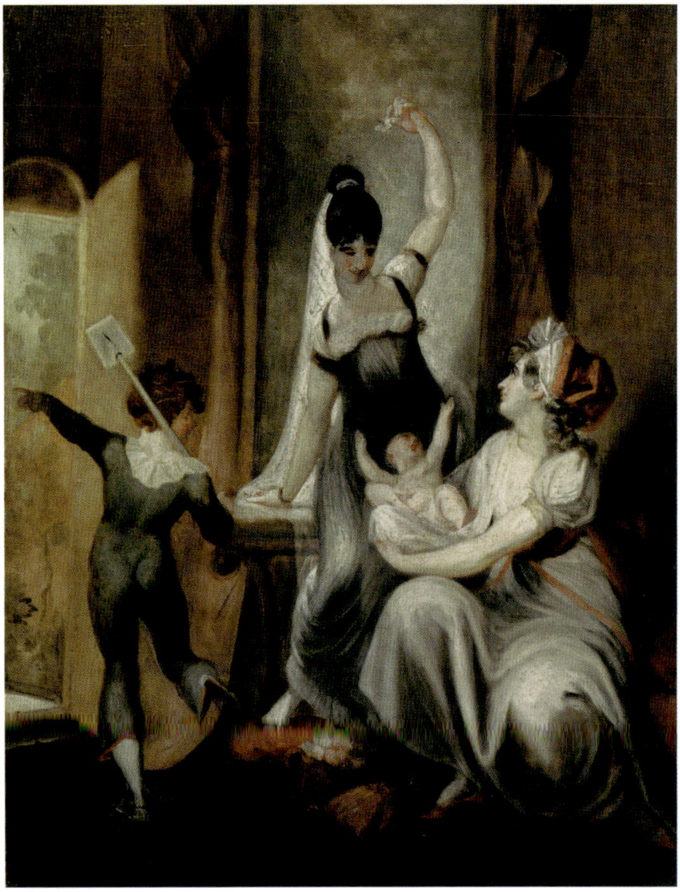

Cat. 28 *The Newspaper in the Country*, 1806–07

Cat. 29 *A Mother with her Family in the Country*, 1806–07

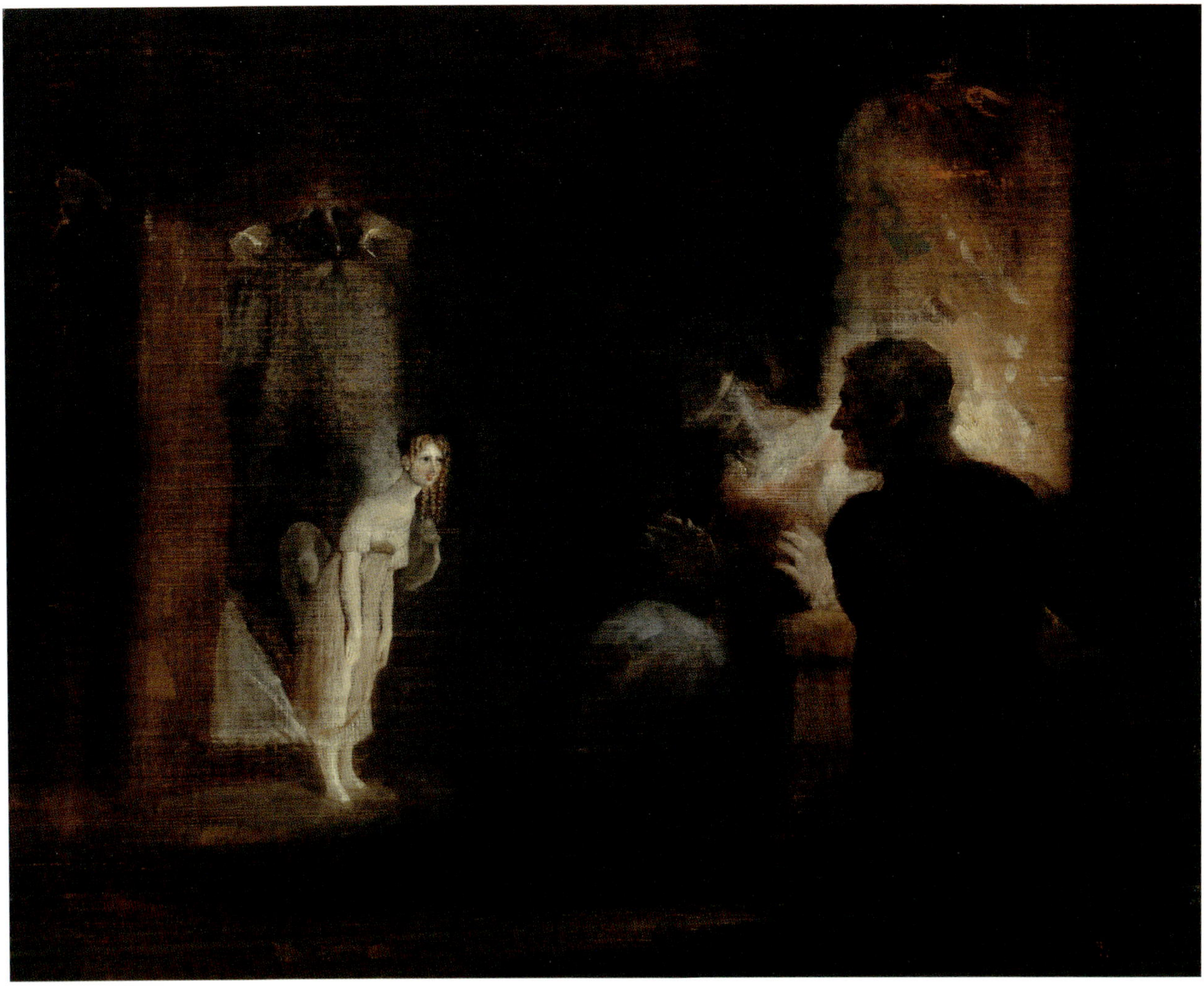

Cat. 30 *Undine Enters the House of the Fisherman and his Wife*, 1821

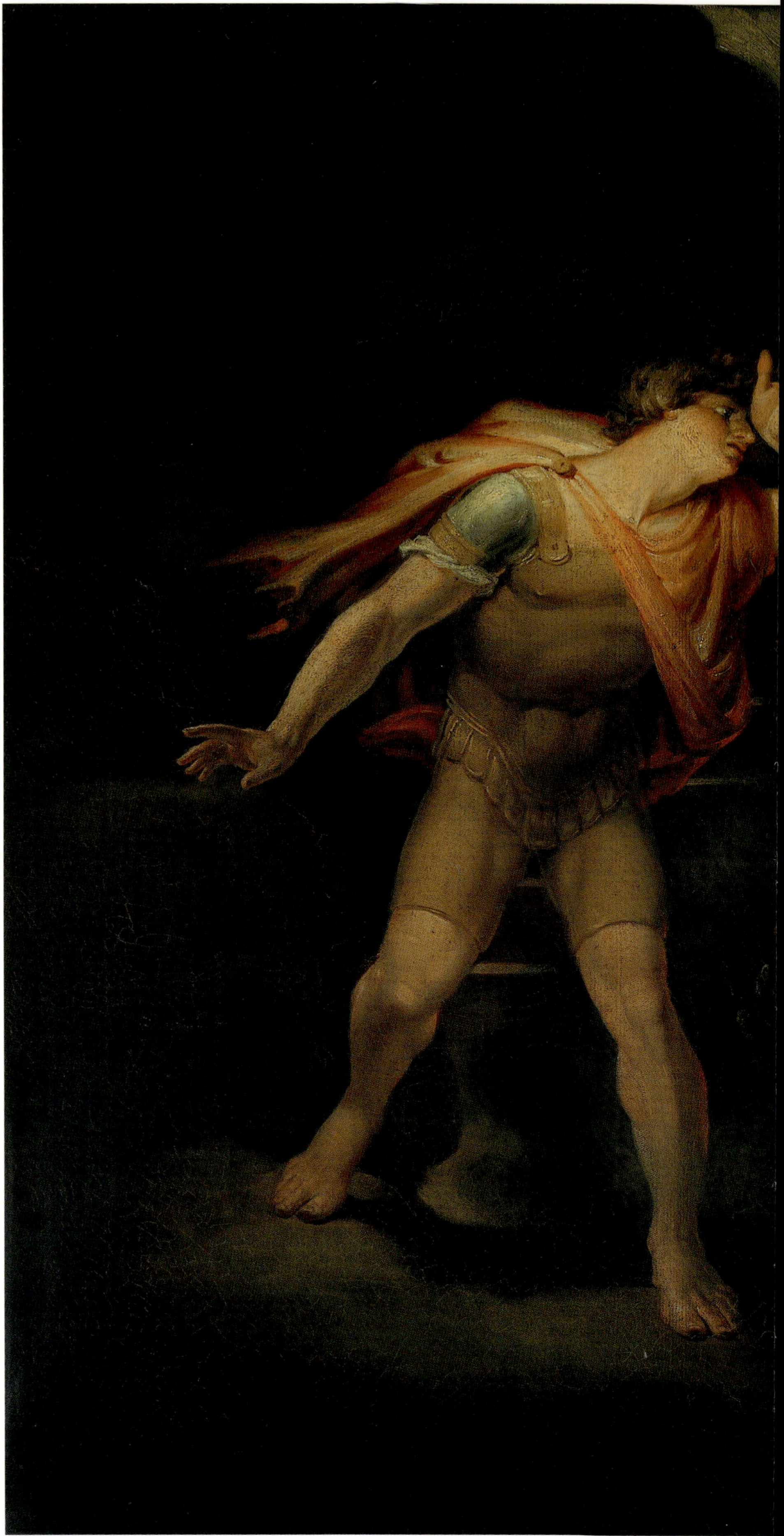

Cat. 31 *The Fire King*, c. 1801–10

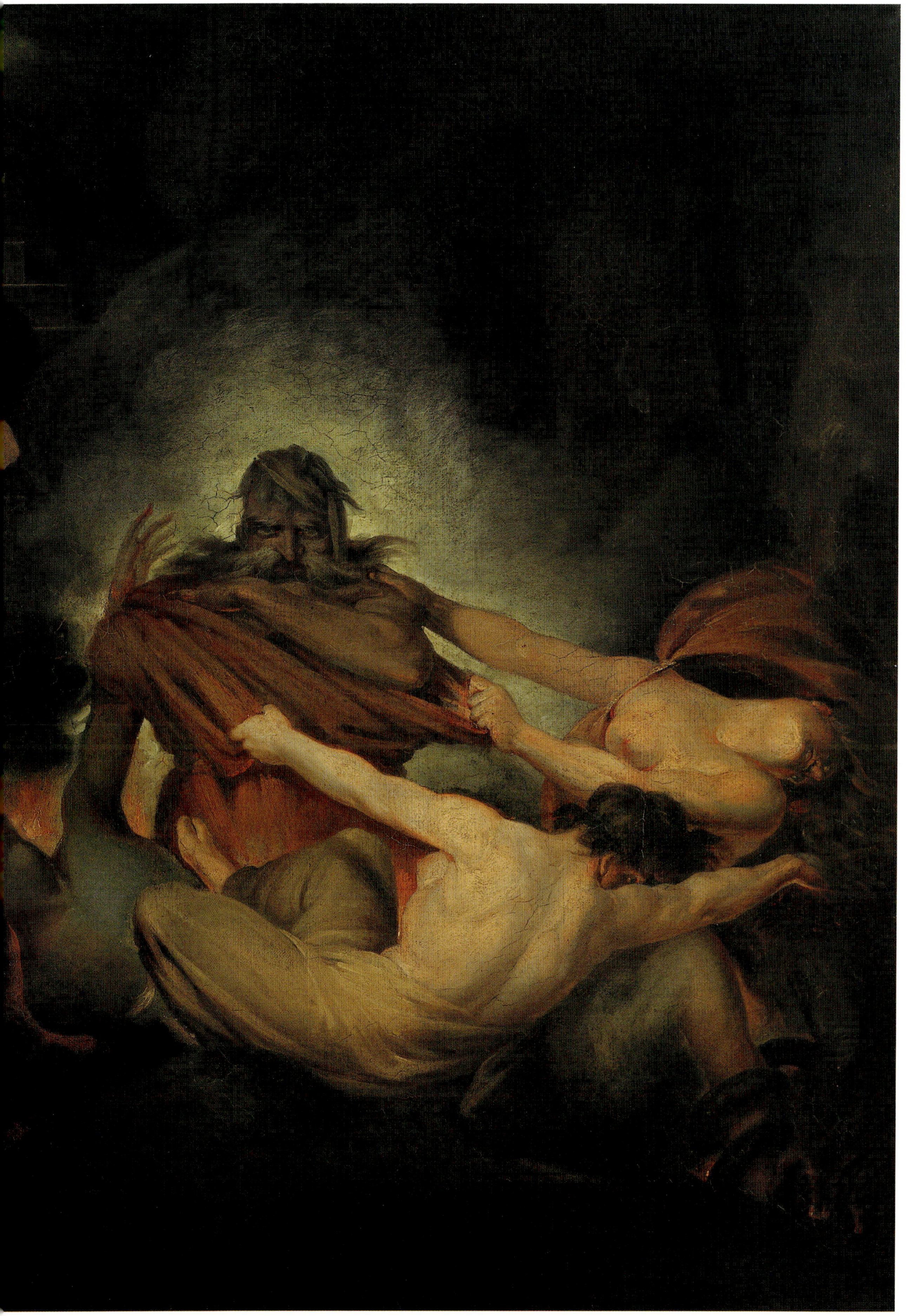

Shakespeare

The plays of Shakespeare offered Fuseli everything he relished as an artist – sublime moments, supernatural visions, extreme emotions. Engagement with the work of 'the supreme master of passions and the ruler of our hearts',[1] as he called the playwright, runs like a leitmotif through his oeuvre. Early on, as a student of Johann Jakob Bodmer in Zurich, he attempted to translate *Macbeth* into German, and in 1763 his sketches on subjects taken from *Macbeth* and *King Lear* prompted the British ambassador to the Prussian court in Berlin to recommend that he move to London.[2] His imagination was fired by visits to the theatre there, where he experienced the famous actor David Garrick as Richard III and Macbeth. During his years in Rome, long before knowledge of the writer's work became widespread on the Continent, Fuseli was already considered a 'Shakespeare painter'.[3] In 1777, under the influence of Michelangelo's frescoes in the Sistine Chapel, he even sketched some ideas for a memorial hall in the author's honour (see p. 24, fig. 3).[4]

By the time Fuseli returned to London from Rome the Shakespeare revival of the previous decades had borne valuable fruit. Adaptations of the plays in obedience to contemporary taste (which decreed, for instance, that Lear should not die) could still be seen on the stage, but several annotated editions of his works had become available and at the Theatre Royal in Drury Lane Garrick was endeavouring to mount productions faithful to the originals. Shakespeare had come to epitomise British culture, in fact: the public was familiar with the principal scenes from the plays, and pictures of them were an established sub-genre of history painting.

The canvases that Fuseli contributed in the 1780s and '90s to the Shakespeare galleries of John Boydell (cats 35, 36) and James Woodmason (cats 32, 34, 44, 48), and to the Poets' Gallery set up by Thomas Macklin (cat. 16, see cat. 39), belong among his finest works. They did not fit in, however, with either of the accepted genres of theatrical painting: scenes from plays and portraits of actors. The influence of actual performances is apparent in the expansive, formal gestures of Fuseli's heroes, in his sure grasp of key emotional moments and in references to such celebrated actors as Garrick, Sarah Siddons and her brother John Philip Kemble. Yet he developed his compositions principally from an imaginative reading of the plays and from a delight in the mysterious realm inhabited by terror and the sublime. He engaged with all areas of Shakespeare's writing for the stage, with the comedies, including *Much Ado About Nothing* (cat. 38) and *A Midsummer Night's Dream*, with the tragedies, such as *Macbeth* (cats 42–45), *King Lear* (cat. 41), *Hamlet* (cat. 48) and *Romeo and Juliet* (cats 46, 47), and with the history plays, among them *Henry VIII* (cat. 39). His take on them fostered both the extravagance of his visual imagery and his powers of invention. These he wedded to a representational mode founded in extreme chiaroscuro contrasts and in a figure style, as reductive as it was extreme, that he culled from the study of classical models in Rome.

In his approach to Shakespeare, Fuseli, for all his admiration for, and close textual acquaintance with, the playwright's works, shows himself to be far more than an illustrator. The paintings relating to *A Midsummer Night's Dream*, for instance, expand Shakespeare's fairy world associatively to reflect the artist's knowledge of English folklore and his scientific interest in butterflies and moths. Fuseli explored other supernatural elements in the plays, and captured them on canvas, with the same passionate intensity – witches and ghosts, for example, phenomena that contemporary critics accorded special praise for their originality and eccentricity and liked to think of as typically English.[5] It is thus no accident that the ghost of Hamlet's father and the three witches from *Macbeth* figured among his best-known Shakespearean pictorial inventions. The extent to which he saw himself as an independent interpreter of the plays is reflected not least in his conviction that his painting could make good omissions in the author's writing.[6] ER

1 Knowles 1831, vol. 2, p. 145.
2 Cunningham 1859, p. 226.
3 Herder 1889, p. 85, referring to Fuseli as 'a Shakespeare worshipper and now a Shakespeare painter'.
4 Sillars 2006, pp. 109–10.
5 West 2012, p. 248.
6 Knowles 1831, vol. 1, p. 189.

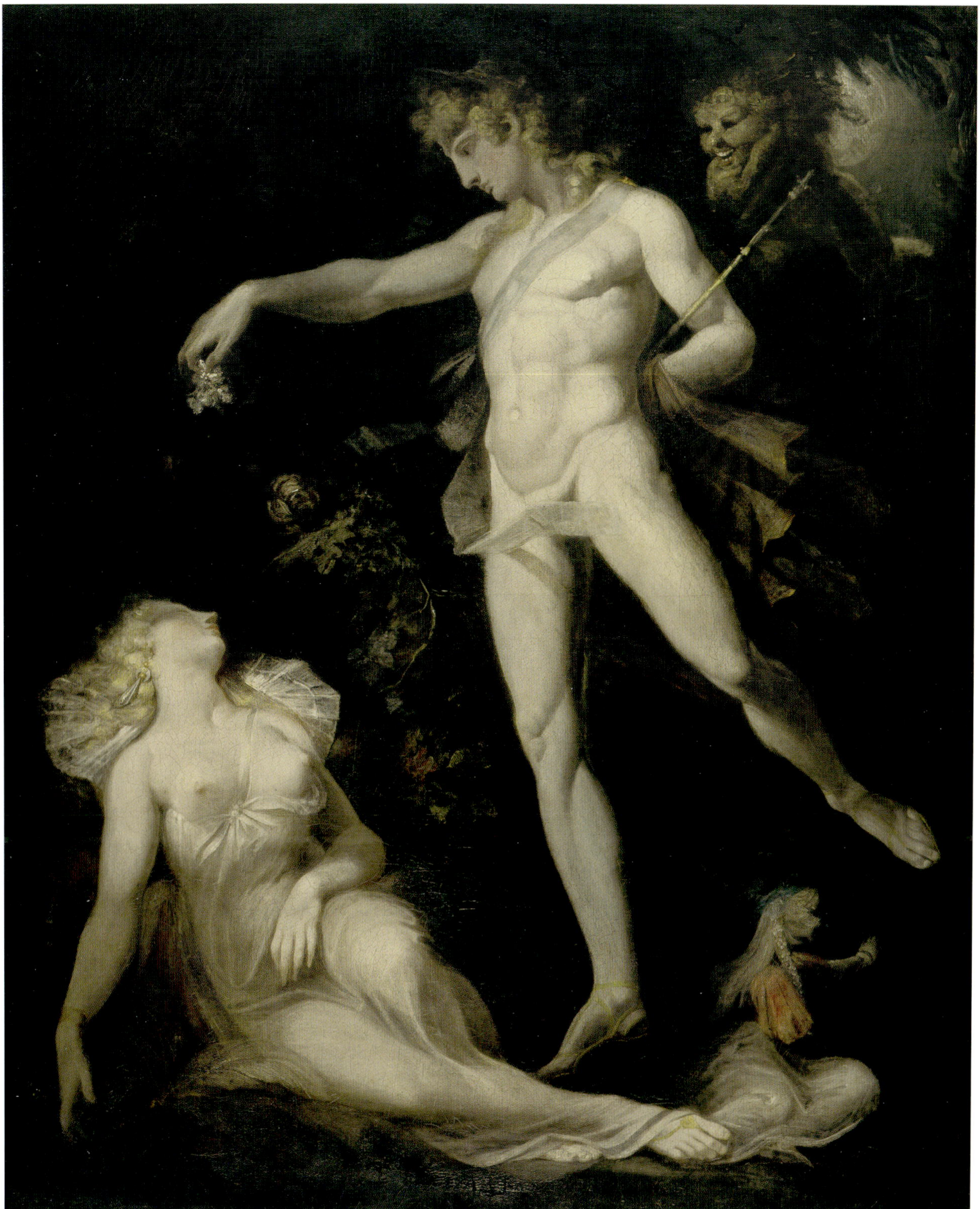

Cat. 32 *Oberon Squeezing the Juice onto Titania's Eyelids*, 1793

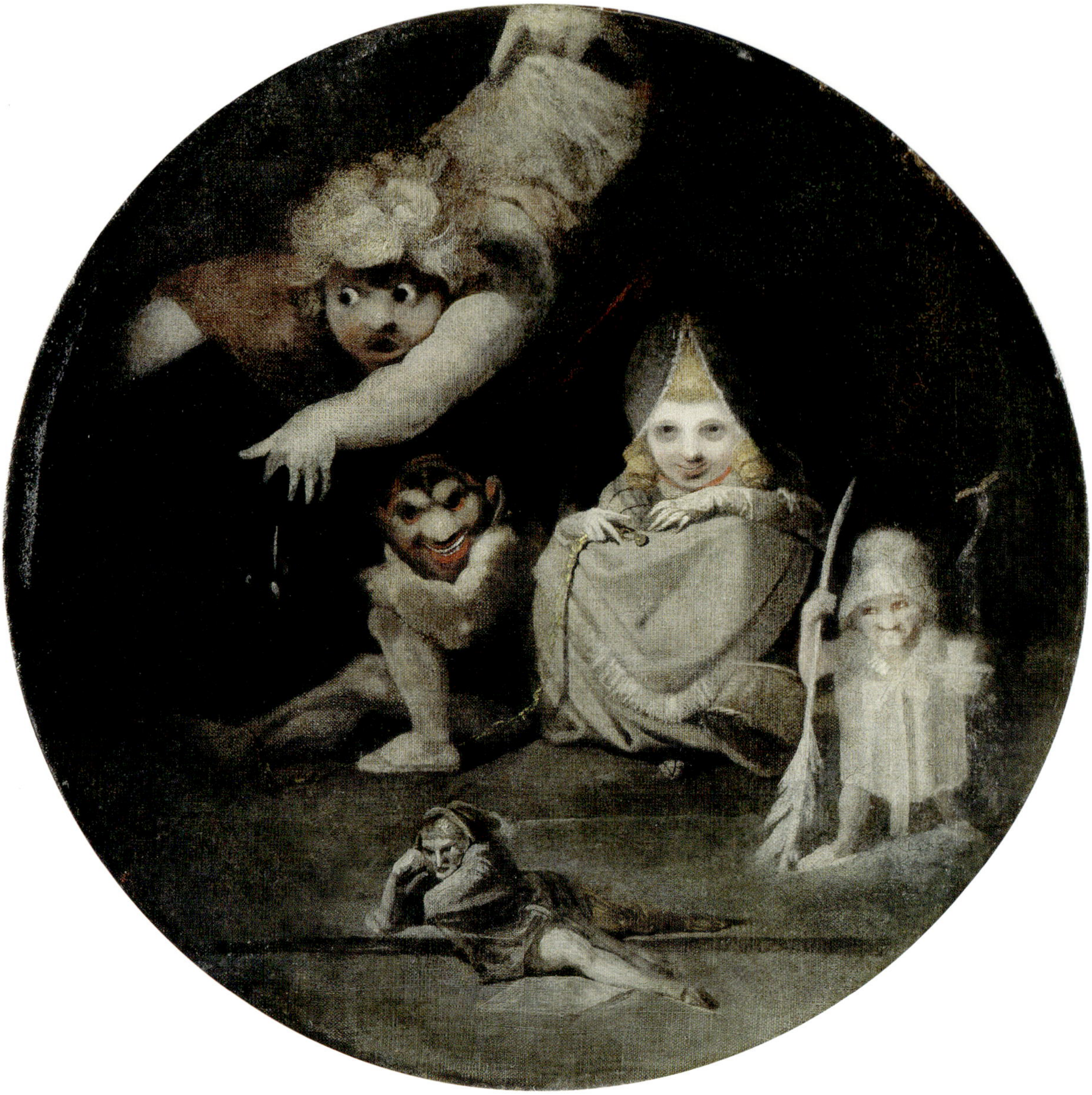

Cat. 33 *Cobweb*, 1785–86

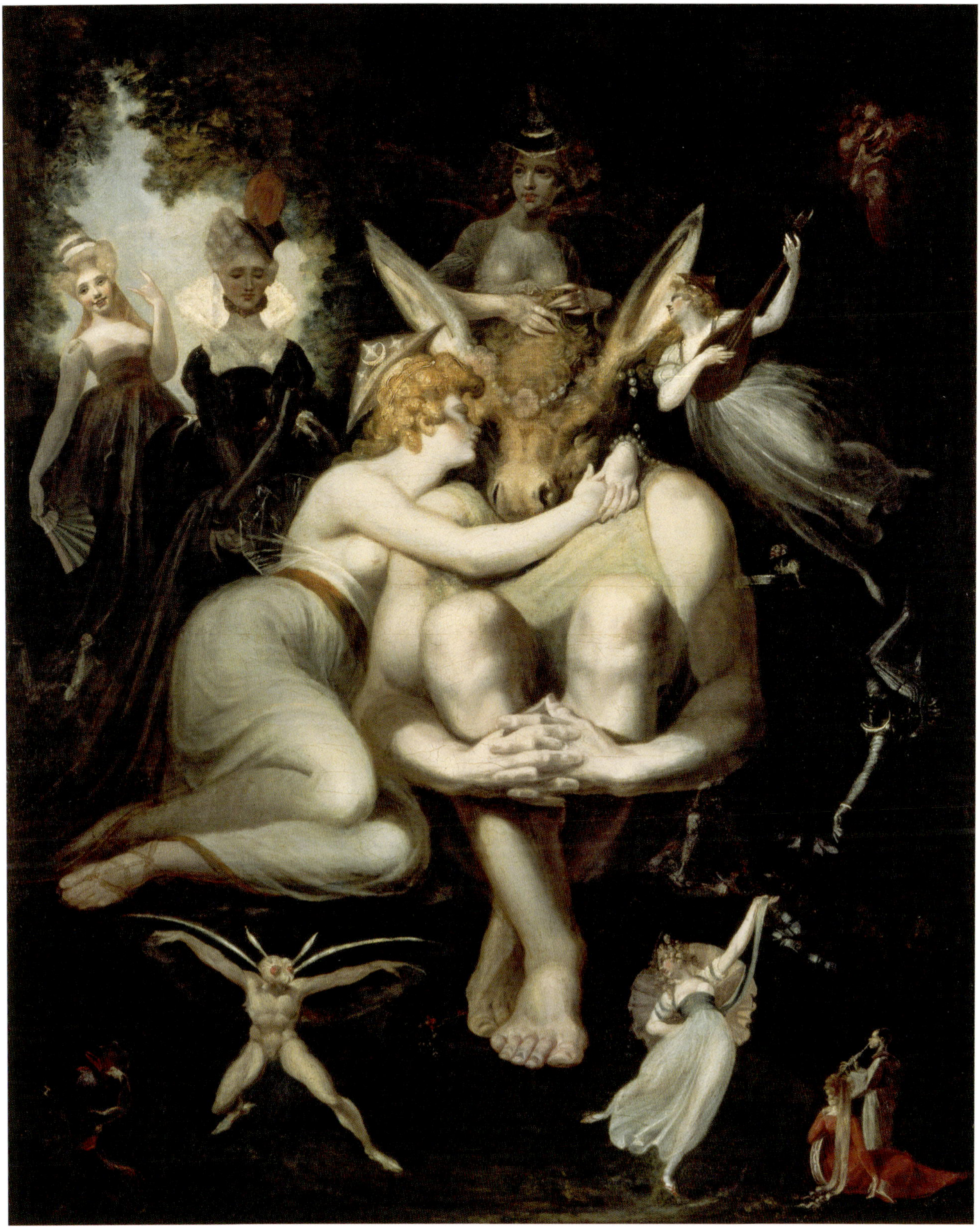

Cat. 34 *Titania and Bottom*, 1793–94

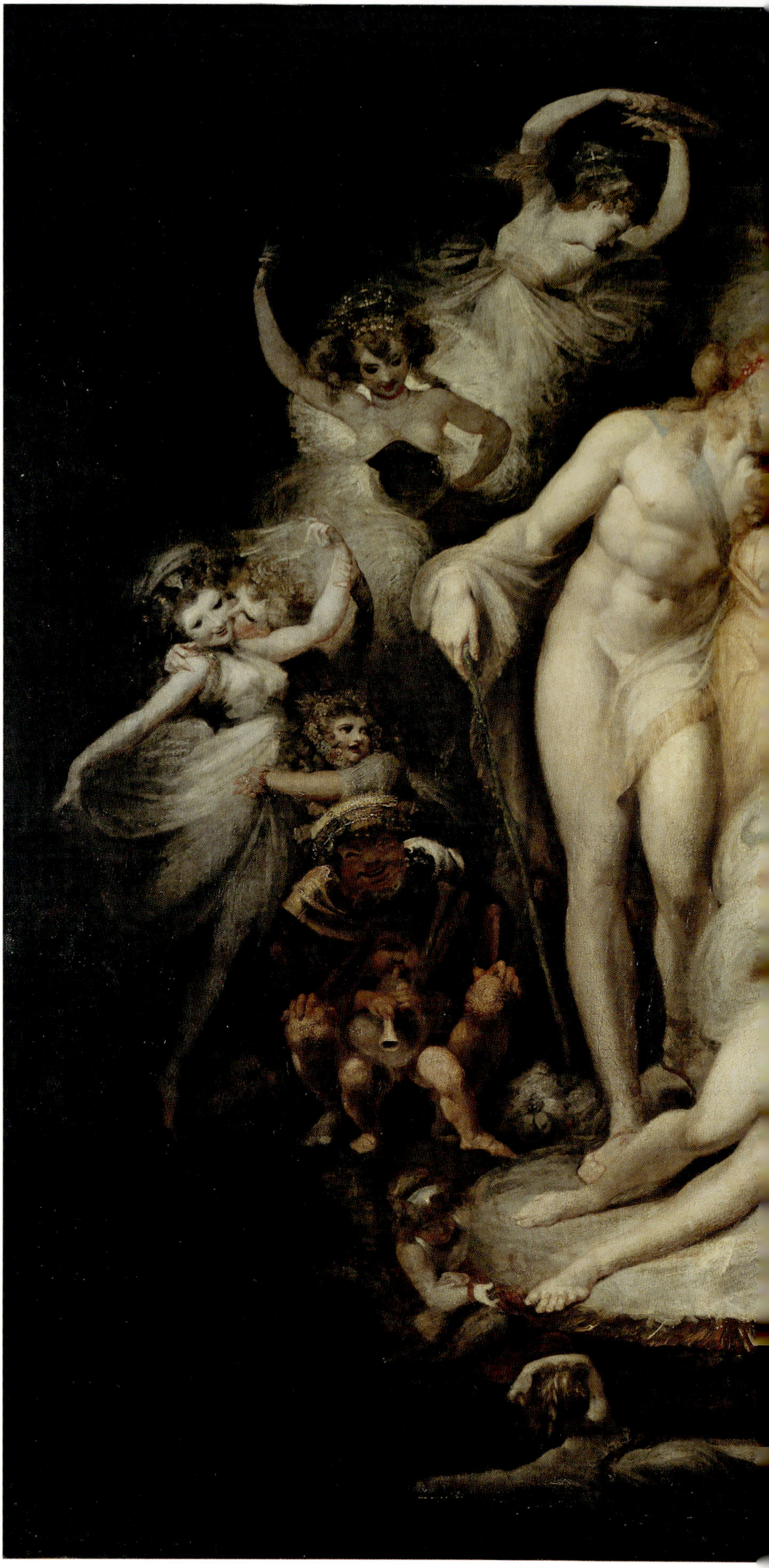

Cat. 35 *Titania's Awakening*, 1785–90

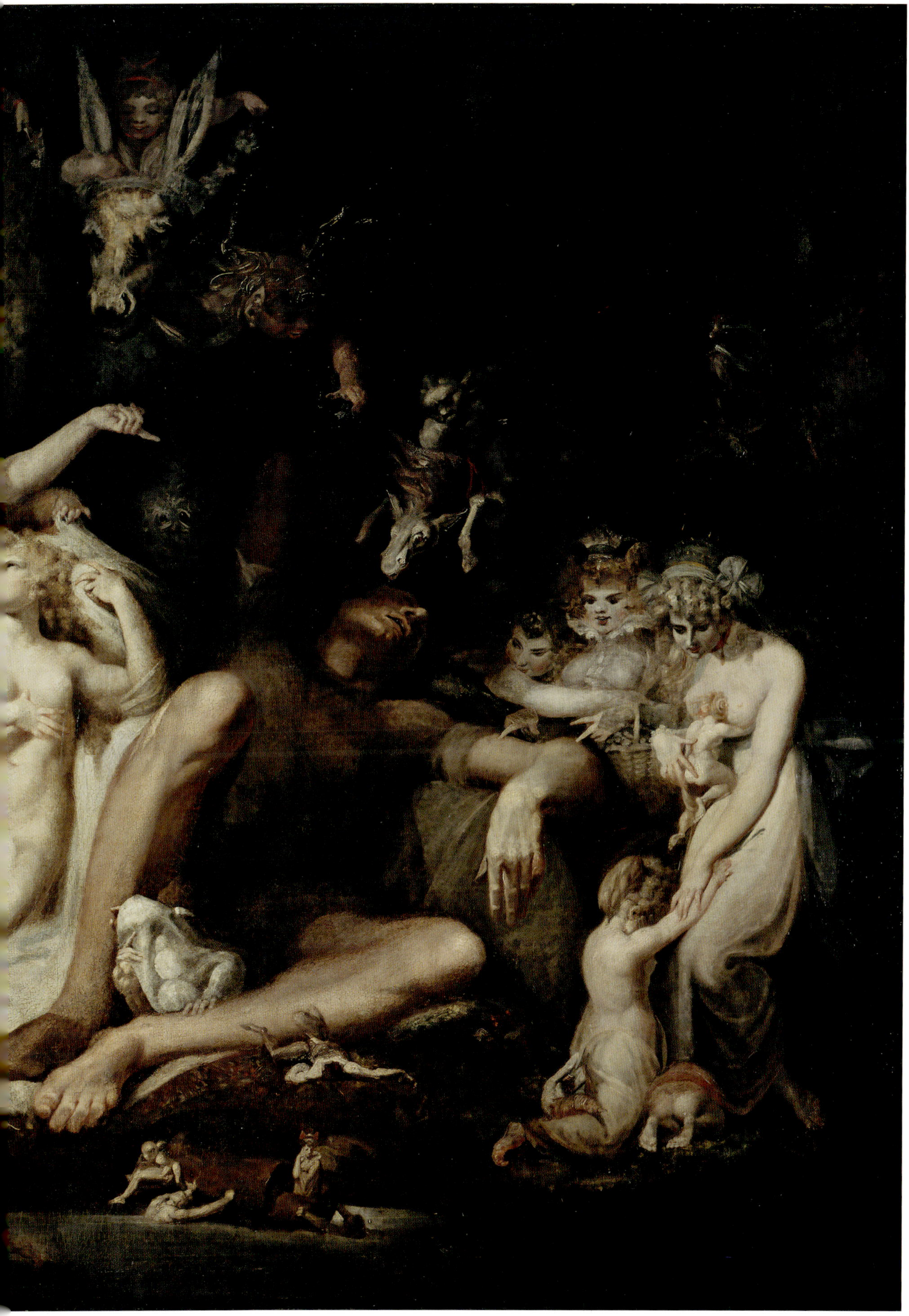

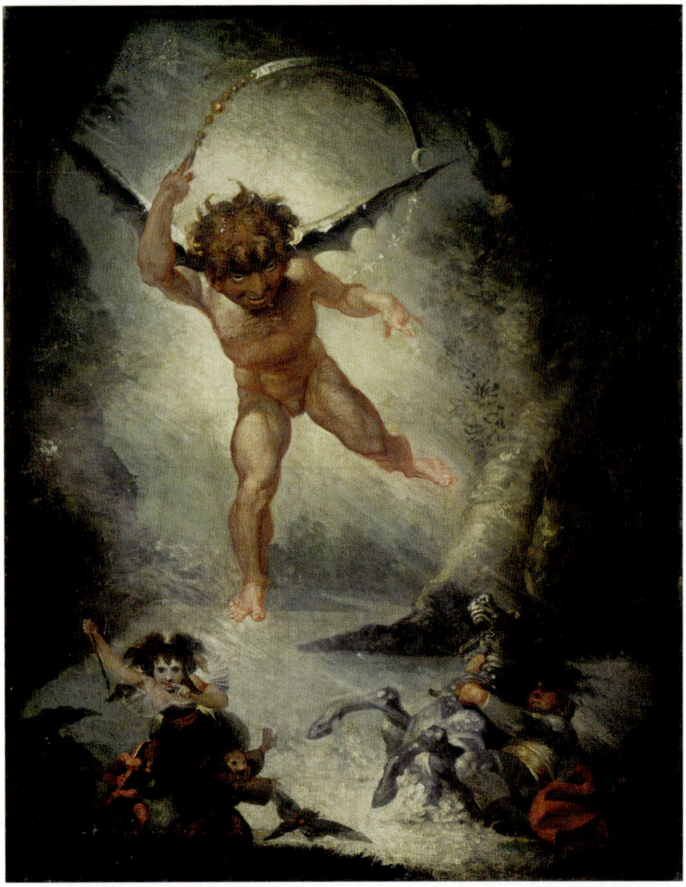

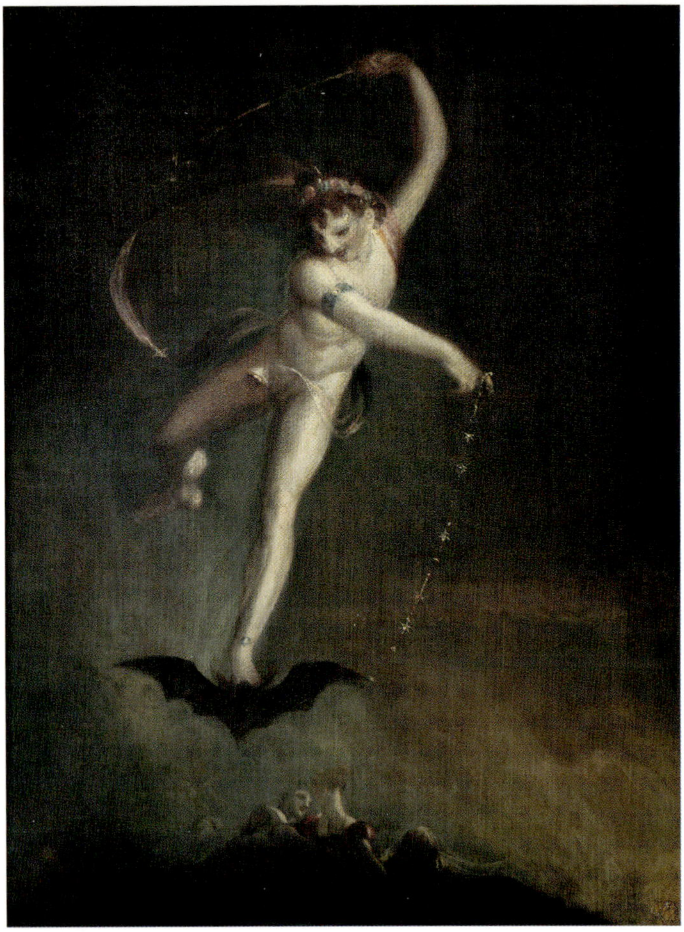

Cat. 36 *Robin Goodfellow (Puck)*, 1787–90

Cat. 37 *Ariel*, 1800–10

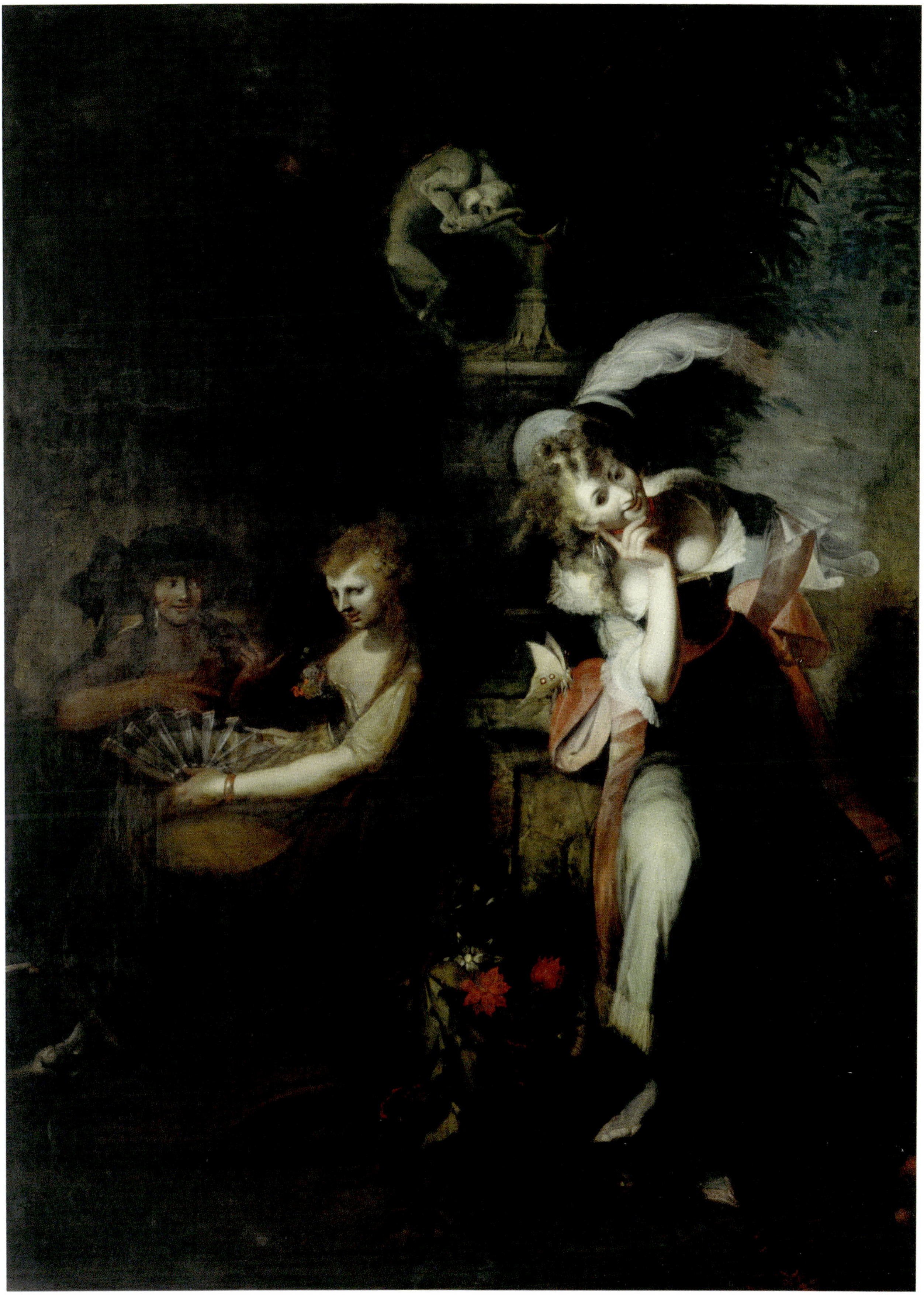

Cat. 38 *Beatrice Eavesdropping on Hero and Ursula*, 1789–91

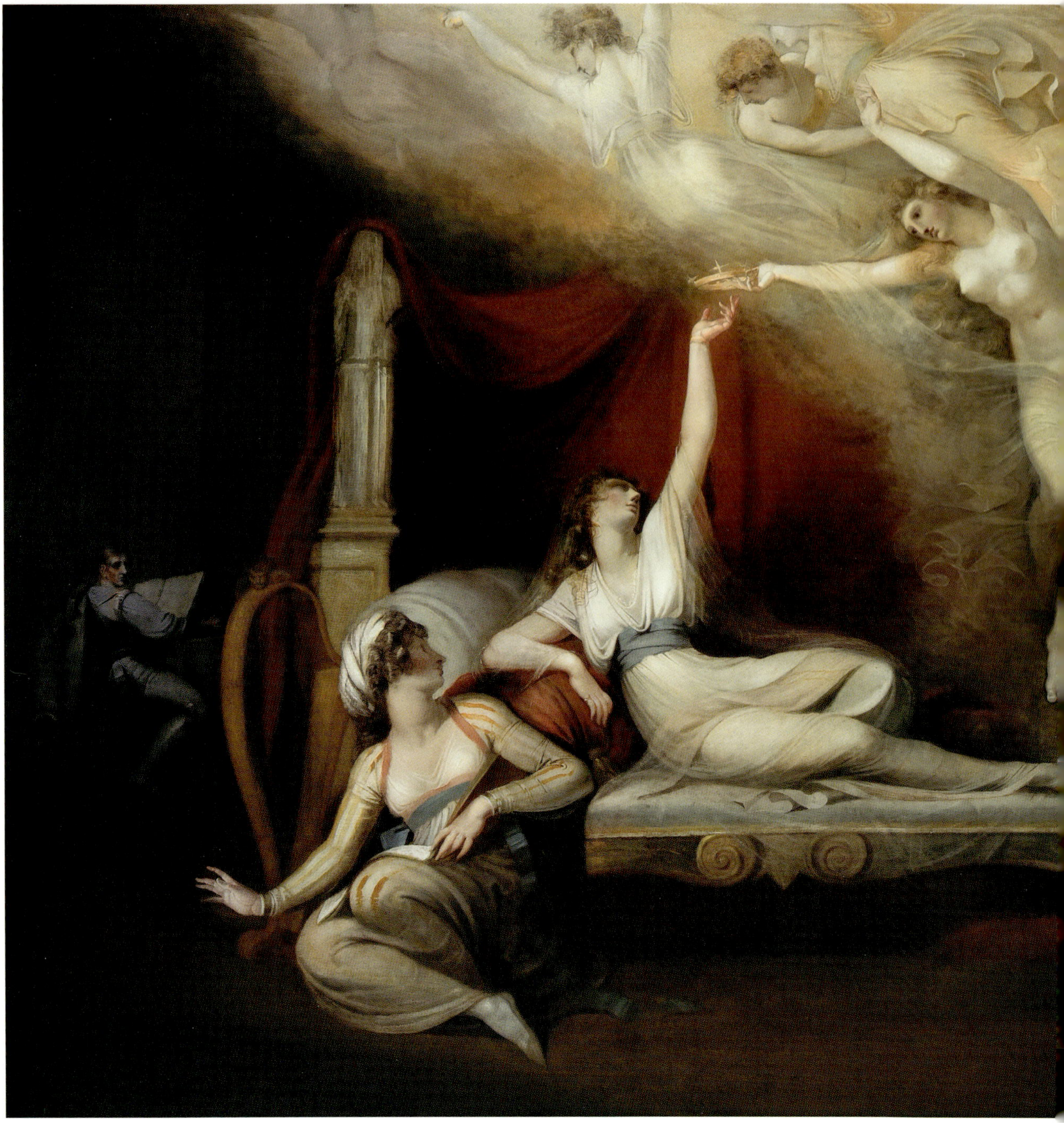

Cat. 39 *Queen Katherine's Dream*, 1781

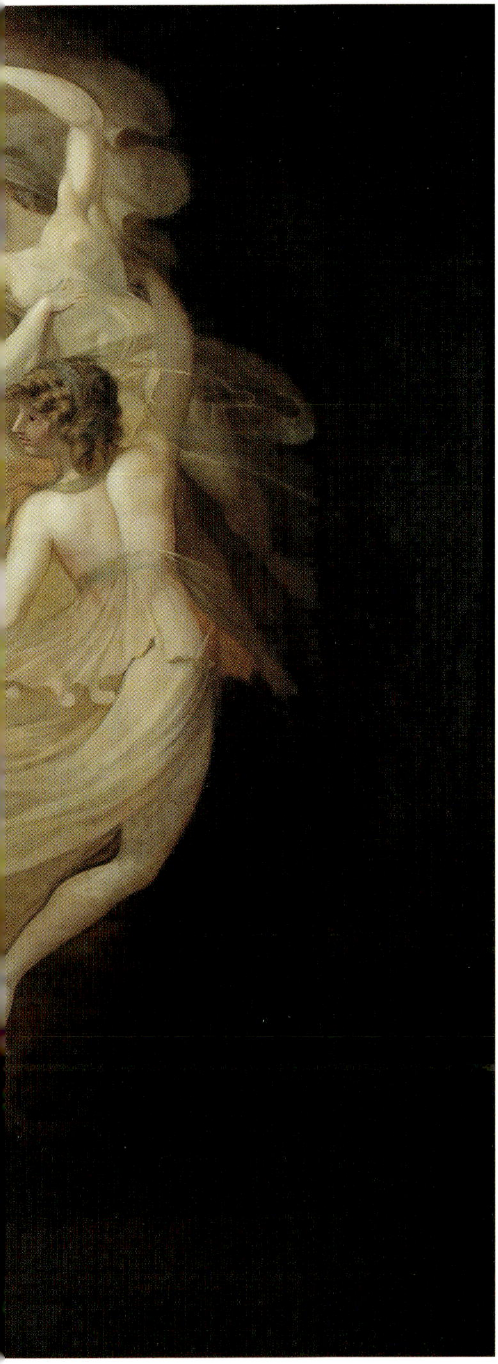

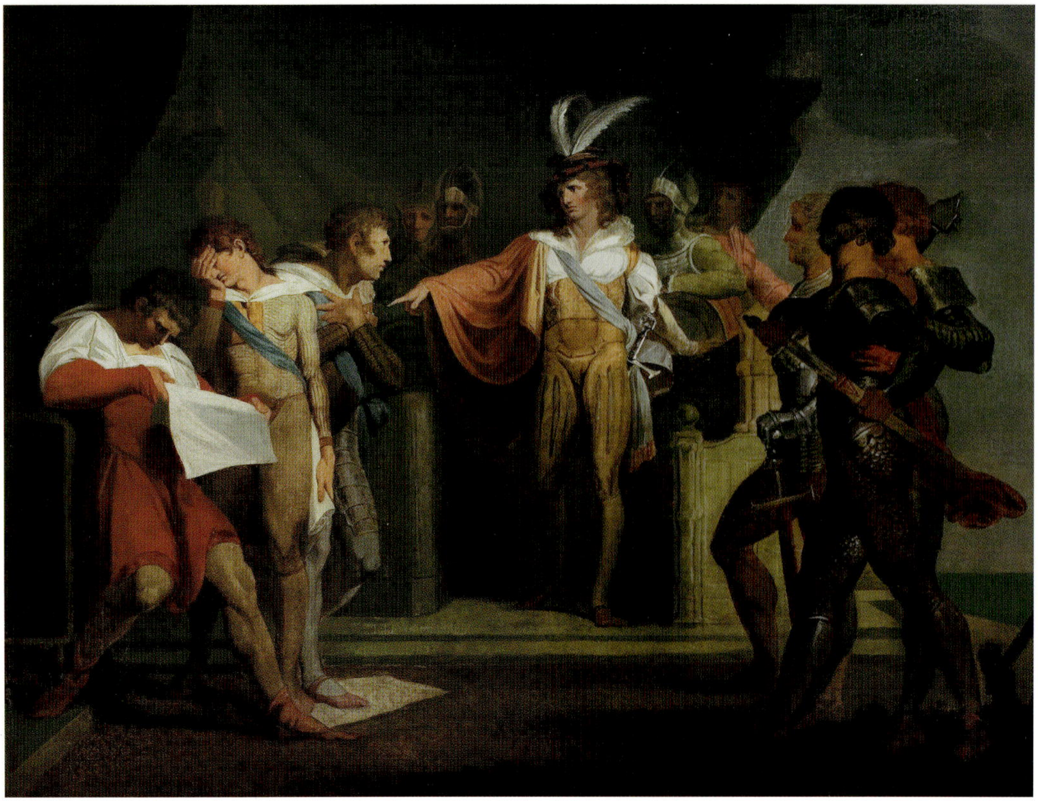

Cat. 40 *Henry V Discovering the Conspirators*, 1786–89

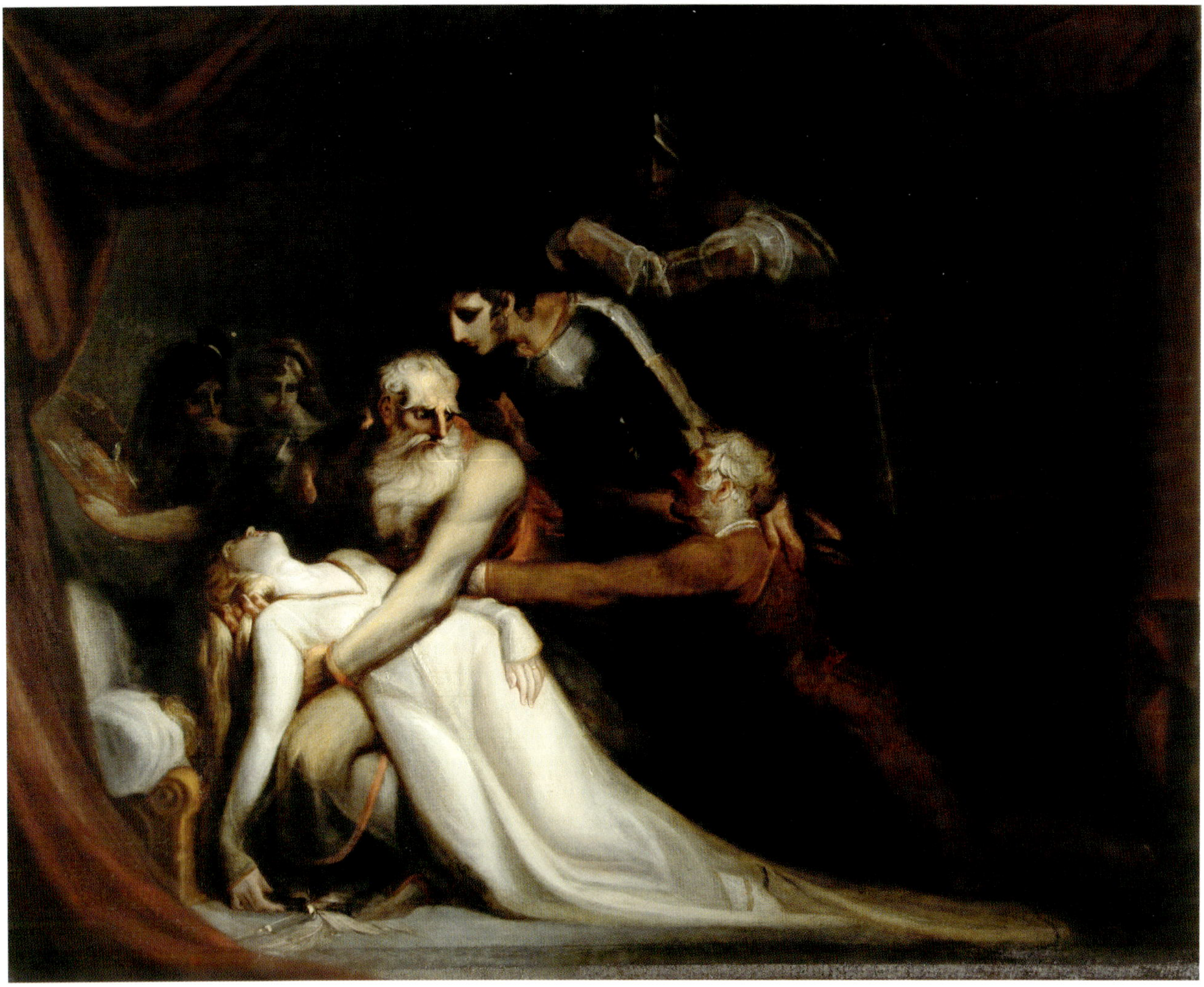

Cat. 41 *The Death of Cordelia*,
1810–20

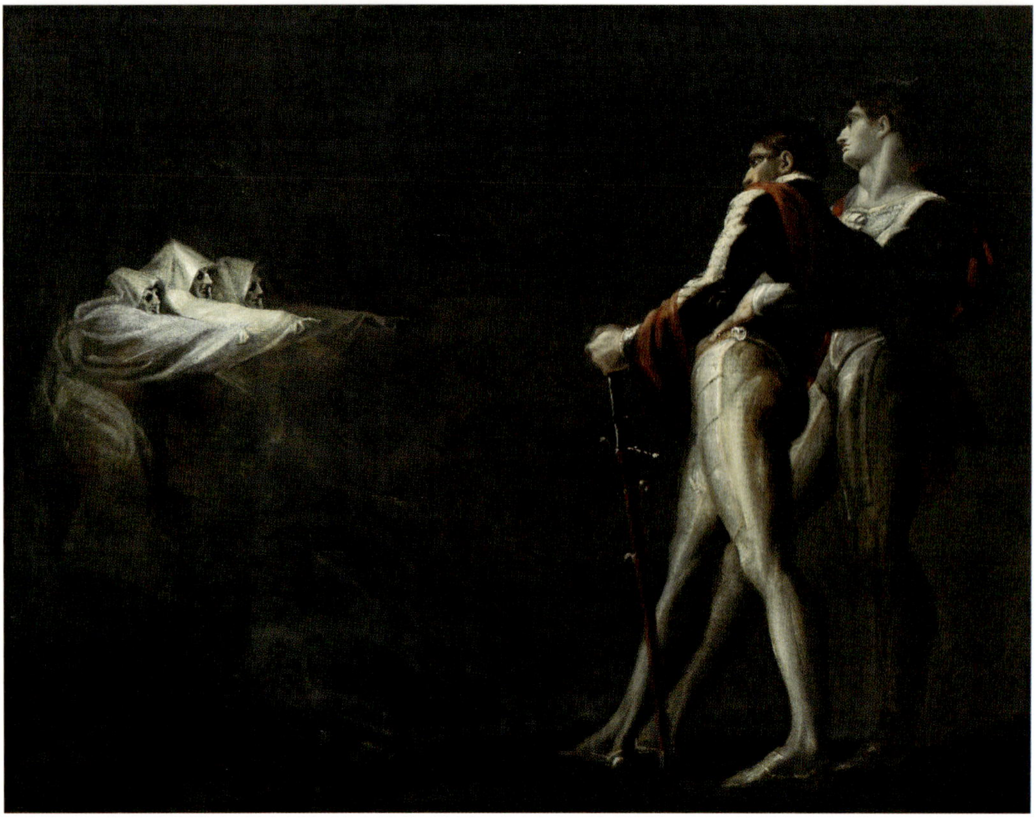

Cat. 42 *The Three Witches Appearing to Macbeth and Banquo*, 1800–10

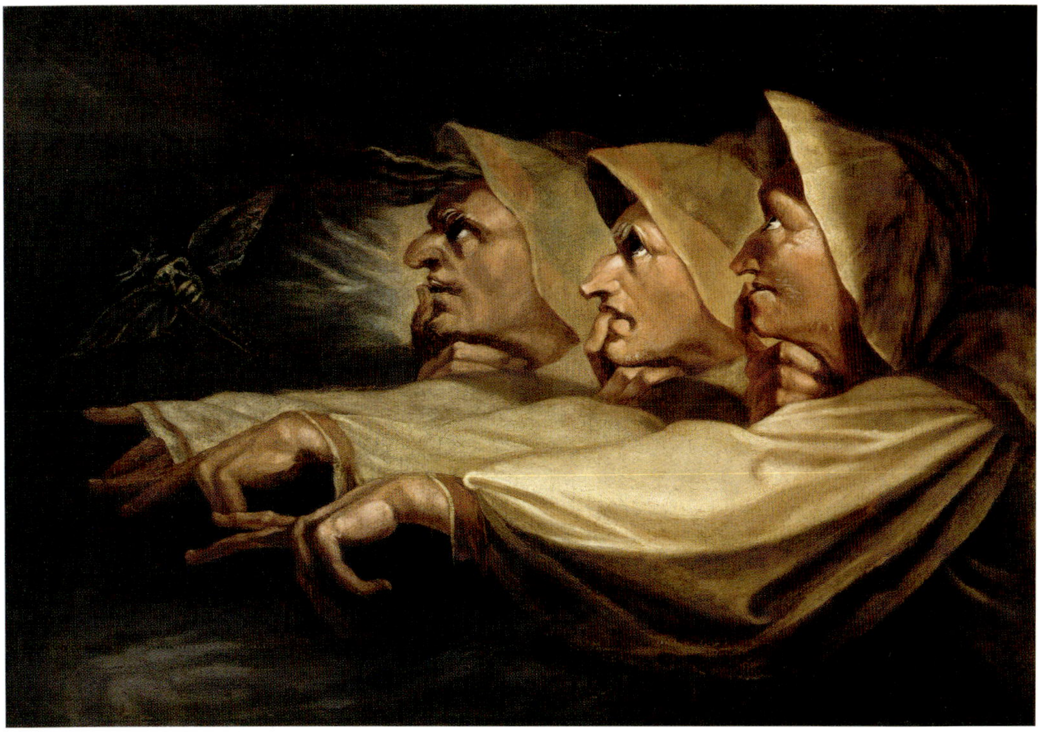

Cat. 43 *The Three Witches*, 1783

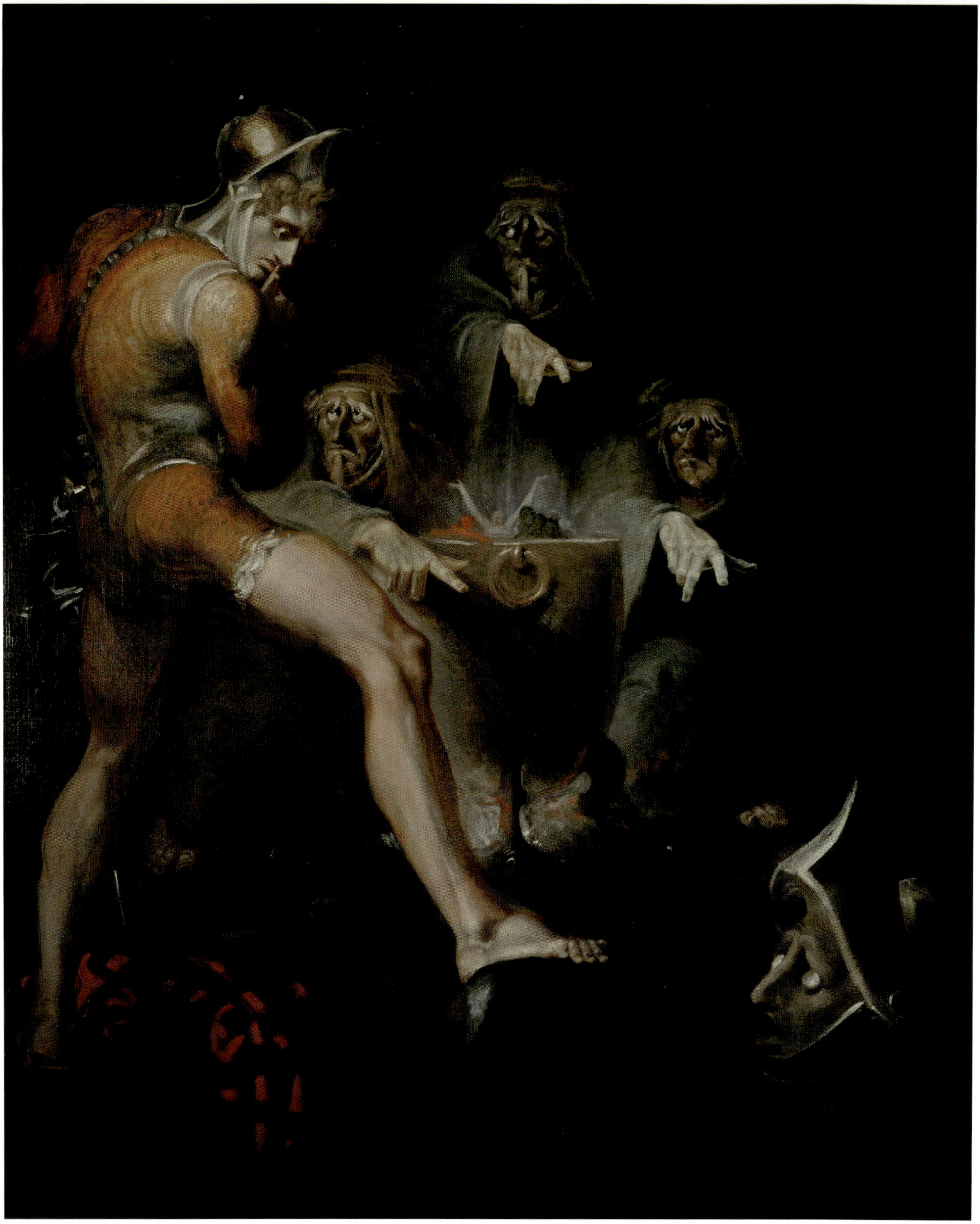

Cat. 44 *Macbeth Consulting the Vision of the Armed Head*, 1793–94

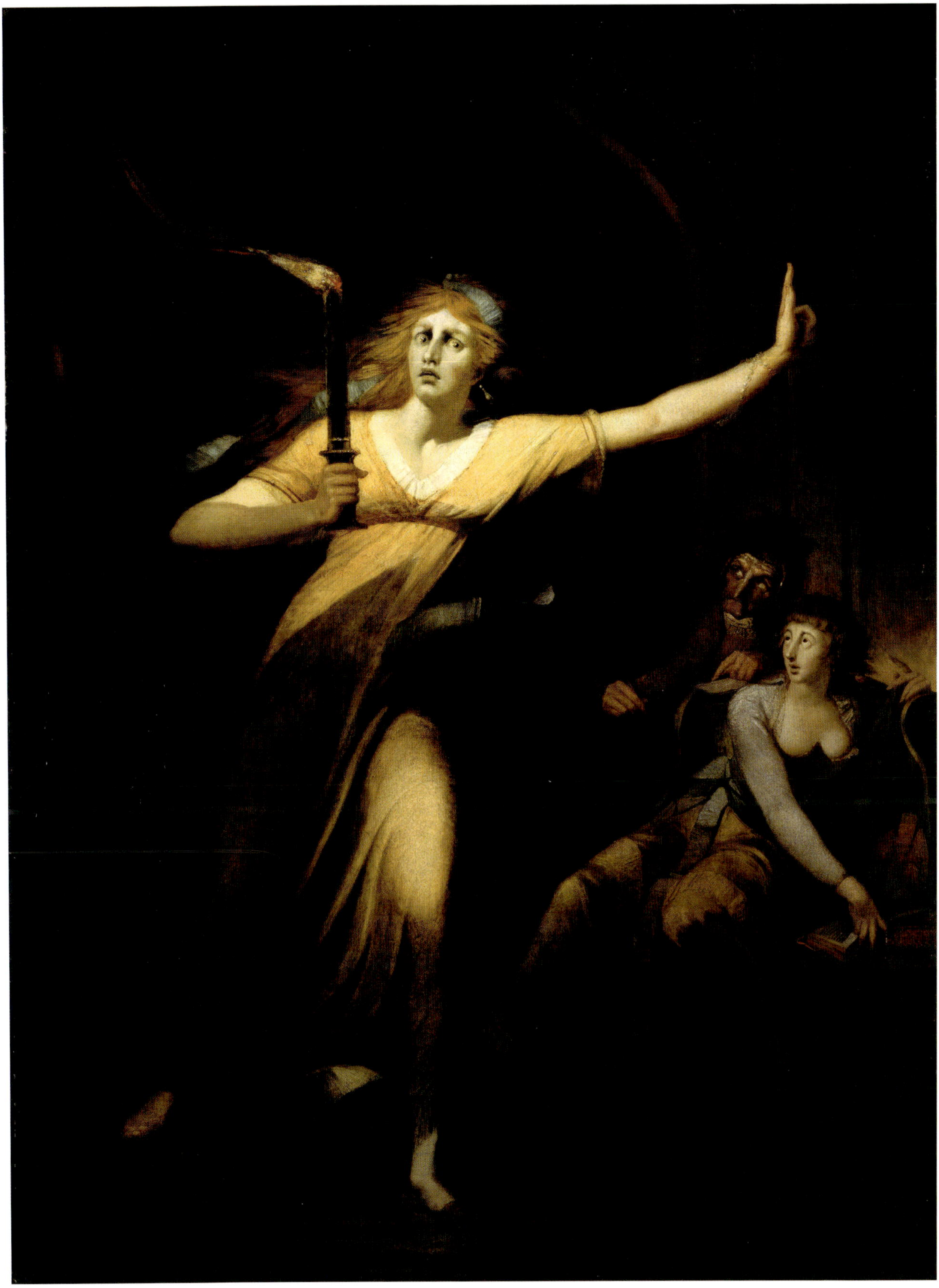

Cat. 45 *Lady Macbeth Sleepwalking*, c. 1783

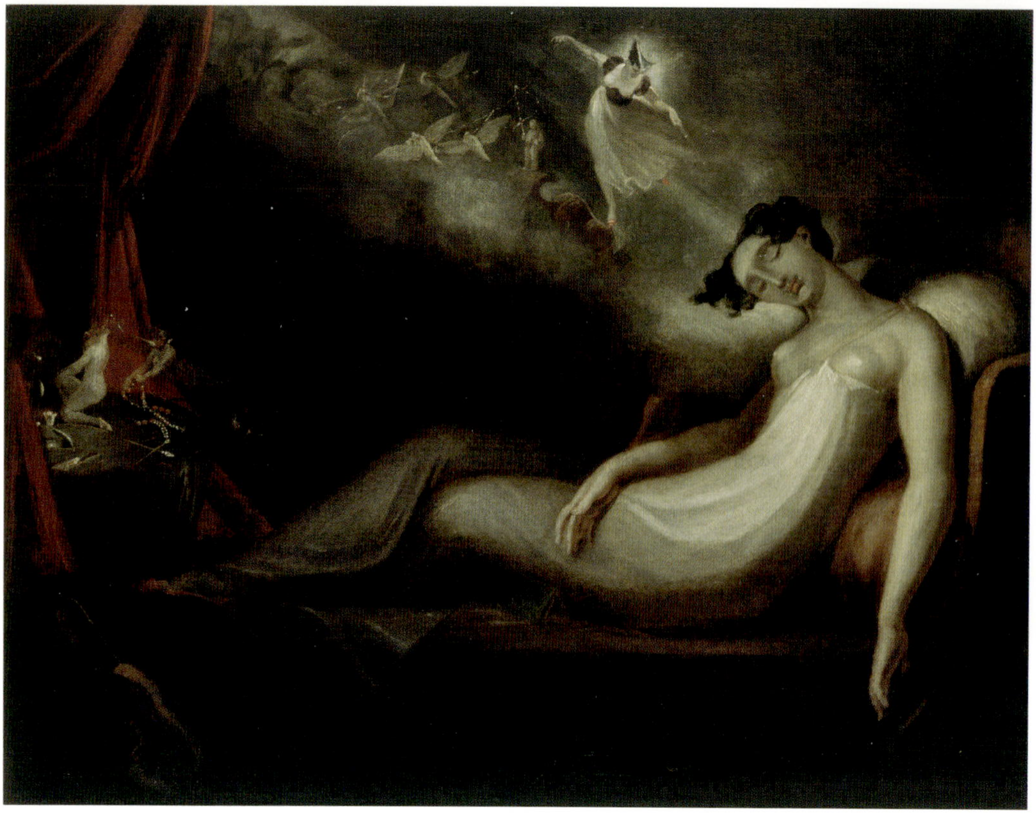

Cat. 46 *Queen Mab*, 1814

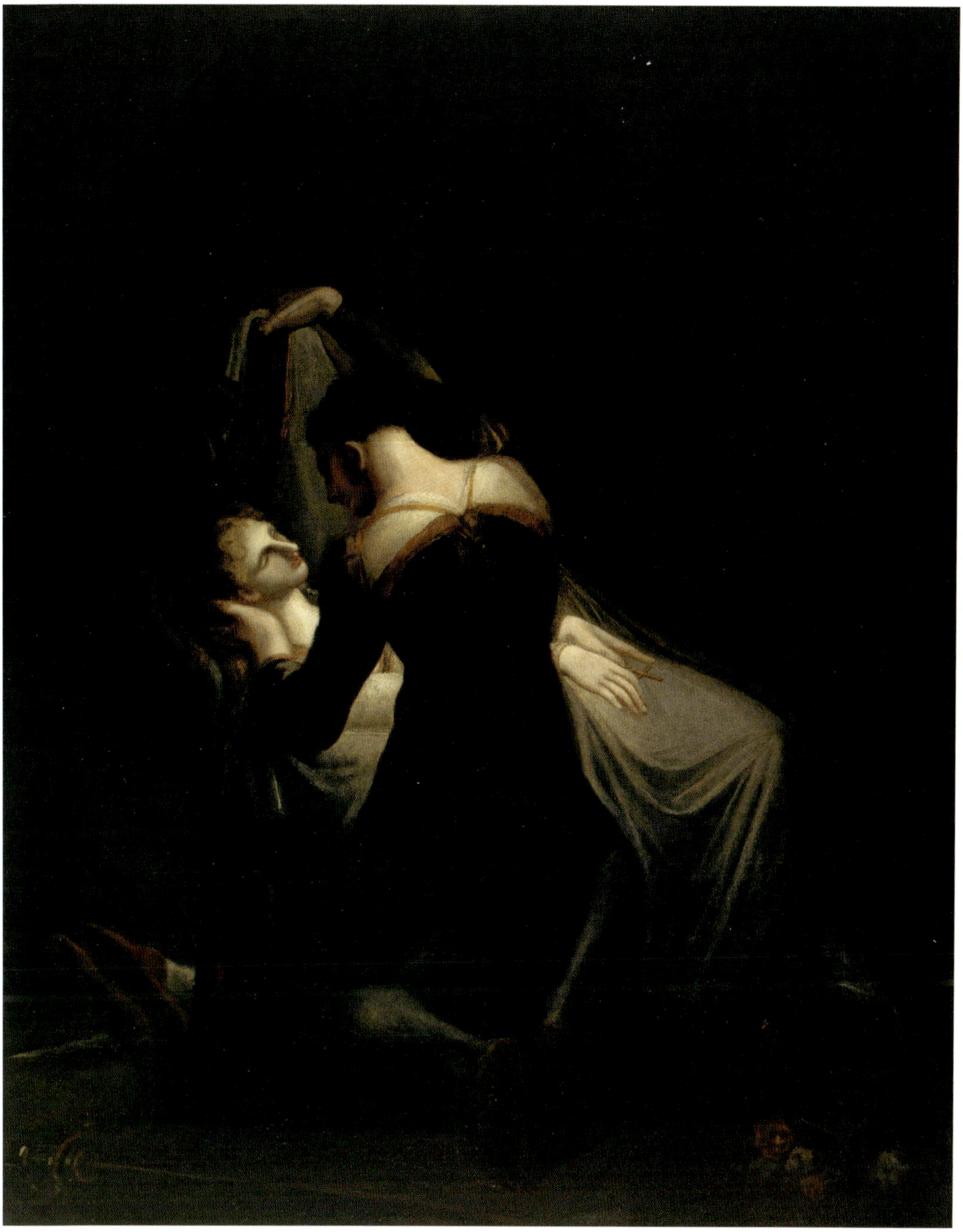

Cat. 47 *Romeo at Juliet's Bier*, 1809

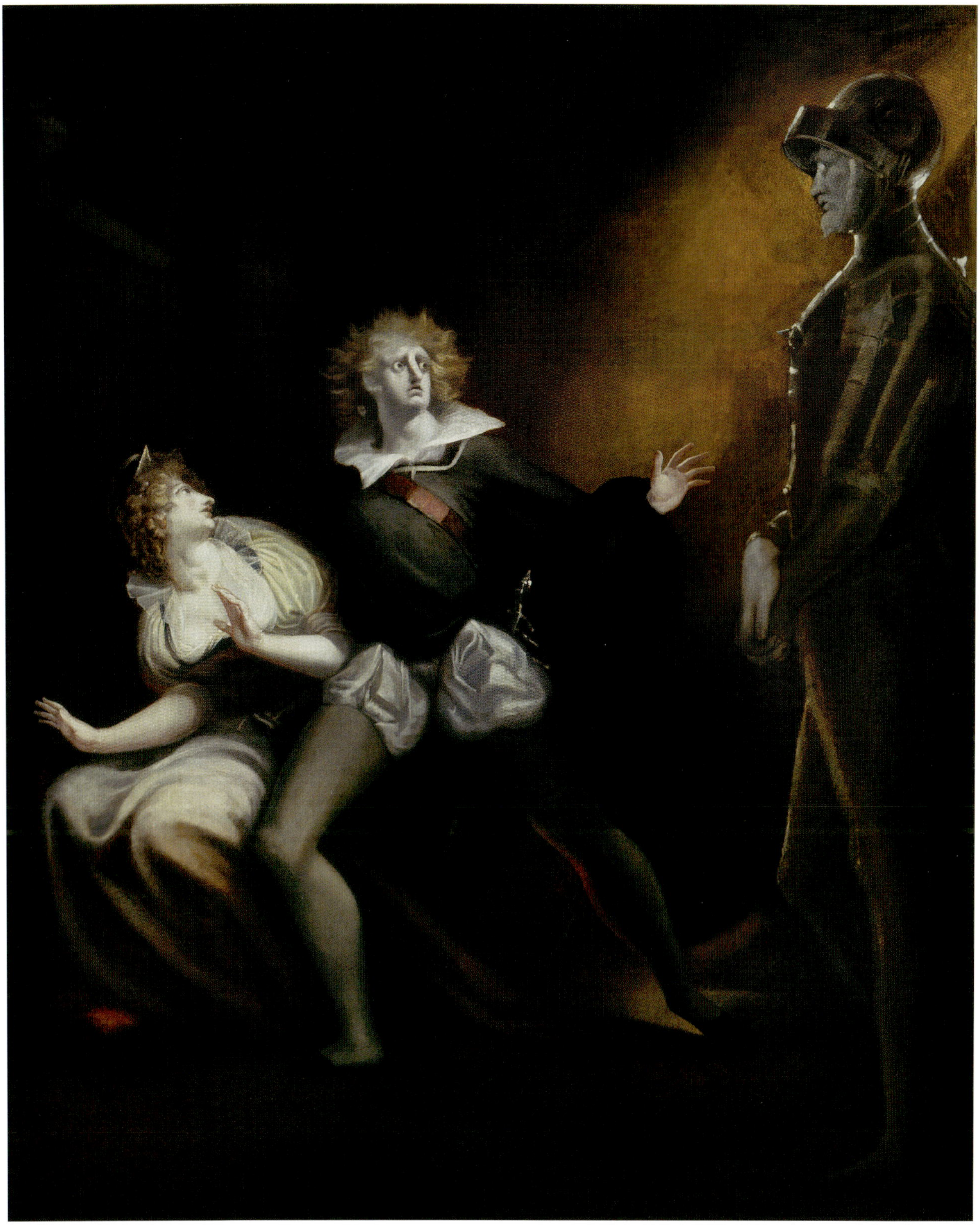

Cat. 48 *Gertrude, Hamlet and the Ghost of Hamlet's Father*, 1793

Milton

Johann Jakob Bodmer had acquainted Fuseli with the work of Milton during his student days in Zurich.[1] By the final decade of the century it had become one of the artist's most important sources of inspiration.[2] Indeed, the most extensive, ambitious and hazardous undertaking of his career was rooted in the evocative language and powerful imagery of England's second national poet. Set up exclusively in accordance with Fuseli's wishes over a period of almost ten years, the Milton Gallery contained forty paintings, some on a very large scale, when it opened on 20 May 1799 and forty-seven the following year, when a second exhibition was mounted.[3] The greater part of these – twenty-seven in the first year, thirty in the next – took their cue from the epic poem *Paradise Lost* (cats 52, 53, 55); the remainder addressed subjects from its sequel, *Paradise Regained*, from the poems *Il Penseroso*, *Lycidas* and *L'Allegro* (cat. 58), from the masque *Comus* and from other works, all rounded out by scenes from the poet's life (cats 59, 63).[4] Add to these a few paintings not included in the gallery (cats 61, 62) and those produced in connection with engravings illustrating Francis Isaac Du Roveray's 1802 edition of *Paradise Lost*, and the poet's outstanding place in Fuseli's oeuvre becomes even clearer.[5] During the genesis of the gallery, which was fraught with difficulty, he also came increasingly to identify with Milton, feeling that they shared a number of biographical similarities (see 'Pictures of Authors, Free Inventions', pp. 159–61).[6]

Fuseli was neither the first nor the only painter to engage with the religious pathos and moral force of *Paradise Lost*,[7] but the number and aesthetic coherence of his series of canvases, their perceptive treatment of the poem's content and their pictorial strategies were without precedent.[8] Often he favoured personal interpretation over faithfulness to the text. Nowhere is that more obvious than in his fixation on Satan, who with him, even more than with Milton, is the real hero of the piece.[9]
Fuseli's mammoth Milton Gallery project took wing from the

failure of another venture of the same kind. Since about 1790 the publisher Joseph Johnson, inspired by the success of John Boydell's Shakespeare Gallery (see 'Shakespeare', pp. 119–20), had been devising a similar compendium of the writings of Milton and was counting on Fuseli to create no less than thirty paintings as models for engravings.[10] When this undertaking collapsed, the artist decided to continue it at his own risk, willing to face years of hardship and effort in certain anticipation of considerable profits.[11] His expectations turned out to be unfounded: the Milton Gallery ended in a financial disaster so large that it almost ruined Fuseli. Both exhibitions had to close within a few weeks owing to poor takings, the envisaged reproduction of the paintings in the form of engravings never got off the ground and the canvases themselves initially proved to be more or less unsaleable.[12] On the other hand, despite the obvious lack of success, the Milton Gallery brought Fuseli praise and recognition from artistic circles in London and enhanced his reputation to the extent that it must have helped his election to Professor of Painting at the Royal Academy in 1799.[13]

Why did the Milton Gallery fail? In the first place, Milton was less popular than Shakespeare and, in the second, the very large dimensions of many of the canvases will have reduced the number of potential buyers.[14] In addition, the general decline in importance of the reproductive print, which set in shortly before 1800, doubtless affected this project as it did others.[15] Over and above these factors, however, there existed a basic conflict of interest between Fuseli's uncompromising focus on his artistic concerns and the expectations and tastes of the wider public, on whom the artist depended for refinancing. Ultimately, many visitors and critics were probably overtaxed or frightened off by highly dramatic and deeply pessimistic pictorial imagery that inhabited a world of its own, dominated by extreme chiaroscuro effects in combination with dark backgrounds. GD

1 See the essay by Alexander Honold in the present volume, pp. 37–57.
2 Tomory 1974, p. 10; Stuttgart 1997, pp. 10–11.
3 Schiff 1963, pp. 22, 27.
4 Schiff (ibid., pp. 141–61) prints a list of the paintings in the Milton Gallery in their original sequence and with the text passages cited by Fuseli.
5 The engravings are Weinglass 165–70.
6 Schiff 1973, vol. 1, pp. 189–92.
7 Pointon (1970) provides a survey of Milton illustrations before and beyond Fuseli.
8 For the pictorial strategies, which cannot be examined here, see especially the detailed discussion in Calè 2006.
9 Schiff 1963, pp. 32–33.
10 Stuttgart 1997, pp. 12–13.
11 Altick 1985, pp. 53–54.
12 Schiff 1963, pp. 25–27.
13 Stuttgart 1997, pp. 17–18; Lentzsch 2005, p. 231.
14 Schiff 1963, p. 25.
15 Hattendorff 1997, p. 84.

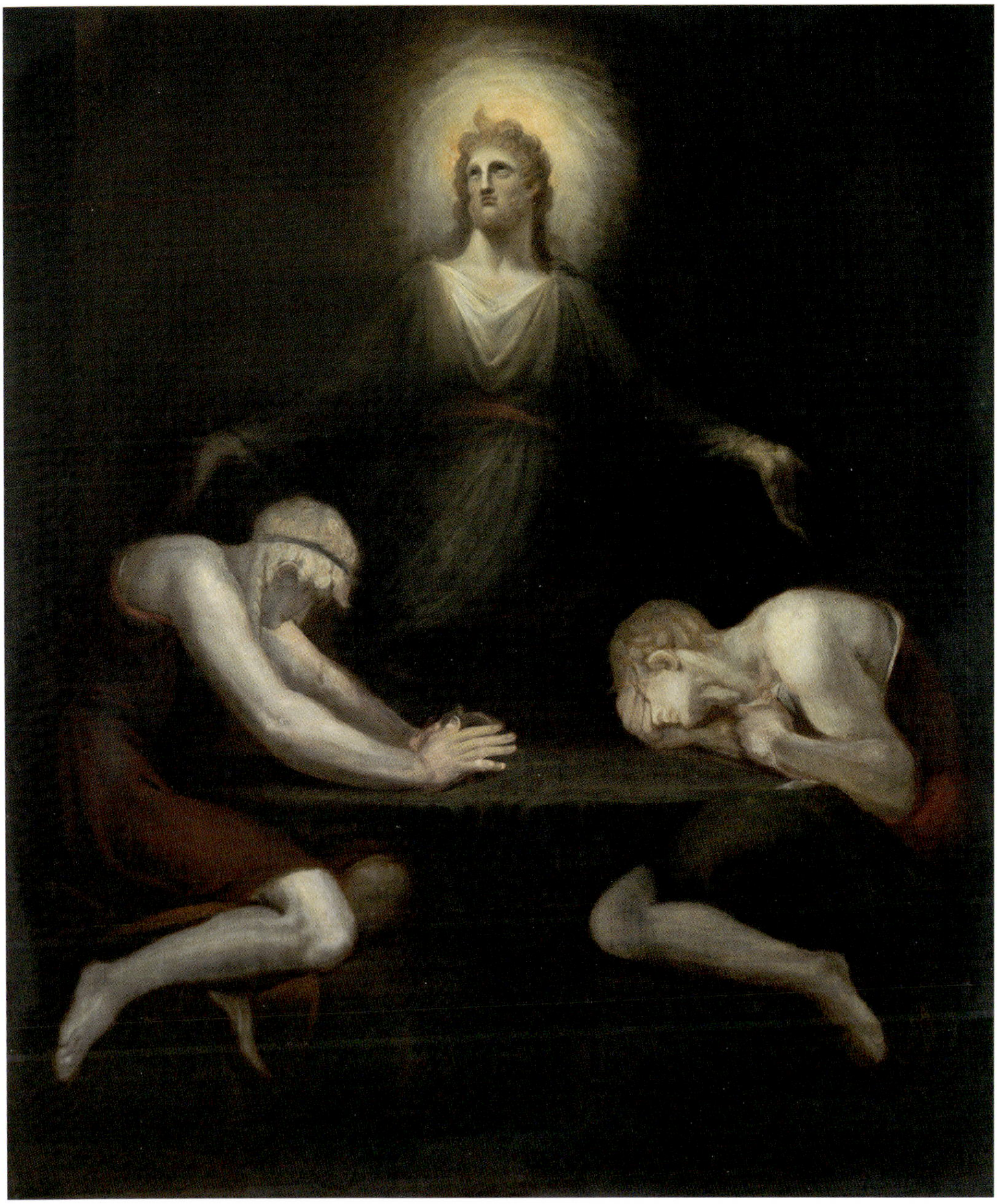

Cat. 49 *Christ Disappearing at Emmaus*, 1792

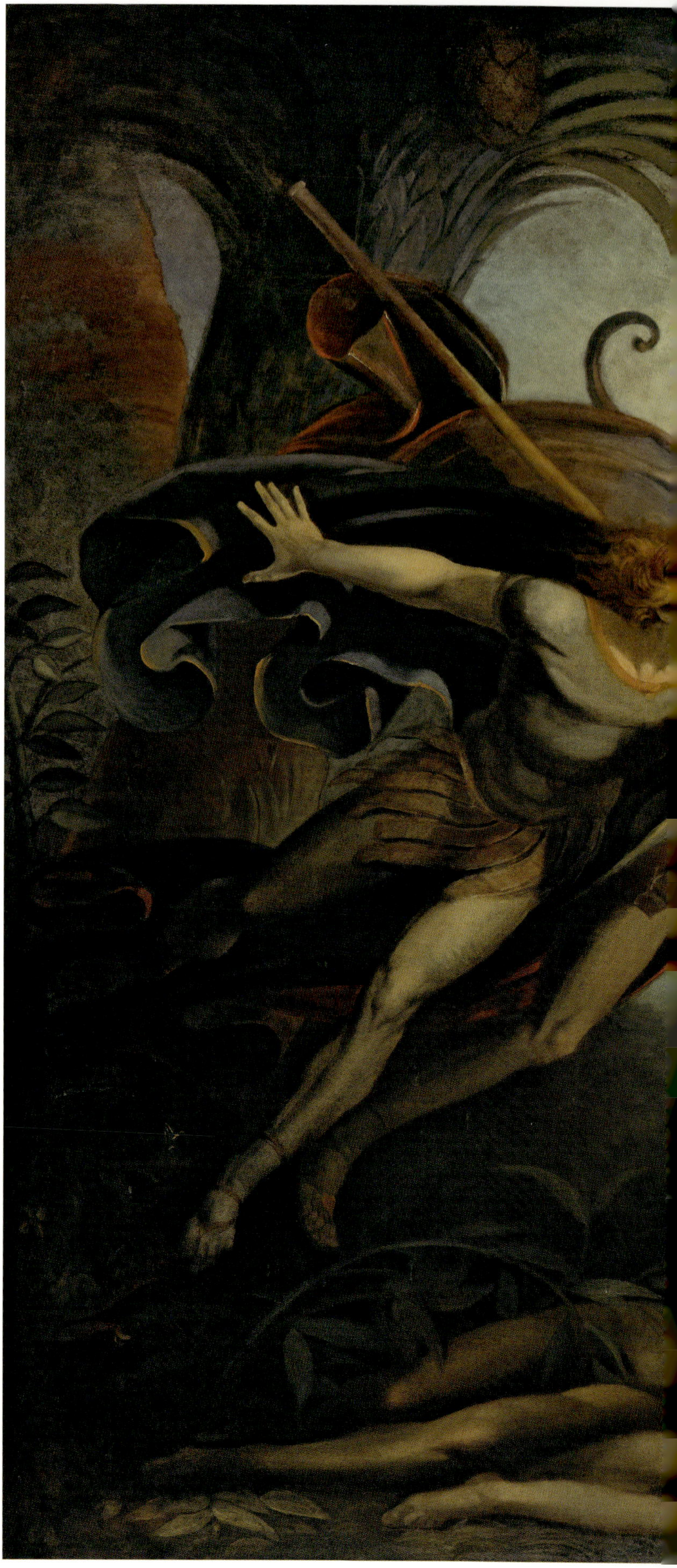

Cat. 50 *Satan Starting from the Touch of Ithuriel's Spear*, 1779

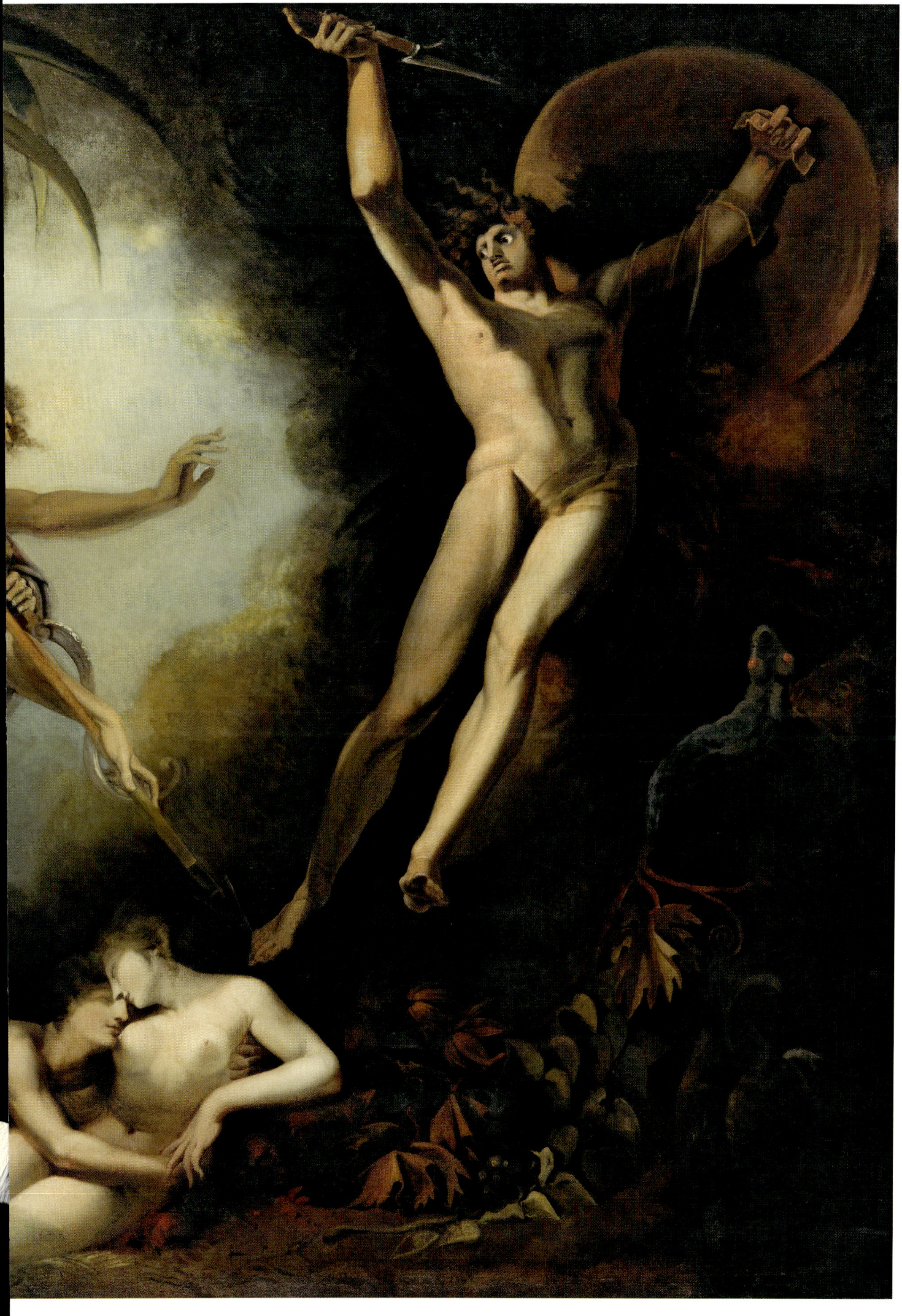

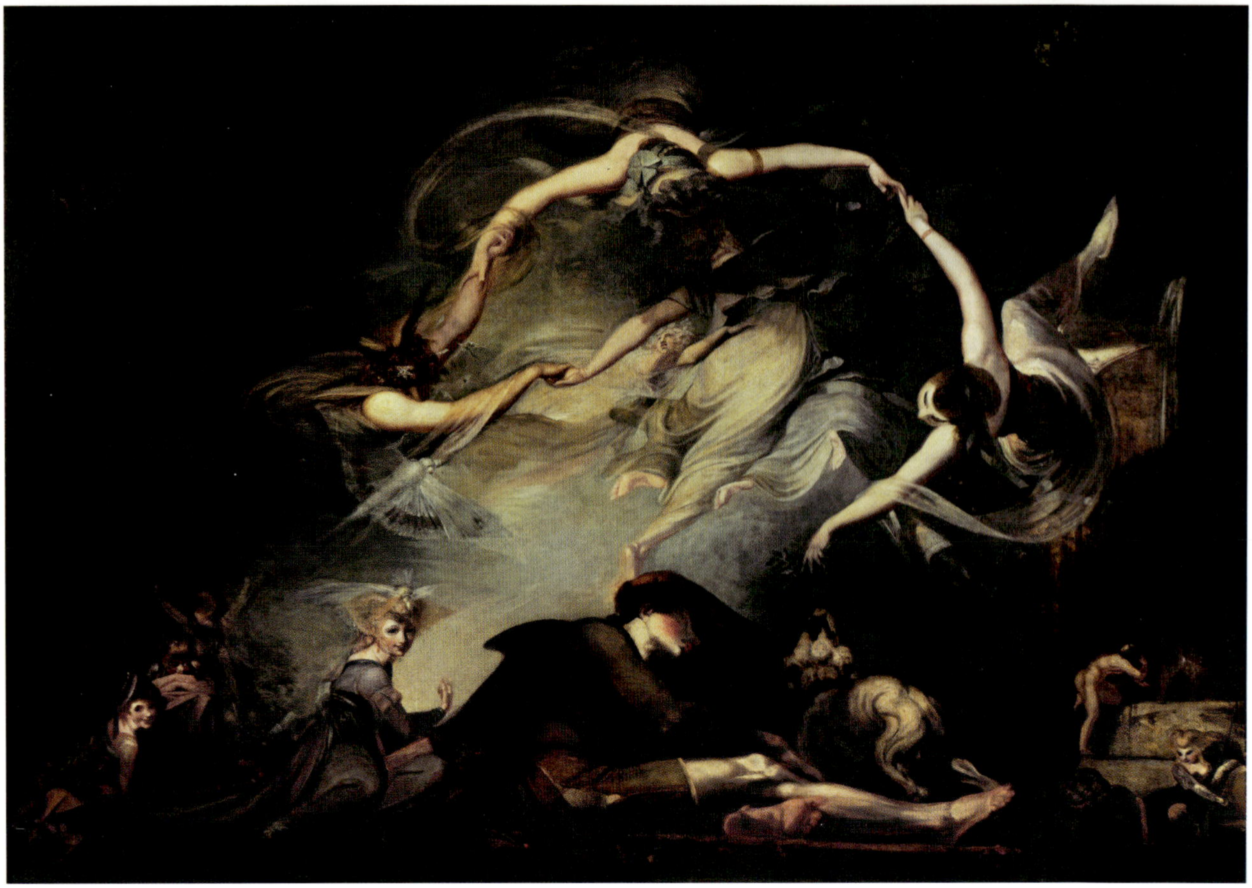

Cat. 51 *The Shepherd's Dream*, 1793

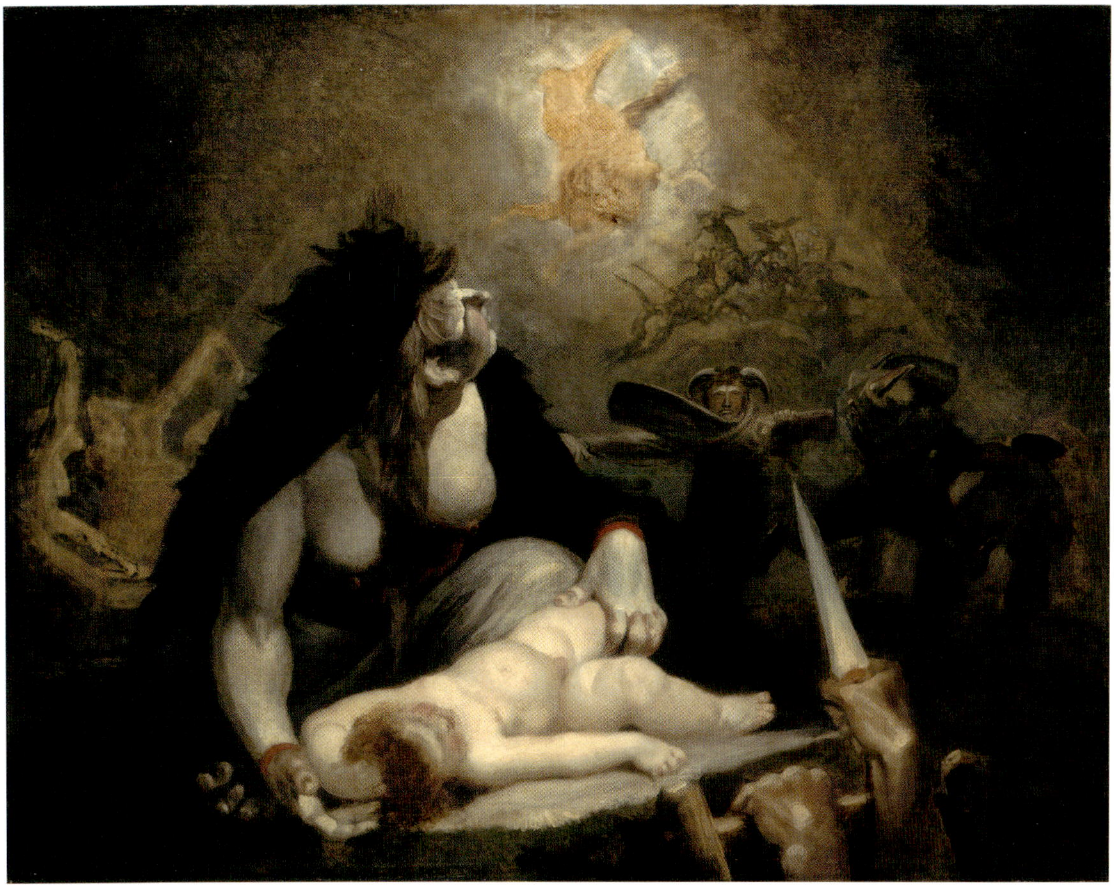

Cat. 52 *The Night Hag Visiting the Lapland Witches*, 1794–96

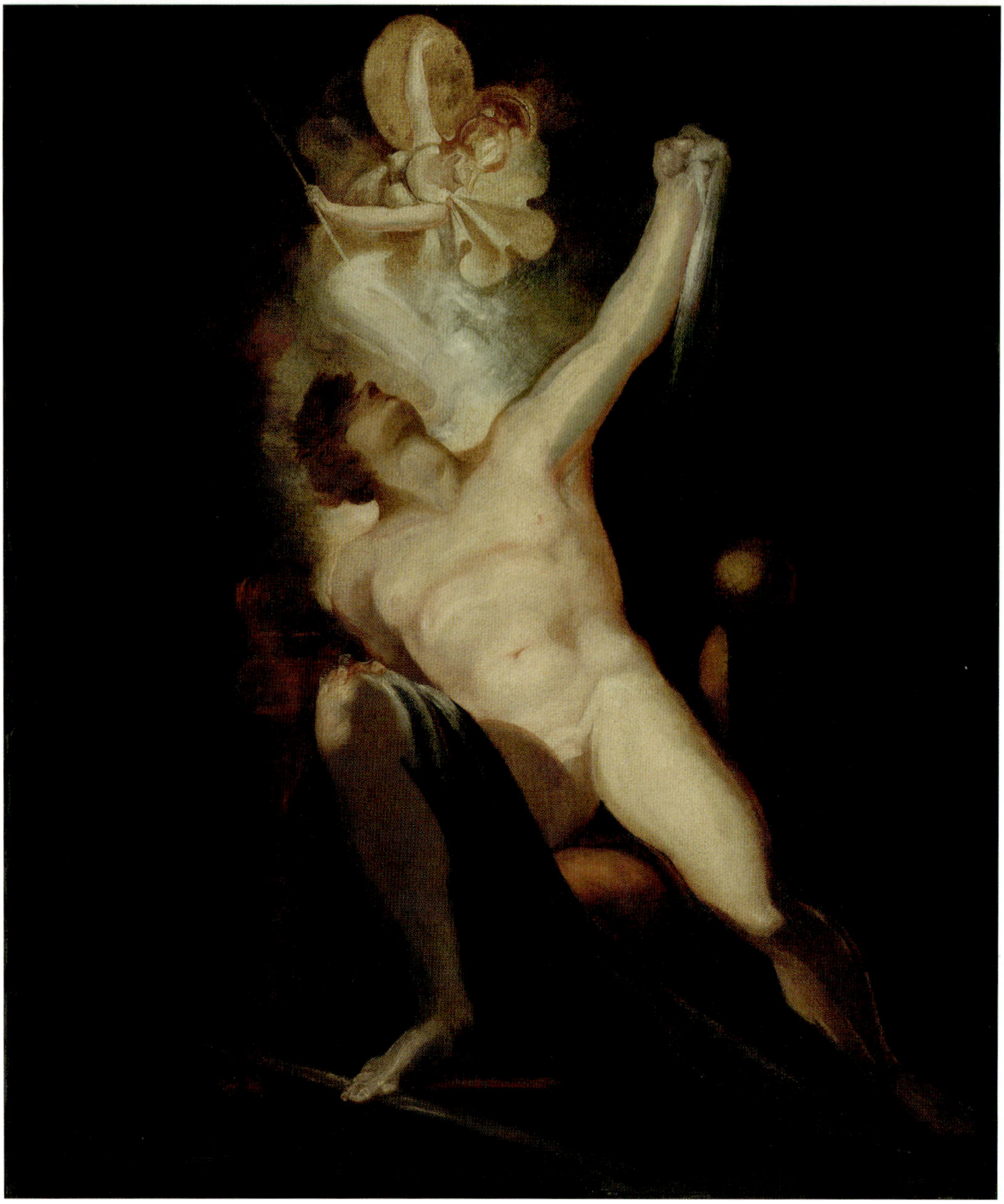

Cat. 53 *Satan and the Birth of Sin*,
c. 1796–99

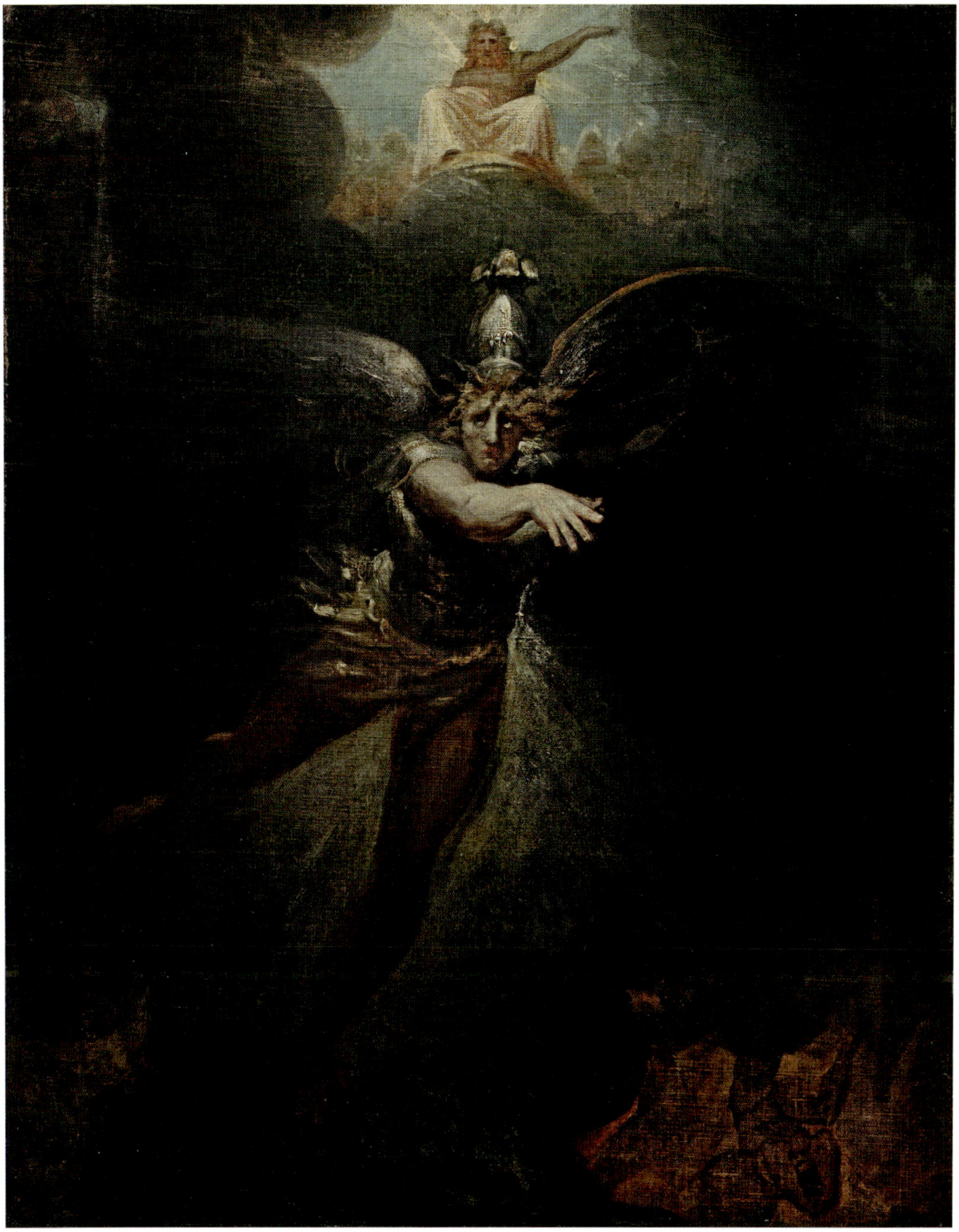

Cat. 54 *The Triumphant Messiah*, 1802

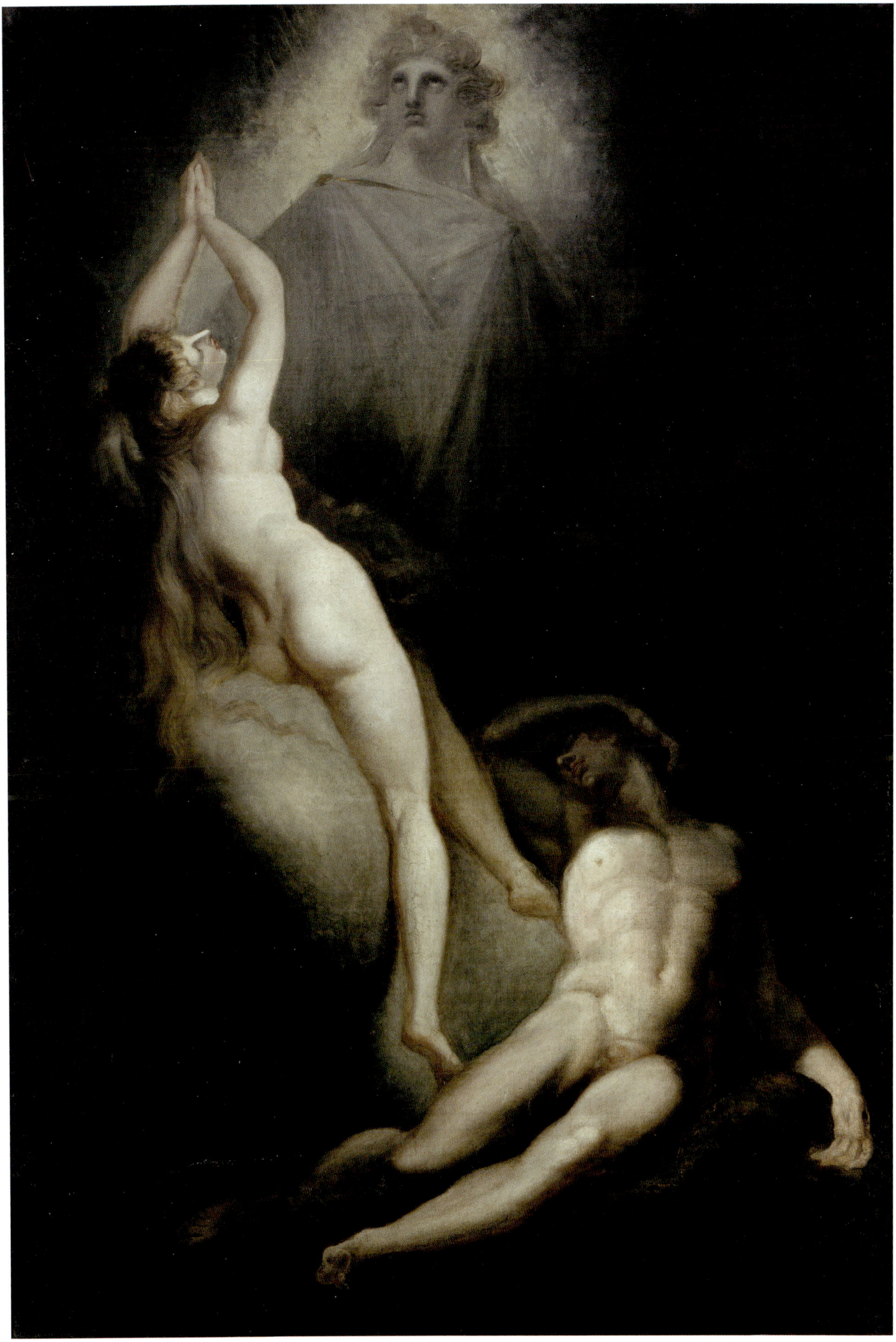

Cat. 55 *The Creation of Eve*, 1793

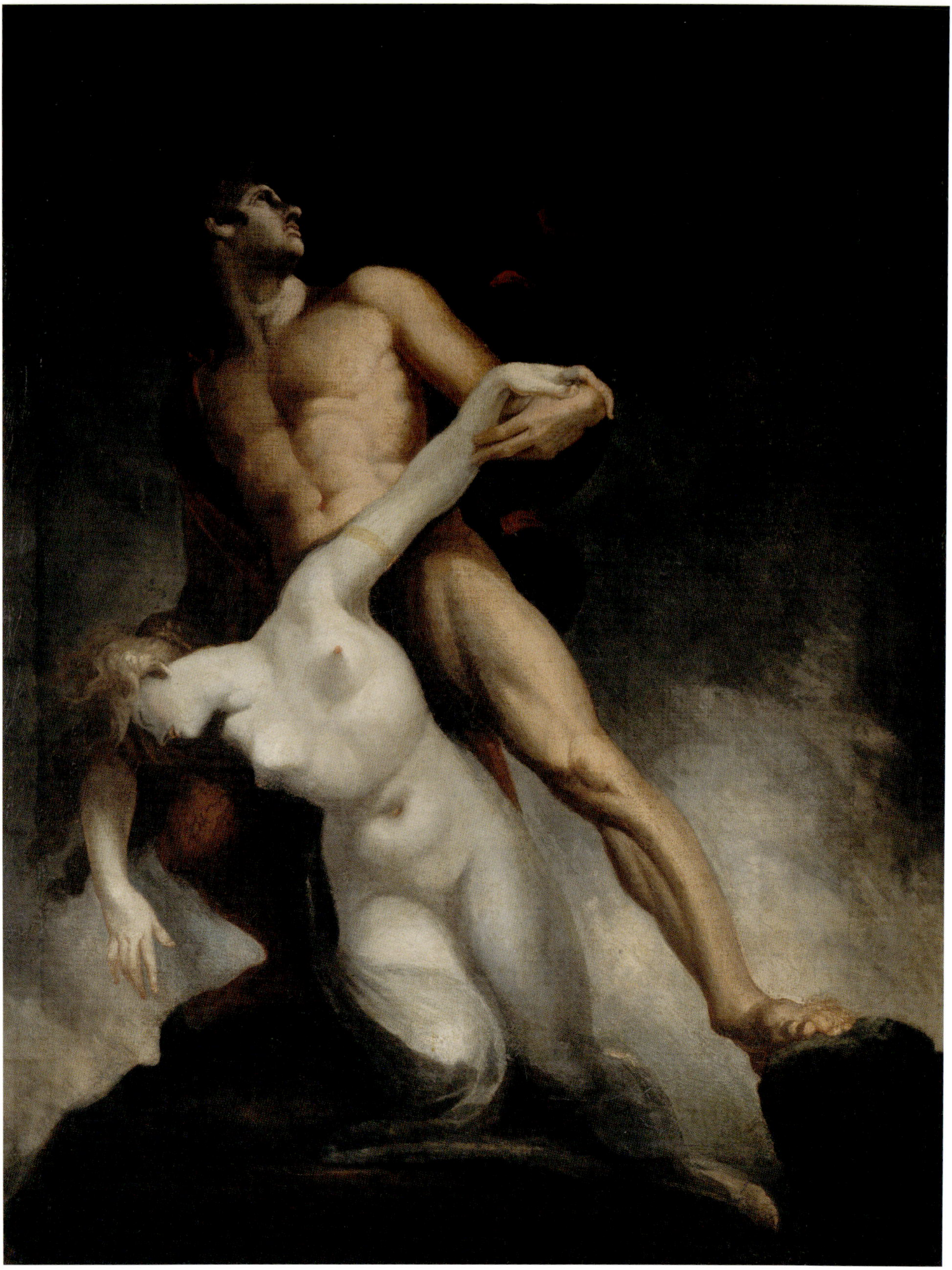

Cat. 56 *The Vision of the Flood*, c. 1800

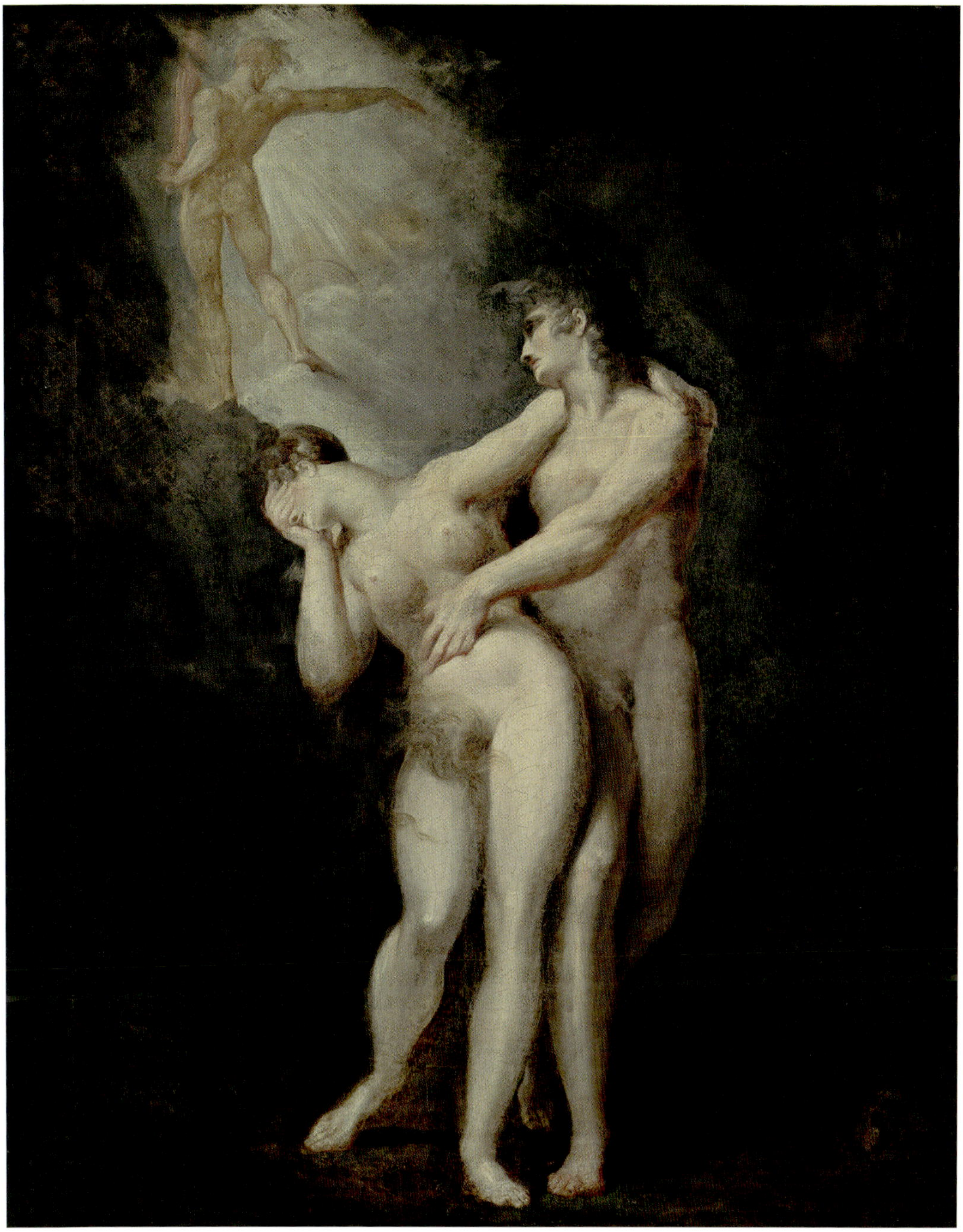

Cat. 57 *The Expulsion from Paradise*, 1802

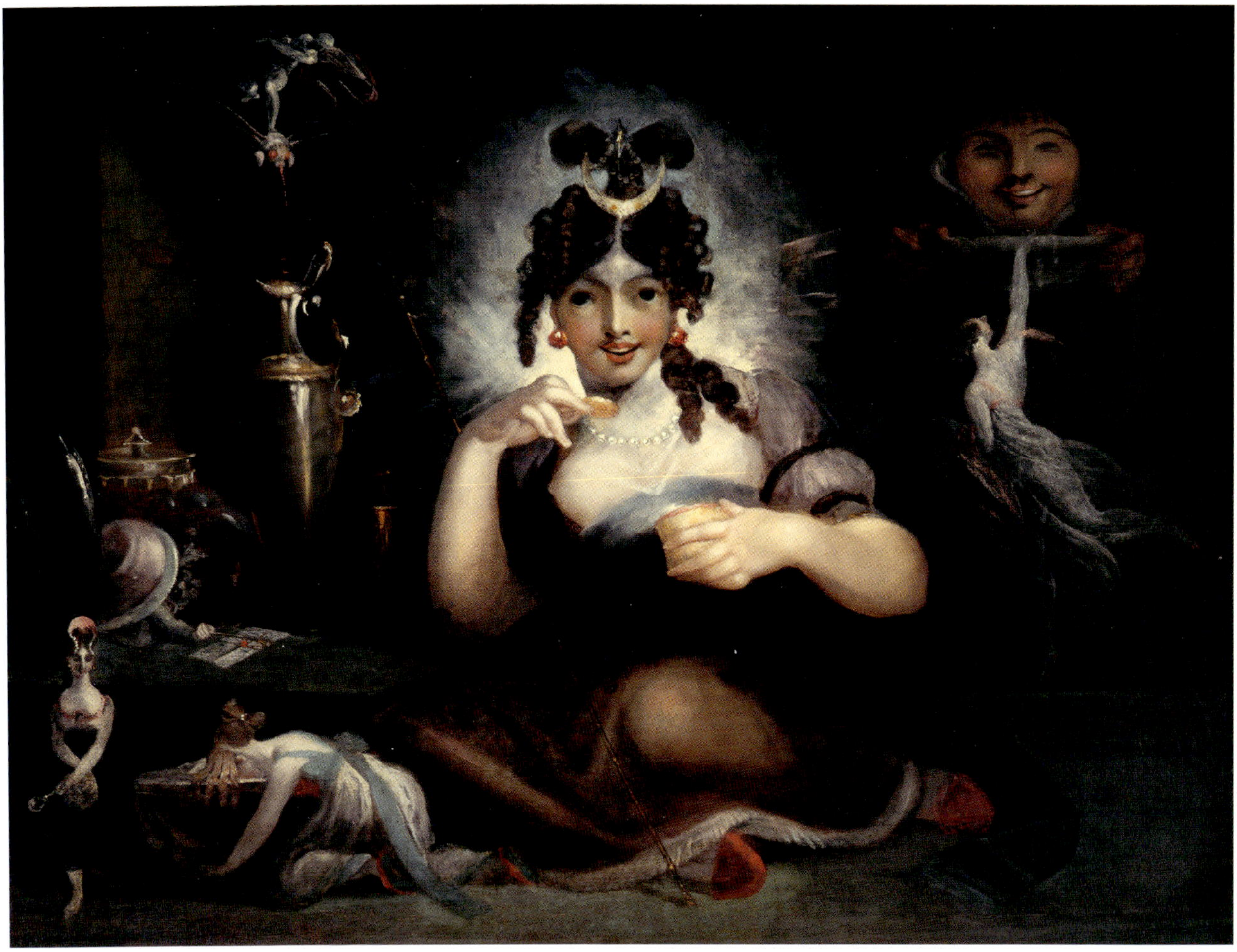

Cat. 58 *Fairy Mab*,* 1815–20

Pictures of Authors, Free Inventions

When Fuseli's Milton Gallery opened in London on 20 May 1799 (see 'Milton', pp. 141–43) the final three paintings in the exhibition showed scenes from the poet's life, anecdotal, genre-like images untypical of his work as a whole. He added two further pictures of this kind to the second exhibition the following year. These five biographical canvases, which have received little attention from scholars, embody key aspects of the artist's engagement with the poet, reinforcing at various levels his identification with Milton and addressing his own views on artistic inspiration.[1]

Three of the paintings take their subjects from the biographies customarily included in complete editions of the poet's work in the eighteenth and nineteenth centuries. Two of them, *The Return of Milton's First Wife, Mary Powell* and *Milton Dictating to his Daughter*, relate exclusively to Milton (cats 61, 63); the third, *Milton when a Youth*, draws on a trope familiar to contemporaries from transfiguring descriptions of both Milton's and other writers' lives (cat. 60). In addition to his abiding fascination with Milton's work, Fuseli repeatedly drew parallels between his own life and that of the poet. In the woman in *Milton when a Boy, Instructed by his Mother*, for example, Gert Schiff sees the idealised features of the artist's own mother (cat. 59).[2]

The first exhibition at the Milton Gallery did not bring the success Fuseli had anticipated. This prompted him to compare the scant cognizance taken by Milton's contemporaries of the difficulties involed in the creation of his principal work, *Paradise Lost*, with his own precarious situation during the almost ten years that he spent setting up the gallery. In a letter to a patron, the Liverpudlian banker William Roscoe, he wrote bitterly: 'The Nation that left Milton poor will not make me rich, but this I knew before.'[3] Fuseli doubtless employed this 'self-pity and histrionic ... self-stylisation', as Schiff calls it,[4] quite deliberately as a means of self-promotion. That, at any rate, is one interpretation that can be put on his words.[5]

The Infant Shakespeare between Tragedy and Comedy and *The Poet's Vision*, the latter forming the basis of the frontispiece to an edition of poems by William Cowper published in 1807 by Joseph Johnson, reveal a different aspect of Fuseli's engagement with literature (cats 64, 65). In these paintings he focuses on the genesis of the writers' works and on creative inspiration in general, a theme that he repeatedly linked to sleep and its dreams and visions. Two of the paintings on the life of Milton, *Milton when a Youth* and *Milton's Vision of his Second Wife*, belong in this context (cats 60, 62). In each case the sleeping or dreaming poet is visited by a female muse. Fuseli's teachers in Zurich, Johann Jakob Bodmer and Johann Jakob Breitinger, had both examined in theoretical terms the value of fantasy in relation to reason. His friend Johann Georg Sulzer, who had asked the artist for assistance with his *Allgemeine Theorie der schönen Künste* (General Theory of the Fine Arts), considered imagination the mother of the fine arts, as he explained in the chapter 'Begeisterung' (Enthusiasm).[6]

The scholar Robert Burton saw melancholy as playing an essential part in artistic stimuli. In *The Anatomy of Melancholy* (1621) he wrote that the imaginative capacities of melancholy people are particularly strong and inform 'forcibly' the work of poets and painters.[7] It is therefore scarcely coincidental that Fuseli shows the young Shakespeare finding nourishment first at the breast of Melpomene, the muse of tragedy, before he turns to Thalia, the muse of comedy (cat. 64). Beyond their obvious primary functions as personifications of tragedy and comedy – that is, of two of the theatrical genres favoured by Shakespeare – the female figures can be read as allegorical representatives of the conflicting emotions involved in the creative act.

Fuseli's freely invented images, whether *Percival Delivering Belisane from the Enchantment of Urma* or the work that vouchsafed him a spectacular breakthrough in the English art world in 1782, *The Nightmare*, appear also to illustrate literary sources (cats 67, 69). In the former case, however, the artist adamantly claimed the subject as of his own devising. Hence

Fuseli's pictures of authors and his free inventions each address in their different ways the creative process and the freedom of the artistic imagination. CB

1 Women play a crucial role in all five images, each of them different, but always related to Milton's poetry. See Tomory 1972, pp. 168–81; Tomory 1986; and the essay by Alexander Honold in the present volume.

2 Schiff 1973, vol. 1, p. 219.

3 Letter from Fuseli to Roscoe, 12 June 1799; qtd. in Fuseli 1982, p. 201.

4 Schiff 1973, vol. 1, p. 190.

5 Bätschmann 1997, p. 9.

6 Sulzer 1792–94, vol. 1, p. 353.

7 'In melancholy men this faculty [phantasy or imagination] is most powerful and strong, and often hurts, producing many monstrous and prodigious things.... In poets and painters imagination forcibly works, as appears by their several fictions, antics, images'. Burton 1857, pp. 102–03.

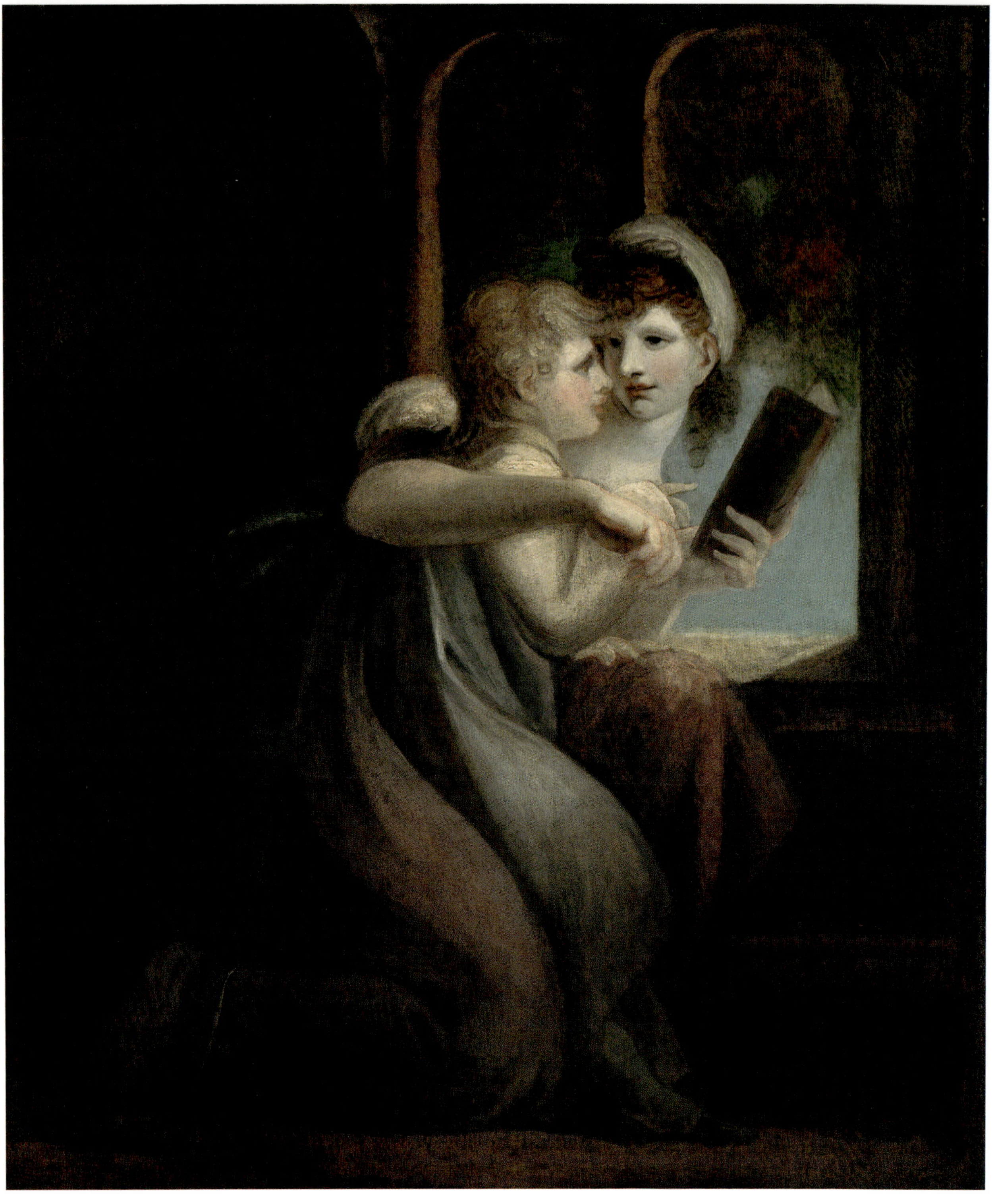

Cat. 59 *Milton when a Boy, Instructed by his Mother*, 1796–99

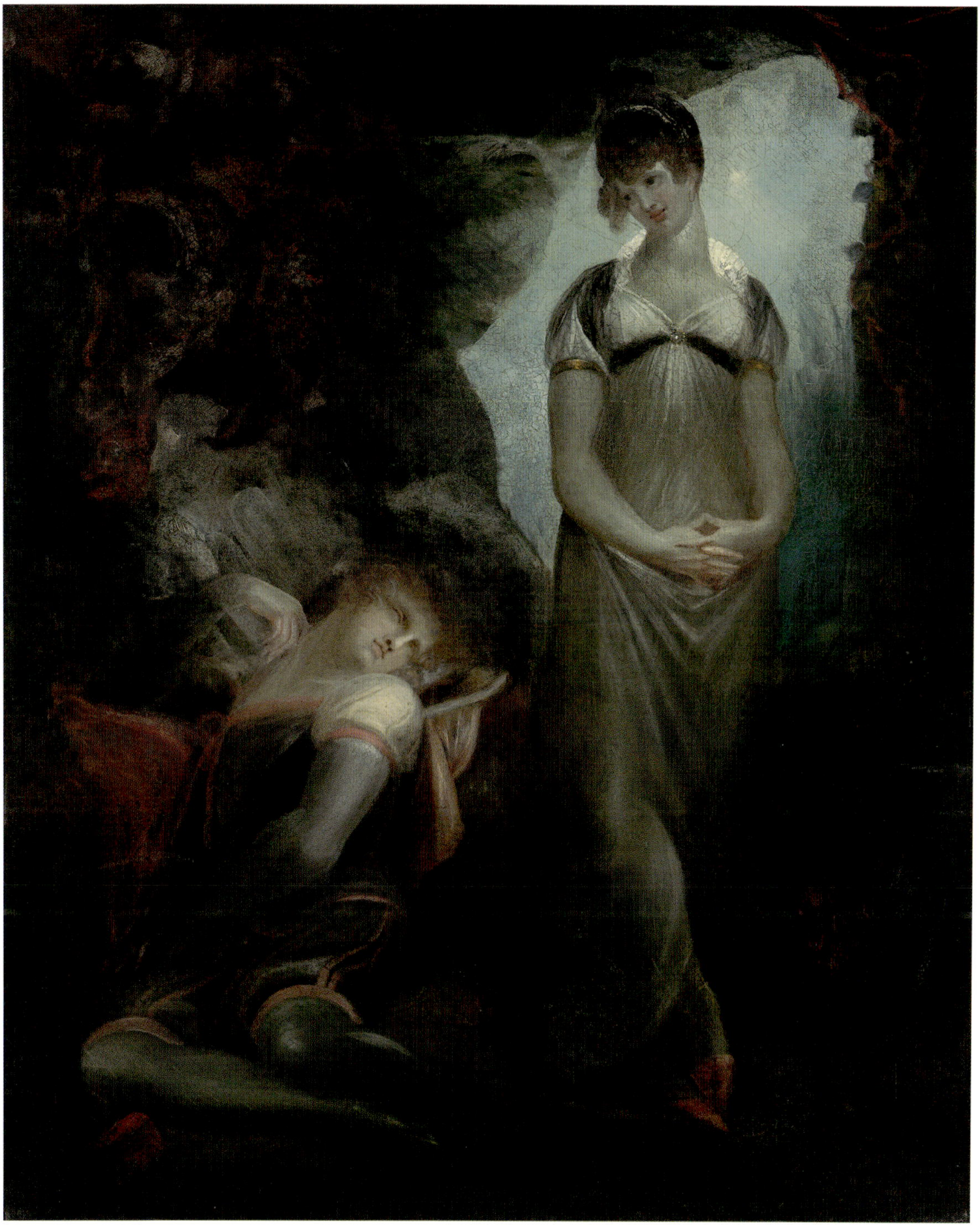

Cat. 60 *Milton when a Youth*, 1796–99

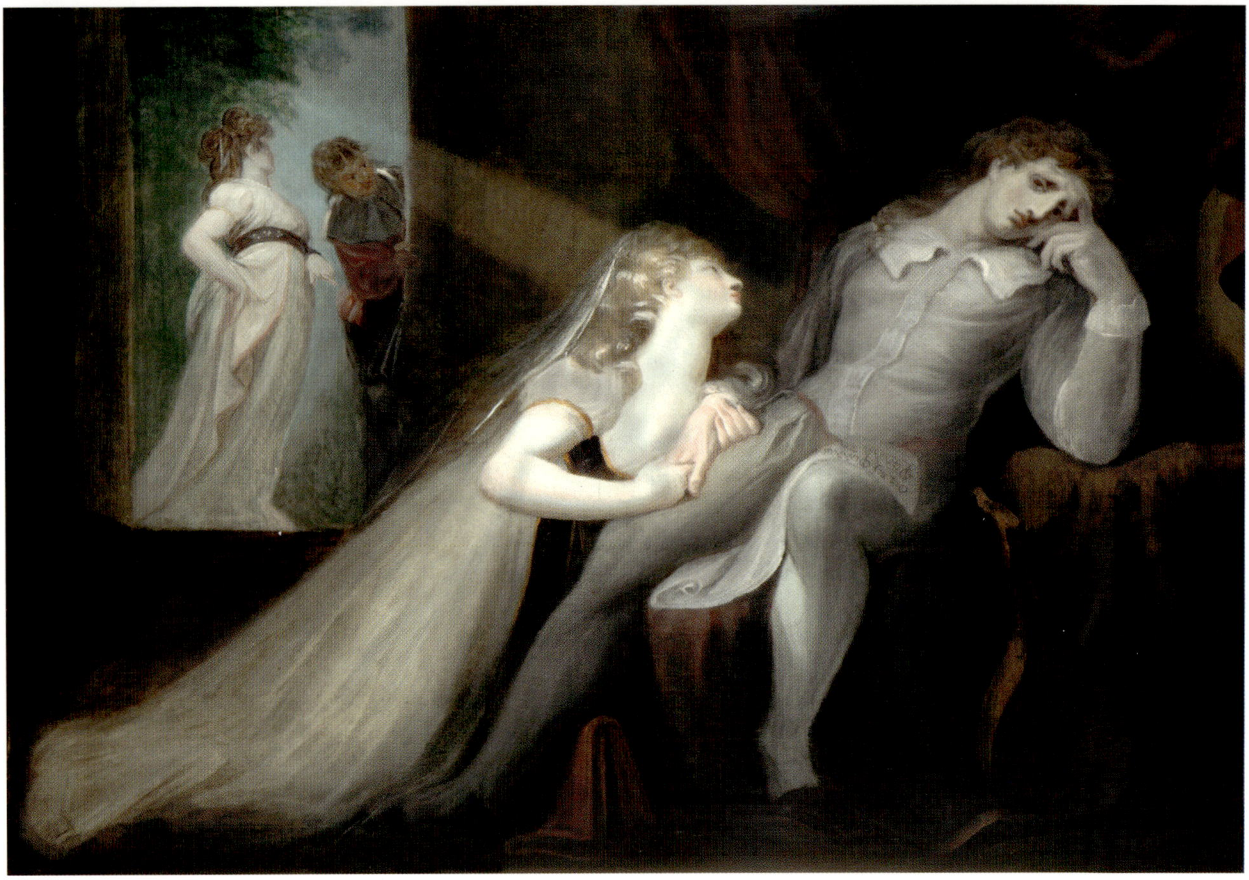

Cat. 61 *The Return of Milton's First Wife, Mary Powell*, 1799–1800

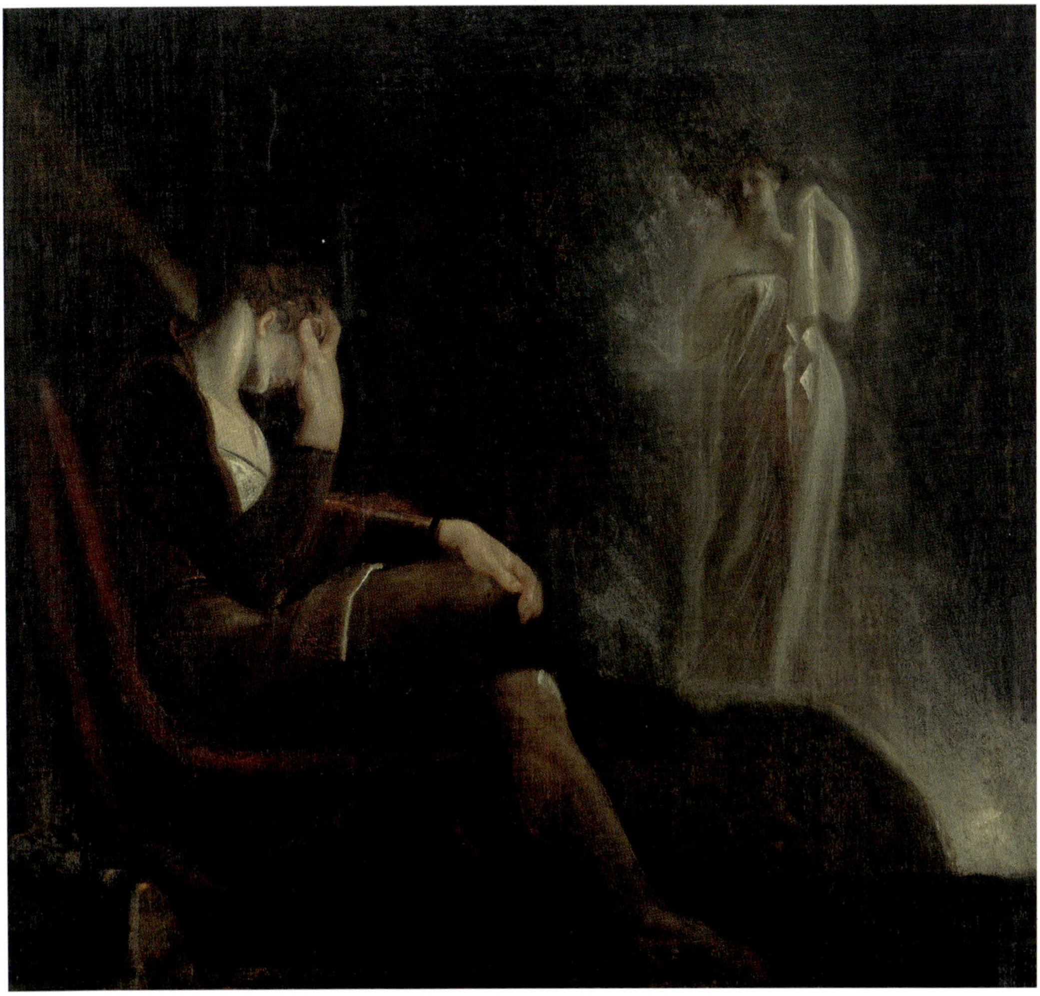

Cat. 62 *Milton's Vision of his Second Wife*, 1799–1800

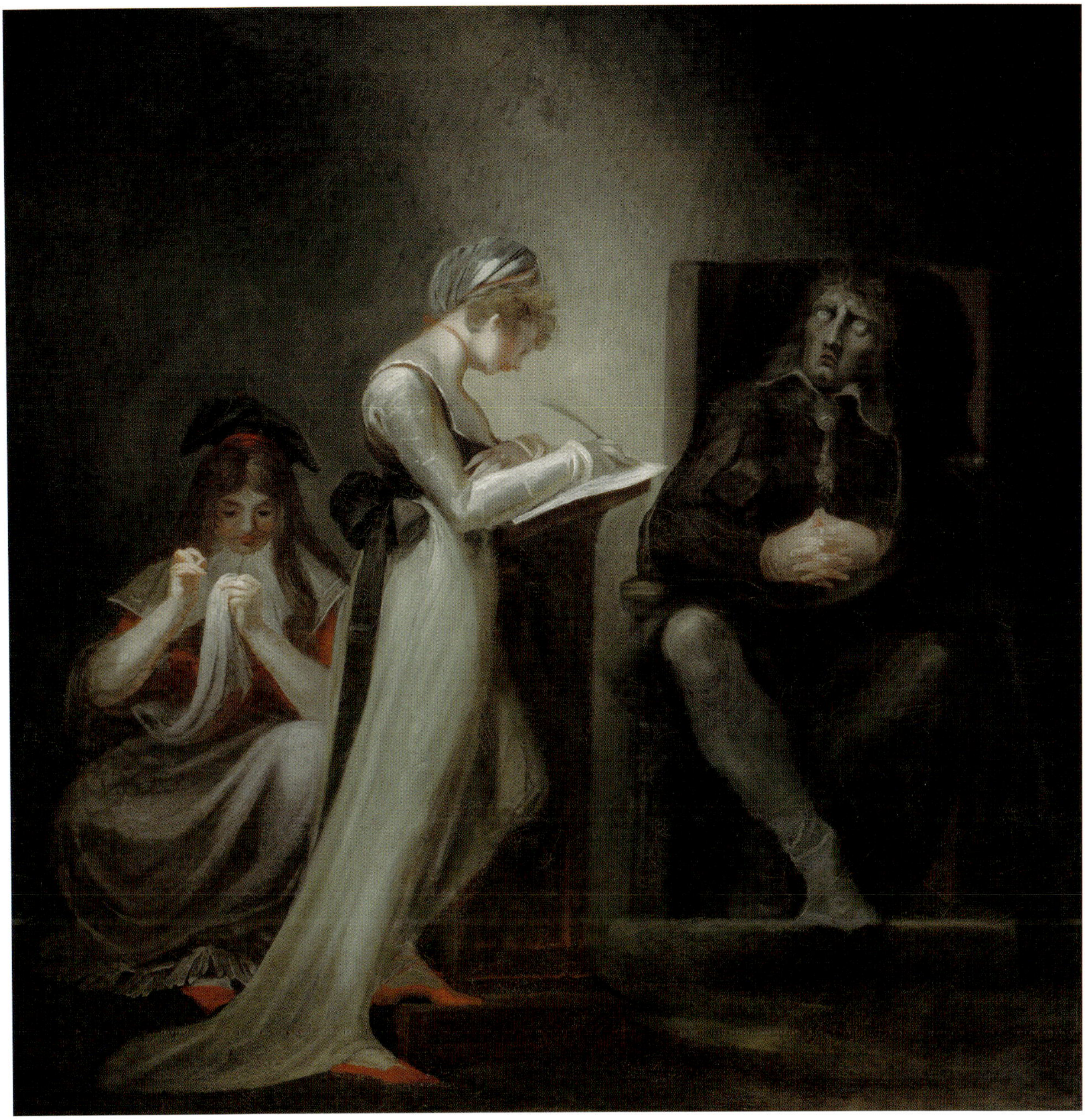

Cat. 63 *Milton Dictating to his Daughter*, 1794

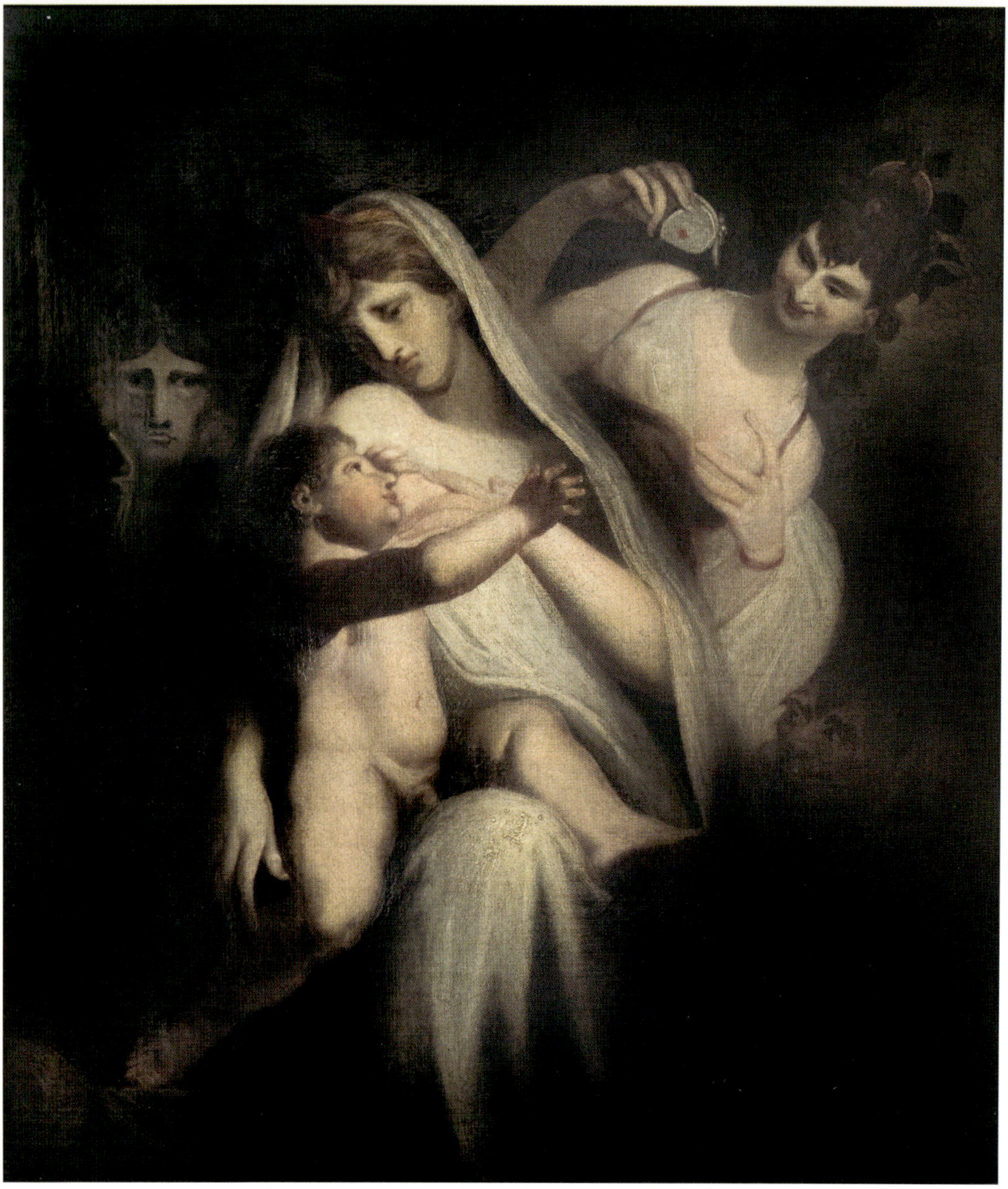

Cat. 64 *The Infant Shakespeare between Tragedy and Comedy*, 1805–06

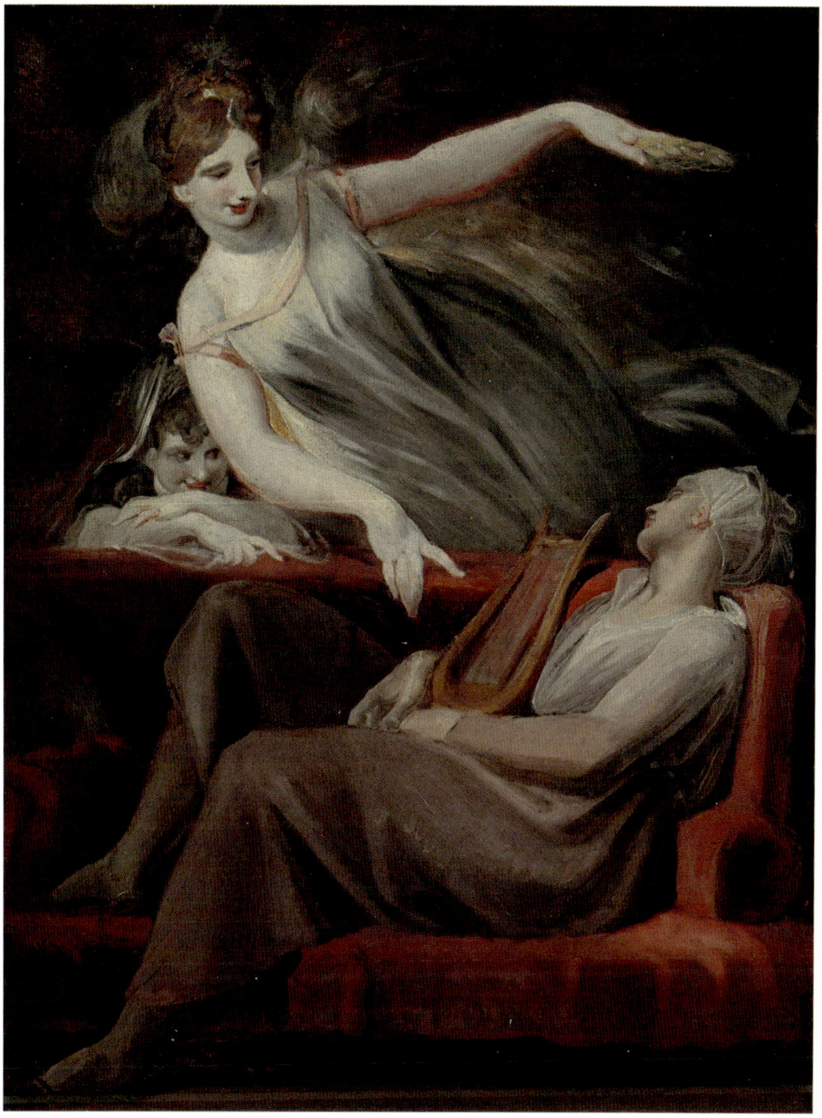

Cat. 65 *The Poet's Vision*, 1806–07

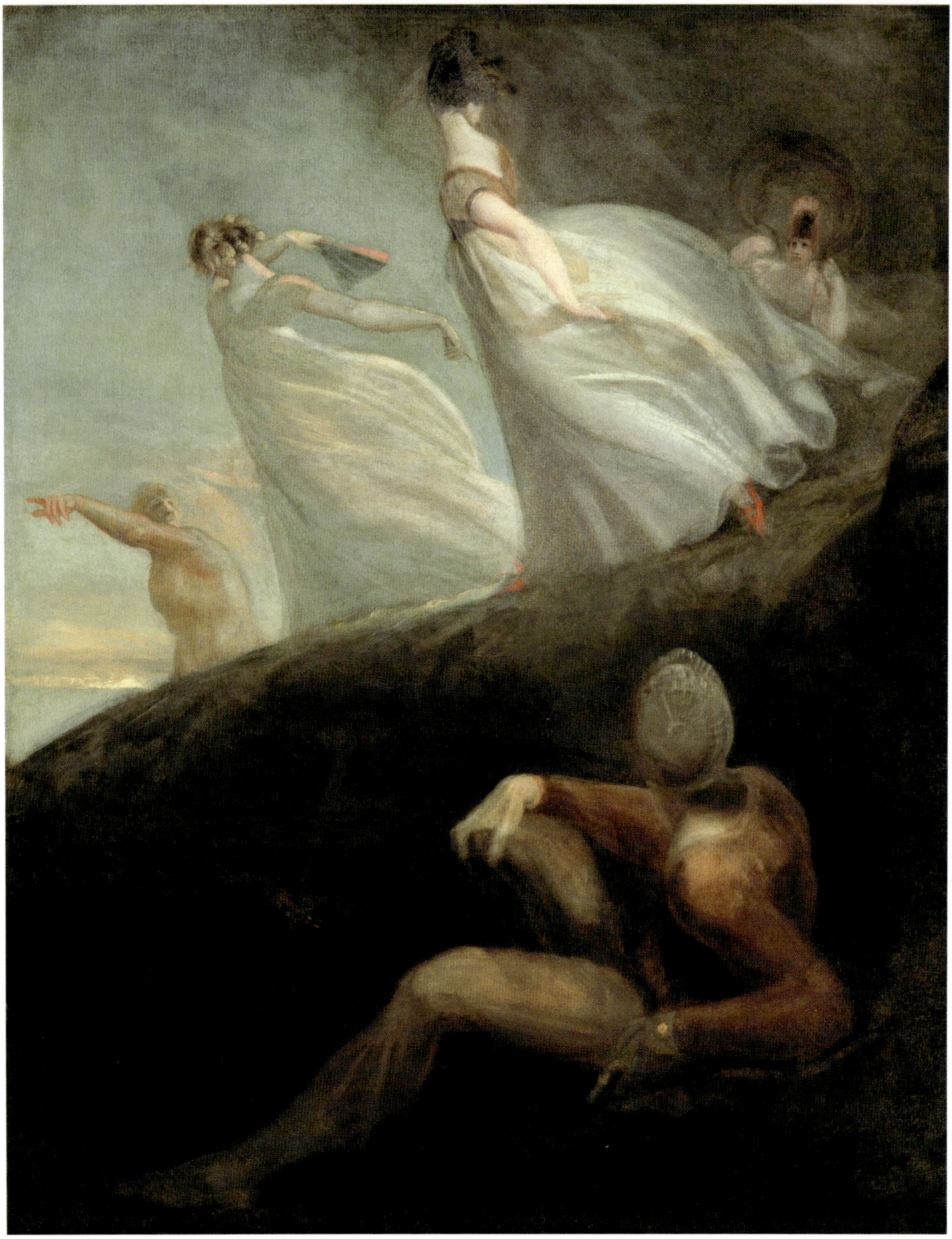

Cat. 66 *The Ladies of Hastings*,
1798–1800

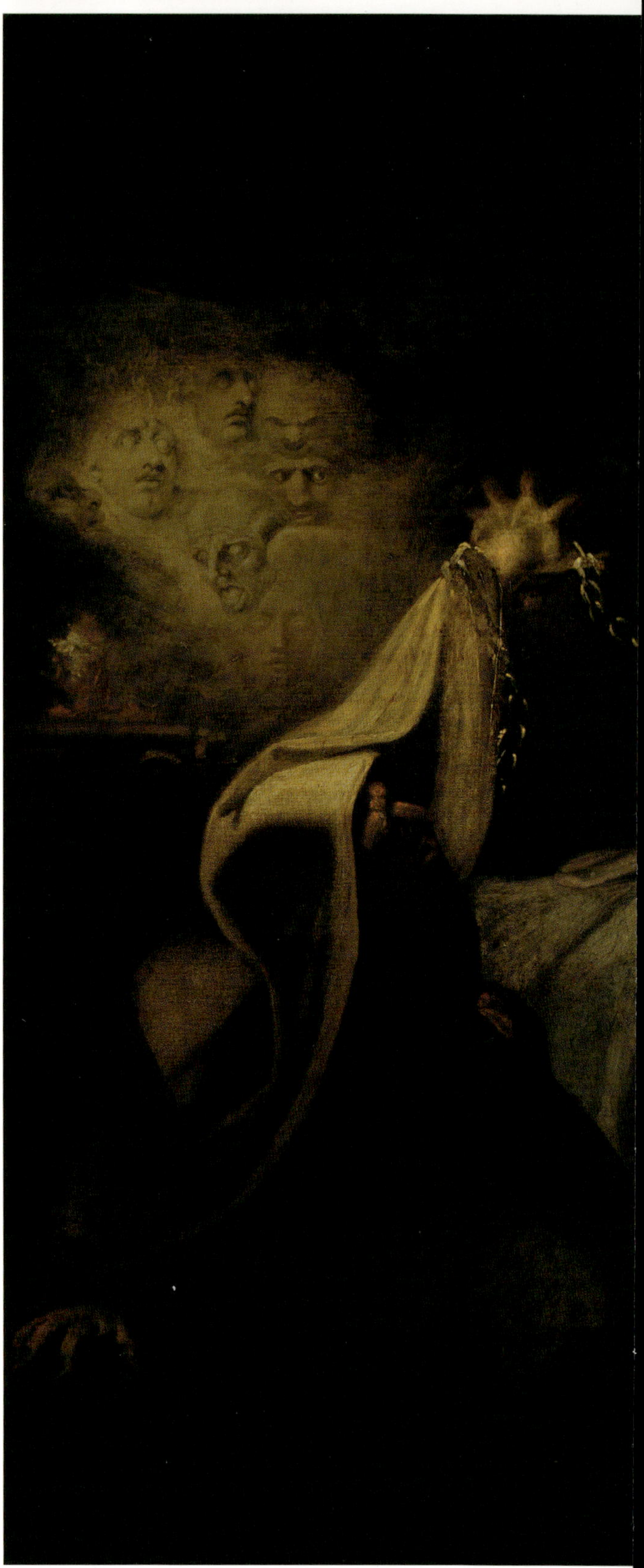

Cat. 67 *Percival Delivering Belisane from the Enchantment of Urma*, 1783

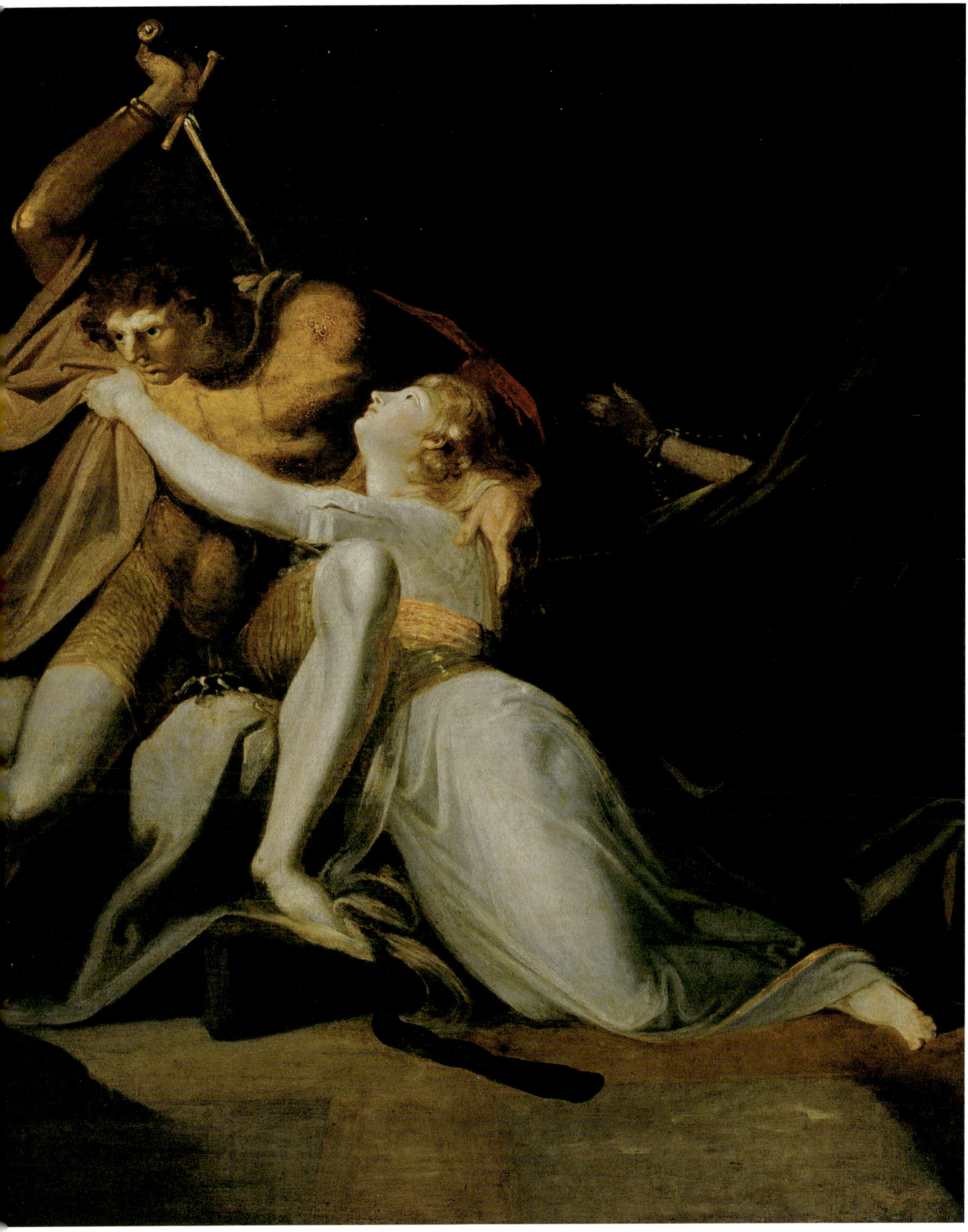

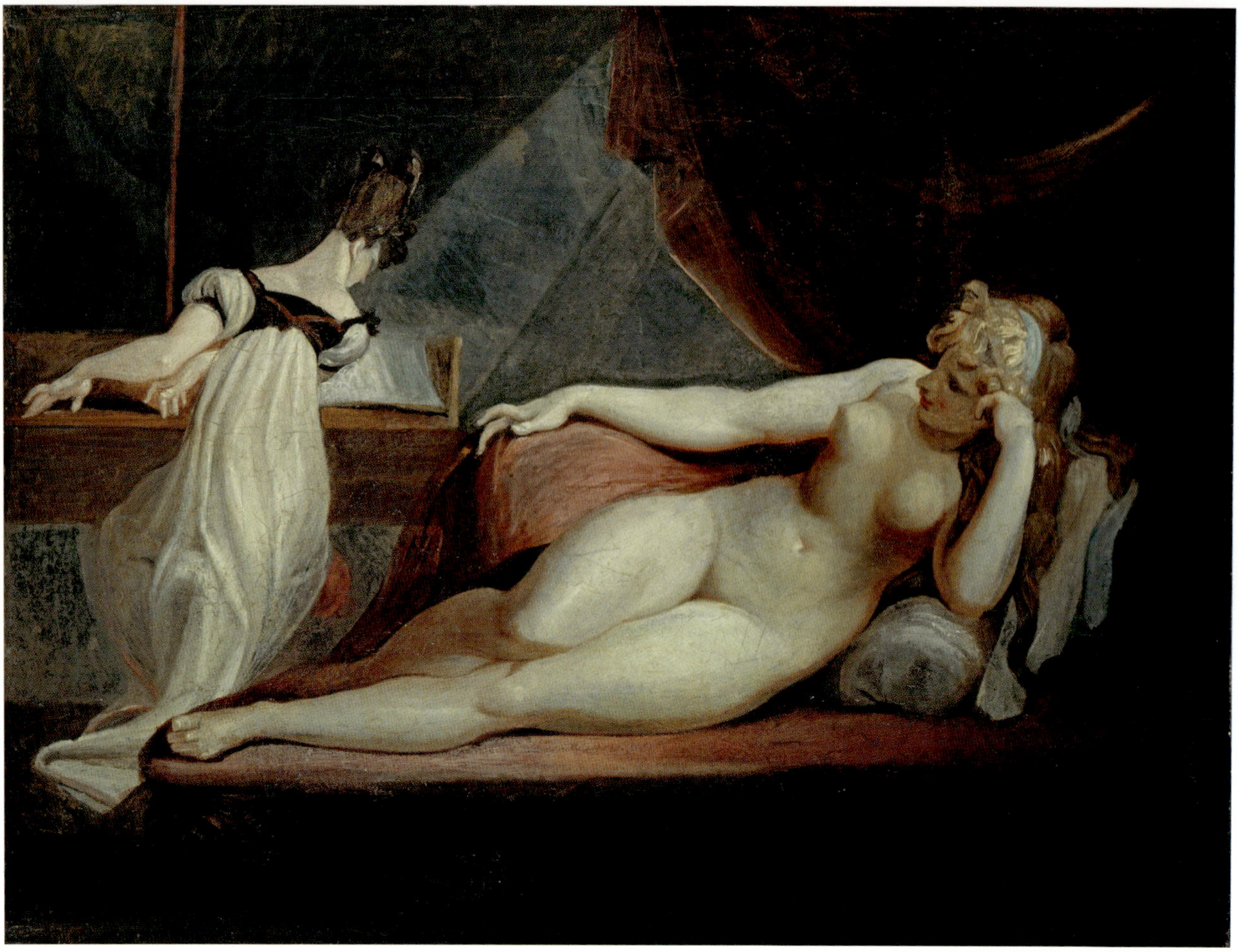

Cat. 68 *Reclining Female Nude with a Pianist*, 1799–1800

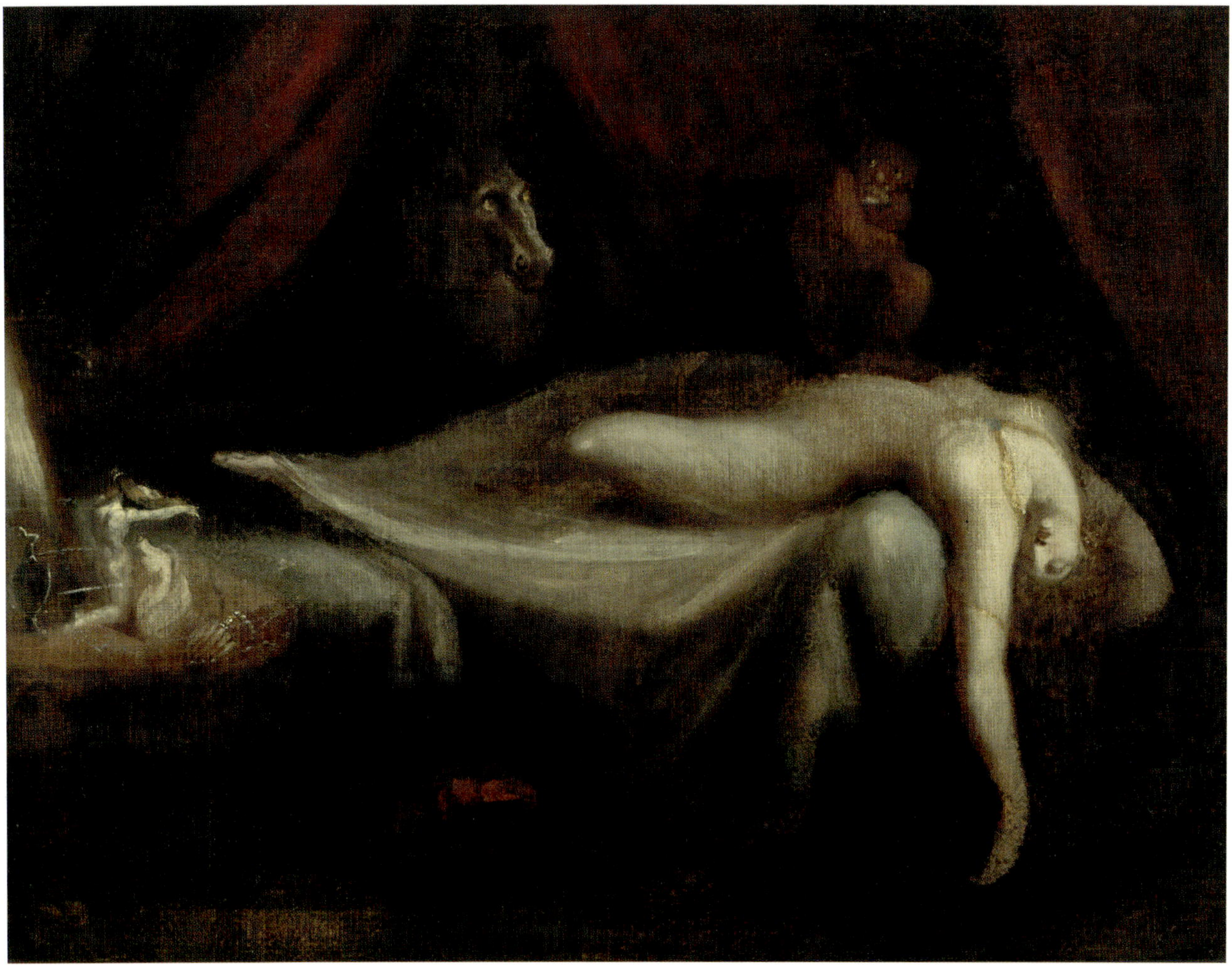

Cat. 69 *The Nightmare*, 1810

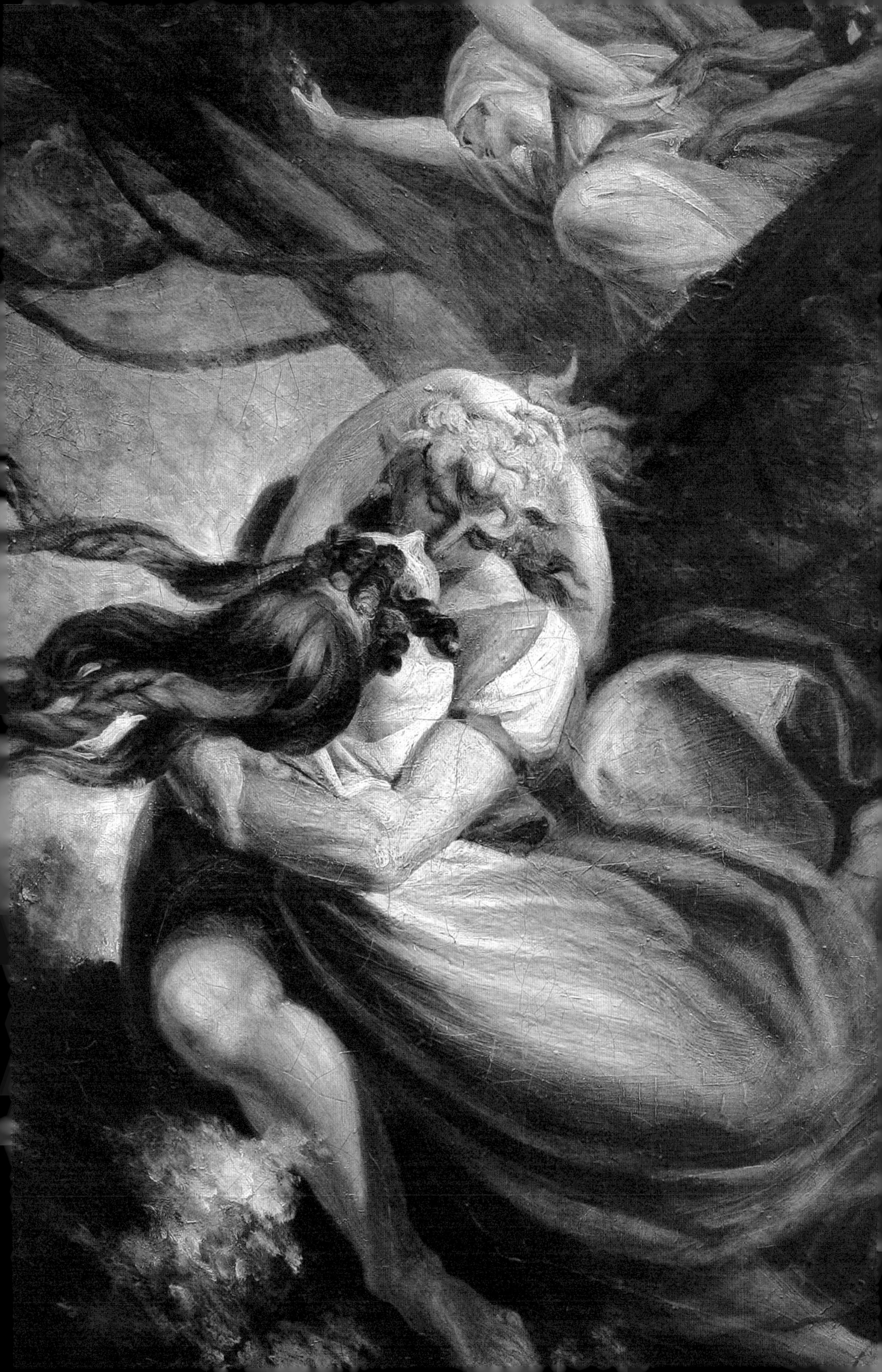

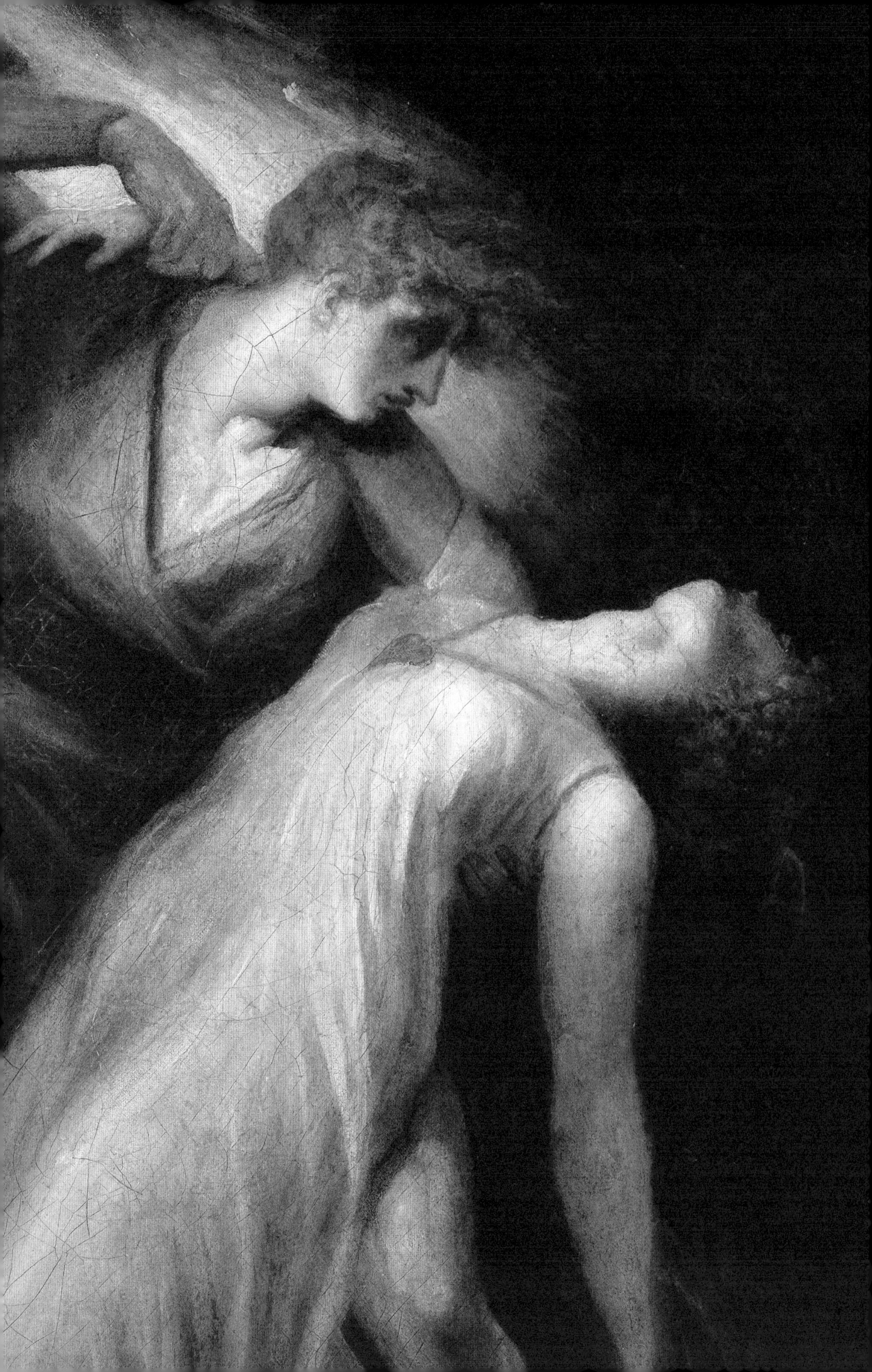

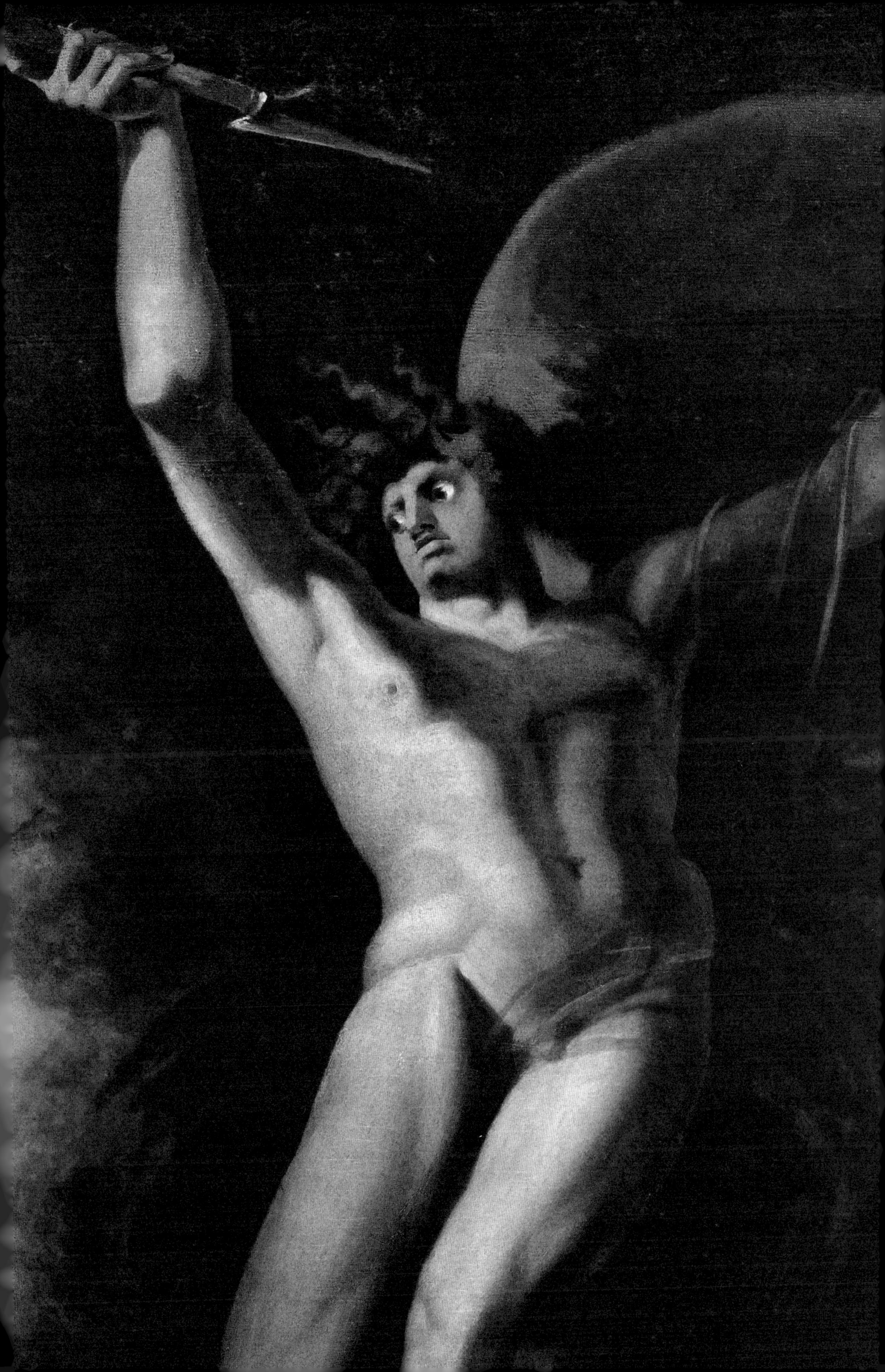

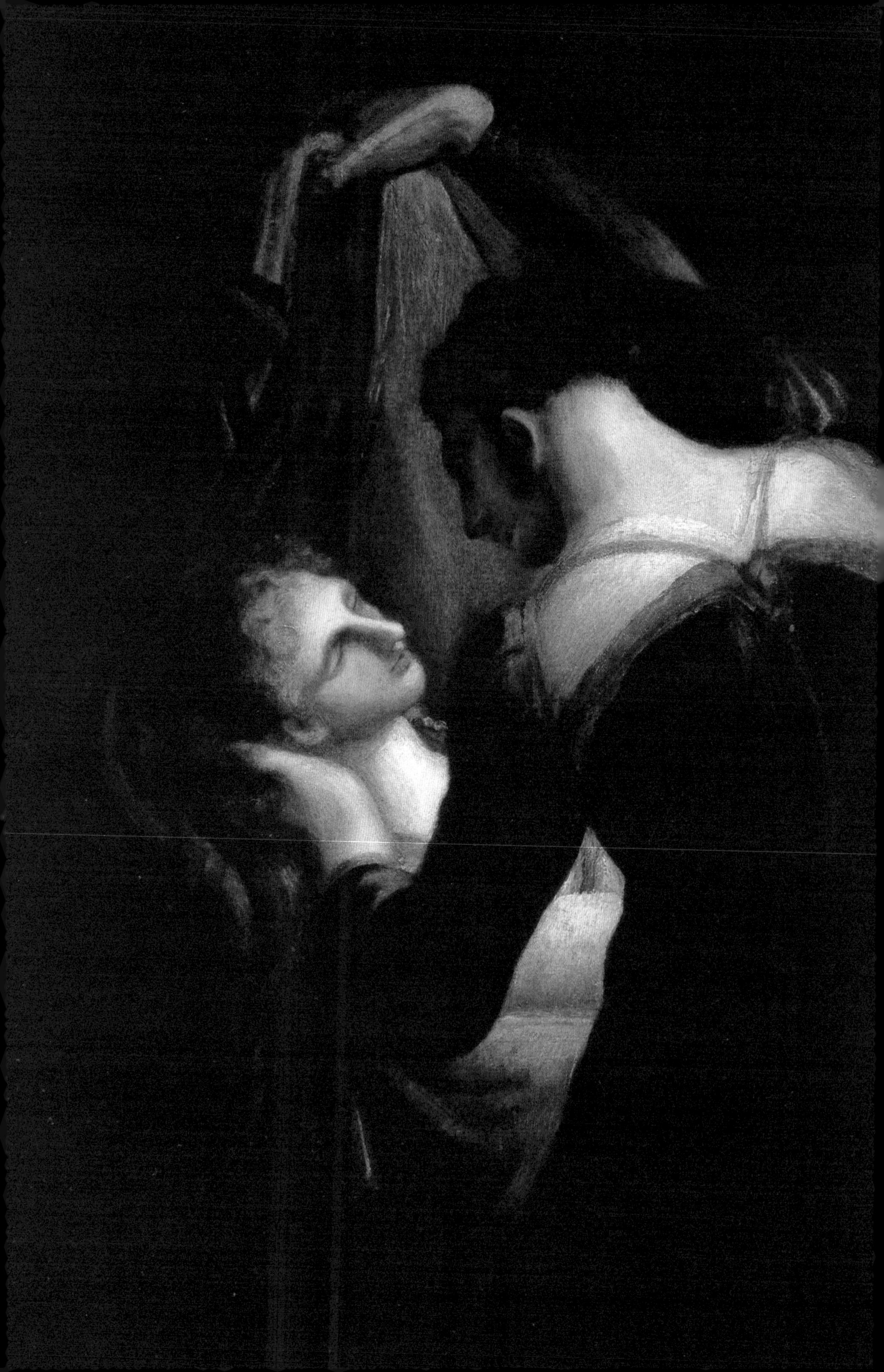

On Fuseli

Thom Luz

Nothing could be more terrifying than returning to one's home one night to find it already inhabited by someone who entirely resembles oneself – this, in brief, is how Henry Fuseli attempts to explain the feeling of the uncanny.[1] By extension, one could add that nothing is more uncanny than visiting a museum and encountering oneself there, seeing oneself looking at pictures. This thought pervaded the beginning of my work on Fuseli, whom I approached from a theatrical perspective and using theatrical means. Fuseli's personal interest in the world of theatre and its dramatic literature aside, the parallels are numerous: Fuseli's canvas is his proscenium stage. Like a stage director, he arranges his tableaux, creates tension through spatial choreography and extreme lighting, and tells stories with mute gestures, unspoken dramas and facial expressions. These are essentially technical, craftsmanlike operations that indicate a painter committed to achieving powerful effects. So why is it that, despite their obviousness, these tricks and techniques derived from the world of theatre make a more profound and lasting impression in Fuseli's imagery than in other forms of craftsmanship of the same epoch which were equally designed to impress? What magical third element does Fuseli add? This same question impels those of us who work in the theatre in our daily tasks of rehearsal and performance. What distinguishes one performance from another, when both were apparently identical and yet one felt like cheap histrionics with fake noses and smoke screens, while the next day the same production created a magical atmosphere in which the actress seemed to become Lady Macbeth herself? Incidentally, in its original definition the word magic meant the rearrangement of symbols – in language or pictures – to purposefully trigger in the addressee of these symbols – the spectator or beholder – an altered state of consciousness. Whether deliberately or accidentally, like all mages or alchemists Fuseli succeeds in this.

My work on Fuseli, which I have consequently named *On Fuseli* and which, a little reluctantly, I call a video installation, explores these issues. It takes place in the actual museum space occupied by the beholder beholding it. By means of Fuseli's above-mentioned techniques transposed into a different discipline, the installation depicts the beholder, thereby opening a window onto a parallel world or time which has already passed or not yet come to pass. The actors of Theater Basel explore the moment of transformation of a mortal acting body into an immortal literary figure. In seemingly random configurations of space and people, the museum visitors change into Percival, Puck and Hamlet for fleeting moments. Though minute, almost imperceptible even, save perhaps in the eye of the beholder, the transformation becomes colossal for a moment – until the very next moment when the image dissolves at the turn of the prism. It is precisely these evanescent moments of awestruck silence which Fuseli captured and which, in the theatre, we seek to achieve throughout our lives.

1 "What, I would ask, would be a greater object of terror to you, if, some night on going home, you were to find yourself sitting at your own table, either writing, reading, or otherwise employed? would not this make a powerful impression on your mind?" Henry Fuseli, qtd. in Knowles 1831, vol. 1, p. 190.

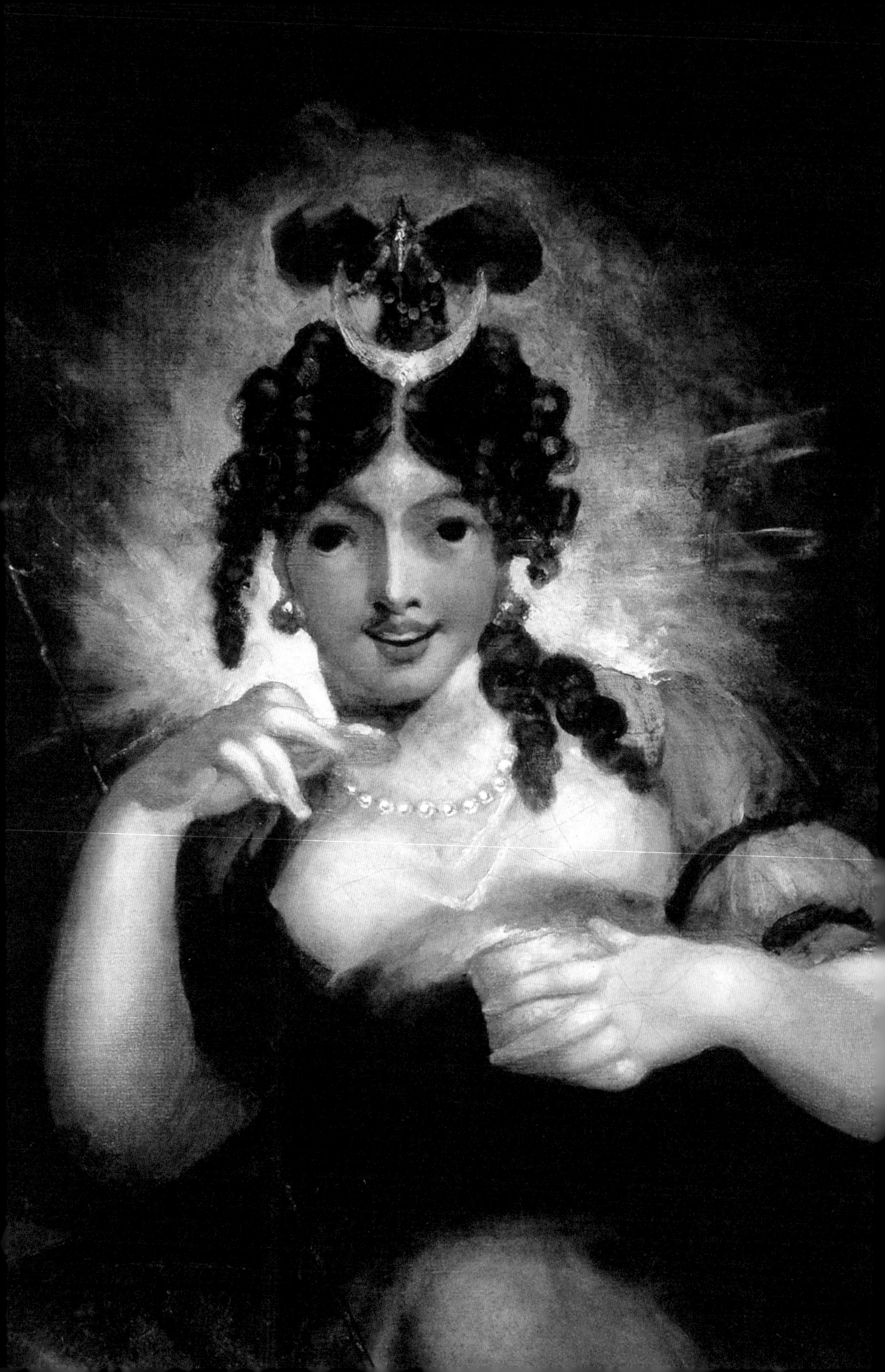

Henry Fuseli's Paintings: Materials, Techniques and Conservation Issues

Caroline Rae

In order to interpret Fuseli's paintings fully it is important for art historians – and perhaps more crucially, for painting conservators who may treat the artist's works – to understand the artist's working processes, including his artistic intentions, materials and techniques, and how his works may have changed over time. Shifts in taste and the inaccessibility of Fuseli's style and subject matter today may explain why little technical study has been carried out on this fascinating artist's work to date, although it is commonplace for authors to bemoan the condition of his paintings, which often display cracks, darkened areas or wrinkles that have been invariably attributed by past scholars to his use of bitumen. In 2009 an in-depth investigation of six paintings from the collections of the National Trust and King's College London (see Table on pp. 196–97 for details) was carried out at the Courtauld Institute of Art with the aim of gaining a holistic view of Fuseli's workshop practice and in order to perform an initial exploration into potential causes of degradation in the artist's works. These focus paintings were examined using ultra-violet light, X-radiography, infra-red reflectography (1–3μm) and optical microscopy, with elemental analysis of samples undertaken using SEM-EDX. Samples of organic material were sent to the Instituut Collectie Nederland (ICN) for analysis using Gas Chromatography-Mass Spectrometry (GCMS) in January 2010. Paintings at the Kunsthaus Zürich; Victoria and Albert Museum, London; Walker Art Gallery, Liverpool; Tate, London; and Hatchlands Park were examined *in situ* using microscopy, 5 × magnification (Optivisor) and portable UV light.[1]

A study of contemporary artists' manuals, Fuseli's *Lectures on Painting* given at the Royal Academy (1801–23), his *Aphorisms* (1818) and correspondence also formed part of the research. Contemporary accounts of Fuseli's working practice given by his biographer John Knowles, his pupils and other contemporary sources were considered, as were the catalogues of the sales of Fuseli's estate carried out in 1825 and 1827 after his death. Such sources should not be regarded as historic fact. Nevertheless, they provide interest when they illuminate further or contradict what can be seen through technical examination.

Fuseli's preferred support was canvas, with only two known works on panel.[2] Fuseli preferred to paint on plain weave canvas, and occasionally used twill for larger scale paintings (for example, *The Three Witches Appearing to Macbeth and Banquo*, Petworth House, National Trust, Schiff 880, examined during the study; *Titania and Bottom*, cat. 34; and *Titania's Awakening*, cat. 35). There are four known double-sided paintings in Fuseli's oeuvre, including *The Nightmare*, 1781, Detroit Institute of Arts, Schiff 757, which bears a portrait of a young woman on the verso. One of these double-sided works (*Five Courtesans*/a scene from *The Wife of Bath's Tale*, Petworth House, National Trust, Schiff 924, 1201) was included in the study (fig. 1). Examination of extant works and Fuseli's correspondence indicates that he used standard sizes prepared by colourmen[3] and that he also had canvases made up in different sizes when necessary (for example, his Milton gallery canvases).[4] Canvas-stamps discovered on the verso of two works relate to two London based colourmen (J. Poole and Thomas Brown) who occupied the same premises in High Holborn, near Fuseli's Somerset House studio, at different dates.[5]

Although there are some variations (for example in the number of his ground layers, and whether these were artist or colourman applied, see Table, pp. 196–97), it can be ascertained that Fuseli appears to have preferred to paint directly onto a white surface, most typically comprised of lead white and chalk bound in oil. However, counter to advice he gave to his RA students, Fuseli occasionally experimented with the coloured grounds which were popular at the time, including vibrant salmon pink and light brown.[6] Examination in infra-red reflectography did not reveal carbon-based underdrawing. Instead Fuseli used fluid underpainting to sketch out his compositions.

Fuseli's core palette included lead white, orpiment and realgar, Prussian blue, yellow ochre, bone black, vermilion, red lake, iron oxide red and an organic brown pigment (identified by optical microscopy, perhaps

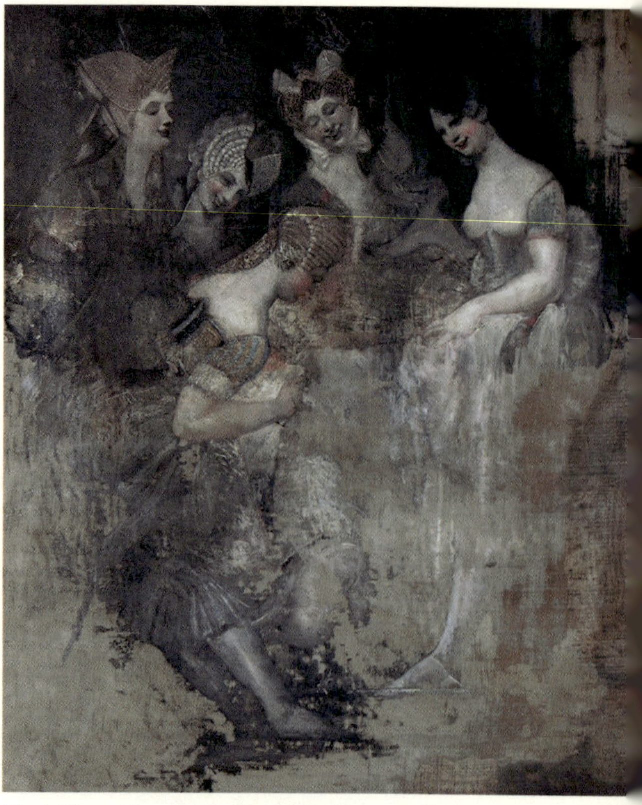

Fig. 1: Henry Fuseli, *Five Courtesans*, 1790, oil on canvas, 91 × 71 cm (verso of a scene from *The Wife of Bath's Tale*, 1812; Schiff 1201), National Trust, Petworth House (Schiff 924)

bitumen); less frequently used in his works were green earth, Naples yellow, charcoal black, blue ochre 'vivianite' and a copper blue or green (perhaps verdigris). These pigments were readily available and commonly used at the time. The most characteristic feature of Fuseli's palette is his extensive use of orpiment. Orpiment was unpopular at the time due to its poisonous nature, dangerous fumes and offensive smell.[7] It was only occasionally used by contemporaries such as Joshua Reynolds.[8] However, it was found in nearly every sample taken from paintings by Fuseli (see Table, pp. 196–97).

Fuseli affected to disdain the flamboyant use of colour and instead adopted a kind of chiaroscuro, perhaps better suited to his dramatic themes and dynamic compositions. This choice may also have, in reality, related to Fuseli's struggles with colour. Fuseli admitted that he had 'courted and still [continued] to court Colour as a despairing lover courts a disdainful mistress',[9] and such difficulties were clearly revealed in the examination of *Five Courtesans* (fig. 1). This work is somewhat unusual within Fuseli's oeuvre in its extensive use of bright pure colours. Fuseli reworked the painting, toning down the bright hues with grey paint (fig. 2), then attempted to scrape the composition off using a palette knife or implement with a sharp edge before abandoning it altogether.

Fuseli appears to have frequently altered his compositions while painting. Although he declared that 'second thoughts are admissible in painting and poetry only as dressers of the first conception; no great idea was ever formed in fragments',[10] scraping down of paint layers was found on two further paintings: *Mamillius in Charge of a Lady of the Court* (Hinton Ampner, National Trust, Schiff 744) and *The Infant Shakespeare between Tragedy and Comedy* (cat. 64). Such dramatic interventions have contributed to uneven surface textures, visible in both raking and ordinary light (fig. 3).

Contemporary accounts, such as the following by Fuseli's pupil Margaret Patrickson, vividly illustrate his somewhat chaotic manner of working:

'Fuseli began one morning to alter the drapery of Pluto, much to my regret, and by no means to his own satisfaction.

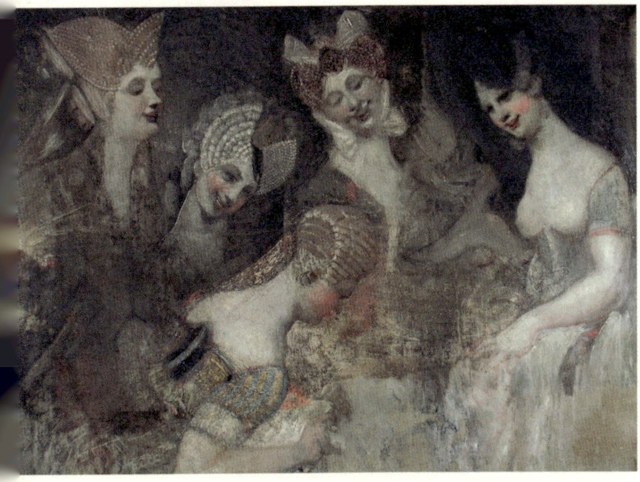

Fig. 2: Henry Fuseli, *Five Courtesans*, detail photograph showing reworking of the unfinished composition using grey paint and areas which have been scraped down to the ground layer (bottom right of image).

The space it occupied on the canvas was immense, and the amount of colour he expended on it was great. He stamped, swore, called himself an ass, a fool and a blockhead, while the rapidity with which he almost flew up and down from his frail perch terrified me exceedingly. Its construction was two large tables placed beside each other, with a chair, and a small flight of stairs upon them, and he used either as he found it convenient. As he never liked the confinement of his palette on his thumb, for he used the brush with equal facility in either hand, that he might reach it when on the top step, he had put three of the small boxes or stools from the Academy in a pile, and still he had to stoop greatly to take up his colour… I durst not speak, for I had objected to the alteration, and he bestowed upon me from time to time some grim smiles. At length he flew out of the room, making the opening of every door be well heard, and returned with a very excellent shirt, which he unfolded very deliberately, took a survey of, and then tore into large pieces. By using nearly the whole of this, and the aid of turpentine, he scrubbed out his whole day's work.'[11]

Other aspects which reveal Fuseli's impetuous approach include runnels of paint and rough passages (for example, the ragged line used to delineate the arm of the left-hand figure of *The Oath on the Rütli*, cat. 15). However, Fuseli was also capable of some beautiful and unusual painting techniques. A startling example is the face of Falstaff (*Falstaff in the Washing Basket*, Kunsthaus Zürich, Schiff 883), where he has scored boldly into wet paint with a sharp implement to vividly create the illusion of eyebrows (fig. 4).

Wrinkling and drying cracks are present in many works by Fuseli (see, for example, drying cracks visible in raking light, *The Infant Shakespeare*, fig. 3). These are a result of mechanical stresses within the paint film caused by inherent weaknesses in materials and/or techniques. Such drying deformations are

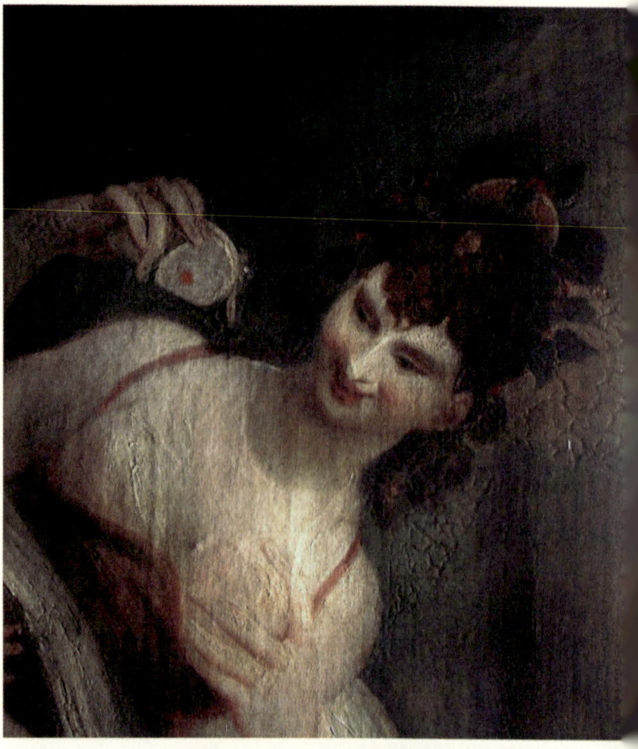

Fig. 3: Henry Fuseli, *The Infant Shakespeare between Tragedy and Comedy*, oil on canvas, 1805–06, 103 × 91 cm, King's College London. Detail photograph, raking light. Image shows the uneven surface texture of this area, caused by the artist's scraping down of the paint layers and also drying cracks in the paint film.

common in this period due to artists' experimentation with materials. Historically these have been blamed by authors such as the Redgraves on Fuseli's use of bitumen and megilps.[12]

The presence of bitumen (in samples taken from light and dark passages of alligatored paint) was indeed indicated on one painting (*Macbeth and Banquo*). Analysis of medium was carried out using GCMS.[13] It was also possible to argue that megilps were likely the primary binding medium used in two paintings which display small scale wrinkling of the paint layers, and paint layers which fluoresce in ultra-violet light.[14] Examination of drying defects in the remaining works suggested a more varied and complex range of causes including reworkings and poor technique. In order to fully characterise these causes, further scientific analysis of media used in a larger number of paintings by Fuseli is required. Also of interest for further investigation into possible causes of the formation of drying defects in the artist's work is his reputed extensive use, as a medium, of 'gold size' (a combination of oil, red lead, litharge, 'copperas', gum amine and turpentine prepared by boiling, which was considered the most powerful drier available at the time).[15]

As oil paint layers age, they become more transparent. Visible pentimenti in *Falstaff in the Washing Basket* and *The Ladies of Hastings* (cat. 66) are likely due to this phenomenon. The darkened appearance of Fuseli's works has previously been associated with bitumen. Examination in ultra-violet light revealed that this may in fact often have been caused by partial cleaning. Darker passages of paint are more likely to be medium-rich or resin based, and so more sensitive to traditional varnish removal methods using solvents. Such areas were often left untouched and covered in layers of yellowed, aged varnish by historic restorers. However, discoloured varnish was often removed from paler passages, known to be more durable due to the presence of the highly stable (and extensively used) pigment lead white. This has often resulted in tonal imbalances between impenetrable dark area and pale statuesque figures. *Titania and Bottom* (cat. 34) is an example of a painting which

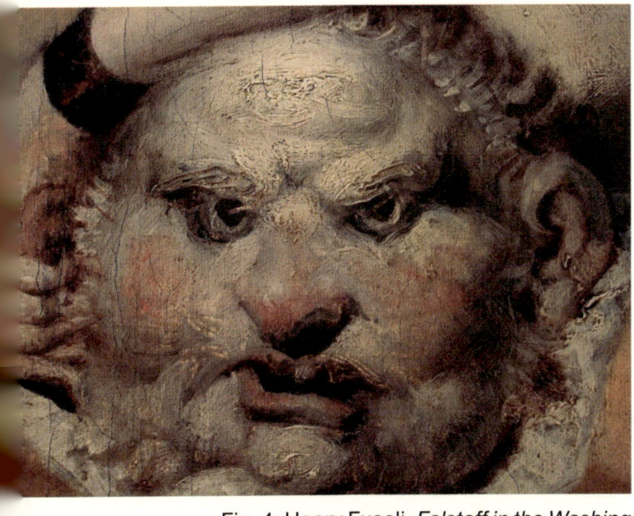

Fig. 4: Henry Fuseli, *Falstaff in the Washing Basket*, 1792, oil on canvas, 135.5 × 170.5 cm Kunsthaus Zürich. Detail of the head of Falstaff, revealing scoring technique used by the artist to create the illusion of hair in the eyebrows.

has been cleaned in such a manner. A further likely contributing factor to the paleness of figures in many of Fuseli's works is the fading of glazes and red delineatory lines due to the highly fugitive nature of the pigment red lake. Such red lines, which can be seen on the hand and arm of the background figure in *The Ladies of Hastings*, were consistently used by Fuseli to delineate flesh and are another striking characteristic of his painting technique.

This initial study, the first holistic technical study of Fuseli's works, has provided an insight into the artist's beautiful and unusual paintings, and its findings suggest that any interpretation of the work, be it in relation to the extreme and dramatic chiaroscuro effects or Fuseli's strangely pale figures, should take into account the ageing processes described, as well as historic conservation practices.

1 Samples for SEM-EDX analysis were taken from *Salome with the Head of John the Baptist*, 1780–90, Lord Egremont, Hatchlands Park (Schiff 710), one of the works which was examined *in situ*.

2 *King Lear casts out his Daughter Cordelia*, 1785–90, Goethe-Museum, Frankfurt am Main, (Schiff 739); *The Temptation of Eve*, 1804, City Art Gallery, Auckland (Schiff 1215).

3 For example, Fuseli mentions 'three large half-lengths', 'three small half-lengths' and 'two kit kats' in a letter to William Roscoe, 9th August 1796. (David H. Weinglass, ed., *The Collected English Letters of Henry Fuseli*, New York, 1982, p. 155).

4 Letter from Fuseli to Roscoe, 16th February 1795 (Weinglass, 1982, p. 127).

5 *Kriemhild throws herself over Siegfried's body*, 1817, Kunsthaus Zürich (Schiff 1491); and *Salome with the Head of John the Baptist*, 1780–90, Lord Egremont, Hatchlands Park (Schiff 710). On Brown and Poole see: Jacob Simon, *British Artists' Suppliers, 1650 -1950*, http://www.npg.org.uk/research/programmes/directory-of-suppliers/b.php

6 See RA Lecture VIII, in: Knowles, 1831, vol. 2, pp. 338–39.

7 Rosamond D. Harley, *Artists' Pigments c.1600 -1835* (2nd edition), UK, 1982, p. 93.

8 B. A. Buckley, 'Sir Joshua Reynolds: The Ladies Annabel and Mary Jemima Yorke', in: Bulletin of the Cleveland Museum of Art, 73, 1986, 9, pp. 350–71.

9 Knowles, 1831, vol. 2, p. 333.

10 Aphorism 71, in: Knowles, 1831, vol. 3, p. 85.

11 Letter from Patrickson to Allan Cunningham, 14th September 1830 (Weinglass, D. H. 1982, p. 530).

12 Richard Redgrave and Samuel Redgrave, *A Century of Painters of the English School*, London, 1866, vol. 2, p. 61, pp. 592–94.

13 Hopanes and alkanes, considered two of the characteristic markers of bitumen, were discovered by Henk van Keulen (ICN) during GCMS analysis in January 2010.

14 Caroline Rae and Christina Young, 'A Technical Study of Three Paintings on a Shakespearian Theme by Henry Fuseli RA', in: *The Picture Restorer*, 39, 2011, pp. 12–15.

15 See: Knowles, 1831, vol. 1, p. 397, Leslie Carlyle, *The Artist's Assistant: Oil Painting Instruction Manuals and Handbooks in Britain 1800-1900*, London, 2001, p. 37.

	Painting	Date	Ground	White	Yellow
six CIA focus painting	*Mamillius in Charge of a Lady of the Court* (National Trust, Hinton Ampner); Schiff 744	1785/86	White, one layer includes lead white, natural chalk and a little iron oxide. Includes one blue particle (unidentified)	Lead white	Orpiment
	Perdita (National Trust, Hinton Ampner); Schiff 745	1785/86	Thin layer of pale grey comprised of lead white, bone black, yellow ochre, vermillion and chalk below two layers of white ground comprised lead white/chalk (upper layer also contains Si)	Lead white	Orpiment, yellow ochre
	Five Courtesans (verso of *The Wife of Bath's Tale*, National Trust, Petworth House); Schiff 924	1790	Two thick white layers, lead white and natural chalk separated by an animal glue size layer. Lower layer also contains charcoal black, earth pigments (including iron oxide red), Si.	Lead white	Orpiment
	The Three Witches Appear to Macbeth and Banquo (National Trust, Petworth House); Schiff 880	1794	White, one layer, chalk and lead white (one sample also included a small quantity of unidentified carbon black, another contained carbon bacl and earth pigments)	Lead white	Orpiment
	The Infant Shakespeare between Tragedy and Comedy (King's College London)**; cat. 65	1805	White, one layer, lead white and chalk	Lead white	Orpiment, yellow ochre
	The Wife of Bath's Tale (National Trust, Petworth House); Schiff 1201	1812	No clear ground layer	Lead white	Orpiment, yellow ochre
Kunsthaus Zürich	*Sin pursued by Death**; Schiff 892	1794–96	Report notes white in colour	Lead white	Yellow ochre
	*Almansaris visits Huon in Prison**; cat. 26	1804/1805	Report notes grey/ beige coloured	Lead white	Yellow ochre
London, Victoria and Albert Museum	*Sprites: Queen Katherine's Dream**** (not in Schiff)	1781	Light brown in colour, contains lead white and challk	Lead white	Orpiment, Naples yellow

Table showing pigments and ground layers used by Henry Fuseli, discovered during the study.

Blue	Green	Red And Orange	Brown	Black	Additions
One particle, sample 1, unidentified, indigo/ Prussian blue?	None sampled	Vermilion	Organic pigment	Bone black	Glass, chalk
Blue ochre "vivianite"	Green earth	Vermilion, iron oxide red	None sampled	Bone black	Glass, lead
Peaks for Fe, may be blue ochre "vivian-ite"?	None sampled	Vemilion, realgar, red lake	Earth pigments	Bone black	Glass, chalk
Copper green/ blue (verdigris?), blue ochre "vivianite"	Copper green/ blue (verdigris?)	Vermilion red lake, iron oxide red	Organic pigment, earth pigments	Bone black, unidentified carbon black	Glass, lead
Prussian blue	Green earth	Iron oxide red, vermilion, realgar, red lake	Mix vermilion/ green earth/ iron oxide red/ Prussian blue, yellow ochre; mix orpiment/bone black/vermilion/ red lake	Bone black	Glass, lead
Only a few particles - unidentified	None sampled	Iron oxide red, realgar, vermilion, red lake	Organic pigment	Bone black charcoal black, unidentified carbon black	Glass
Prussian blue	None sampled	Vermilion	Burnt umber	Bone black	None found
Prussian blue	None sampled	Vermilion, red lake	None sampled	charcoal black	Glass
Prussian blue	Mixture blue and yellow (unspecified in report)	Vermilion	None sampled	None sampled	None sampled

* FTIR carried out in July 1998 at instruction of Kunsthaus Head Conservator, Hanspeter Marty

** Prussian blue identified by raman spectroscopy, carried out by Janet Ambers, British Museum, 5th January 2010

*** XRF carried out in July 1987 during technical examination/conservation campaign by M. Bustin (intern, V&A Museum) and L. Scalisi (Paintings Conservator, V & A Museum)

1741
According to his biographer John Knowles, Henry Fuseli was born on the 7th of February in Zurich. His father Johann Caspar Füssli (1706–1782) was a portrait painter at the imperial court in Vienna before settling in Zurich in 1740. Johann Caspar also published his writings, for example the *Lives of the Helvetic Painters* in 1755–1757. Among his friends were the scholars Johann Jakob Bodmer (1698–1783), Johann Jakob Breitinger (1701–1776) and Johann Joachim Winckelmann (1717–1768), and artists such as Anton Raphael Mengs (1728–1779), Anton Graff (1736–1813) and Angelika Kauffmann (1741–1807). The paternal art collection consisted of plaster casts of antique sculptures and works by German, Dutch and Swiss Old Masters.

From 1756
Through his studies of theology at the Collegium Carolinum– which he attends with Johann Caspar Lavater (1741–1801) – Fuseli increasingly comes under the influence of Breitinger and Bodmer, the latter an acknowledged authority on German and English literature who has translated works by William Shakespeare and John Milton into German, and is a friend of Christoph Martin Wieland (1733–1813). Knowles reports that Fuseli has himself tried his hand at a German translation of Shakespeare's *Macbeth*. He expands his knowledge of languages and, through his teachers, comes into contact with the great works of literature that will later preoccupy him in his art.

1759
Fuseli's mother Elisabeth, née Waser– described as an delicate, ailing woman with a lively spirit – dies at the age of 44. Fuseli was very close to her; according to Gert Schiff, her features later appear in the painting *Milton when a boy, instructed by his mother* (Cat. 59).

1762
With Lavater and Felix Hess (1742–1768), who also studied at the Collegium Carolinum, Fuseli writes an – initially anonymous – indictment entitled *Der ungerechte Landvogt oder Klagen eines Patrioten (The Unjust Bailiff or A Patriot's Complaints)* which exposes the machinations of the corrupt bailiff Grebel in Grüningen, and demands an investigation by the authorities. The philosopher Johann Georg Sulzer (1720–1779) from Winterthur, who holds a professorship in Berlin but is living in Zurich at the time, takes a close interest in the young men's fight against injustice. He offers to take them with him on his return to Germany.

Early 1763
Fuseli, Lavater and Hess travel first to Berlin in the company of Sulzer. Later he takes them to Barth in Swedish Pomerania, where they are the guests of the German enlightenment theologian Johann Joachim Spalding (1714–1804). On Sulzer's recommendation Fuseli is introduced to Sir Andrew Mitchell (1708–1771), the British ambassador to the Prussian court, with the aim of establishing a regular literary exchange between England, Germany and Switzerland.

Late 1763–1769
Following his move to England, Fuseli writes on Jean-Jacques Rousseau (*Remarks on the Writings and Conduct of J. J. Rousseau*, 1767), translates Winckelmann's *Thoughts on the Imitation of Greek Works in Painting and Sculpture* into English and begins to draw again – a passion that he has pursued since his youth. Through Mitchell, he is introduced to the intellectual and cultural society of London. Fuseli encounters the lively London theatre scene, often attending performances at Covent Garden or Drury Lane, where he witnesses the work of the famous actor David Garrick (1717–1779), who is then at the height of his career. He also presents himself to Joshua Reynolds (1723–1792), the preeminent British painter of the time, and shows him his drawings. Reynolds encourages him to try his hand at oil painting.

1769/70
Fuseli is now determined to visit the 'great art school' of Italy. Towards the end of 1769 he travels via Milan and Florence to Rome, which he reaches in early February 1770. In Rome he studies mainly the principles on which the Renaissance masters based their designs; besides the seemingly unreachable ideal of antiquity he finds a model in the art of Michelangelo. He admires the Sistine Chapel, which influences his ideas for a Shakespeare memorial hall.

1776
An early drawing on the theme of *Satan Starts at the Touch of Ithuriel's Spear* (Stockholm, Swedish National Museum) documents his attentive reading of Milton's *Paradise Lost*.

1777
For the first time, Fuseli sends a painting – depicting a scene from *Macbeth* – from Rome to the annual exhibition at the Royal Academy in London.

1778/79
From Rome Fuseli travels back to his home town of Zurich after an absence of sixteen years, arriving there at the end of October 1778. During his six-month stay he begins work on his painting of *The Oath on the Rütli* (cat. 15), among others. In April 1779 Fuseli returns to London via France and the Netherlands, after the father of Anna Landolt, whom he admires, refuses to agree to their marriage.

1780

In the Royal Academy exhibition Fuseli presents – among other paintings – his *Satan Starts at the Touch of Ithuriel's Spear* (cat. 50). As his biographer Knowles records, he is hailed by the most renowned critics as an artist of the first rank for this work.

1781/82

In 1781 Fuseli paints the first version of his *The Nightmare* (Detroit Institute of Arts). In the following year, he exhibits the scandal-provoking picture at the Royal Academy.

1785

After his return from Italy, Fuseli meets the banker William Roscoe (1753–1831), who becomes one of his most important patrons and invites him to Liverpool.

1786

Through the publisher Joseph Johnson (1738–1809) Fuseli gains access to the manuscript of William Cowper's (1731–1800) translation of Homer's *Iliad* into English blank verse. His suggestions for changes recommend him as a competent advisor, leading to a significant revision of Cowper's project; however the poet and the painter never meet in person.

The same year, John Boydell (1719–1804) begins to put together works for his Shakespeare Gallery. Fuseli contributes nine paintings (see cats 35, 36) to the project. A year later he paints a scene for Thomas Macklin's (1752/53–1800) Gallery of Poets. Fuseli meets William Blake (1757–1827), with whom he cultivates an intellectual exchange.

1788–1790

Fuseli marries the considerably younger Sophia Rawlins from Batheaston. In the same year, he submits his application to the Royal Academy. He is accepted first as an associate member, advancing to full membership in 1790 (see cat. 13).

During this time, he meets the writer and advocate of women's rights Mary Wollstonecraft (1759–1797), with whom he corresponds intensively, but whose love for him remains unrequited.

From 1790

Fuseli has barely finished his work for Boydell when he embarks on the major undertaking of an illustrated edition of the collected works of Milton, which he plans to realize in collaboration with Johnson and Cowper. Fuseli is staying with Johnson in Ramsgate when he writes to his patron Roscoe about the project in August. When it fails – probably due to Cowper's mental illness – Fuseli decides to pursue it independently, following the example set by the Shakespeare Gallery.

1792

The English edition of Lavater's studies in physiognomy, illustrated and with a foreword by Fuseli, is published by Johnson as *Essays on Physiognomy*.

1799

Fuseli is offered a professorship in painting at the Royal Academy.

1799/1800

The two exhibitions by Fuseli at the Milton Gallery are a commercial failure but attract considerable attention in artistic circles.

1802

On a trip to Paris, Fuseli visits the Musée Napoléon and the studio of Jacques-Louis David.

1804–1810

In 1804 Fuseli is made a Keeper of the Royal Academy and simultaneously resigns his professorship. He is re-elected as professor in 1810.

1818–1823

The *Aphorisms*, which Fuseli has been working on since 1788, are completed. In addition, his *Lectures on Painting* are published between 1820 and 1823.

1825

In January Fuseli gives his last lectures. As Knowles tells us, the artist maintained his lively mind until the end; his last words were reputedly spoken in Latin. On the morning of the 16th of April 1825 Fuseli dies in the house of the Countess of Guilford in Putney Hill.

CB

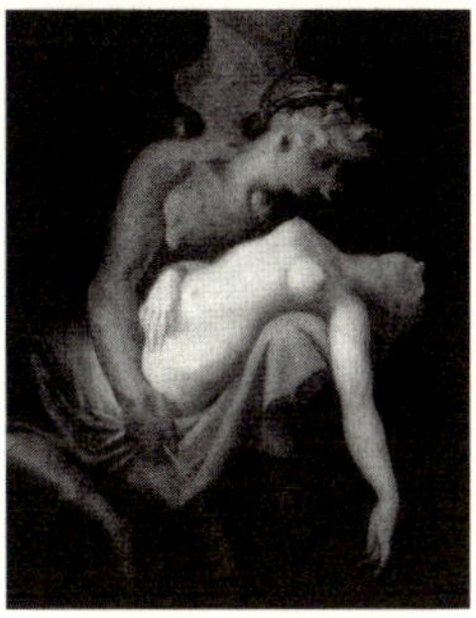

Cat. 1 *Amor and Psyche*, c. 1810
oil on canvas, 125 × 100 cm
Zurich, Kunsthaus Zürich,
Gift of the Union Bank of
Switzerland 1994, 1994/12
(Schiff, 'Verlorene Werke', 75)

Psyche, the daughter of a king, is so beautiful that veneration of the goddess Venus among mortals suffers as a result. Venus' anger increases when her son, Cupid, also falls in love with the young woman. To avenge herself Venus sets Psyche four virtually impossible tasks. The last of these takes her to the underworld, where Proserpina gives her a sealed box full of divine beauty to take back to Venus. Psyche is unable to resist the temptation of opening the box and out comes not the essence of beauty, but a hellish sleep. She falls to the ground as if dead. Cupid finds her, drives the sleep back into its box and resuscitates his beloved by touching her with the tip of one of his arrows. (Apuleius, *Metamorphoses [The Golden Ass]*, VI, 21.) At his request, Jupiter grants Psyche immortality and the couple are able to marry.

Fuseli colours Cupid's white wings black, and the hairstyle and black headband, too, recall his depiction of death and sleep in cat. 4. There can be no doubt, however, that the painting shows the god of love, for it adopts the compositional arrangement of a *Pietà*, and, in this way, though reversing the genders of the two figures, gives expression to the close bond between them. The artist may even have taken his cue from a *Pietà* by Ercole de' Roberti owned by his patron William Roscoe (Liverpool, Walker Art Gallery). BB

References: Noëlle Icard-Gianolio, 'Psyche', in LIMC, vol. 7, 1994, pp. 577–78. – Holm 2006, p. 205. – Zürich 2007a, p. 67. – Zürich 2007b, p. 95. – Brooke 2017, p. 84.

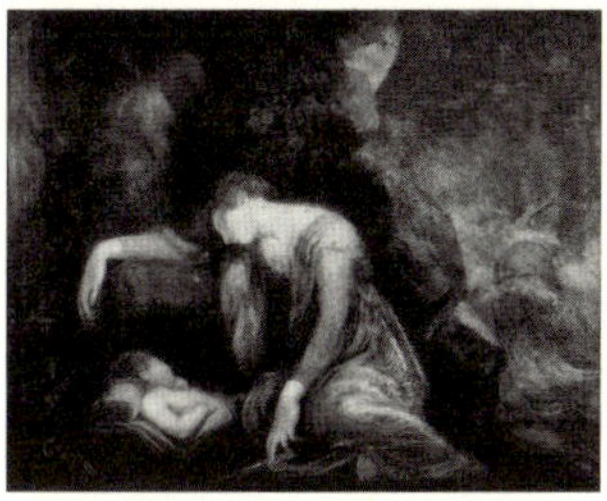

Cat. 2 *Danaë and Perseus on Seriphos (?)*, c. 1785–90
oil on canvas, 101.3 × 127 cm
New Haven, CT, Yale University
Art Gallery, University Purchase,
Associates in Fine Arts Fund,
1958.65 (Schiff 756)

Danae is the daughter of Acrisius, king of Argos, who has her incarcerated when an oracle predicts that he will die by his grandson's hand. Zeus, father of the gods, enters her prison through the roof in the form of a shower of golden rain and pours into her lap while she sleeps. As a result, she gives birth to a son, Perseus, and Acrisius has both of them thrown into the sea in a wooden chest. Poseidon, Zeus' brother and god of the sea, prevents the chest from sinking by calming the waves, and mother and son are washed up on the Cycladic island of Seriphos. Fuseli shows Poseidon on the left, disappearing afterwards into the open sea in his hippocampus-drawn chariot.

Perseus grows up on Seriphos to become one of the greatest heroes in Greek mythology, featured in many exploits. He beheads Medusa, conquers Atlas, frees Andromeda (daughter of the Ethiopian king Cepheus) and then marries her. While throwing the discus in games he takes part in on a journey home, he accidentally hits and kills his grandfather. Thus the prophecy is fulfilled. BB

References: Jean-Jacques Maffre, 'Danae', in LIMC, vol. 3, 1986, pp. 325–37. – New Haven 1992, p. 147. – Linda Jones Roccos, 'Perseus', in LIMC, vol. 7, 1994, pp. 332–48.

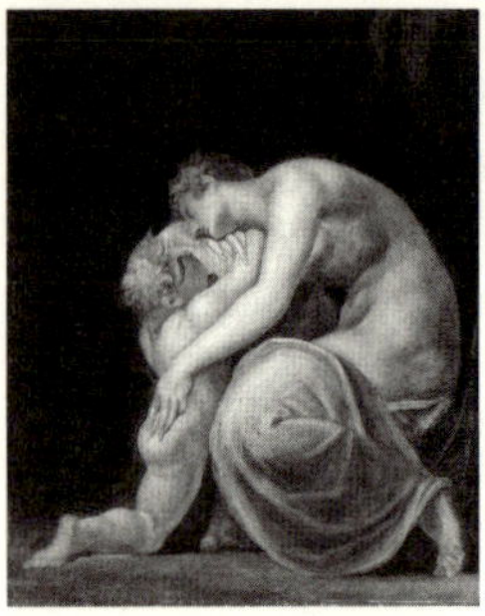

Cat. 3 *Tekemessa and Eurysakes*, c. 1800–10
oil on canvas, 103.8 × 89.2 cm
New Haven, CT, Yale Center for British Art, Paul Mellon Collection, B1976.7.29
(Schiff 1196)

This is a fragment of a painting whose subject and composition can be reconstructed with the aid of two drawings from Fuseli's Roman period (Schiff 389, 390). Both show the group of a woman and child in the lower right corner and, behind them, a young man gesticulating wildly in one drawing and dying on his sword in the other. This is Ajax, a principal hero on the Greek side in the Trojan war, who emerges empty-handed when the slain Achilles' belongings are distributed and therefore seeks revenge on his comrades. In a fit of rage he decides to attack Odysseus and the other Greeks at night, but is sent mad by the goddess Athena and in fact kills only a ram and Odysseus' herd of sheep. Ashamed of his dishonourable deed, he commits suicide the following morning and is mourned by his faithful concubine, the slave Tekemessa and their son Eurysakes.

In Sophocles' *Aias* (ll. 530–584) Tekemessa and Eurysakes play only minor roles – and the boy's is even silent – yet Fuseli evidently based his painting on the tragedy. One of Ajax's legs is just discernible to the left of Eurysakes in the fragment and gives some idea of the size of the original canvas. BB

References: Schiff 1977, pp. 102–03. – Odette Touchefeu, 'Aias II', in LIMC, vol. 1, 1981, p. 349.

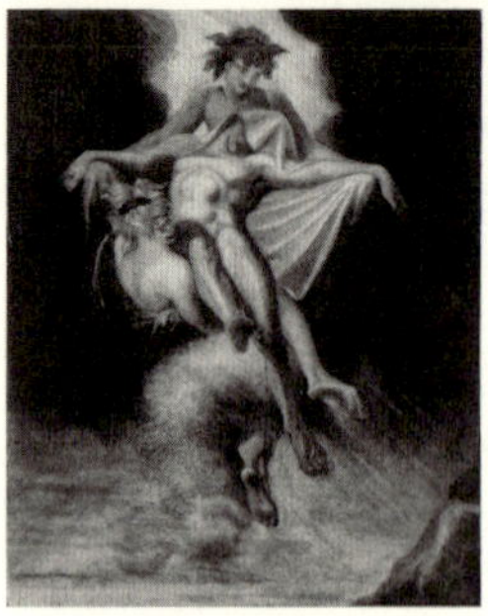

Cat. 4 *Sleep and Death Bear the Body of Sarpedon Away to Lycia*, 1803
oil on canvas, 91.4 × 71 cm
Zurich, Kunstsammlung des Kantons Zürich, 1800_30
(Schiff 1190)

Engraved by James Stow, 1806 (Weinglass 232)

The *Iliad* tells how Sarpedon, king of Lycia and son of Zeus, chief of the gods, fought on the side of the Trojans and was killed in battle by Patroclus, Achilles' comrade. After the Greeks and Trojans have fought for possession of Sarpedon's corpse, the former seizing his armour, Zeus instructs Apollo to abduct the body, cleanse it and anoint it. Hypnos and Thanatos, the gods of sleep and death respectively, are then ordered to carry him back to Lycia for burial. Homer prefaces his description of the battle, as broad in conception as it is bloody in detail, with a conversation between Zeus and Hera, his wife. In this, Zeus considers rescuing his son from the fatal encounter with Patroclus and taking him alive to Lycia. Hera objects that this would disrupt the Olympic order and recommends intervening only after Sarpedon has been killed, advice her husband follows. (Homer, *Iliad*, XVI, 431–683.)

The parallels between Sarpedon's fate and Christ's sacrificial death on the cross may have prompted Fuseli to base his painting on religious iconographical models. His composition recalls images of the Trinity amid clouds that feature Christ's body seen from the front with arms outstretched, but without the cross. Examples include two by Lucas Cranach the Elder (Leipzig, Museum der bildenden Künste, 248; Innsbruck, Tiroler Landesmuseum Ferdinandeum). BB

References: Hamburg 1974, p. 176. – Dietrich von Bothmer, 'Sarpedon', in LIMC, vol. 7, 1994, pp. 696–700.

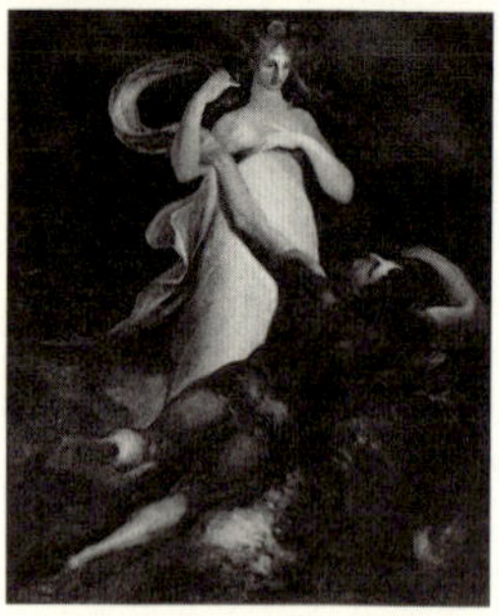

Cat. 5 *Odysseus, on the Raft, Receives the Sacred Veil from Ino–Leucothea*, c. 1805–10
oil on canvas, 175.5 × 138.5 cm
Private collection (Schiff 1193)

Not engraved by William Bromley, 1806, as claimed by Gert Schiff and David Weinglass (Weinglass 237)

Ino, the mortal foster mother of Dionysus, drowned herself in the sea and was admitted to the ranks of the marine deities as Leucothea, the 'white goddess'. She comes to Odysseus' rescue when his raft, constructed with the aid of the nymph Calypso, threatens to capsize in a tempest unleashed by Poseidon. (Homer, *Odyssey*, V, 333–353.) Rising from the depths 'like a sea-mew on the wing' (ibid., 337), she sits down beside the hero on the raft and tells him to undress and jump into the sea. If he stretches her sacred veil beneath his chest, he will be able to swim to land. Despite initial doubts, he does as bidden and reaches the coast of Scheria, the hospitable land of the Phaeacians (ibid., 452–453).

Leucothea, dressed in white, stands upright on the heeling raft. With her left index finger she points to the veil, which she is holding in her other hand as Odysseus, lying on the raft, reaches out for it with his left hand. The rear-view figure of the hero may have been inspired by one of the personifications of the four winds in John Flaxman's illustration of the same subject, which it closely resembles in reverse. Fuseli's Leucothea, on the other hand, is a variation on the *Venus Genetrix*, a standard figure type (see, for example, Rome, Galleria Colonna, a statue that has been altered to form an image of Flora). BB

References: Anne Nercessian, 'Ino', in LIMC, vol. 5, 1990, pp. 657–61. – Basel 2014, p. 111.

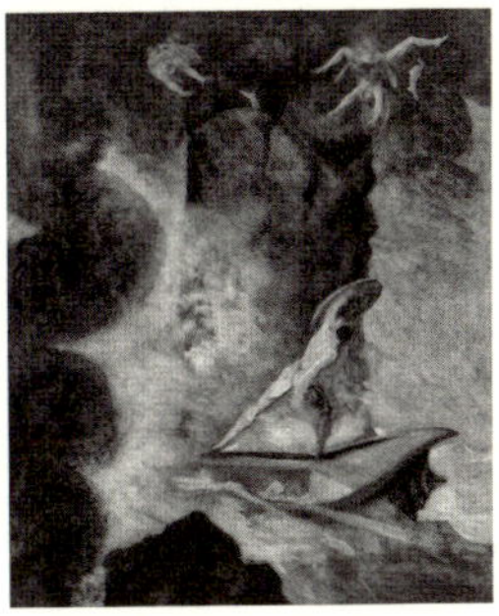

Cat. 6 *Odysseus between Scylla and Charybdis*, c. 1794–96
oil on canvas, 126 × 101 cm
Aarau, Aargauer Kunsthaus, Gift of Freunde der Aargauischen Kunstsammlung, 884 (Schiff 894)

Painting no. 12 in the Milton Gallery

'Picture XII / ULYSSES between SCYLLA and CHARYBDIS. An exemplification of SATAN straitened in his passage to Light / – Harder beset / Than when Ulysses on the larboard shunn'd / Charybdis, and by th' other whirlpool steer'd / So he with difficulty and labour hard / Mov'd on, with difficulty and labour he. Milton, Paradise Lost, Book II v. 1019.'

('A Catalogue of the Milton Gallery', in Knowles 1831, vol. 1, p. 209 [Without noting it, Fuseli suppresses here Milton's similarly brief comparison with the Argonauts between 'harder beset' (l. 1016) and 'when Ulysses' (l. 1019) in ll. 1017–18.])

Homer describes the monsters Scylla and Charybdis on either side of a sea channel that later classical authors identified with the straits of Messina. He does not detail the physical characteristics of Charybdis, who generates whirlpools in the sea, but notes that Scylla, her body stuck in a cave half-way up a tall cliff, has twelve claws and six horrific heads. She devours 'only' six of Ulysses' companions when the hero passes through the straits at the prow of his ship. He had been prepared, taking the advice of the enchantress Circe and ordering his steersman to stay closer to Scylla than to the even more forbidding Charybdis. (Homer, *Odyssey*, XII, 85–141, 201–259.)

Illustrating Homer's text was a secondary consideration for Fuseli, since the painting formed part of his Milton Gallery, in the catalogue of which he quotes the passage from Book II of *Paradise Lost* (see above) in which the poet compares the affliction caused by Satan with Odysseus' situation in the straits of Messina. Little more than an aside in Milton's epic – the passage encompasses only two lines – the poet states that Odysseus kept Charybdis out of reach on the port side of the ship. Fuseli therefore had to show the hero at the stern of the ship, since he depicts it travelling towards the left, and that is indeed indicated by the position of the shadowy form of the steersman. Thus, in following Milton, the artist contradicts Homer, who, in addition, has Odysseus reaching for two spears in this scene and not for a shield (Homer, *Odyssey*, XII, 229). He modelled Odysseus' body on an antique sculpture much admired in the eighteenth century, the *Borghese Gladiator*, then in the villa in Rome after which it is named (Paris, Musée du Louvre). BB

References: Hamburg 1974, p. 160. – Odette Touchefeu-Meynier, 'Odysseus', in LIMC, vol. 6, 1992, pp. 945, 964. – Marie-Odile Jentel, 'Skylla I', in LIMC, vol. 8, 1997, pp. 1137–45. – Zürich 2005, pp. 230–31, 271.

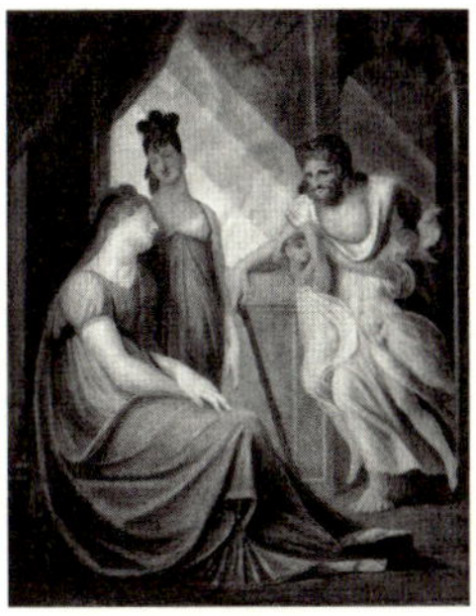

Cat. 7 *Thetis Asks Hephaestus to Provide Achilles with Armour*, 1803
oil on canvas, 91 × 71 cm
Zurich, Kunsthaus Zürich, 1941, 2561 (Schiff 1191)

Engraved by Edward Smith, 1805 (Weinglass 233)

The sea-nymph Thetis is the mother of Achilles, who outside Troy is deprived of his armour, once a wedding present from the gods to his father, Peleus. Achilles had lent it to his friend and comrade Patroclus, who then fell in battle against Hector. Thetis seeks out Hephaestus, the god of fire and metalworking, to request new armour for Achilles. (Homer, *Iliad*, XVIII, 369–617.) Hephaestus is beholden to her because she rescued and brought him up when his crippled leg and other birth defects had prompted his mother, Hera, to throw him from Olympus into the sea.

Thetis is received by Aglaea, one of the Three Graces (or Charites). In Homer and Hesiod, Aglaea, not Aphrodite, is Hephaestus' wife. Bidding her visitor to be seated, she goes to fetch her husband, who is just making the last of twenty wheeled, self-driving tripods to be used in running errands to the gods (*Iliad*, XVIII, 373–377) – objects unfortunately not depicted by Fuseli! Hephaestus joins the two women, assisted, according to Homer, by robots of his own construction: artificial handmaidens made of gold, equipped with speech and intelligence, capable of undertaking mechanical tasks and, it would seem, of floating in mid-air (this last is Fuseli's improvement on Homer and, indeed, on John Flaxman's well-known cycle of Homer illustrations). The handmaiden robots 'support' the limping god (ibid., 417), who could therefore do without the knotty walking-stick and carry a sceptre instead, as he does with Flaxman. There are doubtless philological reasons for the difference: William Cowper (whose *Iliad* translation was revised critically by Fuseli) interpreted 'σκῆπτρον παχύ' (ibid., 416) as signifying a 'sturdy staff' and not, like Alexander Pope ('huge sceptre') and Johann Heinrich Voss before him, a royal insignium. Ironically, the engraving after Fuseli's painting was originally intended for an edition of the Iliad in Pope's translation. The printed sheets of that publication were destroyed in a fire, and so the illustrations based on Fuseli came to be used in an edition containing Cowper's version.

Fuseli apparently had no desire to depict the 'withered legs' mentioned by Homer in his description of Hephaestus. (*Iliad*, XVIII, 411). Yet his way of showing the god, using a walking-stick and 'suffering' from heptadactyly ('seven-toe-hood'), gives the impression that Hephaestus' robotic assistants are somehow glued to him and are carrying, rather than supporting, him. A further anomaly occurs on the right, where the automaton's left foot disappears into a trumeau as though kicking open a concealed door. BB

References: Hamburg 1974, p. 176. – Antoine Hermary and Anne Jacquemin, 'Hephaistos', in LIMC, vol. 4, 1988, pp. 627–54. – Rainer Vollkommer, 'Thetis', in LIMC, vol. 8, 1997, pp. 6–14. – Zürich 2005, p. 271. – Zürich 2007a, p. 65.

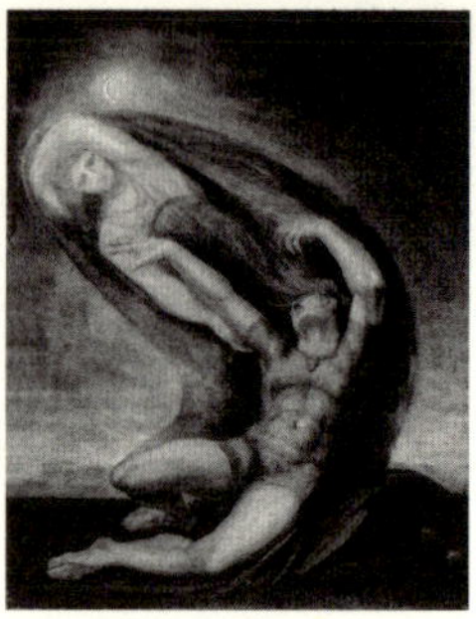

Cat. 8 *Achilles Grasping at the Shade of Patroclus*, 1803
oil on canvas, 91 × 71 cm
Zurich, Kunsthaus Zürich, 1941, 2562 (Schiff 1192)

Engraved by James Heath, 1806 (Weinglass 235)

The shade of Patroclus appears to Achilles as he lies asleep by the sea. After asking Achilles to bury his corpse swiftly, Patroclus prophesizes that his friend and comrade, too, will soon die in battle. Then the spirit requests that the bones of both heroes, who have known each other since childhood, be laid to rest in a single urn. Consenting in his dream, Achilles asks Patroclus to embrace him and reaches out towards the wraith. The apparition disappears like smoke sinking to the ground and Achilles awakes. (Homer, *Iliad*, XXIII, 62–109.)

Fuseli depicts Patroclus as required by the text, which states that his shade agreed in size, appearance and dress with his actual person (ibid., 66–67), and surrounds the dimly outlined figure with a black aureole because Greek mythology maintained that the dead existed as fleeting shadows. The wraith casts a shadow on Achilles' naked body, yet the indeterminate lighting makes it seem like a transparent, skin-tight body stocking. Pose and frontal view of the hero's muscular torso would appear to have been inspired by the *Barberini Faun* (Munich, Glyptothek) and by Michelangelo's figure of Adam at his creation on the ceiling of the Sistine Chapel. BB

References: Hamburg 1974, p. 177. – Odette Touchefeu-Meynier, 'Patroklos', in LIMC, vol. 8, 1997, pp. 948–52. – Zürich 2005, pp. 106, 271. – Zürich 2007a, p. 66.

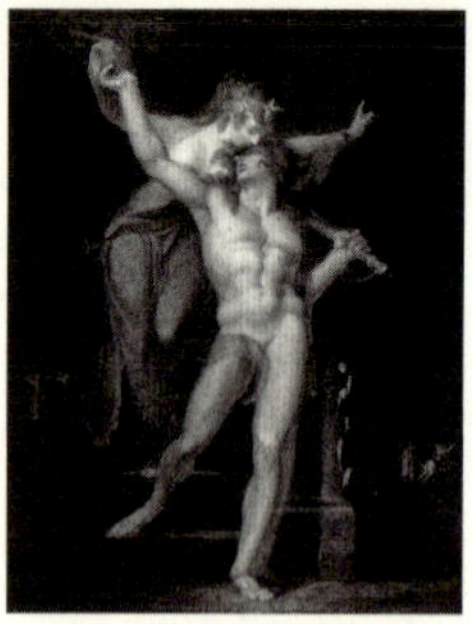

Cat. 9 *Theseus and Ariadne*, 1788
oil on canvas, 96 × 73 cm
Zurich, Kunsthaus Zürich, 1913, 1023 (Schiff 714)

Mezzotint reproduction by John Raphael Smith, 1788 (Weinglass 79)

Minos, king of Crete, demanded from the Athenians a tribute of seven youths and seven girls, to be sent every nine years as food for the Minotaur, a bull/human hybrid imprisoned in a labyrinth designed by the brilliant inventor Daedalus. Theseus, son of the king of Athens, embarks for Crete with the other chosen victims with the aim of putting an end to this practice by killing the monster. Ariadne, one of Minos' two daughters, falls in love with Theseus and furnishes him with a sacred sword and, on Daedalus' advice, a ball of thread. By tying one end of the thread to the entrance of the labyrinth and unwinding it on his passage through the maze, he would be able to find his way out again after slaying the Minotaur.

Fuseli stages the handing over of the thread as an elegant *pas de deux* that brings to mind the contemporaneous *tableaux vivants* performed by Lady Hamilton – her 'attitudes'. As the ball passes from Ariadne's right hand to that of Theseus their mouths converge for a kiss. Since the sword lacks a cross-guard, it cannot be the weapon received from Ariadne, but must be the bronze club belonging to Periphetes, which Theseus seized after overcoming the giant on the road to Athens and which is his most important iconographical attribute.

Several antique authors recorded the tale, including Ovid in the *Metamorphoses* (VIII, 152–173). Fuseli reveals his source as Virgil's *Aeneid* (VI, 27) by inscribing the words 'Hic labor ille domvs [et inextricabilis terror]' (there that house of toil, a maze inextricable; VI, 27) on the base of the stair post.

Gert Schiff sought to link the painting with the relief *Perseus and Andromeda* in the Capitoline Museums in Rome– a work drawn by Fuseli (Schiff 661) – but the relationship is not notably close. Of greater interest is the observation in the Hamburg exhibition catalogue of 1974 that Fuseli ultimately took his cue from Mannerist compositions showing the figures of loving couples one behind the other, such as Bartholomäus Spranger's *Angelica and Medoro* (Munich, Alte Pinakothek) and the same artist's large-scale *Venus and Adonis* (Vienna, Kunsthistorisches Museum). BB

References: Hamburg 1974, p. 138. – Marie-Louise Bernhard and Wiktor A. Daszewski, 'Ariadne', in LIMC, vol. 3, 1986, pp. 1050–70. – Jennifer Neils and Susan Woodford, 'Theseus', in LIMC, vol. 7, 1994, pp. 940–43. – Zürich 2007a, p. 63.

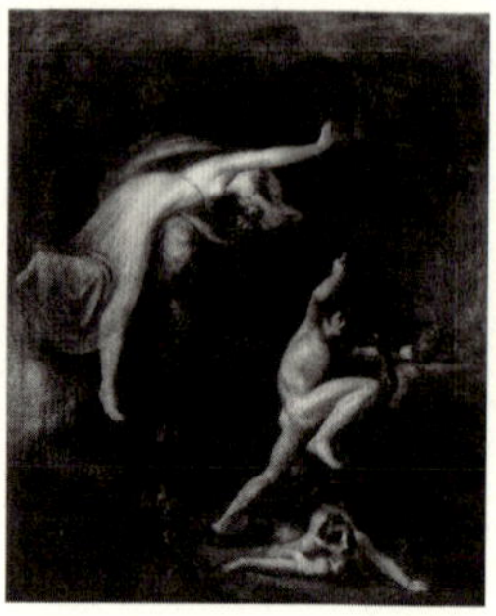

Cat. 10 *Ariadne Watches Theseus Fighting the Minotaur*, c. 1815–20
oil on canvas, 160 × 128 cm
Private collection, Switzerland (Schiff 1488)

The picture, for which a body-colour sketch survives (New Haven, Yale Center for British Art, Paul Mellon Collection, B1977.14.1671; Schiff 1529), was exhibited at the Royal Academy in 1820 and, despite its much later date, is connected with *Theseus and Ariadne* (cat. 9). In a letter of 12 July 1794 to his friend and patron William Roscoe, Fuseli asked whether Arthur Heywood, the owner of a different version of that earlier painting, would like to have a pendant to it showing 'Ariadne looking from a higher part of the Labyrinth on Theseus whilst he is combating the minotaur below'. No commission seems to have resulted from this enquiry, but the present canvas indicates that the artist stuck to his idea.

The architecture, with the stairs on the left and the chain attached to the stair post, corresponds to the entrance to the labyrinth shown in the earlier composition. On the right Theseus is striking the Minotaur, which has fallen on its back. Without a literary source to illustrate– no version of the myth states that Ariadne witnessed the killing – Fuseli could give free rein to his imagination. The princess reacts on the stairs like a sportswoman condemned to play the part of spectator, her muscles instinctively imitating the movements of her team mate down below. A male and a female corpse lie in the foreground – clearly, slain members of the Athenian victim delegation. Curiously, the top body is protruding from a huge vessel, as if ready for serving after it had been cooked. BB

References: Schiff 1973, vol. 1, p. 488. – Cat. 9 in the present volume.

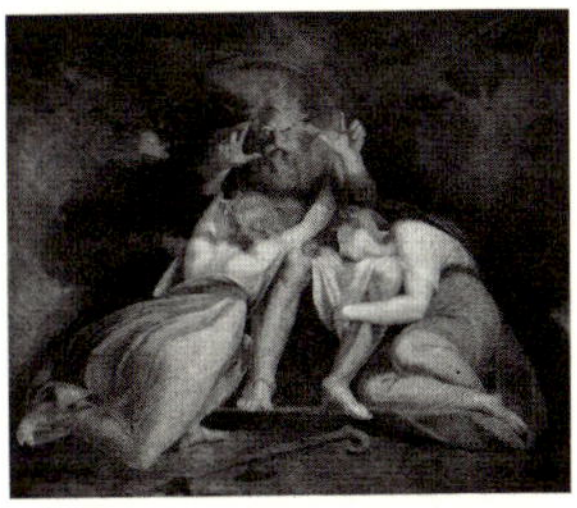

Cat. 11 *The Death of Oedipus*, 1783–84
oil on canvas, 150 × 168 cm
Liverpool, Walker Art Gallery, WAG 1537 (Schiff 712)

Mezzotint reproduction by William Ward, 1785 (Weinglass 74)

The subject comes from Sophocles' *Oedipus at Colonus*, a tragedy completed by his son. The aged King Oedipus, roaming about as a blind beggar after his self-induced banishment from Thebes, is guided by his daughter Antigone to the sacred grove of the Eumenides (the Furies, or goddesses of retribution) on the hill of Colonus near Athens. According to a prophecy, he will find his longed-for death there. When his son Polyneices appears and asks him for support in his feud with his other son, Eteocles, the angry Oedipus predicts that they will eventually kill each other. Fuseli depicted this scene in a painting that Gert Schiff surmises may date from the artist's Roman period (Washington, D. C., National Gallery of Art, Paul Mellon Collection). That canvas was evidently conceived as a pendant to the present picture, which is virtually the same size and shows the king's demise, presaged by thunder and lightning.

Oedipus obviously cannot see the bright shafts of lightning behind him, but he is able to hear the thunder, which he interprets as a message from the father of the gods: 'This winged thunder of Zeus will soon lead me to Hades' (Sophocles, *Oedipus at Colonus*, 1460–61). He looks forward to his death with grim satisfaction, whereas his daughters, Antigone and Ismene, react frantically: 'the maidens shuddered as they heard. They fell weeping at their father's knees, and did not cease from beating their breast, and from wailing loud' (ibid., 1606–09).

Fuseli inscribed the first three lines of this passage on a preliminary drawing dated 1783 that corresponds largely to the painting (New York 2007, lot 95). He will certainly have been aware that the scene he chose to illustrate would never have been seen by audiences at the Dionysia in Athens because it is an instance of teichoscopy (literally, 'viewing from the walls', a narrative technique of antique drama that entailed characters on a real or imaginary city wall describing action that remained hidden from the spectators). In the present case Sophocles put the words into the mouths of a chorus of messengers. BB

References: Haenlein 1974. – Ingrid Krauskopf, 'Oidipus', in LIMC, vol. 7, 1994, pp. 1–15.

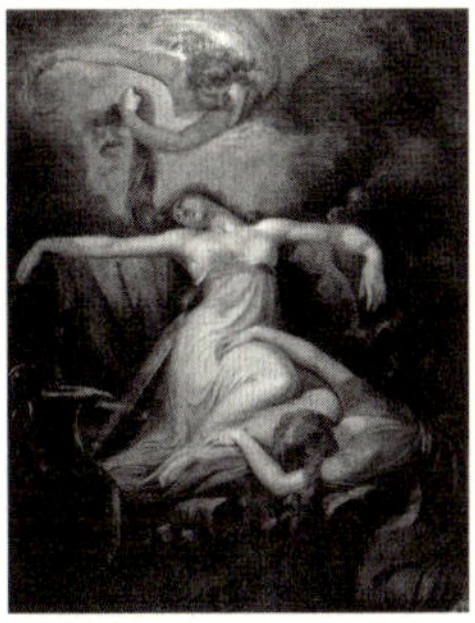

Cat. 12 *Dido*, 1781
oil on canvas, 244.3 × 183.4 cm
New Haven, CT, Yale Center for British Art, Paul Mellon Collection, B1976.7.184 (Schiff 713)

The legend of Rome's foundation, narrated by Virgil in the *Aeneid*, tells how Aeneas and his companions, after the downfall of Troy, were driven by a storm onto the coast of Carthage, where they were received hospitably by Queen Dido. Dido and Aeneas fall in love and neglect their obligations: Dido has sworn an oath never to be unfaithful to her dead husband and Aeneas is bound by fate to travel to Italy and found Rome. Jupiter sends Mercury, the male messenger of the gods, to Aeneas to remind him of his destiny. He thereupon quits Carthage and his lover. Devastated, Dido has a pyre erected in a courtyard of her palace and stacks Aeneas' belongings on it, including their shared bed – indicated in Fuseli's painting by the red cloth. She uses the hero's sword to take her own life and is mourned during her protracted battle with death by her devoted sister, Anna. Eventually, Juno sends Iris, the female messenger of the gods, to cut off Dido's hair and thereby free her soul from her body. (Virgil, *Aeneid*, IV, 475–705.)

Not coincidentally, Dido's pose and the arrangement of the three figures recall the group in cat. 4, for both paintings revolve around the theme of death and the release of the soul. Though Fuseli follows the *Aeneid*'s dramatic description of 'the blade reeking with blood' (ibid., 664–665), he foregoes showing how 'the deep-set wound gurgles in her breast'. BB

References: Hamburg 1974, p. 138. – Erika Simon, 'Dido', in LIMC, vol. 9, 1997, pp. 559–62. – London 2006, p. 10. – New Haven 2015, pp. 12–14.

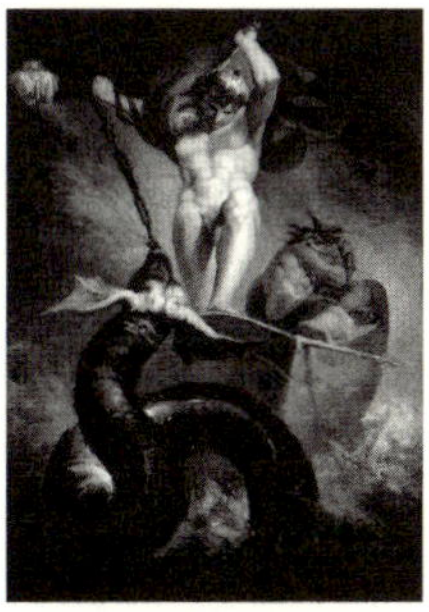

Cat. 13 *Thor Battering the Midgard Serpent*, 1790
oil on canvas, 133 × 94,6 cm
London, Royal Academy of Arts, 03/995 (Schiff 716)

This painting was Fuseli's diploma work for election as a full member of the Royal Academy in 1790. Its subject comes from the lay 'Hymiskviða' (Hymir's Poem) in the *Poetic Edda* and was known to the artist from the expanded, English edition of Paul Henri Mallet's *Introduction à l'histoire de Dannemarc*, published in 1770.

Thor, the god of thunder, persuades the reluctant giant Hymar to accompany him on a fishing trip. He rows with superhuman strength so far out to sea that, as Hymar remarks, they are in danger of running into the world-spanning sea serpent Midgard. Thor throws a bull's head overboard attached to a very tough fishing line. The monster rises to the bait, but resists so powerfully that Thor, pulling on the line, pushes both his feet through the bottom of Hymar's boat and lands on the bed of the ocean, where he continues the battle. While Thor is battering the serpent with his club, the giant, fearing for his leaking boat, cuts the line with a knife. The Midgard serpent escapes into the depths of the sea.

Familiarity with the text explains why Fuseli, though representing the end of the fishing line as a series of chain links, shows its continuation as a rope wound round Thor's arm: Hymar could not have cut through a chain with a knife. Thor's cloak billows behind him in obedience to classical pictorial convention, but the detail is not well thought through, because his club would have become entangled in the cloth. Moreover, by depicting Thor in a standard walking pose at the prow of the boat, the artist ignores the narrative's turning-point– Thor's falling though the floor of the boat – which, in leading the god to do battle with the monster throughout the sea's depths, lends the tale a cosmic dimension. It would have taken pictorial imagination of Goyaesque force to do justice to such an awe-inspiring theme, however, and Fuseli focuses instead on the contrast between the god's heroism and the giant's fear, showing Hymar anxiously clutching the helm as he apparently appeals for aid to Odin, the supreme god, who has emerged from amid the clouds. BB

References: Mallet 1770, vol. 2, pp. 135–36. – Hamburg 1974, p. 140. – Zürich 2005, pp. 152, 270. – London 2006, p. 88.

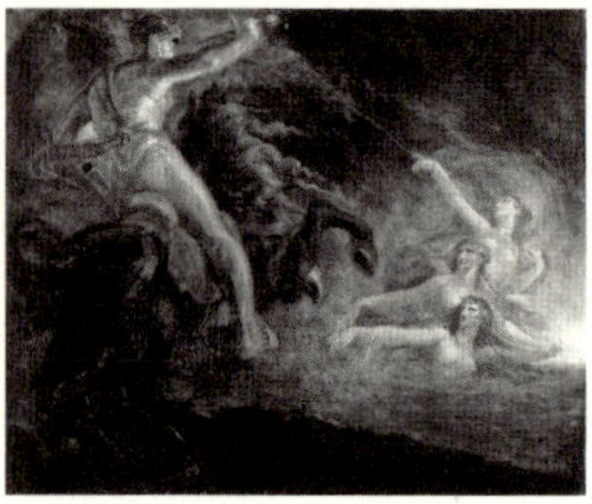

Cat. 14 *Hagen and the Nymphs of the Danube*, c. 1800–15
oil on canvas, 118 × 142 cm
Zurich, Kunsthaus Zürich, Gift of Dr. Martin Hürlimann to the city of Zurich, 1978, 1978/10 (Schiff 1199)

Although fearing an ambush, the Nibelungs accept Kriemhild's invitation to visit the court of her second husband, Etzel, in Hungary. Riding on ahead in search of a ferry across the Danube, Hagen of Tronje encounters the water-nymphs Hadburg and Siegelind. They are bathing, and he steals their clothes. In exchange for them the nixies offer him the benefit of their prophetic gifts. When Hadburg forecasts a stay full of glory at Etzel's court, Hagen returns the water-sprites' clothes. Only then does Siegelind warn that all the Nibelungs except the king's chaplain will lose their lives there. Ignoring the prophecy, Hagen asks the nymphs where he can find a ferry and they direct him to one. (*Nibelungenlied*, XXV, 1592–1608.)

Disregarding the text, Fuseli adds a third water-nymph pointing Michelangelo's Adam on the ceiling of the Sistine Chapel. The effect is rather contrived, yet the gesture is evidently intended to carry a significance of comparable weight to that of its predecessor, for a red ray issuing from the hand generates flashes of lightning at the upper left that reveal the black, shadowy head of Siegfried (?), whom Hagen had murdered. BB

References: Von Graberg 1970, pp. 24–25. – Hamburg 1974, pp. 181–82. – Zürich 2005, pp. 159–60. – Zürich 2007a, p. 67.

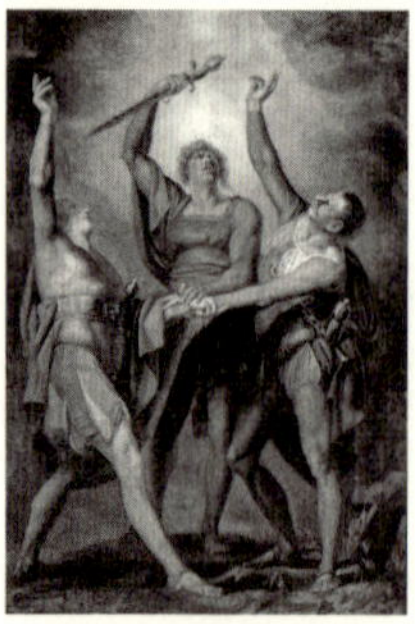

Cat. 15 *The Oath on the Rütli*, 1779–81
oil on canvas, 267 × 178 cm
Zurich, Kunsthaus Zürich, on loan from the canton of Zurich, 1989, 1989/15 (Schiff 359)

Engraved by Franz Hegi, 1807–1809 (Weinglass 282)

Since early modern times legends surrounding the foundation of the Swiss Confederacy have included an oath of allegiance sworn on the Rütli meadow, near the shore of Lake Uri, by Werner Stauffacher, Walter Fürst and Arnold von Melchtal as the representatives of the cantons of Schwyz, Uri and Unterwalden. The *Bundesbrief* (federal charter) of 1291 was discovered in 1758 but did not become the dominant element in the liberation narrative until the nineteenth century. The best-known historical source for the event is the *Chronicon Helveticum* by Aegidius Tschudi (1505–1572). First published in Basel in 1734–36 (vol. 1, p. 236), this dates the oath to 1307.

While staying in Zürich on his way back from Italy to England in the winter of 1778–79, Fuseli was persuaded by his friend and former fellow student Johann Caspar Lavater to accept the commission for the present painting, financed by prominent Zürich citizens and intended for the local town hall. His signature and the date of 1780 at the lower edge were added later in another hand: in fact, he did not finish the picture until 1781, in London.

Fuseli took as his model not a sixteenth-century Bible woodcut, as Andrei Pop fancies, but a far more recent source: David Herrliberger's illustration on the title page of an edition in German and French of the poem *Die Alpen* by Albrecht von Haller (1773), which shows the three figures in exactly the same arrangement. The position of the clasped hands, too, corresponds precisely to that in the etching. Gert Schiff noted the similarities, but was so in thrall to Fuseli's genius, and to the cult of the genius in general, that he found it impossible to believe that the artist had not himself invented these elements. That does not mean that Fuseli felt no need to improve on the sober naturalism of the book illustration. Two preliminary drawings (Klassik Stiftung Weimar, Graphische Sammlungen, Kunsthaus Zürich, Grafische Sammlung, Schiff 411, 412) and an oil sketch (Art Institute of Chicago; not in Schiff) show him experimenting with the stances of the figures and their raised right arms in the interests of a more heroic image. He then incorporated his solutions into Herrliberger's composition. In addition, he monumentalised the figures by availing himself of an old trick of history painting, depicting their lower legs and feet from above and their throats and heads from below. BB

References: Schiff 1973, vol. 1, pp. 94–98. – Debrunner 1996, p. 159. – Zürich 2005, pp. 34, 269. – London 2006, p. 82. – Zürich 2007a, p. 62. – Gonon 2007. – Pop 2015, pp. 63–68.

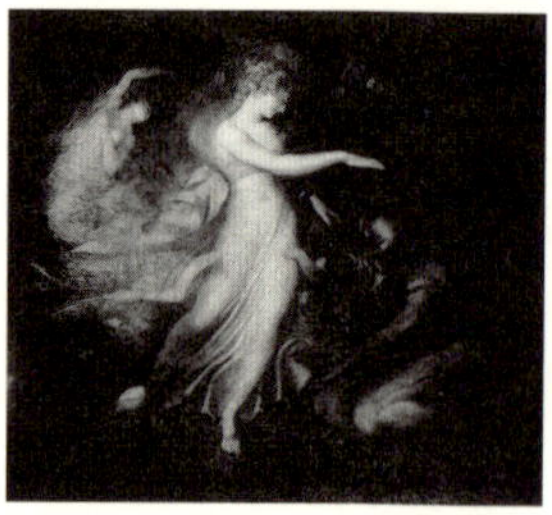

Cat. 16 *Prince Arthur and the Fairy Queen*, 1785–88
oil on canvas, 100.5 × 106.9 cm
Basle, Kunstmuseum Basel, 1566 (Schiff 721)

Aquatint reproduction by Peltro W. Tomkins, 1788 (Weinglass 78)

Edmund Spenser, *The Faerie Queene*, I, 9, 13

For-wearied with my sports, I did alight / From loftie steed, and downe to sleepe me layd; / The verdant gras my couch did goodly dight, / And pillow was my helmet faire displayd: / Whiles every sence the humour sweet embayd, / And slombring soft my hart did steale away, / Me seemed, by my side a royall Mayd / Her daintie limbes full softly down did lay: / So faire a creature yet saw never sunny day.

(Spenser 1978, p. 149)

The 'Faerie Queene' in Edmund Spenser's *chef d'oeuvre* is called Gloriana and is an allegorical representation of Elizabeth I. Spenser (1552/53–1599) dedicated his epic poem to her and she rewarded him with a pension for life. In one of its principal scenes Gloriana appears in a dream to Prince Arthur, a character based on the legendary figure of King Arthur.

In 1787 Thomas Macklin followed in the footsteps of John Boydell and his Shakespeare Gallery by commissioning paintings for a Poets' Gallery. They included Fuseli's picture of Prince Arthur's dream, a subject hitherto ignored by eighteenth-century illustrators of Spenser's poem. The painting is much faded and the small sprites accompanying the queen are therefore no longer visible, but they are documented by the print reproducing the image.

Fuseli's composition is essentially a reversed version of Anthony van Dyck's paintings *Rinaldo and Armida*, then owned by Earl Fitzwilliam of Wentworth Woodhouse, Yorkshire, and now in Baltimore (Museum of Art, Jacob Epstein Collection). The figure of Prince Arthur, however, is not related directly to Van Dyck's Rinaldo, as Gert Schiff claims, but was put together from two ignudi in the north-western corners of Michelangelo's *The Creation of Eve* and *The Separation of Land and Water* on the ceiling of the Sistine Chapel. BB

References: Schiff 1973, vol. 1, p. 490. – Bradley 1979–80, p. 39.

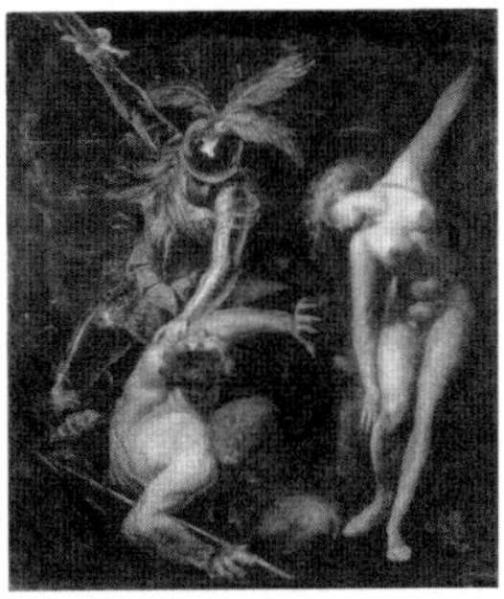

Cat. 17 *Britomart Freeing Amoretta from the Spell of Busirane*, 1824
oil on canvas, 182.8 × 153.2 cm
Frankfurt am Main, Freies Deutsches Hochstift, Frankfurter Goethe-Museum, IV-1957–088 (Schiff 1494)

Edmund Spenser, *The Faerie Queene*, III, 12, 30–39

So mightily she smote him, that to ground / He fell halfe dead; next stroke him should have slaine, / Had not the Lady, which by him stood bound, / Dernly unto her called to abstaine / From doing him to dy. For else her paine / Should be remedilesse, sith none but hee / Which wrought it, could the same recure againe. Therewith she staid her Hand, loth staid to bee; / For Life she him envy'd, and long'd Revenge to see.

(Spenser 1978, p. 558)

Busirane, a wicked sorcerer who separates loving couples, abducted Amoretta from the nuptial bed she shared with Scudamour and held her captive by binding her around the waist to a bronze pillar (verse 30), aiming to torture her to death. Britomart, a female virgin knight who is subjected to many trials in Edmund Spenser's epic poem, enters the magician's castle and beats him to the ground. As she is about to deal Busirane the death blow Amoretta stops her, because only the wizard himself can undo the spells he casts on his prisoners. That is the moment Fuseli chose to depict. Immediately afterwards, the two women force Busirane to break the spell.

As in the *Roman de la Rose* and other works of medieval literature, the main characters in *The Faerie Queene* each personify an abstract value: Amoretta, for example, embodies conjugal love, and Britomart, patterned on the figure of Bradamante in Ariosto's *Orlando Furioso*, represents chastity and, as her name suggests, British military strength (Spenser borrowed the name from that of the nymph Britomartis, associated with Artemis in classical mythology).

Fuseli relies in his composition on the centuries-old formula for depicting Perseus liberating Andromeda from her fetters on a rock. However, he fails to depict the narrative's turning-point convincingly and therefore misses a crucial aspect: hanging unconscious from her bonds, Amoretta would scarcely be capable of speaking the words that save Busirane's life. The painting's colour, dramatic lighting and free brushwork take their cue from Tintoretto and Titian's late work. BB

References: Frankfurt am Main 2011, pp. 65–66.

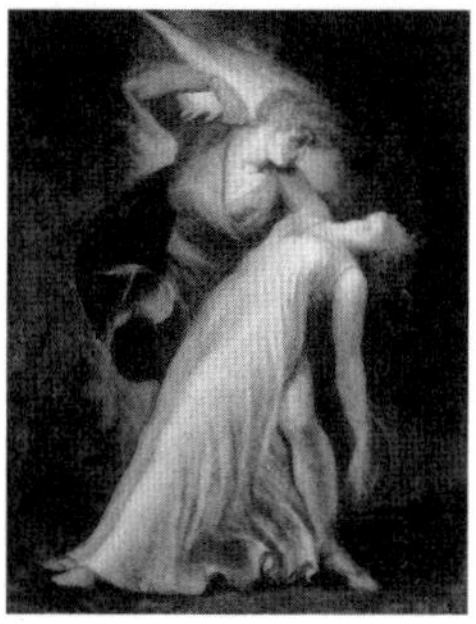

Cat. 18 *Celadon and Amelia*, 1801
oil on canvas, 91.5 × 71.5 cm
Karlsruhe, Staatliche Kunsthalle Karlsruhe, 2470 (Schiff 1218)

Engraved by William Bromley for an edition of James Thomson's The Seasons published by Francis Isaac Du Roveray in 1802 (Weinglass 163)

James Thomson, *The Seasons*, II: 'Summer', 1214–19

… From his void embrace, Mysterious Heaven! that moment, to the ground, / A blackened corse, was struck the beauteous maid. / But who can paint the lover, as he stood, / Pierc'd by severe amazement, hating life / Speechless, and fix'd in all the death of woe?

(Thomson 1793, p. 95)

In 1802 Francis Isaac Du Roveray published a new, de luxe edition of James Thomson's *The Seasons*. The Scottish writer's epic blank verse poem in four 'books' had first appeared complete in 1730, but was still popular at the turn of the century. Du Roveray commissioned Fuseli to produce designs for two illustrations. Only the present picture, for 'Summer' (Book II), has survived; that for 'Winter' (Book IV) is considered lost. In both cases the artist chose scenes redolent of terror: deaths caused by the forces of nature. The tragedy depicted in 'Summer', exhibited at the Royal Academy in 1801, is extreme. Celadon and Amelia, a young couple bound by an undying love and lauded by Thomson as 'unmatched' in their virtue and innocence, live happily and harmoniously in idyllic rural surroundings. Out walking one day, they are surprised by a thunderstorm. Celadon attempts to calm his fearful companion by invoking divine benevolence, but the next moment he finds her dead in his arms, struck down by a shaft of lightning.

In response to the poet's question as to who could paint the desperate Celadon, Fuseli devised a composition reduced to very few elements and therefore all the more compellingly theatrical. Filling almost the entire picture plane and boldly modelled by dramatic lighting, the tragic couple combine to form a whole that unites expressive opposites in the manner of an antique sculpture. This contrasts with the dark background, which appears dissolved in clouds of paint, the thunderstorm and natural surroundings merely hinted at by a few vague shapes and their modelling. The antique group *Menelaus Supporting the Body of Patroclus* (Florence, Uffizi) probably provided a basic template for the work, but Fuseli varied it in a number of ways. He borrowed the figure of Amelia, struck by the lightning appearing behind Celadon's head as a patch of illumination, from the 'dying bacchante' in an antique Bacchus relief (also Florence, Uffizi; see Schiff 372, 373). Her drapery, on the other hand, is remarkably similar to that of the sleeping woman in the first version of Fuseli's *The Nightmare* (fig. 5, p. 25) and to that of the saint in Stefano Maderno's sculpture St Cecilia (1600; Rome, S. Cecilia in Trastevere), which likewise shows the head slightly averted from the viewer and which Fuseli 'genealogists' seem to have overlooked as a source of *The Nightmare* and other works by him (cat. 69). The figure of Celadon, shot through with grief and horror in contrast to the inert body of his dead beloved, represents an upright version of another antique sculpture, a 'dying giant' that Fuseli studied closely in Rome (see a pen and ink drawing in the Kunsthaus Zürich; Schiff 643), although he transformed the 'pathos formula' of arms held behind the head into a gesture of support. Finally, it would be worth investigating whether a hitherto unknown model formed the basis of the striking similarity between Fuseli's group and a reversed *bozzetto* that Berthel Thorvaldsen created for his *Achilles and Penthisileia* at perhaps exactly the same time in Rome (Copenhagen, Thorvaldsens Museum). GD

References: Schiff 1973, vol. 1, pp. 342–43. – Frankfurt am Main 2017, p. 92. – London 1973, p. 47.

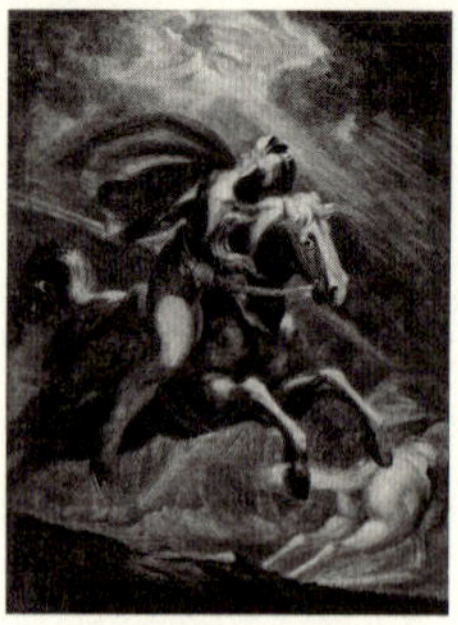

Cat. 19 *Sherasmin and Huon Fleeing from Oberon*, 1804–05
oil on canvas, 61 × 45 cm
Zurich, Städtische Kunstsammlung, 4964 (Schiff 1220)

Engraved by Francis Engleheart, 1806 (Weinglass 245)

Christoph Martin Wieland, *Oberon*, II, 29–31

'Oh, fly, sir! Your life's not worth a song!' – / Sir Huon strives, indeed, but strives in vain; / The old man speeds in fullest flight amain, / And after him drags Huon's horse along: / O'er stock and stone, thro' bush and brake they race, / Nor hedge nor ditch impedes their desperate pace: / Nor ceas'd the wight to scamper, fear-pursu'd, / Till, clear from out the compass of the wood, / They find themselves at last amid an open space.

A tempest, wing'd with lightning, storm, and rain, / O'ertakes our pair: around them midnight throws / Darkness that hides the world: it peals, cracks, blows, / As if the uprooted globe would split in twain: / The elements in wild confusion flung, / Each warr'd with each, as fierce from chaos sprung. / Yet heard from time to time amid the storm / The gentle whisper of th' aërial form / Breath'd forth a lovely tone that died the gales among –

'Why dost thou fly? thy happiness thou fly'st! / 'Come back, come, Huon! dare in me confide – / 'Hear me! to happiness thy path I guide I' – / 'If thou delay'st a moment, sir, thou dy'st! / 'Away! away! your finger in your ear! / 'He means no good – 'tis death his voice to hear!' / Onward, through thick and thin, they dash again, / Beat by the blast, and flooded by the rain – / When lo! a cloister wall impedes their rash career.

(Wieland 1805, vol. 2, pp. 53–54.)

Huon, the youthful hero of Christoph Martin Wieland's epic poem *Oberon*, first published in 1780, is tricked into killing one of Emperor Charlemagne's sons. The vengeful emperor punishes the unwitting murderer by sending him on a 'suicide mission': to attain forgiveness he must slay the intended husband of the sultan of Bagdad's daughter, kiss her as his own bride and bring back four of the sultan's molars and a tuft from his beard as a gift. Setting off intrepidly to accomplish these seemingly impossible tasks, Huon soon encounters the hermit Sherasmin, who had once accompanied Huon's father to the Holy Land as a warrior. Henceforth he will spare no effort to help Huon in the exploits ahead of him.

Ignoring a warning from Sherasmin, Huon takes the shortest route to Bagdad. This leads through a wood rumoured to be enchanted and there the pair discover the castle of the fairy king Oberon. When Oberon appears and invites them to stay, Sherasmin panics and urges Huon to flee. A wild chase ensues, after which it transpires that Oberon is well-disposed towards them. Promising to stand by Huon, he gives him two magic objects that will enable him to survive his trials at the Sutan's court: a horn and a goblet that refills itself with wine.

This episode introduces the character from which the poem takes its name. Wieland describes him as a boy or dwarf, but Fuseli stages his appearance like a Late Baroque vision of God, even borrowing his gesture from that of the divine judge in Michelangelo's *Last Judgement* in the Sistine Chapel. A further unexpected echo of Christian iconography emerges from the combination of the supernatural apparition with the group of the horse and rider, which occupies most of the picture plane as Huon turns back to look at Oberon in a variation on the standard composition for depicting the conversion of Saul. In surroundings whose drama is enhanced by a blurred backdrop of unfettered natural forces, and by the contrary movements of Huon's ghostly horse and his companion's mount, which is disappearing out of the picture at the right, Fuseli focuses attention on the character and emotions of the young hero: fearless on his galloping horse, he establishes contact with his future protector by turning towards him with a mixture of scepticism and curiosity. GD

References: Schiff 1973, vol. 1, p. 326. – Zürich 2005, pp. 85, 271, no. 91.

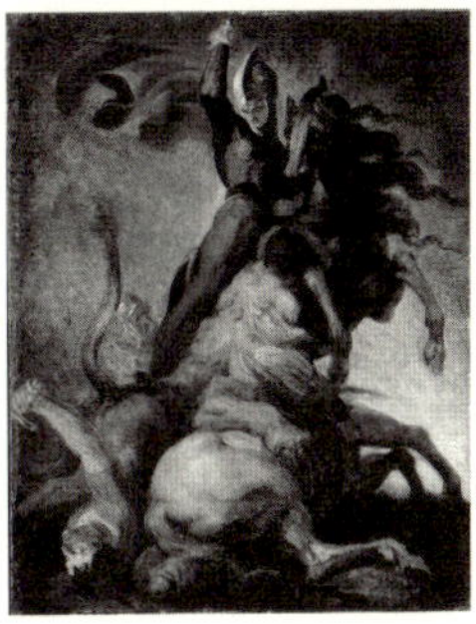

Cat. 20 *Huon Freeing Babekan from the Lion*, 1804–05
oil on canvas, 61.3 × 45 cm
Private collection (Schiff 1222)

Engraved by Charles Warren, 1806 (Weinglass 247)

Christoph Martin Wieland, *Oberon*, IV, 24–25.

As forward darts the beast with hideous roar, / And flashes lightning from his eyes of flame, / Huon divides his flank with sidelong aim: / The wound inflames the forest king the more; / Fiercely he bounds, and rends with headlong spring / The iron plates that round the warrior cling: / Blood from a thousand sources dies the plain: / That single stroke had torn the knight in twain, / Save for the magick force of Angulaffer's ring!

Sir Huon summons his remaining strength, / And though death glar'd before him, undismay'd / Darts in the monster's neck his vengeful blade – / In vain, high rais'd, his tail's enormous length / Swings in the air, and curling to and fro / Had crush'd in instant death his prostrate foe, / If active Huon had not leap'd aside – / In vain his claws gigantick open wide; / Bold Sherasmin draws near, and fells him at a blow!

(Wieland 1798, vol. 1, p. 113.)

Huon must experience further adventures before reaching Bagdad. Together with Sherasmin, he kills a huge lion, for example, thereby freeing the 'Saracen' Babekan from certain death. Scarcely on his feet again, Babekan's dubious character is revealed by Huon's magic goblet, which dries up when he tries to drink from it. Without a word of gratitude, Babekan blasphemes wildly, steals Huon's horse and rides off. It subsequently emerges that he is the betrothed of the sultan's daughter, the very man whom Charlemagne has ordered Huon to slay at a banquet in Bagdad. In this way, a cold-blooded 'contract killing' is transmuted into a just punishment meted out to a dishonourable wrongdoer.

As in cat. 19, Fuseli bases his composition on Christian iconographic models. Frederick Antal pointed out the striking similarity of the battling knight to a painting by Peter Paul Rubens of St George and the dragon (Madrid, Prado). Fuseli shifts the Flemish artist's group of horse and rider, which he may have known from a preliminary study, into a position less firmly aligned with the picture plane, increases its verticality and, showing it from farther below, emphasises its monumentality at the centre of the image. The role of the defeated dragon is taken in Fuseli's composition not by the lion hurling itself at Huon, but by Babekan, who lies desperately on the ground in a pose derived from Leonardo da Vinci's *Battle of the Anghiari* – a configuration that can be seen as pointing to Huon's subsequent murder of Babekan. GD

References: Antal 1956, pp. 159–60. – Schiff 1973, vol. 1, p. 326.

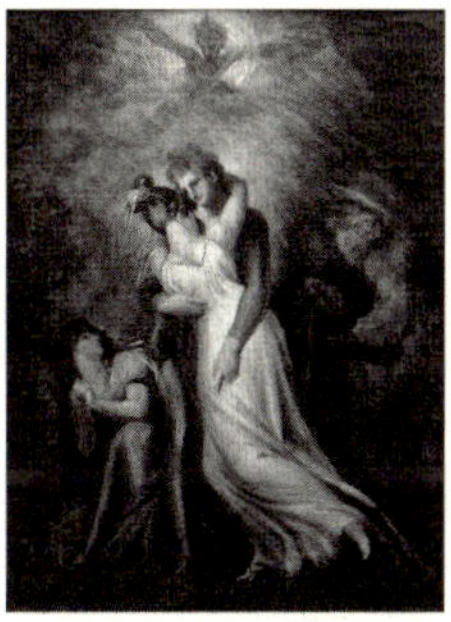

Cat. 21 *Huon and Rezia United, with Fatma, Sherasmin and Oberon*, 1804–05
oil on canvas, 61 × 45 cm
Lucerne, Kunstmuseum Luzern, on loan from a private collection, L 2007.56x (Schiff 1223)

Engraved by James Heath, 1806 (Weinglass 248)

Christoph Martin Wieland, *Oberon*, V, 74–75.

Yet, his first kiss, still thrilling in her heart, / Requires no other aid to swell the flame: / Wealth, glory, splendour, all an empty name: / From these it little seems at once to part, / So the enchanted maid her Huon keeps: / With shame and love o'erpower'd she fondly weeps, / And hides her burning face on Huon's breast; / While rais'd to meet his heart, with rapture prest, / High swells her glowing heart, and 'gainst his bosom leaps.

And gently o'er them Oberon extends / His lily wand, as if in act to place / His nuptial blessing, as their hearts embrace. / Soft from his eye a stealing tear descends / On both their brows – 'So haste, thou matchless pair, / 'On wings of love, my car, that cuts the air, / 'Shall waft you high above terrestrial sight, / 'And place, ere morning melt the shades of night, 'On Askalon's far shore, beneath my guardian care.'

(Wieland 1805, vol. 2, p. 172)

This scene from the conclusion of Canto V, in which Oberon gives his blessing to Huon and Rezia, the Sultan's beautiful daughter, and they sink happily into each other's arms, is both an end and a beginning. On the one hand, Huon has performed the tasks assigned to him by Charlemagne and has fallen madly in love (encouraged by dreams implanted in the couple by Oberon); on the other, the story's ultimate purpose – the reconciliation of Oberon and Titania, his queen, by means of another couple's unconditional love and faithfulness – has yet to be accomplished by the unwitting pair. Soon, they will disobey the fairy king's injunction to remain chaste until they are married in Rome, an order given on threat of severe punishment. As a result, they will be submitted to further trials over a period of several years.

Fuseli depicts the loving couple in an intimate, but chaste, embrace. Rezia's physically precarious pose may be seen as an indication that this moment of happiness will be fleeting, as Gert Schiff suggests. Its rather surprising source lies in depictions of the drunken Silenus in ancient Roman reliefs (see a pen and ink drawing in the Kunsthaus Zürich, 1914/15; Schiff 658). The other three figures offer compelling evidence that, in addition to many other sources, Fuseli took his cue from the relevant 'pathos formulas' of Christian pictorial narrative. Physiognomically, Oberon may resemble Fuseli's goblins and ghosts more than a divine vision, but his appearance as a whole clearly relates to such models as the scenes from the Creation on the Sistine Chapel ceiling. The figure of Sherasmin, blinded by divine light, would work equally well as a bystander in pictures of the Ascension, Assumption or Annunciation to the Shepherds, while Rezia's old nurse, Fatma, shown kneeling in adoration, seems to have strayed in from a religious iconographical context. GD

References: Schiff 1973, vol. 1, p. 326.

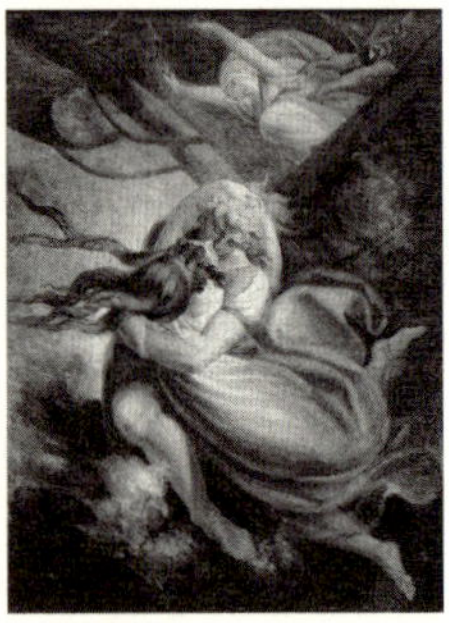

Cat. 22 *Amanda/Rezia Plunges into the Sea with Huon, while Fatme is Held Back*, 1804–05
oil on canvas, 61 × 45 cm
Lucerne, Kunstmuseum Luzern, on loan from a private collection, L 2007.54x (Schiff 1224)

Engraved by James Neagle, 1806 (Weinglass 250)

Christoph Martin Wieland, *Oberon*, VII, 25–26.

The Paladin moves on with steady pace: / At once amid the crew, th' empassion'd fair, / So long the lifeless statue of despair, / Darts wild with woe to Huon's last embrace, / Loose, like a lion's mane, her ringlets sweep / Before the blast! With eyes that cannot weep, / With love to frenzy wrought, with high-swoln breast, And circling arms round Huon closely prest, / She hurls him with herself amid the swallowing deep!

And what but force the trusty Fatme saves / From willing death? She views their clasping forms / Entwin'd like tendrils, by the billowy storms / Roll'd onward, faintly struggling through the waves. / And when, soon lost, she views them, ah! no more, / Her shrieks of anguish ring the vessel o'er. / Who shall assuage her heart-consuming pain? / Who to her arms Amanda bring again? / Who all she lov'd replace, and hope extinct restore?

(Wieland 1805, vol. 2, pp. 13–14.)

Oberon's benevolence towards Huon and Rezia (or Amanda, as she was named after converting to Christianity) changes to implacable enmity when the fire of youthful love induces the couple to disobey the vow of chastity he had demanded of them. When their ship threatens to capsize in a storm, Huon seeks to placate the vengeful king of the fairies by sacrificing his own life. Amanda does not hesitate to join him in death, and they both jump into the surging sea, which quickly becomes calm again. The magic ring, which Amanda has worn since her marriage, rescues the pair of them from drowning and they end up safe and sound on an inhospitable island.

The composition is constructed along the diagonals, tying together the main figures with the sailing ship tilted at a dangerous angle as it dances on the foam. Gert Schiff aptly called this 'probably the most astonishing triumph that temperamental vision has ever won over gross distortion'. Furthermore, with the image of the passionately kissing lovers inextricably united in a bundle of forms amid the unfettered forces of nature Fuseli created a powerful visual counterpart to the theme of love and sexuality lived freely and in opposition to prevailing social convention that is inscribed in Wieland's poem. GD

References: Zürich 1969, p. 31, no. 82. – Schiff 1973, vol. 1, pp. 326–27.

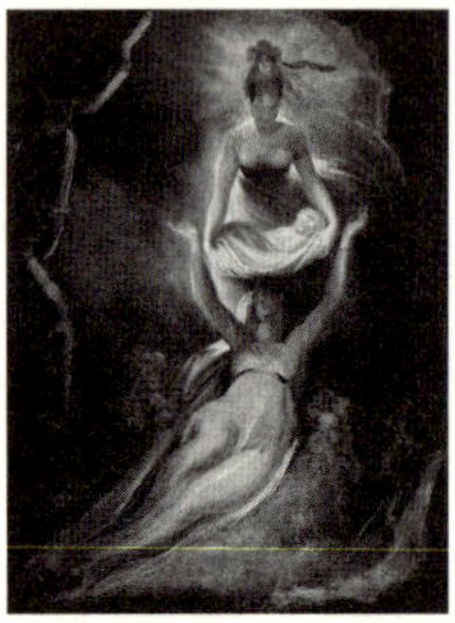

Cat. 23 *Titania Shows Amanda her Son, Born in the Grotto*, 1804–05
oil on canvas, 61 × 45 cm
Zurich, Städtische Kunstsammlung, 4965 (Schiff 1225)

Engraved by Charles Warren, 1806 (Weinglass 251)

Christoph Martin Wieland, *Oberon*, VIII, 73–74

For the last time her higher beating heart / Thrills with a short and softly-silenc'd pain – / The forms are fled away – she swoons again – / And now, without remembrance of a smart, / Wakes to soft notes, and seems afar to hear / Their low-lull'd echoes dying from the ear. / The sister forms are vanish'd from her view, / Alone before her, rob'd in roseate hue, / The gracious elfine queen soft-smiling deigns appear.

Within her arms repos'd a new-born child: / She gives it to Amanda – then, as blown / At distance, in a wink away is flown: Sweet odours breathe where late the fairy smil'd – . / The dreamer opes her disenchanted eyes, / And darts her hand, while now the vision flies, / To catch the hem that gilds her robe of light – / In vain – the whole is vanish'd from her sight – / Her hand but grasps the air – Amanda lonely lies?

(Wieland 1805, vol. 2, pp. 85–86)

Stranded on the desolate island, Huon and Amanda (Rezia) suffer many a hardship, but continue to enjoy the new-found pleasure of physical love. This changes when they encounter the old hermit Alphonso, who encourages Huon to calm Oberon's wrath by exercising sexual abstinence and seeking distraction in hard work. In the meantime Amanda is pregnant with a son and withdraws to a grotto to give birth. There she has a vision of Titania, Oberon's abandoned consort, who just happens to have chosen the same island as a refuge. Unknown to Huon and Armanda, she has for some time been carefully following their exploits, since the couple's unswerving love in the face of all manner of trials has led her to hope for deliverance from her own amorous tribulations. Amanda, waking from her dream, finds the little Huonet lying in her lap.

Fuseli avails himself of one of his favourite compositional devices in the figures of Titania, Huonet and Amanda, using poses, gestures and gazes to bind them together in a single towering group in the centre of the picture (see, for example, cats 4, 49). Moreover, Amanda's theatrically uplifted arms – inspired, among other models, by Raphael's *The Fire in the Borgo* in der Stanza dell'Incendio in the Vatican – is one of his standard motifs. The shape of the entrance to the grotto echoes the opposing gestures of the two main figures in a telling visual equivalent of Huonet's birth, yet narrative logic suffers as a result of the contrived effect of the overall arrangement: Amanda, for instance, is scarcely able to glimpse Titania standing behind her and sees little more of her new-born son than the end of his swaddling clothes. GD

References: Schiff 1973, vol. 1, p. 327. – Hamburg 1974, pp. 190–91.

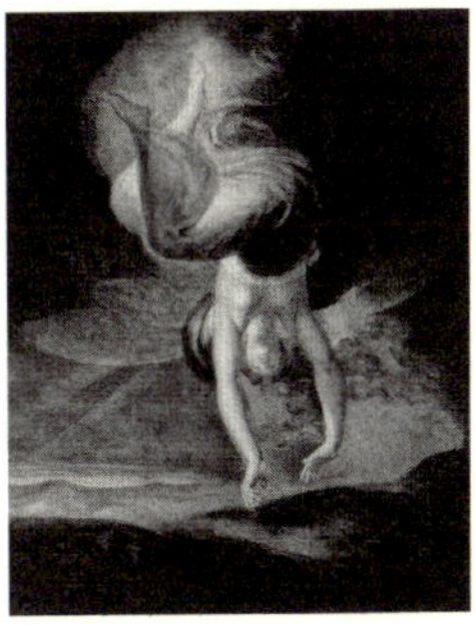

Cat. 24 *Titania Finds the Magic Ring on the Shore*, 1804–05
oil on canvas, 61 × 45 cm
Zurich, Kunsthaus Zürich, 1923, 1575 (Schiff 1226)

Engraved by James Heath, 1806 (Weinglass 253)

Christoph Martin Wieland, *Oberon*, X, 2–3

Titania hears him, wrapt in misty air, / From the far wood in long deep pauses sigh: / She sees the wretch in silent anguish die, / And weeps, and flies away in mute despair. / In vain warm sympathies her soul expand: / In vain she ventures near– a viewless hand / Still drives her back – yet, as she leaves the shore, / Her last long look that rolls the island o'er / Darts on a ring of gold that glitters on the sand.

Reft from Amanda's hand, the ring unseen / Dropt as she struggled with the pirate train; / And as Titania seizes it again, How beat the bosom of the fairy queen! / 'Hail! talisman! by elf and spright ador'd! / 'Soon shall our fate be full, to love restor'd / 'We shall again our nuptial promise flight! / 'This once united, shall again unite, / 'And crown thee, O belov'd! once more my sov'reign lord!'

(Wieland 1805, vol. 2, p. 122)

In her struggle with her abductors Amanda (Rezia) loses the ring that Huon had given her as a mark of their union – the selfsame ring that he had taken from the giant Angulaffer in a previous exploit and that, unbeknownst to him and Armanda, is in fact Oberon's wedding ring. The painting shows how Titania, hovering above the island, finds it and takes it, a stroke of good fortune that nourishes her hopes of rapid reconciliation with her consort.

In more than one respect the image differs from all the other *Oberon* illustrations. In the first place, it contains only a single figure, an entirely self-contained figure not communicating with or related at all to anyone else. In addition, and more importantly, it represents one of the rare instances in Fuseli's oeuvre of a direct borrowing from his younger fellow artist William Blake. Titania, existing outside natural laws, as befits a winged fairy queen, hovers upside-down in the air as she gazes pensively at the precious token of her love. The figure is derived from that of a pearl fisher in Blake's illustrations to Edward Young's *Night-Thoughts* (V, 246), published in 1797, with only the position of the legs and the body's modelling altered. A very similar figure, albeit rising rather than descending, is to be found among the resurrected in Michelangelo's *Last Judgement* in the Sistine Chapel. GD

References: Schiff 1973, vol. 1, pp. 289, 327. – Zürich 2007a, p. 66.

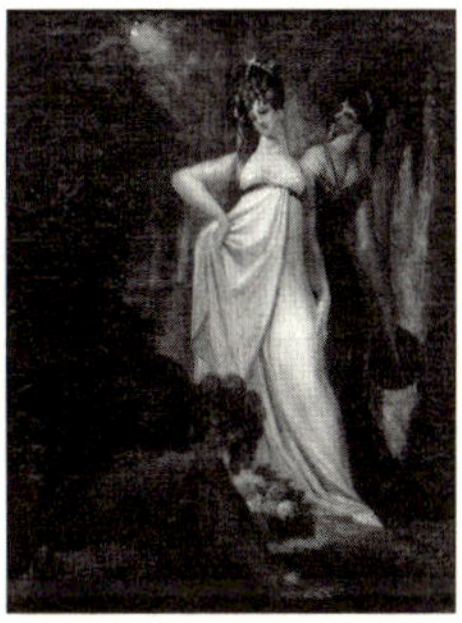

Cat. 25 *Huon, Disguised as a Gardener, Meets Sultana Almansaris Accompanied by Nadine*, 1804–05
oil on canvas, 61 × 45 cm
Lucerne, Kunstmuseum Luzern, L 2007.55x (Schiff 1227)

Engraved by Robert Hartley Cromek, 1806 (Weinglass 254)

Christoph Martin Wieland, *Oberon*, XI, 13–14

The fair sultana naturally starts To see a man, a stranger in her way – / 'What dost thou here?' while passion's fiery ray / Flash'd from her eye, and shot indignant darts / Of pow'r to strike with death each timid slave – / But Huon dar'd th' impending danger brave, / Dar'd with sunk eyelid near the goddess draw, / And lowly bending down, with noble awe, / The fruits and fragrant flowers a graceful offering gave.

''Tis true – for her he had transgress'd the time, / 'To cull for her an offering had presum'd, / 'Fruits of fair growth, and flowers that freshly bloom'd; / 'Had he too rashly dar'd, too great the crime, 'His life must expiate the zealous deed.' – / Yet her soft look a milder death decreed, / While at her feet the beauteous gard'ner lies: / Fixt on his charms she feasts her ravish'd eyes, / And seems with tardy pace unwilling to proceed.

(Wieland 1805, vol. 2, p. 155)

After her abduction Amanda (Rezia) is sold to Almansor, the sultan of Tunis. He is captivated by her beauty, arousing the jealousy of his wife Almansaris. Huon, who has been brought to Tunis by order of Oberon, adopts a false name and, in order to search for his beloved, gains employment as a gardener in the extensive harem precincts. Men are forbidden on pain of death to enter the harem after sunset because at night the sultana and her attendants habitually stroll there and bathe naked. Surprised one day by the quickly lengthening shadows, Huon is discovered at twilight by Almansaris, but succeeds in talking his way out of punishment. The sultana falls in love with the handsome young man and makes several attempts to seduce him. This is the final trial facing the heroic couple.

Fuseli focuses on the ironic and openly erotic tone of the text rather than on the mortal danger facing Huon. The sultana, whose charms Wieland praises in great detail, towers above the hero lying at her feet with the grandeur of a seductress as threatening as she is enticing. Her attendant's suggestive pose indicates complicity in the sexual adventure she envisages. According to the text, Huon resists temptation out of profound love for Amanda, yet his rather exaggeratedly submissive pose could equally well be read as surrender to an Almansaris whom the artist characterises as a *femme fatale*. Her hairdo, as imposing as Titania's (see cat. 34), is capped by a crescent moon, the attribute of the goddesses Luna and Diana. This may allude to the amorous confusion sometimes said to result from the influence of the moon, which is seen shining in the background; but above all Fuseli here takes up the allusion to the goddess of the hunt inherent in the text: men who see Diana bathing are likewise rewarded with death. GD

References: Zürich 1969, p. 32. – Schiff 1973, vol. 1, p. 327.

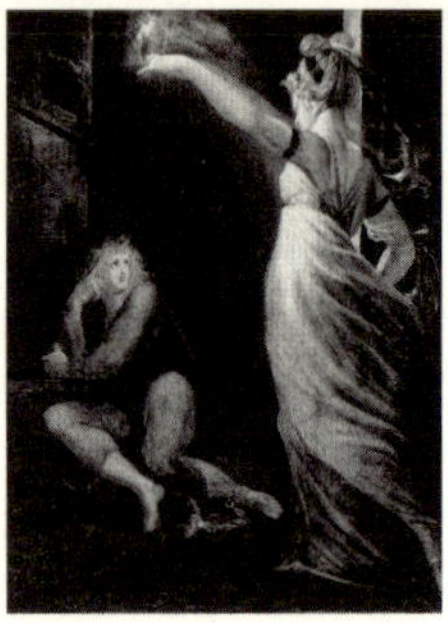

Cat. 26 *Almansaris Visits Huon in Prison*, 1804–05
oil on canvas, 61 × 45 cm
Zurich, Kunsthaus Zürich, 1923, 1576 (Schiff 1228)

Engraved by Robert Hartley Cromek, 1806 (Weinglass 254)

Christoph Martin Wieland, *Oberon*, XII, 31–35

When half the world lay wrapt in sleepless night, / A jarring sound the startled hero wakes: / With grating keys the dungeon hoarse-ly shakes, / The iron door ex-pands: a paly light / Gleams through the vaults, at distance dim descried: / He hears a step draw near – in beauty's pride / A female comes – wide floats her glistening gown, / Her hand sustains a lamp, her head a crown: / Lo! the sultana's self stands graceful at his side!

The smiling queen her beauteous hand extends – / 'Wilt thou forgive that counterfeited part, / 'When dire necessity belied my heart ? / 'O thou belov'd! my life on thine depends! / 'Oh! let this act that transient ill atone! / 'Spite of thy struggles here I come alone, / 'From death to snatch thee, from that flaming pyre, / 'Where the stern tyrant dooms thee to expire, / 'And raise thee to the height thou well deserv'st – a throne.

'Arise! for thee the sunny paths expand / 'Of empire – love conducts thee – wake to fame! / 'Let glory to the world thy deeds proclaim. / 'Go, where love guides thee by this proffer'd hand. / 'The ruthless tyrant dies! his guards retreat! / 'His slaves, like dust, shall fall before thy feet – / 'The harem to my nod obedience yields: / 'Love opes thy prison, love thy bosom shields: / 'Go forth! what love has dar'd, heroick youth! complete.'

'Desist, O queen! the plan thou deign'st propose, / 'Barbs with new pangs the shaft of tort'ring pain. / 'Ah! why against my will my soul constrain / 'To scorn each gift that from thy bounty flows? / 'No deed of guilt shall these vile fetters loose!' – / 'Can folly thus,' she cried, 'thy soul abuse? / 'Wretch! while destruc-tion tow'rs before thy sight, / 'And on yon pile death waves thy funeral light, / 'Canst thou my proffer'd hand, and throne at once refuse?'

'Tell me,' the hero answers, 'tell me, queen! / 'If I can aid thee by my flowing blood, / 'I at thy feet will pour the vital flood: / And, mark! beyond vain words, in action seen, / 'That no ungrateful wretch before thee lies – / 'My life is thine – accept the sacrifice – / 'From honour, faith, I never can depart: / 'Thou know'st me not – forget not who thou art! / 'Nor ask, oh vain request! what fate itself denies!'

(Wieland 1805, vol. 2, pp. 198–200)

The last of the twelve illustrations to Wieland's Oberon does not depict the splendid finale of the dramatic tale, as might be expected, but the last of the hero's trials, the completion of which makes possible the happy ending. Discovering Huon at a tryst arranged by his wife Almansaris without the hero's knowledge, Almansor condemns him to be burned at the stake. The besotted sultana then visits Huon in prison and makes him a tempting offer: he will be spared if he agrees to spend his life at her side and mount the sultan's throne. Huon steadfastly refuses and, since Amanda (Rezia) would similarly rather die than submit to Almansor's advances, the couple succeed in furnishing conclusive proof of their everlasting fidelity. They are thus both saved, and Oberon is able to return to Titania.

Fuseli's image revolves around the contrast between the tall sultana, driven by her desperate love as she energetically besieges Huon with her proposal, and the passive figure of the knight, sitting in the corner resignedly without hope of rescue. Comparison with the very different image of Huon presented in the pictures illustrating the beginning of the tale (see cats 19, 20) serves to point up his development from an innocent young adventurer to a morally mature hero. The artist was clearly satisfied with this pictorial invention, its drama enhanced by the lighting, because he repeated it in a number of variations (for example, Schiff 1209, 1230 and 1395). GD

References: Schiff 1973, vol. 1, p. 327. – Hamburg 1974, p. 192. – Zürich 2007a, p. 66.

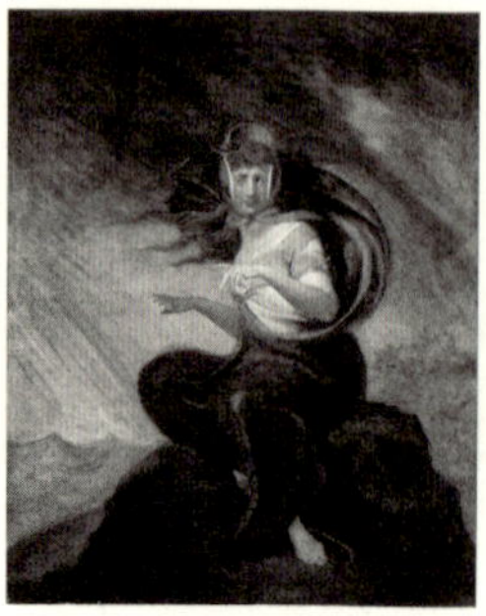

Cat. 27 *Mad Kate*, 1806–07
oil on canvas, 91.8 × 71.5 cm
Frankfurt am Main, Freies Deutsches Hochstift, Frankfurter Goethe-Museum, IV-1955–007 (Schiff 1234)

Engraved by William Bromley, 1804 (Weinglass 272)

William Cowper, *The Task*, I, 534–556

There often wanders one, whom better days / Saw better clad, in cloak of sattin trimm'd / With lace, and hat with splendid ribband bound. / A serving maid was she, and fell in love / With one who left her, went to sea and died. / Her fancy followed him through foaming waves / To distant shores, and she would sit and weep / At what a sailor suffers; fancy too, / Delusive most where warmest wishes are, / Would oft anticipate his glad return, / And dream of transports she was not to know. / She heard the doleful tidings of his death, / And never smil'd again. And now she roams / The dreary waste; there spends the livelong day, / And there, unless when charity forbids, / The livelong night.
A tatter'd apron hides, / Worn as a cloak, and hardly hides a gown / More tatter'd still; and both but ill

conceal / A bosom heaved with never-ceasing sighs. / She begs an idle pin of all she meets, / And hoards them in her sleeve; but needful food, / Though press'd with hunger oft, or comelier cloaths, / Though pinch'd with cold, asks never.— Kate is craz'd.

(Cowper 1995, pp.130–31)

William Cowper's poem *The Task* appeared in 1785. Epic in form, its observations of everyday contemporary life encompass six 'books', the first of which includes the tale of 'mad Kate'. She is well situated and loves a sailor, but her world collapses when she hears of his death at sea. Cowper's description of how she roams about as a beggar conveys a sense of dignity despite her madness. The fact that, over a period of forty years, the poet repeatedly addressed the subjects of stormy seas and sailors who perish in them may reflect his own suffering as a victim of severe depression and mental illness.

Fuseli produced the present picture only a few years after Cowper's death, as a design for an edition of his poems (Weinglass 267–74). The artist follows the text in detail, right down to the pins on Kate's sleeves, and links the unleashed forces of nature to the outbreak of human madness. Reduced to a sequence of stylised waves, the sea rages against the rock on which Kate sits. She has turned round in alarm to stare straight at the viewer, perhaps after looking out to sea. The figure and her wind-blown garment bear witness to Fuseli's study of Michelangelo during his time in Rome, most notably of the Delphic and Libyan sibyls on the Sistine Chapel ceiling. For all this image's stylisation, the artist showed such interest in the extreme psychological state it depicts that he is said to have consulted a physician on the symptoms of female love-induced frenzy. ER

References: Tomory 1972, p. 110. – Frankfurt am Main 2011, p. 62.

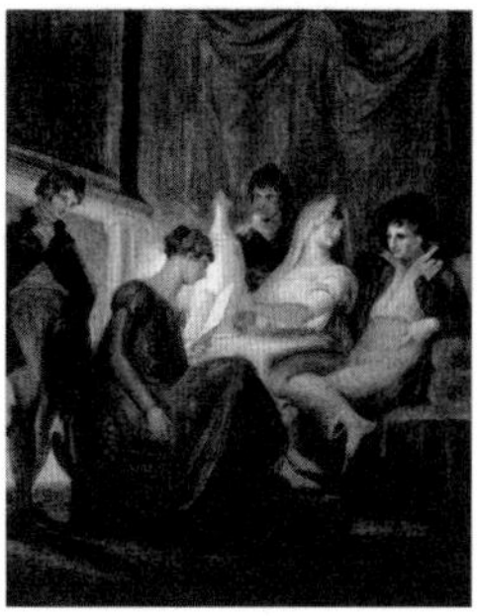

Cat. 28 *The Newspaper in the Country*, 1806–07
oil on canvas, 91.3 × 71 cm
Basle, Kunstmuseum Basel,
G 1986.14 (Schiff 1235)

Engraved by James Neagle, 1807 (Weinglass 273)

William Cowper, *The Task*, IV, 30–33

Or do we grind her still? the grand debate, / The popular harrangue, the tart reply, / The logic and the wisdom and the wit / And the loud laugh – I long to know them all.

(Cowper 1995, pp. 187–88)

The Task (1785) ranks as William Cowper's masterpiece. In the introduction the author relates how it came about: a lady had challenged him to write a piece, not in rhyming couplets, but in blank verse – in other words, in the unrhymed iambic pentameters that Milton had used in *Paradise Lost*. Starting out from a mock-serious disquisition on the sofa, Cowper proceeds to describe life in the country, simple, reclusive and largely untouched by industrial innovation. Fuseli chose for his painting a passage outlining a fireside conversation around the tea-table. Like cats 27, 29, 65, it is one of eight works by the artist reproduced as engravings to illustrate the edition of Cowper's poems published in 1807 by Joseph Johnson. Fuseli translates the meandering thoughts of the poet in concrete terms, into an image of a group of people exchanging news in an apparently tranquil atmosphere. The precise relationship of the figures to one another is unclear, however, and Fuseli's palette invests the warm intimacy conveyed by Cowper with a certain tension. Scholars are not agreed on the location: Edmond Jaloux sees in it a colonial interior in the southern United States, whereas Frederick Antal interprets it as part of a property owned by a wealthy country family. LG

References: Jaloux 1942, pp. 137–38. – Antal 1956, pp. 122–24. – Schiff 1973, vol. 1, pp. 327–34.

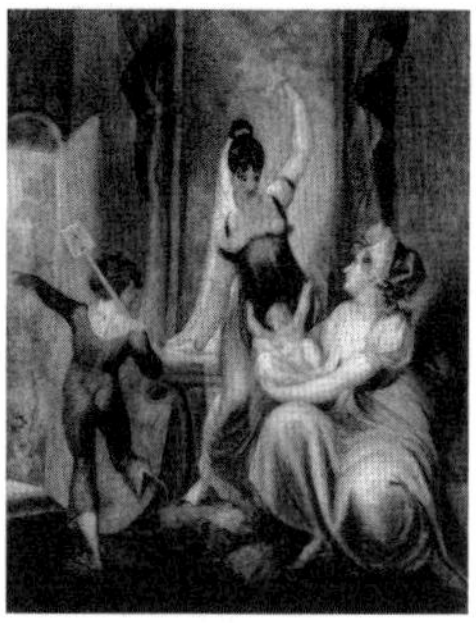

Cat. 29 *A Mother with her Family in the Country*, 1806–07
oil on canvas, 91.5 × 71.3 cm
Basle, Kunstmuseum Basel,
G 1981.6 (Schiff 1232)

Engraved by Richard Rhodes, 1807 (Weinglass 273)

William Cowper, 'Retirement', 175–190

Some minds by nature are averse to noise, / And hate the tumult half the world enjoys, / The lure of av'rice, or the pompous prize / That courts display before ambitious eyes, / The fruits that hang on pleasure's flow'ry stem, / Whate'er enchants them are no snares to them. / To them the deep recess of dusky groves, / Or forest where the deer securely roves, / The fall of waters and the song of birds, / And hills that echo to the distant herds, / Are luxuries excelling all the glare / The world can boast, and her chief fav'rites share. / With eager step and carelessly array'd, / For such a cause the poet seeks the shade, / From all he sees he catches new delight, / Pleas'd fancy claps her pinions at the sight.

Cowper 1980, pp. 382–83.

Like cats 27, 28 and 65, the painting served as the basis of an engraving in the edition of Cowper's poems issued by Joseph Johnson in 1807. The subject here came from one of the author's early didactic works, 'Retirement' (1781), written in praise of the simple rural life and the health-giving benefits of nature. The illustration is accompanied in the book by the lines 'The fruits that hang on pleasure's flow'ry stem, / Whate'er enchants them are no snares to them', a juxtaposition that emphasises the freedom of Fuseli's visual interpretation of the text. A mother stands at the centre of a domestic scene and playfully holds aloft a butterfly by the tips of her fingers, while her baby, held by a nanny, reaches out to it. On the left a boy with a spade slung over his shoulder points through an open door to the garden outside.

Fuseli and Cowper apparently never met, but the painter helped to revise Cowper's translation of Homer and the two men held each other in great esteem. Their projected collaboration on an illustrated edition of Milton's *Paradise Lost*, however, never got beyond the planning stage. LG

References: Antal 1956, pp. 122–24. – Schiff 1973, vol. 1, pp. 327–34. – Zürich 2005, p. 271, no. 13.

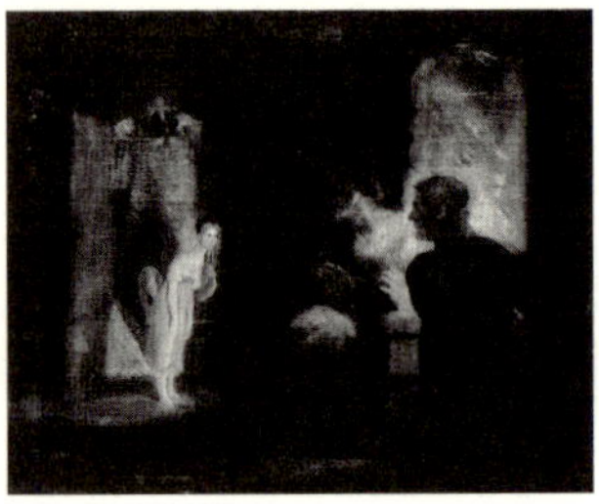

Cat. 30 *Undine Enters the House of the Fisherman and his Wife*, 1821
oil on canvas, 63.5 × 76.4 cm
Basel, Kunstmuseum Basel, 1895 (Schiff 1499)

Friedrich de la Motte Fouqué, *Undine*, chapter 2

That selfsame evening we were sitting, childless and alone, in the cottage. Neither had any pleasure in talk, nor indeed would our tears have allowed it. It seemed better to gaze into the fire and utter never a word. On a sudden, something rustled outside the door, which straightway opened; and lo! a beautiful little girl, clad in rich garments, stood there on the threshold, smiling at us. Marvellously astonied were we; as for me, I wist not whether it might be illusion or reality on which I gazed. But I saw the water dripping from her golden hair and her rich garment, and methought the pretty child had been lying in the water and needed our help.

(De la Motte Fouqué 1909, p. 16)

The subject comes from the fairy-tale novella *Undine* by the German Romantic writer Friedrich de la Motte Fouqué, published in 1811 and translated into English in 1818. The protagonist, a semi-divine water-spirit named Undine, acquires a human soul through her marriage to the knight Huldbrand. Fuseli depicts Undine's arrival at the cottage of a fisherman and his wife, who, having lost their own child, take her in and bring her up. Soaking wet, the water-sprite leans forwards as she stands on the threshold of the parlour. The couple's startled reaction is outlined by their shadowy, partly silhouetted figures, with only the hands, upper body and neck of the seated wife visible. According to Gert Schiff, the mask of the water-spirit Kühleborn, who constantly haunts Undine in her human existence, can be seen above the door.

A sketch reveals Fuseli's concern to find a visual equivalent of the flowing water that runs like a leitmotif through de la Motte Fouqué's narrative (Basel, Kupferstichkabinett, Schiff 1559). The painting's subject was not identified until publication of Schiff's catalogue raisonné in 1973 and the canvas was therefore known before that as *The Fairy, Small Fairy* or *The Nixie*. LG

References: Schiff 1973, vol. 1, pp. 380–81. – Basel 1988, pp. 78–79.

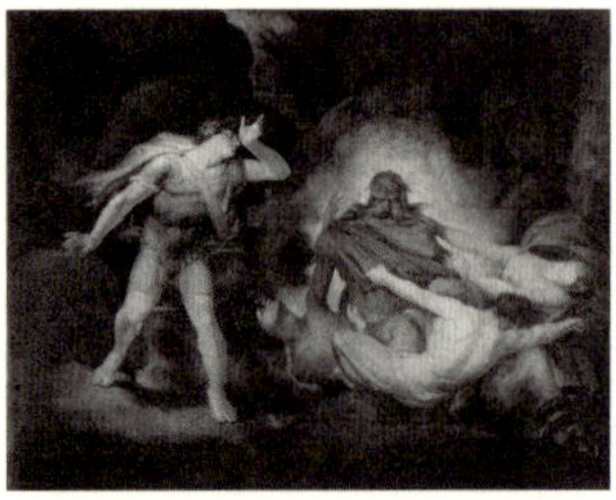

Cat. 31 *The Fire King*, c. 1801–10
oil on canvas, 99 × 124 cm
London, Victoria and Albert Museum, purchase 1885
158–1885 (Schiff 1237)

Walter Scott, 'The Fire King'

Scarce pass'd he the archway, the threshold scarce trod, / When the winds from the four points of heaven were abroad; / They made each steel portal to rattle and ring, / And, borne on the blast, came the dread Fire-King.

Full sore rock'd the cavern whene'er he drew nigh, / The fire on the altar blazed bickering and high; / In volcanic explosions the mountains proclaim / The dreadful approach of the Monarch of Flame.

Unmeasured in height, undistinguish'd in form, / His breath it was lightning, his voice it was storm, / I ween the stout heart of Count Albert was tame, / When he saw in his terrors the Monarch of Flame.

In his hand a broad falchion blue-glimmer'd through smoke, / And Mount Lebanon shook as the monarch he spoke; / "With this brand shalt thou conquer, thus long, and no more, /Till thou bend to the Cross, and the Virgin adore."

The cloud-shrouded Arm gives the weapon – and see! / The recreant receives the charm'd gift on his knee. / The thunders growl distant, and faint gleam the fires / As, born on his whirlwind, the phantom retires.

Count Albert has arm'd him the Paynim among, / Though his heart it was false, yet his arm it was strong; / And the Red-cross wax'd faint, and the Crescent came on, / From the day he commanded on Mount Lebanon.

(Scott 1801, vol. 1, pp. 66–67)

Walter Scott wrote the ballad 'The Fire King' for *Tales of Wonder*, an anthology of horror poems catering to the taste for Gothic novels that was put together by Matthew Gregory Lewis and published in 1801. It tells the story of the crusader Count Albert who, imprisoned in the Holy Land, falls in love with the sultan's daughter, renounces his faith for her sake and enters into a pact with the eponymous Fire King. In a cave this terrifying creature gives him a sword that renders him invincible as long as he does not pray to the Cross or the Virgin Mary. Later, after unwittingly killing Rosalie, his former betrothed, Albert unintentionally breaks this pact with the devil and pays for it with his life.

The circumstances and date of the painting's genesis are both obscure. Choosing to depict the moment at which the Fire King appears, Fuseli once more provides evidence of his freely inventive approach to written sources. The grim monster rises like a prince of hell from a sea of flames, its glow forming an effective foil for his figure and investing his appearance with a ghostly aura (see also cat. 48). Four more or less naked, wildly twisting and turning women hold on to the Fire King. Not mentioned by Scott, they were taken over by the artist from his *Fatal Sisters*, an illustration of Thomas Gray's poem of that title (Schiff 1312). Gert Schiff saw in them spirits tearing off the Fire King's robe in order to 'uncover him in his full majesty'. Yet they might also symbolise the lost souls of the damned, especially since more hands are visible at the edge of the canvas and since a hellish serpent is evidently preventing one of the women from escaping the blaze. The apostate crusader, just descended and shortly to dwell among the lost souls, stands opposite the Fire King and is appalled by what Scott calls the 'terror' of the scene. He sports antique-style armour instead of the turban and caftan he had worn after his change of faith. Fuseli's visualisation of the Fire King's horrific appearance as described by Scott is compellingly original, but the figure of Albert, conceived as a counterpoint to the monstrous creature but exhibiting curiously limp gestures, teeters on the brink of empty theatricality. GD

References: Schiff 1973, vol. 1, pp. 69, 343. – Tomory 1974, p. 122. – London 1975, p. 108. – Altick 1985, p. 425. – http://collections.vam.ac.uk/item/O17298/the-fire-king-oil-painting-fuseli-henry/ (accessed 12 May 2018).

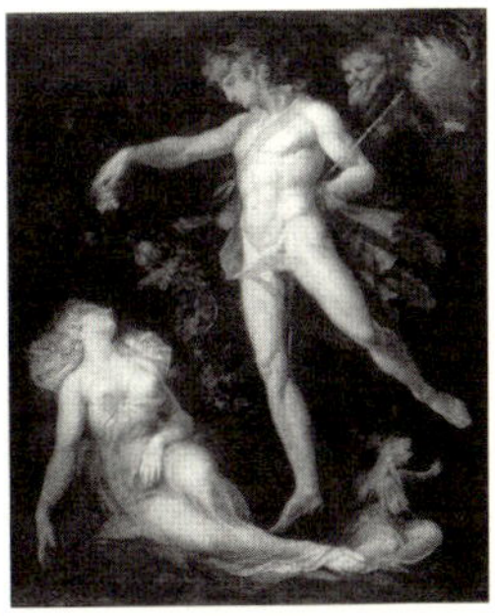

Cat. 32 *Oberon Squeezing the Juice onto Titania's Eyelids*, 1793
oil on canvas, 169 × 135 cm
Zurich, Kunsthaus Zürich, Vereinigung Zürcher Kunstfreunde, 1993, 1984/56 (Schiff 884)

Painting no. 1 in the Woodmason's Shakespeare Gallery
Engraved by Richard Rhodes, 1794 (Weinglass 132)

William Shakespeare, *A Midsummer Night's Dream*, II, 2

Oberon: What thou seest when thou dost wake, / Do it for thy true-love take, / Love and languish for his sake: / Be it ounce, or cat, or bear, / Pard, or boar with bristled hair, / In thy eye that shall appear / When thou wakest, it is thy dear: / Wake when some vile thing is near.

(Shakespeare 1995c, p. 54)

Oberon, king of the fairies, plays a trick on his queen, Titania, after arguing with her. While she sleeps, he squeezes juice from a flower onto her eyelids and casts a spell on her: she will fall in love with the first living being she sees on waking. This turns out to be none of the creatures mentioned in the text, but Bottom, a weaver given an ass's head by another magic spell.

The painting is one of five that Fuseli contributed to James Woodmason's Irish Shakespeare Gallery. Woodmason, a London publisher and bookseller, had lost his family and livelihood in a fire and was seeking to capitalise on the success of John Boydell's similar venture. Gert Schiff identifies the source of the elegantly Mannerist figure of Oberon as the image of a faun reproduced in the *Bronzi di Ercolano* (1767–71), a volume dedicated to the sensational finds made at the ancient Roman site of Herculaneum. The subtle colours, contrasting the ivory-coloured figures with a dark background, make one wonder whether the dramatic chiaroscuro effects in many of Fuseli's works might not have increased over time, as a result of darkening colours, for example, fading red pigments, or partial cleaning. ER

References: Schiff 1973, vol. 1, p. 188. – Essay by Caroline Rae in the present volume.

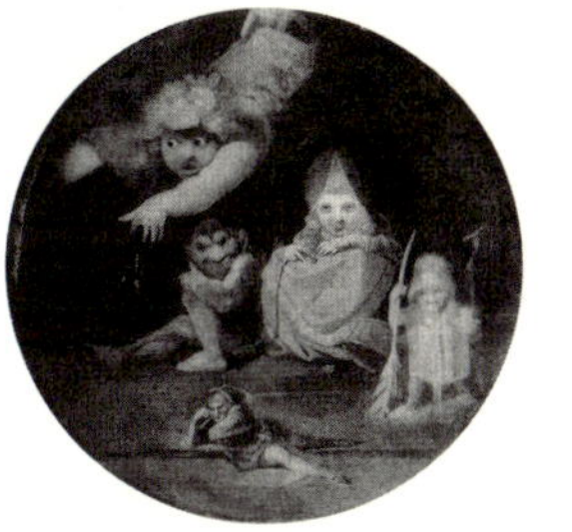

Cat. 33 *Cobweb*, 1785–86
oil on canvas, diam. 45.7 cm
Private collection, Switzerland (Schiff 752)

Cobweb is one of several tondi that Fuseli painted in 1785–86. Two of them, the present canvas and its pendant, feature the fairies in *A Midsummer Night's Dream*; another four address subjects taken from Shakespeare's *A Winter's Tale*. As in the other pictures relating to *A Midsummer Night's Dream*, *Cobweb* attests to his fascination with the fairy myths of British folklore. Shakespeare's influence often caused the queen of the fairies to be called either Titania or Queen Mab, and occasionally the two figures were conflated, but with Fuseli both are quite distinct characters. His versions of Queen Mab vary considerably, ranging from the Rococo-like *Faery Mab* inspired by Milton's *L'Allegro* (cat. 58) to the small, artful-looking creature in the present painting. Seated on the ground to the right of centre, she holds a gnome on a chain grasped in her hand. On her left is Cobweb, with a feather as a broom. Mustardseed, another elf at the court of the fairy queen, appears in the foreground, while the goblin Puck hovers over the group. Fuseli painted the picture for his friend William Roscoe, a notable collector, writer and historian who eventually acquired fifteen works by the artist. ER

References: Becker 2005, pp. 122–23. – Gibson and Esra 2014, pp. 79–80.

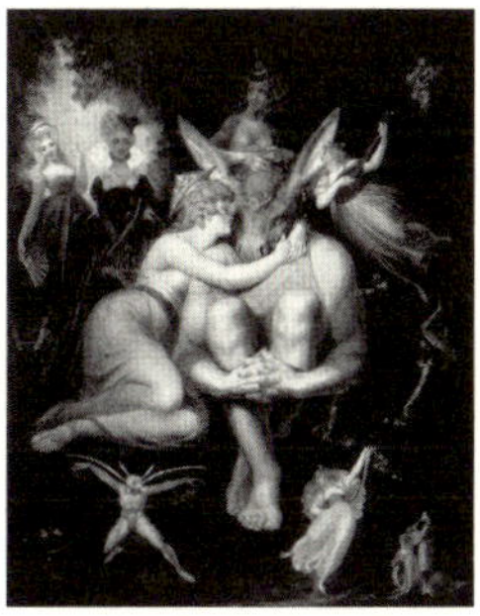

Cat. 34 *Titania and Bottom*, 1793–94
oil on canvas, 169 × 135 cm
Zurich, Kunsthaus Zürich, Vereinigung Zürcher Kunstfreunde, 1941, 2543 (Schiff 885)

Painting no. 2 in Woodmason's Irish Shakespeare Gallery
Engraved by Richard Rhodes, 1794 (Weinglass 133)

William Shakespeare, *A Midsummer Night's Dream*, IV, 1

Titania: Come, sit thee down upon this flowery bed, / While I thy amiable cheeks do coy, / And stick musk roses in thy sleek smooth head, / And kiss thy fair large ears, my gentle joy. / Bottom: Where's Peaseblossom? Peaseblossom: Ready. / Bottom: Scratch my head Peaseblossom. Where's Monsieur Cobweb? / Cobweb: Ready.

(Shakespeare 1995c, p. 115)

This was the second painting that Fuseli contributed to the twenty-seven in James Woodmason's Irish Shakespeare Gallery. It shows the fairy queen Titania after she has fallen in love with the ass-headed weaver Bottom (see cat. 35). Fuseli surrounds the unlikely couple with a company of dancing and music-making goblins and fairies. Some of them, including Peaseblossom, who scratches Bottom's head, appear in contemporary, Rococo-style costume. Gert Schiff identified the figure wearing armour on the right as Cobweb, who is slaying a bee on a thistle and removing its honey for Bottom. Since *A Midsummer Night's Dream* could not be seen on stage in an authentic form at the time the picture was painted, it may be assumed that Fuseli relied on printed sources and his own imagination. Unlike the many-figured narrative paintings on subjects from the play that he produced for John Boydell, the present canvas focuses on the central couple and grants their companions a more ornamental character. ER

References: Hamburg 1974, p. 157. – Sillars 2006, pp. 232–33. – Best.-Kat. Zürich 2007, p. 64

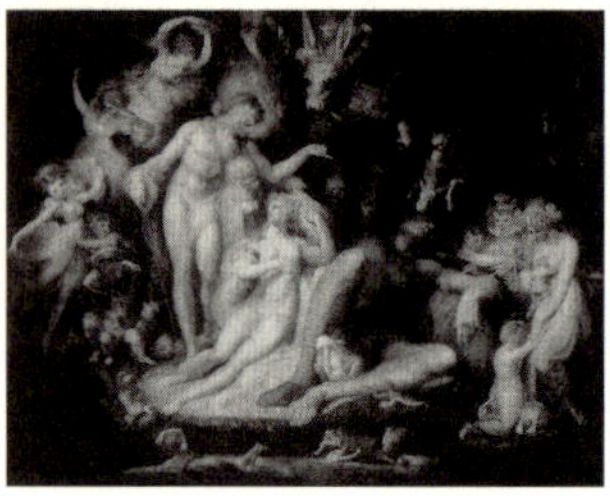

Cat. 35 *Titania's Awakening*, 1785–90
oil on canvas, 222 × 280 cm
Winterthur, Kunst Museum, Geschenk des Galerievereins, 1935, 755 (Schiff 754)

Painting no. 3 in Boydell's Shakespeare Gallery
Stipple engraving by Thomas Ryder, 1803 (Weinglass 119)

William Shakespeare, *A Midsummer Night's Dream*, IV, 1

Oberon: Be as thou wast wont to be; / See as thou wast wont to see: / Dian's bud o'er Cupid's flower / Hath such force and blessed power. / Now, my Titania; wake you, my sweet queen. / Titania: My Oberon! what visions have I seen! / Methought I was enamour'd of an ass.

(Shakespeare 1995c, p. 118)

Fuseli painted nine canvases for the publisher John Boydell's Shakespeare Gallery, three on subjects from *A Midsummer Night's Dream*. From 1791 the present example formed part of the permanent display in the gallery. It shows the fairy queen Titania awaking from her magic sleep to describe to Oberon the things she believes happened to her in a dream. Fuseli also produced a picture of the previous scene, in which Titania commands her elves to care for the ass-headed Bottom, with whom she has fallen in love as a result of Oberon's magic juice (London, Tate). In the Winterthur canvas the fairy king points by way of explanation to the sleeping Bottom. The ass's head, from which Puck has freed him, hovers in the centre of the composition. Approaching Shakespeare's text associatively, Fuseli expands the playwright's fairy world to encompass a whole company of elves and goblins, which, in contrast to the differently conceived pictures on *A Midsummer Night's Dream* that he was to paint for James Woodmason's Shakespeare Gallery (see cats 32, 34, 44, 48), appear as an integral part of the scene. The result of an imaginative engagement with a literary source, the picture also exemplifies Fuseli's surprising conjunctions of subjects involving traditional folklore with the visual legacy of classical antiquity evidenced by the figures. ER

References: London 2006, p. 160. – Dias 2013, pp. 139–40.

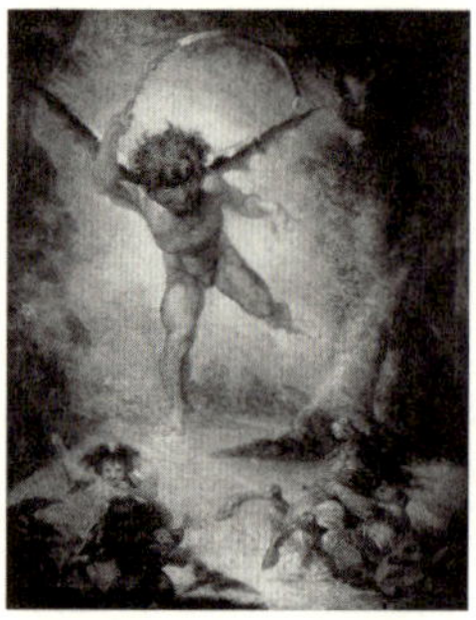

Cat. 36 *Robin Goodfellow (Puck)*, 1787–90
oil on canvas, 106 × 82 cm
Schaffhausen, Museum zu Allerheiligen, Stadt Schaffhausen, A604 (Schiff 750)

Painting no. 9 in Boydell's Shakespeare Gallery
Engraved by James Parker, 1799 (Weinglass 125)

William Shakespeare, *A Midsummer Night's Dream*, II, 1

Fairy: Either I mistake your shape and making quite, / Or else you are that shrewd and knavish sprite / Call'd Robin Goodfellow: are not you he / That frights the maidens of the villagery; / Skim milk, and sometimes labour in the quern / And bootless make the breathless housewife churn; / And sometime make the drink to bear no barm; / Mislead night-wanderers, laughing at their harm? / Those that Hobgoblin call you and sweet Puck, / You do their work, and they shall have good luck: / Are not you he??

(Shakespeare 1995c, p. 36)

Three of the nine pictures that Fuseli painted in 1786–90 for the Shakespeare Gallery set up by the engravings publisher John Boydell address subjects from *A Midsummer Night's Dream*. They consist of two compositions with a large number of figures, *Titania and Bottom* (London, Tate) and *Titania's Awakening* (cat. 35), and the present work, listed as no. 9 in the gallery.

Puck, in the folklore of the Elizabethan era the name given to a domestic sprite or goblin, is in Shakespeare's play a tiny vassal of the fairy king Oberon. Also known as Robin Goodfellow or Friar Puck, he traditionally possessed both positive and negative characteristics. Fuseli focuses in his painting on Puck's mischievous habit of leading travellers astray at night. His huge figure, sporting bat's wings and a devilish grin, gleefully hovers above a horseman he has caused to fall from his mount while crossing a stream. The artist may have derived the scene from Milton's description of an evil spirit in *Paradise Lost* (IX, 634–642), while the belt glittering with pearls and stars that the demon wields doubtless alludes to words spoken by Puck in Act II of *A Midsummer Night's Dream*: 'I'll put a girdle round about the earth in forty minutes.' ER

References: Schaffhausen 1989, pp. 100–101. – Bown 2001, pp. 27–28.

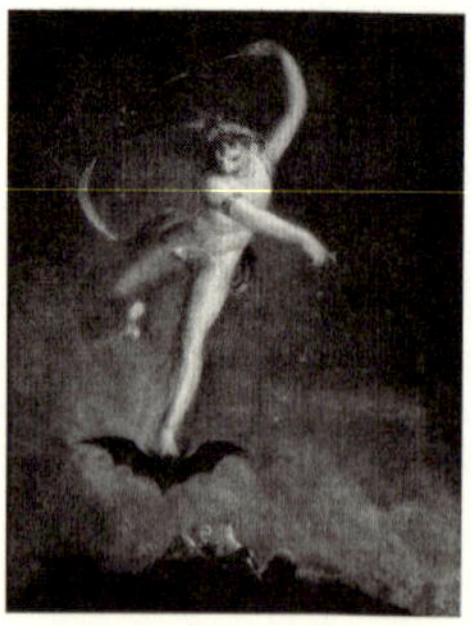

Cat. 37 *Ariel*, 1800–10
oil on canvas, 92.7 × 71.5 cm
Washington, D. C., Folger Shakespeare Library, FPa22 (Schiff 1208)

William Shakespeare, *The Tempest*, V, 1
Ariel (*sings and helps [Prospero] to attire*):

Where the bee sucks, there suck I; / In a cowslip's bell I lie; / There I couch when owls do cry. / On the bat's back I do fly / After summer merrily. / Merrily, merrily shall I live now / Under the blossom that hangs on the bough.

(Shakespeare 1996, p. 148)

Ariel is an 'airy spirit' bound to serve Prospero after the prince and magician is stranded on an island with his daughter, Miranda, when their ship capsizes in a storm. In the course of the play Ariel causes Miranda to fall in love with Ferdinand, Prince of Naples.

'On the bat's back I do fly' sings Ariel, and Fuseli depicts him doing just that. Prospero, however, is missing from the painting, which at the bottom shows Miranda and Ferdinand lying in each other's arms – a motif later repeated by the artist in a drawing (Kunstmuseum Basel, Kupferstichkabinett; Schiff 1555).

Ariel's strikingly exuberant pose recalls that of *Puck* (cat. 36), a similarity that Stuart Sillars sees as reflecting the 'moral dualism' of both beings. Pentimenti in the area of the legs show Fuseli trying out variations on the pose. The figure also brings to mind Raphael's painting *St Michael Vanquishing Satan* and Giambologna's sculpture *Mercury* (both Paris, Musée du Louvre). CB

References: Washington 1993, pp. 64–65. – Sillars 2006, pp. 240–43.

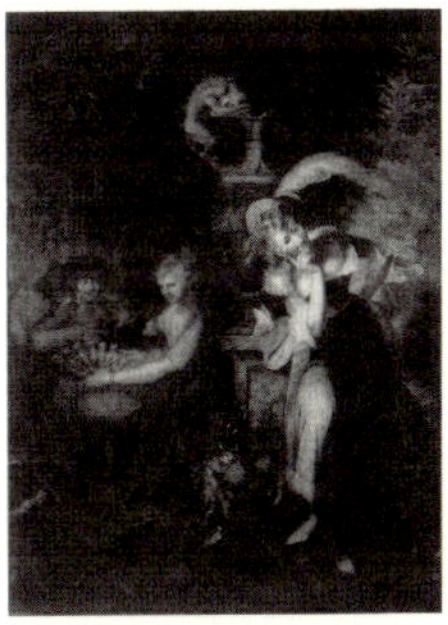

Cat. 38 *Beatrice Eavesdropping on Hero and Ursula*, 1789–91
oil on canvas, 222 × 159 cm
Gemäldegalerie Alte Meister, Staatliche Kunstsammlungen Dresden, 798 E (Schiff 748)

Mezzotint reproduction by John Jones, 1791 (Weinglass 113)

William Shakespeare, Much Ado About Nothing, III, I

Hero: Now, Ursula, when Beatrice doth come, / As we do trace this alley up and down, / Our talk must only be of Benedick. / When I do name him, let it be thy part / To praise him more than ever man did merit: / My talk to thee must be how Benedick / Is sick in love with Beatrice. Of this matter / Is little Cupid's crafty arrow made, / That only wounds by hearsay. / *Enter Beatrice, behind* / Now begin; / For look where Beatrice, like a lapwing, runs / Close by the ground, to hear our conference. / Ursula: The pleasant'st angling is to see the fish / Cut with her golden oars the silver stream, / And greedily devour the treacherous bait: / So angle we for Beatrice; who even now / Is couched in the woodbine coverture. / Fear you not my part of the dialogue. / Hero: Then go we near her, that her ear lose nothing / Of the false sweet bait that we lay for it. / *Approaching the bower* / No, truly, Ursula, she is too disdainful; / I know her spirits are as coy and wild / As haggerds of the rock.

(Shakespeare 2001, pp. 80/82)

With the exception of this scene, *Much Ado About Nothing* and its humorous amorous intrigues do not figure in Fuseli's oeuvre. Beatrice and Benedick are to be tricked into admitting their love for each other. Hero and Ursula are shown discussing Benedick's alleged affection for Beatrice while fully aware that the latter is listening to them, a fact conveyed in the painting by Hero's sideways gaze and Ursula's gesture. A number of fantastical, almost grotesque elements appear in the evening garden setting.

Fuseli painted two versions of *Beatrice Eavesdropping on Hero and Ursula*. That shown in 1789 at the Royal Academy exhibition in Somerset House was probably the present canvas, more striking in its large format and its colour than the other. In a critique published anonymously in the *Analytical Review* the artist discussed in detail the figure of Beatrice in the picture, noting that he had depicted her as a spirited young lady, playful in her innocence and thoroughly decorous in her 'propriety and dignity'. Gert Schiff, however, sees Fuseli's Beatrice as marked by an 'irrepressible desire to uncover the secrets of others' and accuses the artist of 'pharisaic self-promotion'. CB

References: Posse 1927. – Schiff 1973, vol. 1, p. 147. – Dresden 1992, pp. 205. – Mamiano di Traversetolo 1997, pp. 84–85.

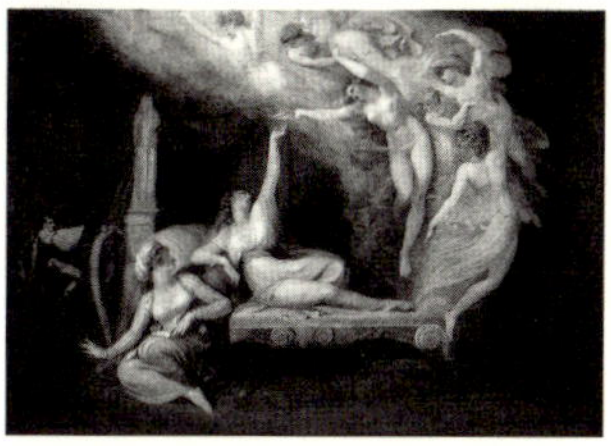

Cat. 39 *Queen Katherine's Dream*, 1781
oil on canvas, 151.1 × 212.1 cm
Lytham St Annes Art Collection, Fylde Borough Council, 52 (not in Schiff)

William Shakespeare, *Henry VIII*, 4, 2

Griffith: [*to the woman*] She is asleep. Good wench, let's sit down quiet / For fear we wake her. Softly, gentle Patience. / *The vision. Enter, solemnly tripping one after another, six personages clad in white robes, wearing on their heads garlands of bays, and golden visors on their faces. They carry branches of bays or palm in their hands. They first congé unto Katherine, then dance; and, at certain changes, the first two hold a spare garland over her head; at which the other four make reverent curtsies. Then the two that held the garland deliver the same to the other next two, who observe the same order in their changes, and holding the garland over her head. Which done, they deliver the same garland to the last two, who likewise observe the same order. At which, as it were by inspiration, she makes in her sleep signs of rejoicing, and holdeth up her hands to heaven. And so in their dancing vanish, carrying the garland with them. The music continues.* / Katherine: [*waking*] Spirits of peace, where are ye? Are ye all gone, / And leave me here in wretchedness behind ye?

(Shakespeare 1986, p. 1370)

Henry VIII (c. 1613) deals with events in 1533 that led to the crown's break with the Catholic church. Seeking divorce from Katherine of Aragon in order to marry Anne Boleyn, Henry banishes Katherine to Kimbolton Castle, where she falls ill and dies. Fuseli was the first to make the vision of eternal bliss she has shortly before her death the subject of a painting. The six dancing figures, clad in white, who appear to Katherine in a dream are shown wafting upwards elegantly into a light-filled realm. They extend a diadem to the queen, rather than the garland mentioned in the text. The space occupied by Katherine and her attendants, which resembles a stage set, is mostly plunged into darkness. Fuseli later took over some elements from this image in his paintings on *A Midsummer Night's Dream* (cats 32 and 35) and in *The Shepherd's Dream* (cat. 51). The present picture, one of seven commissioned from the artist by his patron Sir Robert Smyth, was shown at the Royal Academy in 1781 together with *Dido* (cat. 12). Another version, preserved in fragmentary form, was commissioned by the print seller and picture dealer Thomas Macklin for his never-to-be-completed Poets' Gallery (London, Victoria and Albert Museum). ER

References: London 2006, p. 152. – Gerkens 2009, pp. 67–68.

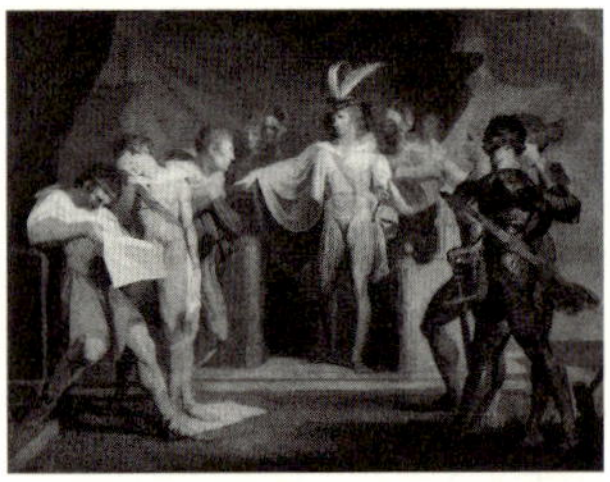

Cat. 40 *Henry V Discovering the Conspirators*, 1786–89
oil on canvas, 48.3 × 61 cm
Stratford-upon-Avon, Royal Shakespeare Company, STRPG:A:1993.50 (Schiff 725)

William Shakespeare, *Henry V*, II, 2

King Henry V: Alas, your too much love and care of me / Are heavy orisons 'gainst this poor wretch! / If little faults, proceeding on distemper, / Shall not be wink'd at, how shall we stretch our eye / When capital crimes, chew'd, swallow'd and digested, / Appear before us? We'll yet enlarge that man, / Though Cambridge, Scroop and Grey, in their dear care / And tender preservation of our person, / Would have him punished. And now to our French causes: / Who are the late commissioners? / Cambridge: I one, my lord: / Your highness bade me ask for it to-day. / Scroop: So did you me, my liege. / Grey: And I, my royal sovereign. / King Henry V: Then, Richard Earl of Cambridge, there is yours; / There yours, Lord Scroop of Masham; and, sir knight, / Grey of Northumberland, this same is yours: / Read them; and know, I know your worthiness. / My Lord of Westmoreland, and uncle Exeter, / We will aboard to night. Why, how now, gentlemen! / What see you in those papers that you lose / So much complexion? Look ye, how they change! / Their cheeks are paper. Why, what read you there / That hath so cowarded and chased your blood / Out of appearance? / Cambridge: I do confess my fault; And do submit me to your highness' mercy. / Grey, Scroop: To which we all appeal.

(Shakespeare 1999, pp. 128/130)

The canvas is probably a preparatory work for painting no. 6 in John Boydell's Shakespeare Gallery, a canvas that has not survived. A replica of this design exists in a private collection.

The almost symmetrically composed scene shows Henry V slightly off-centre. He is pointing to the document he has just passed to the conspirators, supposedly an order, but in fact an indictment for a capital offence. Cambridge is reading the document in disbelief, while the gestures of Scroop and Grey convey admission of guilt in the one case and a plea for mercy in the other. Gert Schiff notes that the three traitors' reactions seem 'rather formulaic', but the scene as a whole is convincing in psychological terms. The light, coming from the upper right, strikes the three accused men, whereas the loyal Exeter, Bedford and Westmoreland stand in the shade, the first of them with his head averted from the viewer as he draws his sword.

The composition strongly resembles that of the artist's *King Lear Casting Out his Daughter Cordelia*, no. 7 in Boydell's gallery. A small version of that painting is in Frankfurt am Main (Goethe-Museum; Schiff 740). CB

References: Merchant 1959, p. 237. – Schiff 1973, vol. 1, p. 144.

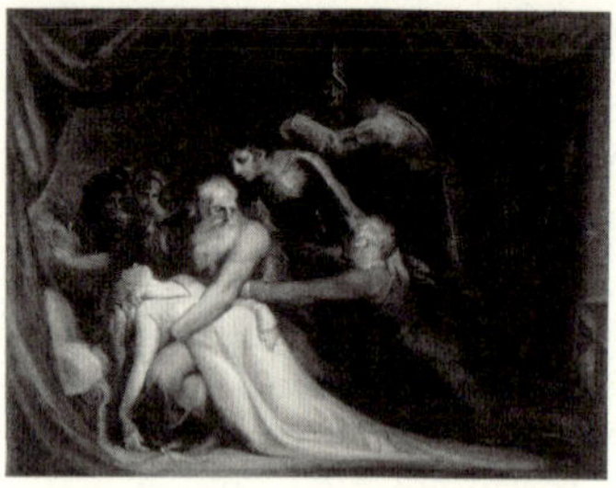

Cat. 41 *The Death of Cordelia*, 1810–20
oil on canvas, 117.1 × 142.6 cm
Frankfurt am Main, Freies Deutsches Hochstift / Frankfurter Goethe-Museum, on loan from the Adolf and Luisa Haeuser Foundation for Art and Cultural Affairs, IV-2003–005 (not in Schiff)

William Shakespeare, *King Lear*, V, 3

Lear: Howl, howl, howl, howl! O, you are men of stones: / Had I your tongues and eyes, I'ld use them so / That heaven's vault should crack. She's gone for ever! / I know when one is dead, and when one lives; / She's dead as earth. Lend me a looking-glass; / If that her breath will mist or stain the stone, / Why, then she lives. / Kent: Is this the promised end? / Edgar: Or image of that horror? / Albany: Fall, and cease! / Lear: This feather stirs; she lives! if it be so, / It is a chance which does redeem all sorrows / That ever I have felt. / Kent *(kneeling)*: O my good master! / Lear: Prithee, away. / Edgar: 'Tis noble Kent, your friend. / Lear: A plague upon you, murderers, traitors all! / I might have saved her; now she's gone for ever! / Cordelia, Cordelia! stay a little. Ha! / What is't thou say'st? Her voice was ever soft, / Gentle, and low, an excellent thing in woman. / I kill'd the slave that was a-hanging thee. / Captain: 'Tis true, my lords, he did. / Lear: Did I not, fellow? / I have seen the day, with my good biting falchion / I would have made them skip: I am old now, / And these same crosses spoil me. Who are you? / Mine eyes are not o' the best: I'll tell you straight.

(Shakespeare 1997, pp. 260/262)

Recovering his sanity, the old Lear realises that he had behaved unjustly in banishing his daughter Cordelia and his faithful follower Kent. Cordelia has been hanged in her prison by order of Edmund and now lies dead in her father's lap. Kent, Edgar and Albany mourn with Lear. Fuseli conveys a sense of Cordelia's innocence and loyalty through the white of her robe and a dramatic use of chiaroscuro. Her pose and attire recall those of the sleeping woman in *The Nightmare* (cat. 69). The main figures, arranged in the form of a pyramid, are accommodated in a stage-like setting. Red curtains flank the scene, alluding to the location of the action – the British military camp near Dover – and also evoking the theatre, even if the action in Fuseli's day customarily took place on the apron stage, not behind the proscenium arch. For Erin C. Blake, the curtains enhance the image's portrait character, especially as paintings of specific scenes could be read as 'portraits' of Shakespeare's plays. In addition, Petra Maisak and Gerhard Kölsch convincingly interpret the two main figures as representing a secular Pietà in reverse, as it were, with the father lamenting the daughter as a victim of his wrongdoing.

A pen and ink drawing shows that Fuseli had already addressed the subject in Rome in 1774 (Kunsthaus Zürich; Schiff 465). It attests to his long-standing knowledge of Shakespeare's original plays, for in the eighteenth century *King Lear* was performed in an adaptation by Nahum Tate in which neither Cordelia nor Lear dies. CB

References: Mamiano di Traversetolo 1997, pp. 106–07. – Frankfurt am Main 2011, pp. 62–65. – Blake 2011. – Maisak 2017b.

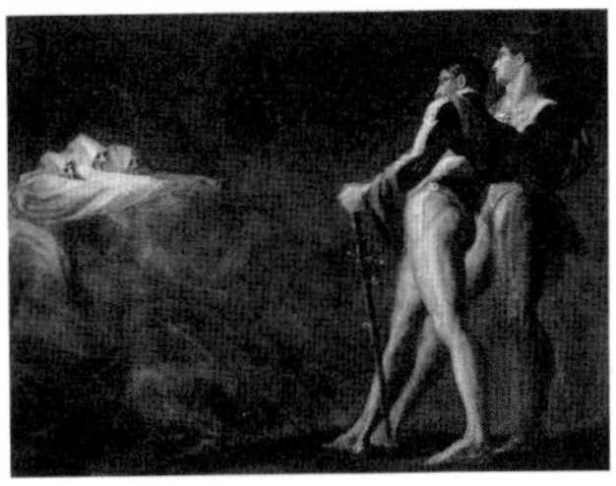

Cat. 42 *The Three Witches Appearing to Macbeth and Banquo*, 1800–10
oil on canvas, 87.3 × 111.7 cm
Private collection (Schiff 1205)

William Shakespeare, *Macbeth*, I, 3

Macbeth: So foul and fair a day I have not seen. / Banquo: How far is't call'd to Forres? What are these / So wither'd and so wild in their attire, / That look not like the inhabitants o' the earth, / And yet are on't? Live you? or are you aught / That man may question? You seem to understand me, / By each at once her chappy finger laying / Upon her skinny lips: you should be women, / And yet your beards forbid me to interpret That you are so. / Macbeth: Speak, if you can: what are you?

(Shakespeare 1995a, p. 18)

Fuseli's engagement with *Macbeth* revolved primarily around the three witches, whose fateful prophecies ultimately bring about the tragic hero's downfall. In 1783 the artist depicted the 'weird sisters' in isolation (cat. 43), then showed them for the first time in a scene from the play in a painting produced in the late 1780s for John Boydell's Shakespeare Gallery. That picture, which survives only in the form of an engraving (Schiff 1748; Weinglass 120), represents the supernatural beings appearing to Macbeth and Banquo as the generals return from battle. In a review of the Shakespeare Gallery, published anonymously, Fuseli referred to the scene as sublime and lauded Macbeth as a character too great to be daunted by an extraordinary event. He returned to the subject in 1793–94 in connection with James Woodmason's Irish Shakespeare Gallery. That version (Petworth House, National Trust; Schiff 880), in the vertical format required by Woodmason, includes part of the generals' army. The present, horizontal variant dates from Fuseli's time as Professor of Painting at the Royal Academy and focuses on the two men's encounter with the witches. ER

References: Fuseli 1789, p. 111. – Weinglass 1994, p. 137.

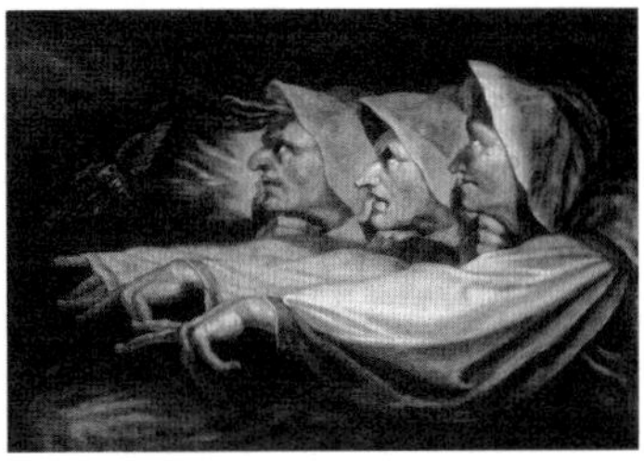

Cat. 43 *The Three Witches*, 1783
oil on canvas, 65 × 91.5 cm
Zurich, Kunsthaus Zürich, 1941 2540 (Schiff 733)

Mezzotint reproduction by John Raphael Smith, 1785 (Weinglass 73)

William Shakespeare, *Macbeth*, I, 3
See cat. 42 for literary source

Fuseli painted this picture of the three witches from *Macbeth*, his first version of the subject, in 1783. He repeated the composition, showing the figures grouped densely behind one another and pointing forwards in a threefold reiterated gesture, on several occasions. The gnarled, distorted facial features and the staggered arrangement can be traced to Leonardo da Vinci's drawings of grotesque heads as reproduced in contemporary prints. With their strikingly masculine profiles, the figures contradict their description as witches or 'weird sisters', a duality addressed by Shakespeare when he has Banquo exclaim: 'you should be women, / And yet your beards forbid me to interpret / That you are so'. Words from Aeschylus' *Eumenides* cited in another version of the painting (private collection), and presumably reproducing an original inscription by the artist, also allude to the figures' sexual ambiguity: 'yet not women, / But Gorgons rather'. The death's-head hawkmoth echoing the witches' gestures may hint at the crimes to come. Prints made Fuseli's composition widely known and variants of it even appeared in political cartoons. ER

References: Tomory 1972, pp. 95–96, no. 72 – London 2006, p. 130, no. 80 – Best.-Kat. Zürich 2007, S. 63

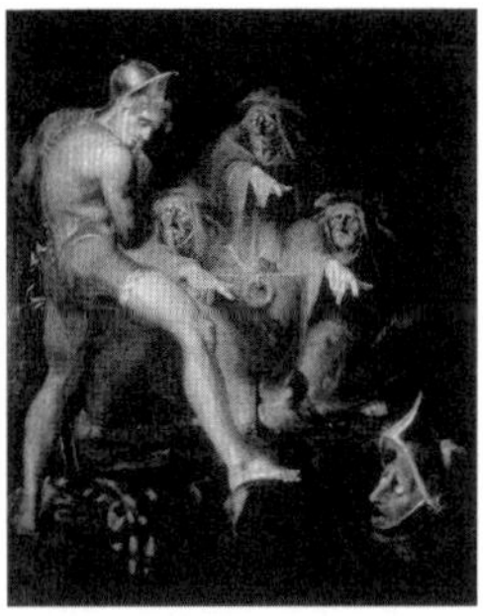

Cat. 44 *Macbeth Consulting the Vision of the Armed Head*, 1793–94
oil on canvas, 163 × 130 cm
Washington, D. C., Folger Shakespeare Library, FPa27 (Schiff 881)

Painting no. 4 in Woodmason's Shakespeare Gallery

William Shakespeare, *Macbeth*, IV, 1

Macbeth: Call 'em; let me see 'em. / First Witch: Pour in sow's blood, that hath eaten / Her nine farrow; grease that's sweaten / From the murderer's gibbet throw / Into the flame. / All: Come, high or low; / Thyself and office deftly show! / *Thunder. First Apparition, an armed Head* / Macbeth: Tell me, thou unknown power, – / First Witch: He knows thy thought: / Hear his speech, but say thou nought. / First Apparition: Macbeth! Macbeth! Macbeth! / beware Macduff; / Beware the Thane of Fife. – Dismiss me. – Enough. / *Descends*

(Shakespeare 1995a, pp. 124/126)

In his younger years, long before published translations existed, Fuseli had tried his hand at rendering *Macbeth* in German. Shakespeare's tragedy developed into one of his principal sources of inspiration, his fascination aroused in particular by its descriptions of supernatural beings. The present painting, one of five he created for James Woodmason's Irish Shakespeare Gallery, shows the first of three apparitions that fuel Macbeth's thirst for power and drive him to commit further murders. The 'armed head' conjured up by the witches warns Macbeth, now king of Scotland, to be on his guard against the nobleman Macduff. A previous version of the subject by Fuseli, produced in Rome, belongs, according to Schiff (363), among his earliest paintings.

Fuseli justified his depiction of the supernatural head as a mirror image of Macbeth by claiming that nothing is more sinister than an encounter with oneself. The painting has the vertical format stipulated by Woodmason, which facilitated the reproduction of the composition in the form of prints that could easily be incorporated into a bound publication. Fuseli's biographer, John Knowles, acquired the canvas in the artist's lifetime and reported that he had considered it one of his 'best poetical conceptions'. To Knowles he also explained that the liberties he sometimes took in interpreting literary subjects stemmed from a desire to include aspects 'deficient in the poetry'. ER

References: Knowles 1831, vol. 1, p. 189. – Washington 1993, p. 55, no. 24.

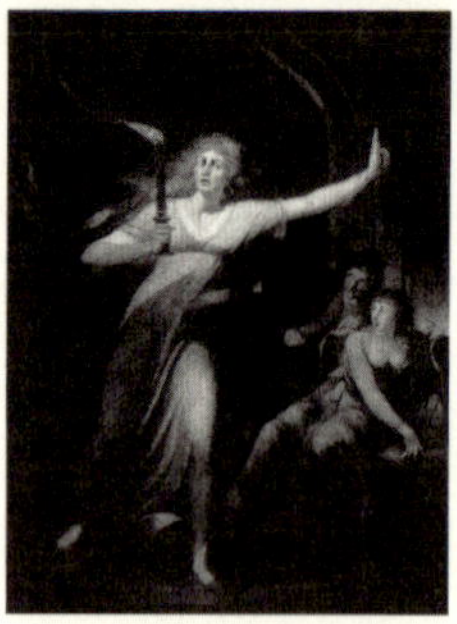

Cat. 45 *Lady Macbeth Sleepwalking*, c. 1783
oil on canvas, 221 × 160 cm
Paris, Musée du Louvre, Département de Peintures, R. F. 1970–29
(Schiff 738)

Mezzotint reproduction by John Raphael Smith, 1784 (Weinglass 71)

William Shakespeare, *Macbeth*, V, 1

Doctor: How came she by that light? / Gentlewoman: Why, it stood by her: she has light by her continually; 'tis her command. / Doctor: You see, her eyes are open. / Gentlewoman: Ay, but their sense is shut.

(Shakespeare 1995a, p. 160)

The terrible crimes that Lady Macbeth has committed with her husband in the pursuit of power cause her to lose her mind. Depictions of madness and other extreme emotional states occur repeatedly in Fuseli's art (see also cat. 27). In the present case he shows the conscience-stricken figure gesturing wildly as she emerges sleepwalking from the nocturnal gloom. Her face, distorted in terror, is dramatically illuminated by the light of the torch in her hand. Not only does the yellow of her robe invoke the colour's traditionally negative connotations, it also enhances the stark chiaroscuro contrast used here and in many other works by Fuseli to increase an image's power. The doctor and gentlewoman, small in comparison with the dominant main figure, are shown commenting on the scene in the whispered tones suggested by the text. One of the most compelling of all representations of Shakespeare's 'fiend-like queen', the painting was exhibited at the Royal Academy in 1784, but the artist had already addressed the subject in several works on paper dating from the 1770s (see Schiff 460, 461). Gert Schiff views the clear differentiation of the facial features and other details in the painting as evidence of Fuseli's renewed acquaintance with actual performances in the London theatre. William Merchant goes further, proposing that the canvas represents the celebrated actress Sarah Siddons, although she did not take the role of Lady Macbeth, at the Theatre Royal, Drury Lane, until 1785. ER

References: Merchant 1959, p. 80. – Sillars 2006, pp. 224–25. – Smith 2010, pp. 37–38.

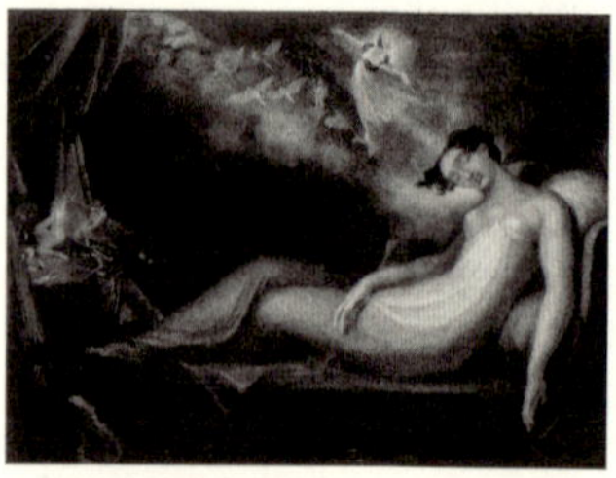

Cat. 46 *Queen Mab*, 1814
oil on canvas, 71.5 × 91.5 cm
Schaffhausen, Museum zu Allerheiligen, on permanent loan from the Sturzenegger Foundation, A 1749 (Schiff 1496)

William Shakespeare, *Romeo and Juliet*, I, 4

Romeo: I dream'd a dream to-night. / Mercutio: And so did I. / Romeo: Well, what was yours? Mercutio: That dreamers often lie. / Romeo: In bed asleep, while they do dream things true. / Mercutio: O, then, I see Queen Mab hath been with you. / She is the fairies' midwife, and she comes / In shape no bigger than an agate-stone / On the fore-finger of an alderman, / Drawn with a team of little atomies / Athwart men's noses as they lie asleep; / Her wagon-spokes made of long spiders' legs, / The cover of the wings of grasshoppers, / The traces of the smallest spider's web, / The collars of the moonshine's watery beams, / Her whip of cricket's bone, the lash of film, / Her wagoner a small grey-coated gnat, / Not half so big as a round little worm / Prick'd from the lazy finger of a maid; / Her chariot is an empty hazel-nut Made by the joiner squirrel or old grub, / Time out o' mind the fairies' coachmakers. / And in this state she gallops night by night Through lovers' brains, and then they dream of love; / O'er courtiers' knees, that dream on court'sies straight, / O'er lawyers' fingers, who straight dream on fees, / O'er ladies' lips, who straight on kisses dream, / Which oft the angry Mab with blisters plagues, / Because their breaths with sweetmeats tainted are: / Sometime she gallops o'er / a courtier's nose, / And then dreams he of smelling out a suit; / And sometime comes she with a tithe-pig's tail / Tickling a parson's nose as a' lies asleep, / Then dreams he of another benefice: / Sometime she driveth o'er a soldier's neck, / And then dreams he of cutting foreign throats, / Of breaches, ambuscadoes, Spanish blades, / Of healths five-fathom deep; and then anon / Drums in his ear, at which he starts and wakes, / And being thus frighted swears a prayer or two / And sleeps again. This is that very Mab / That plats the manes of horses in the night, And bakes the elflocks in foul sluttish hairs, / Which once untangled, much misfortune bodes: / This is the hag, when maids lie on their backs, / That presses them and learns them first to bear, / Making them women of good carriage: / This is she – / Romeo: Peace, peace, Mercutio, peace! / Thou talk'st of nothing.

(Shakespeare 1995b, pp. 48/50)

Like Edmund Spenser's Faerie Queene and Shakespeare's own Titania, the Queen Mab described in detail by Mercutio in *Romeo and Juliet* was a familiar literary queen of the fairies from the sixteenth century onwards. Her influence can be both beneficial and harmful. Among other things, she causes unruly dreams and likes eating at night, which is why wise farmers seek to gain her favour by leaving junkets for her.

Fuseli shows Queen Mab as a tiny dancer pointing her magic wand at a young woman reclining on a recamier. This 'fairy-stroke' puts the woman into a deep sleep, and immediately two fairies begin rummaging in the jewellery on the dressing table surrounded by a red curtain on the left.

Petra Maisak surmises that the painting represents a positive, literary complement to the negative *Nightmare* (Detroit Institute of Arts; Schiff 757) of 1781. She further suggests that it may have formed a pendant to a late version of that picture (cat. 69). CB

References: Weinglass 1998. – Becker 2005. – Maisak 2017a.

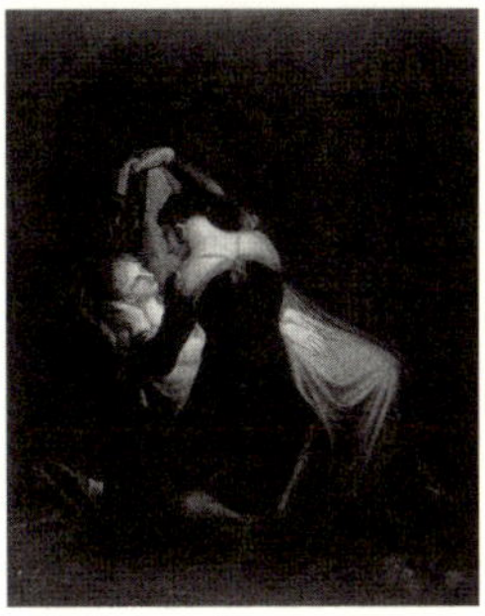

Cat. 47 *Romeo at Juliet's Bier*, 1809
oil on canvas, 143 × 112 cm
Basle, Kunstmuseum Basel, on permanent loan from a private collection, Switzerland, Dep 123 (Schiff 1207)

William Shakespeare, *Romeo and Juliet*, V, 3

Romeo: … O my love! my wife! Death, that hath suck'd the honey of thy breath, / Hath had no power yet upon thy beauty: / Thou art not conquer'd; beauty's ensign yet / Is crimson in thy lips and in thy cheeks, / And death's pale flag is not advanced there. / Tybalt, liest thou there in thy bloody sheet? / O, what more favour can I do to thee, / Than with that hand that cut thy youth in twain / To sunder his that was thine enemy? / Forgive me, cousin! Ah, dear Juliet, / Why art thou yet so fair? shall I believe / That unsubstantial death is amorous, / And that the lean abhorred monster keeps / Thee here in dark to be his paramour? For fear of that, I still will stay with thee; / And never from this palace of dim night / Depart again: here, here will I remain / With worms that are thy chamber-maids; O, here / Will I set up my everlasting rest, / And shake the yoke of inauspicious stars / From this world-wearied flesh. Eyes, look your last! / Arms, take your last embrace! and, lips, O you / The doors of breath, seal with a righteous kiss / A dateless bargain to engrossing death! / Come, bitter conduct, come, unsavoury guide! / Thou desperate pilot, now at once run on / The dashing rocks thy sea-sick weary bark! / Here's to my love! / *Drinks* O true apothecary! / Thy drugs are quick. Thus with a kiss I die.

(Shakespeare 1995b, p. 226)

Fuseli bathes the scene, which takes place just after sunset, in a muted light. Kneeling at Juliet's bier, Romeo lifts her shroud while cradling her head in his left hand, ready to kiss her for a last time, unaware that she is still alive. The artist thus records this key instant in what is perhaps the most tragic of all love stories as an endlessly prolonged moment of devotion.

The pervading gloom combines with a glossy varnish to all but obscure both the crucifix in the background, echoed by the cross resting near Juliet's hands, and the red-shod feet of Paris, who has just been killed by Romeo with the dagger lying in the foreground. Juliet will awaken shortly, when the effect of the death-simulating sleeping draught wears off. She has avoided marriage with the hated Paris, but will find her beloved Romeo dead beside her and will take her own life as a result. CB

References: Schiff 1973, vol. 1, p. 322. – Zürich 2005, ill. p. 236.

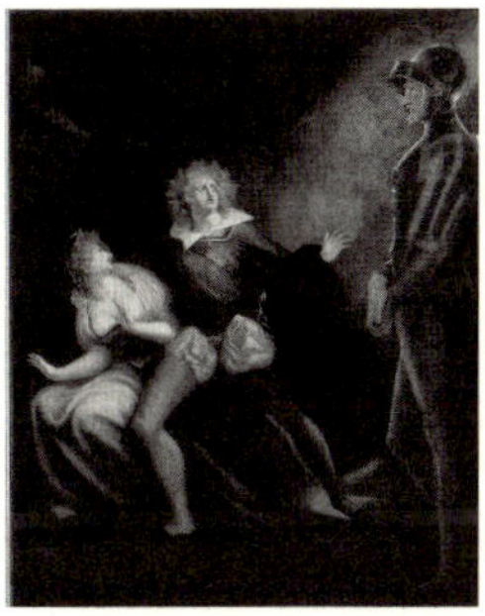

Cat. 48 *Gertrude, Hamlet and the Ghost of Hamlet's Father*, 1793
oil on canvas, 165.5 × 134 cm
Mamiano di Traversetolo, Parma, Fondazione Magnani Rocca, 199 (Schiff 1747)

Painting no. 15 in Woodmason's Shakespeare Gallery

William Shakespeare, *Hamlet*, III, 4

Hamlet: A king of shreds and patches, – / *Enter Ghost.* / Save me, and hover o'er me with your wings, / You heavenly guards! What would your gracious figure? / Queen Gertrude: Alas, he's mad! / Hamlet: Do you not come your tardy son to chide, / That, lapsed in time and passion, lets go by / The important acting of your dread command? O, say! / Ghost: Do not forget: this visi tation / Is but to whet thy almost blunted purpose. / But, look, amazement on thy mother sits: O, step between her and her fighting soul: / Conceit in weakest bodies strongest works: / Speak to her, Hamlet. / Hamlet: How is it with you, lady? / Queen Gertrude: Alas, how is't with you, / That you do bend your eye on vacancy / And with the incorporal air do hold discourse? / Forth at your eyes your spirits wildly peep; / And, as the sleeping soldiers in the alarm, / Your bedded hair, like life in excrements, / Starts up, and stands on end. O gentle son, / Upon the heat and flame of thy distemper / Sprinkle cool patience. Whereon do you look? / Hamlet: On him, on him! Look you, how pale he glares! / His form and cause conjoin'd, / preaching to stones, / Would make them capable. Do not look upon me; / Lest with this piteous action you convert / My stern effects: then what I have to do / Will want true colour; tears perchance for blood. / Queen Gertrude: To whom do you speak this? / Hamlet: Do you see nothing there? / Queen Gertrude: Nothing at all; yet all that is I see. / Hamlet: Nor did you nothing hear? / Queen Gertrude: No, nothing but ourselves. / Hamlet: Why, look you there! / look, how it steals away! / My father, in his habit as he lived! / Look, where he goes, even now, out at the portal! / *Exit Ghost.*

(Shakespeare 1995d, pp.188–92)

The painting depicts one of the most dramatic events in *Hamlet*, a scene that in eighteenth-century book illustration had come to stand for the play as a whole. It shows the confrontation between Hamlet and his mother. Hamlet is convinced that Gertrude, by marrying the brother of his father, the former king, has wed the latter's murderer. The ghost of his father suddenly appears and exhorts Hamlet to exact revenge. A drawing of the subject by Fuseli dating from 1780–82 (Schiff 819) includes Polonius, whom Hamlet has just killed, while the painting focuses on the emotions of the two principal characters and captures a classic moment in the play. Ashen-faced, Hamlet alone sees the ghost, his features expressing the utmost terror as he recoils from the apparition in a traditional pose used in many versions of the scene since the beginning of the eighteenth century. Gertrude, for her part, gazes fearfully at her son, thinking that he has become deranged. David Weinglass conjectures that Hamlet's dress may have been inspired by costumes worn by John Philip Kemble when performing the role in the theatre. ER

References: Mamiano di Traversetolo 1997, p. 70. – Young 2002, pp. 230–31.

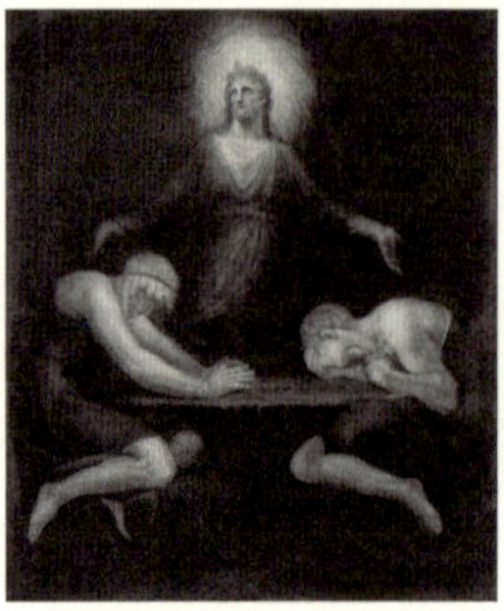

Cat. 49 *Christ Disappearing at Emmaus*, 1792
oil on canvas, 143.5 × 118.1 cm
New Haven, CT, Yale Center for British Art, Paul Mellon Collection, B.1981.25.92
(Schiff 1759)

Luke 24, 30–31

And it came to pass, as he sat at meat with them, he took bread, and blessed it, and brake, and gave it to them. And their eyes were opened, and they knew him; and he vanished out of their sight.

Excluding works inspired by quotations from the Bible in literary contexts, such as the Adam and Eve cycle inspired by Milton (see cats 55, 57), the number of authentically biblical subjects in Fuseli's oeuvre is relatively small. The series of illustrations on subjects from the Old Testament and the life of Christ that he contributed to Francis Willoughby's *Practical Family Bible* in 1772 (Weinglass 25–35) can virtually be discounted, as a commission welcome to a young artist in which artistic considerations doubtless played a secondary role. No series of biblical images is known from later periods in his career, yet the present painting might mark the beginnings of such an undertaking. Still labouring under the financial disaster of his Milton project (see 'Milton', pp. 141–43), he may have sought with this picture to commend himself to the publisher and bookseller Thomas Macklin, who was planning a cycle of illustrations to the Bible. It can only be surmised how the mature artist would have depicted scenes from the life of Christ, but his version of the supper at Emmaus certainly suggests that he would have followed his customarily free approach to textual sources and arrived at unusual iconographical solutions that questioned conventional interpretations. Ignoring an extensive pictorial tradition relating to the passage from St Luke's Gospel, he chooses to show not the moment when the disciples recognise Christ, generally rendered as reactions on their part that range from shock to hope and joy, but the end of the episode, when Jesus disappears. Apart from the tabletop, he omits all narrative accessories, including the location and the bread, and focuses on the figures of Christ, Cleopas and his fellow disciple, uniting them in a pyramidal composition illuminated in stark chiaroscuro. The two slumped disciples, who seem to float in front of the dark background, have already turned from Jesus in sadness and despair as he departs this world and confers his blessing on them. GD

References: Schiff 1973, vol. 1, pp. 170, 294. – Tomory 1974, p. 110.

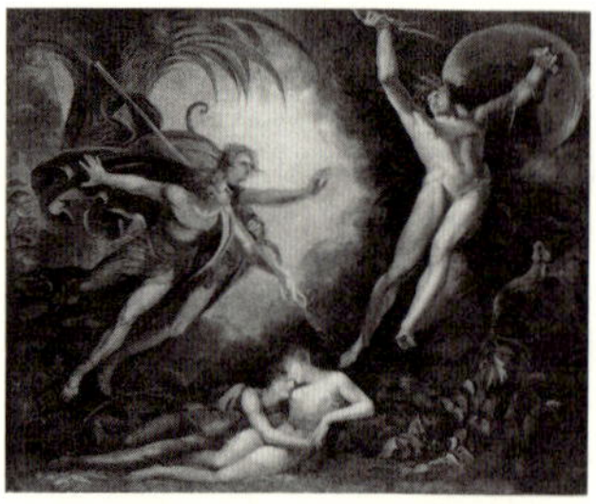

Cat. 50 *Satan Starting from the Touch of Ithuriel's Spear*, 1779
oil on canvas, 230.5 × 276.3 cm
Stuttgart, Staatsgalerie Stuttgart, acquired with lottery funds 1995, 3708 (Schiff, 'Verlorene Werke', 18)

John Milton, *Paradise Lost*, IV, 810–19

Him thus intent Ithuriel with his spear / Touch'd lightly; for no falsehood can endure / Touch of celestial temper, but returns
Of force to its own likeness: up he starts, / Discover'd and surpris'd. As when a spark / Lights on a heap of nitrous powder, laid / Fit for the Tun some Magazin to store / Against a rumord Warr, the Smuttie graine / With sudden blaze diffus'd, inflames the Aire: / So started up in his own shape the Fiend.

(Milton 1796, pp. 160–61)

Fuseli had known Milton's *Paradise Lost* since his youth and, together with the works of Shakespeare, it became his chief source of artistic inspiration. The present painting depicts Satan's unsuccessful attempt to destroy the human beings created by God. Poised to attack Adam and Eve sleeping peacefully in Paradise, Satan, discovered in his disguise as a toad, suddenly returns to his 'own likeness' and is driven away by the archangels Zephon and Ithuriel.

The picture was among those that the artist exhibited at the Royal Academy in 1780 after returning from Rome. Preparatory drawings dating from 1776 (Schiff 482, 483) may reflect contact in Rome with the Scottish painter Alexander Runciman, who in 1773 had shown a work on the same subject at the Royal Academy. Fuseli's large, notably ambitious composition was one of several commissioned from him by Sir Robert Smyth. Gert Schiff listed it as lost, but it turned up in the 1980s and, before entering the collection of the Stuttgart Staatsgalerie, had been owned by the famous Russian ballet dancer Rudolf Nurejev. The artist painted another picture on the subject years later in connection with his Milton Gallery, but that canvas has not survived. He also produced a version to serve as the basis for an engraving in the edition of Milton's epic poem published by Francis Isaac Du Roveray in 1802. ER

References: Pointon 1970, p. 113. – Stuttgart 1997, pp. 19–20. – London 2006, no. 37, pp. 78–79.

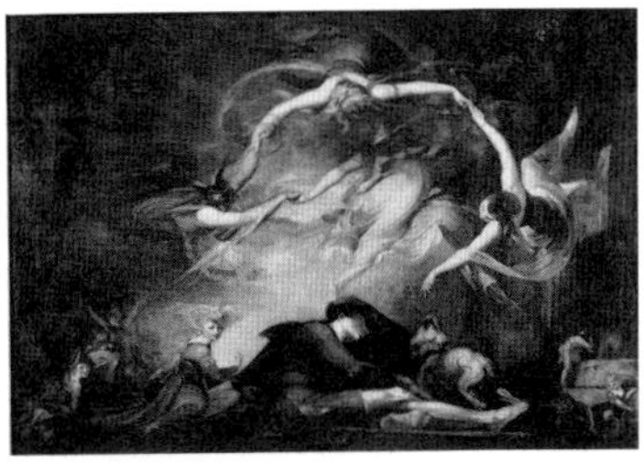

Cat. 51 *The Shepherd's Dream*, 1793
oil on canvas, 154.3 × 215.3 cm
London, Tate, purchase 1966, T00876 (Schiff 1762)

John Milton, *Paradise Lost*, I, 775–88

So thick the airy crowd Swarm'd and were straiten'd; till, the signal given, / Behold a wonder! they but now who seem'd / In bigness to surpass earth's giant sons / Now less than smallest dwarfs, in narrow room / Throng numberless, like that pygmean race / Beyond the Indian mount, or faery elves, / Whose midnight revels, by a forrest side / Or fountain some belated peasant sees, / Or dreams he sees, while over-head the moon / Sits arbitress, and nearer to the earth / Wheels her pale course, they on their mirth and dance / Intent, with jocund music charm his ear; / At once with joy and fear his heart rebounds.

(Milton, 1796, p. 35)

At the end of Book I of *Paradise Lost* Milton describes how Satan amasses his legions and how the lower ranks of fallen angels reduce their size to ensure that they all fit inside the Hall of Pandemonium. In this connection the poet compares the fallen angels to dancing music-making fairies beguiling a shepherd in his dreams. That is the subject of Fuseli's painting. On the one hand, the depiction of a dream featuring the airy dance of graceful figures relates it to his picture of Queen Katherine's dream from Shakespeare's *Henry VIII* (cat. 39); on the other, the presence of Puck, who is hovering in front of the moon, and Queen Mab, who sits on the steps on the right, link it to his canvases illustrating *A Midsummer Night's Dream* (cats 32–36).

Painting no. 4 in the Milton Gallery addresses the same subject, but Martin Myrone (London 2006) identifies the present work as that which Fuseli exhibited at the Royal Academy in 1786 and described in a letter of 22 January 1785 to his patron Brooke Boothby as a 'large Fairie Scene of the Sleeping Shepherd'. According to Myrone, the Milton Gallery canvas was smaller. ER

References: London 2006, p. 154. – Calè 2006, p. 84.

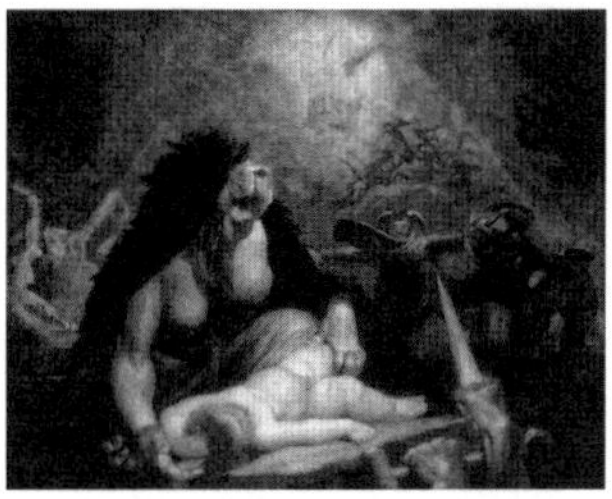

Cat. 52 *The Night Hag Visiting the Lapland Witches*, 1794–96
oil on canvas, 101.6 × 126.4 cm
New York, The Metropolitan Museum of Art, Purchase, Bequest of Lillian S. Timken, by exchange, and Victor Wilbour Memorial, The Alfred N. Punnett Endowment, Marquand and Charles B. Curtis Funds, 1980, 1980.411
(Schiff, 'Verlorene Werke', no. 35)

Painting no. 8 in Fuseli's Milton Gallery

John Milton, *Paradise Lost*, II, 662–66

...follow the night-hag, when call'd / In secret, riding through the air she comes / Lur'd with the smell of infant blood, to dance / With Lapland witches, while the labouring moon / Eclipses at their charms.

(Milton, 1796, p.68)

Fuseli worked on his ambitious project to create a Milton Gallery from 1790 to 1800, producing forty-seven paintings on the poet's life and work. The gallery catalogue lists the present scene as no. 8, titled *Lapland Orgies; the Hell-hounds round Sin.* As in *The Shepherd's Dream* (cat. 51), the artist took his cue from a simile in the text, here voiced during a discussion of the nature of sin. The painting shows nocturnal demons drawn to a witch preparing to sacrifice an abducted child. A pack of hell-hounds follows the approaching 'Night-Hag'. That epithet was frequently applied to the goddess Hecate, who was associated with the moon, the underworld and magic, but Lawrence Feingold argues that Fuseli's image corresponds to more general notions of mounted female demons as bringers of nightmares. The subject of *The Night Hag Visiting the Lapland Witches* would then be related to that of the artist's well-known *The Nightmare* of 1781 (see p. 25). In 1808 he sold the painting to his future biographer John Knowles, remarking that it was one of his finest works. ER

References: Feingold 1982, p. 54. – London 2006, p. 140. – Calè 2006, pp. 162–71.

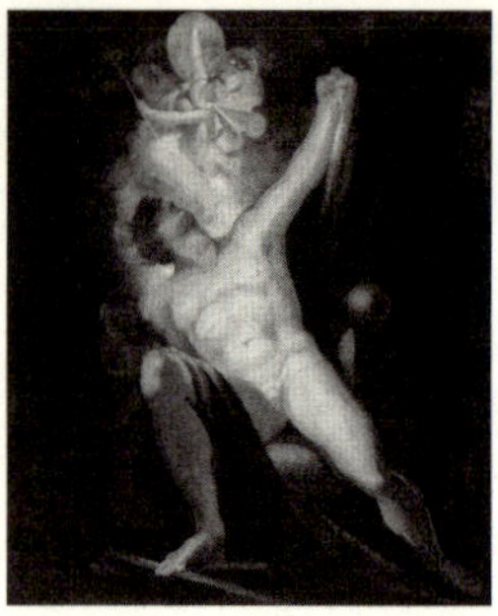

Cat. 53 *Satan and the Birth of Sin*, c. 1796–99
oil on canvas, 142.6 × 118.8 cm
Dallas Museum of Art, Foundation of the Arts Collection, Mrs. John B. O'Hara Fund, 1996.104FA
(Schiff, 'Verlorene Werke', 34)

Painting no. 6 in Fuseli's Milton Gallery
Engraved by Abraham Raimbach, 1806
(Weinglass 261)

John Milton, *Paradise Lost*, II, 746–60

To whom thus the portress of hell-gate reply'd: / Hast thou forgot me then? and do I seem / Now in thine eye so foul? once deem'd so fair / In Heaven, when at the assembly, and in sight / Of all the Seraphim with thee combin'd / In bold conspiracy against Heaven's King, / All on a sudden miserable pain / Surpris'd thee, dim thine eyes, and dizzy swum / In darkness, while thy head flames thick and fast / Threw forth, till on the left side opening wide, / Likest to thee in shape and countenance bright, / Then shining heavenly fair, a goddess arm'd / Out of thy head I sprung: amazement seiz'd / All the host of Heaven; back they recoil'd afraid / At first, and call'd me Sin…

(Milton, 1796, pp. 71–72)

At the gates of Hell Satan encounters Death and Sin, who have been banished there to act as terrifying and invincible guards. The battle that immediately ensues between Satan and Death is stopped by Sin, who reveals to the astonished combatants that they are closely related through incest. She, Sin, had been born at the moment of Satan's resolve to rebel against God, when she emerged from his painfully opening head. Satan's lust had then led him to impregnate his own daughter and thus unwittingly to become father to the offspring that resulted from this mésalliance – Death. The latter had, in turn, repeatedly raped his own mother and thereby sired the host of witches and hellhounds. Satan promises them both rich booty in the form of God's latest creation, humankind, whereupon Sin unlocks the gates.

Fuseli takes his cue from Milton's parody of the story of Athena as related by Hesiod in his *Theogony*. She, too, first saw the light of day literally as a brainchild when Hephaistos split open Zeus' skull with an axe as a remedy for his inexplicable headaches. To everyone's surprise out came Athena, fully armed, the head of the gods having previously swallowed her pregnant mother, his first wife, Metis. That explains why Fuseli's Sin, although she appears as ethereal and supple as his winged fairies, bears the shield, spear and helmet that are the attributes of Athena. In an allusion to his future role as lord of the underworld Satan leans backwards in a throne-like armchair, despite the fact that Sin's birth occurs before the fall of the rebel angels (see cat. 55). The antique progenitor of his figure was not the 'pedagogue' in the *Niobe* group (Florence, Uffizi), as Gert Schiff claims, but an even more famous sculpture: *Laocoon*, whose upper body and extended arm with the clenched fist (the figure had been incorrectly restored in Fuseli's day) appear reversed in the painting. Satan's body, like Laocoon's, is shot through with physical and emotional tension. The lighting generates a Caravaggesque chiaroscuro typical of several of the artist's Milton images and helps to lend the ghostly scene a degree of dramatic expression that is perhaps a mite overdone. GD

References: Schiff 1963, pp. 51, 143. – Stuttgart 1997, pp. 30–32. – Calè 2006, p. 160. – See Weinglass 261.

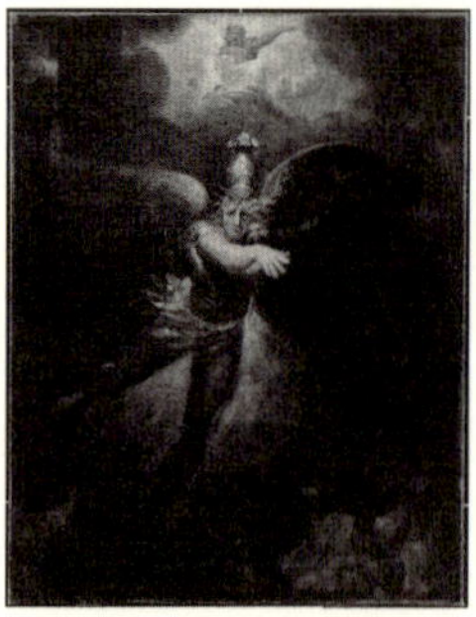

Cat. 54 *The Triumphant Messiah*, 1802
oil on canvas, 91 × 71 cm
Kunst Museum Winterthur, loan
(Schiff 1213)

Engraved by Charles Warren, 1802
(Weinglass 169)

John Milton, *Paradise Lost*, VI, 852–65

Yet half his strength he put not forth, but check'd / His thunder in mid volley; for he meant / Not to destroy, but root them out of Heaven: / The overthrown he rais'd, and as a Herd / Of goats or timorous flock together throng'd, Drove them before him thunder-struck, pursued / With terrors and with furies to the bounds And crystal wall of Heaven, which opening wide, / Roll'd inward, and a spacious gap disclos'd / Into the wasteful deep; the monstrous sight / Struck them with horror backward, but far worse / Urg'd them behind; headlong themselves they threw / Down from the verge of Heaven, eternal wrath / Burnt after them to the bottomless pit.

(Milton 1796, p. 250)

In a dream Satan implants in Eve a longing for the forbidden fruit of the Tree of Knowledge. God thereupon despatches the archangel Raphael to Paradise to warn the first parents of the consequences of succumbing to this temptation and to urge them to obey God's will. Raphael describes to them in detail the rebellion against the divine order undertaken by Satan and his allies before the Creation and how God's own son had put an end to it: at the height of the decisive battle between good and evil he had mercilessly driven back the insurgents in his vast chariot and hurled them down through the opening wall of Heaven into the jaws of Hell. Regaining strength there, they planned to tempt the entire newly created human race in revenge for their defeat.

Fuseli produced his painting, like cat. 7, as the basis of an illustration in Francis Isaac Du Roveray's edition of *Paradise Lost* of 1802. Its effectiveness derives principally from the unusual vantage point: watched at the top by the enthroned Messiah and his heavenly legions, viewers witness the fall of the rebel angels from far below and find themselves in the position of the vanquished. The illusion of participating directly in the events depicted is increased by the fact that the huge descending figure of Satan, his arm seemingly invading the beholder's space, appears almost tangibly close and threatens to collide with the viewer. Although defeated now, the prince of Hell stretches out his shield defiantly, if powerlessly, towards the superior forces of Heaven and is apparently already meditating revenge. Claudia Hattendorf has rightly pointed out that Milton's text offers no justification for this focus on

Satan during the fall of the rebel angels. The empathy with the tempter that it evinces is, however, characteristic of Fuseli's interpretation of Milton, which for much of the time privileges Satan as the real hero of the poem. In the subsidiary figure in the lower right corner the artist once more reveals his penchant for models derived from Michelangelo's *Last Judgement* in the Sistine Chapel (see, for example, cats 19, 24). GD

References: Schiff 1973, vol. 1, p. 564. – Stuttgart 1997, p. 89.

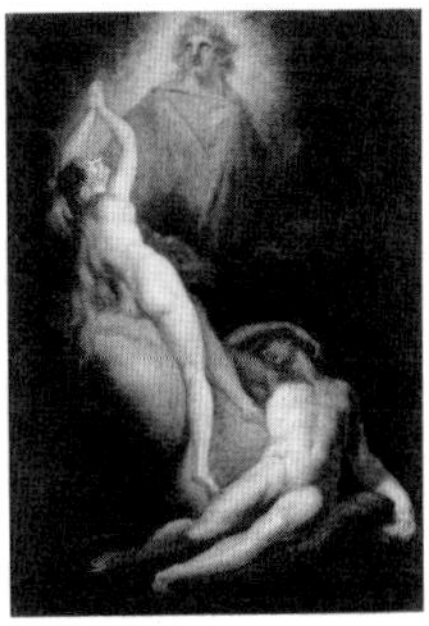

Cat. 55 *The Creation of Eve*, 1793
oil on canvas, 307 × 207 cm
Hamburg, Hamburger Kunsthalle
(Schiff 897)

Painting no. 17 in Fuseli's Milton Gallery

John Milton, *Paradise Lost*, VIII, 460–77

Mine eyes he clos'd, but open left the cell / Of fancy my internal sight, by which / Abstract as in a trance methought I saw, / Though sleeping, where I lay, and saw the shape / Still glorious before whom awake I stood; / Who stooping open'd my left side, and took / From thence a rib, with cordial spirits warm, / And life-blood streaming fresh; wide was the wound, / But suddenly with flesh fill'd up and heal'd: / The rib he form'd and fashion'd with his hands; / Under his forming hands a creature grew, / Manlike, but different sex, so lovely fair, / That what seem'd fair in all the world, seem'd now / Mean, or in her summ'd up, in / her contain'd / And in her looks, which from that time infus'd / Sweetness into my heart, unfelt before, / And into all things / from her air inspir'd / The spirit of love and amorous delight.

(Milton 1796, pp. 307–08)

Having described to the first parents the failed rebellion in heaven (cat. 50) and the creation of the world, the archangel Raphael is ready to return heavenwards, yet Adam first acquaints him with everything he can remember since his creation. In this way, Raphael learns how Eve had been created from one of Adam's ribs and how Adam thus acquired the companion he had longed for.

Fuseli's choice of subject was not particularly original, of course, but for this monumental painting, among the many larger canvases produced for the Milton Gallery, he devised an unusual composition that is compelling in formal terms. It focuses on the first parents, starkly illuminated against a dark background, and the figure of the creator, with its perhaps excessive pathos and ambivalent character. In a letter to William Roscoe Fuseli refused to accept the identification of this figure as God the Father, although the text and iconographical tradition stipulate precisely that. Instead, he envisaged an interpretation as either the Messiah or a higher being providing succour, depending on the viewer's confession. Formally, he linked the three figures both in the shape of a large, arabesque-like S-shape and as the embodiment of an upward motion extending from Adam asleep in the foreground, via Eve raising her arms in prayer, to the ghostly apparition at the rear, all arranged around an imaginary axis in the manner of a *figura serpentinata*.

Here, too, Fuseli evinces a creative and flexible approach to models that served him as archetypes. His Adam, for instance, is a cross between a free interpretation of the *Barberini Faun* (Munich, Glyptothek) and the legs of Michelangelo's Adam in *The Creation of Eve* on the ceiling of the Sistine Chapel (see also the figure of Eve in cat. 57). Ten years later he re-used this Adam in a very different context, changing only the position of the arms (cat. 8). Eve in the present canvas, her pose eminently unsuited to a seated figure, is derived from one of the blessed at the left edge of Michelangelo's *Last Judgement* (also in the Sistine Chapel), which offered Fuseli a seemingly inexhaustible store of gestures, poses and psychological motifs (see, for instance, cat. 54). GD

References: Schiff 1963, pp. 66–70. – Hamburg 1974, p. 160. – Stuttgart 1997, pp. 42–43.

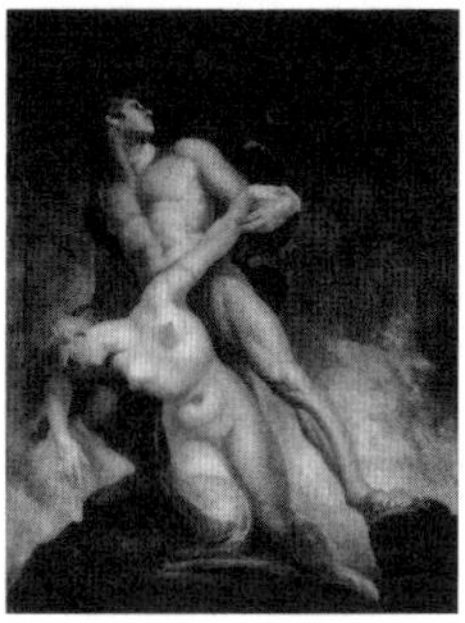

Cat. 56 *The Vision of the Flood*, c. 1800
oil on canvas, 158 × 119 cm
Kunst Museum Winterthur,
Gift of Georg Reinhart, 1946, 637
(Schiff 901)

Probably a second version of painting no. 25 in the Milton Gallery

John Milton, *Paradise Lost*, XI, 738–45, 754–61

Meanwhile the south-wind rose, and with black wings / Wide hovering, all the clouds together drove / From under Heaven; the hills to their supply / Vapor, and exhalation dusk and moist, / Sent up amain; and now the thicken'd sky / Like a dark ceiling stood; down rush'd the rain / Impetuous, and continued till the Earth / No more was seen. / … / How didst thou grieve then, Adam, to behold / The end of all thy offspring, end so sad, / Depopulation; thee another flood, / Of tears and sorrow' a flood thee also drown'd, / And sunk thee as thy sons; till gently rear'd / By the' Angel, on thy feet thou stood'st at last, / Though comfortless, as when a Father mourns / His children, all in view destroy'd at once.

(Milton 1796, p. p.455–56)

After Satan has brought about the Fall of Man through guile and seductive powers of persuasion, God sends a host headed by the archangel Michael to drive the disobedient first parents from Paradise. Full of remorse, Adam and Eve beg God for forgiveness through the mediation of the Messiah. God accepts their prayers but insists on carrying out the punishment he had decided on. Eve then bewails her fate at length, while Adam submits devoutly to God's will. Before they leave Paradise (see cat. 57), Michael, leaving Eve behind asleep, leads Adam to a hill, where he is shown a vision of all that will happen to sinful humanity, from Cain's fratricide and the Flood to redemption by the Messiah and the Last Judgement.

Fuseli's composition, probably a second version, smaller and slightly altered, of the painting for the Milton Gallery, is an example par excellence of the artist's often free approach to his sources, privileging artistic invention, emotional force and compelling immediacy over literal accuracy. In addition, he here arrives at an iconographical solution susceptible to more than one interpretation. The painting either depicts two victims of the Flood who resemble exactly the artist's figures of the first parents and have sought refuge on a rock while awaiting their end, or it shows Adam and Eve themselves, who, in a departure from Milton's narrative, have both been led to the hill, although the image agrees with the poem inasmuch as Eve's collapse means she does not see the vision presented by Michael. Either way, the picture reveals Fuseli's skill as a painter–director, for the audience witnesses the horror of the Flood only indirectly, via the gestures and facial expressions of figures. As so often in his work, those figures take their cue from antique sculptures and are seen starkly illuminated against a dark background in a dramatic view from below. The harrowing scenes of mass death, and the people and animals saved in Noah's ark, are left to the spectator's foreknowledge and imagination. In this respect the painting goes one step further than its lost predecessor, which included the desperately raised hand of a person drowning next to the figure of Eve. GD

References: Schiff 1963, pp. 74, 151. – Stuttgart 1997, pp. 49–50. – Winterthur 2005, pp. 73–75.

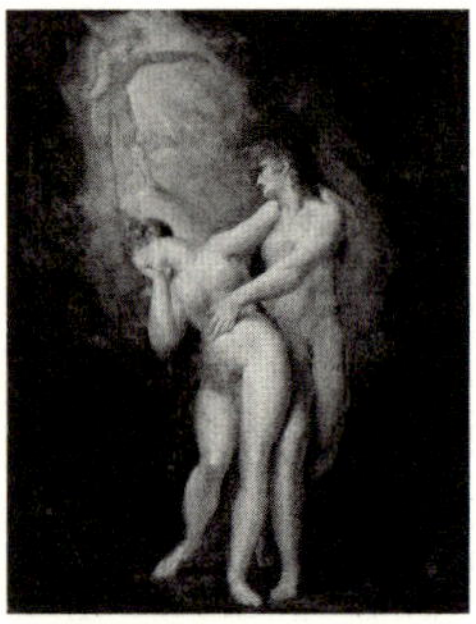

Cat. 57 *The Expulsion from Paradise*, 1802
oil on canvas, 92 × 71 cm
Basle, Kunstmuseum Basel, on permanent loan from a private collection, Switzerland, Dep 26
(Schiff 1214)

Engraved by Anker Smith, 1802
(Weinglass 170)

John Milton, *Paradise Lost*, XII, 637–44

In either hand the hast'ning Angel caught / Our lingering parents, and to the' eastern gate / Led them direct, and down the cliff as fast / To the subjected plain; then disappear'd. / They looking back, all the' eastern side beheld / Of Paradise, so late their happy seat, / Wav'd over by that flaming brand, the gate / With dreadful faces throng'd and fiery arms:

(Milton 1796, p. 493)

Adam, vouchsafed a vision of the future encompassing both the suffering caused by the Fall of Man and the redemption of the human race in the distant future (see cat. 56), and Eve, granted an image of hope in a God-given dream, are led from the Garden of Eden by the archangel Michael. Outside, the first parents look back and see Michael sealing the Paradise they have now lost with his flaming sword. Profoundly shaken, but with their sights firmly fixed on the future, they then set out on their joint path into an unknown world. And, with that, Milton's poem ends.

The relatively small picture did not form part of the Milton Gallery, but was painted later, as the basis for a mezzotint in an edition of *Paradise Lost* published in 1802 by Francis Isaac Du Roveray, to which Fuseli contributed six of the twelve illustrations. Comparison with a second version of the lost original from the Milton Gallery (Houston, Sarah Campbell Blaffer Foundation, suggests that the present canvas is a generally faithful replica of that composition. That certainly applies to the monumental figures of the first parents, the bold lighting rendering them powerfully three-dimensional and setting them off against the neutral background as they literally hold on to one another. Eve is still prey to remorse and despair, while Adam supports her and seeks to comfort her. Gert Schiff convincingly argued that the figure of the sword-wielding Michael in the background, altered slightly in the mezzotint, is a partly reversed reproduction of the henchman in Raphael's *Judgement of Solomon* in the Stanza della Segnatura in the Vatican. GD

References: Schiff 1963, vol. 1, p. 74. – Schiff 1973, 'Verlorene Werke', 45. – Stuttgart 1997, pp. 52, 84–85, 87.

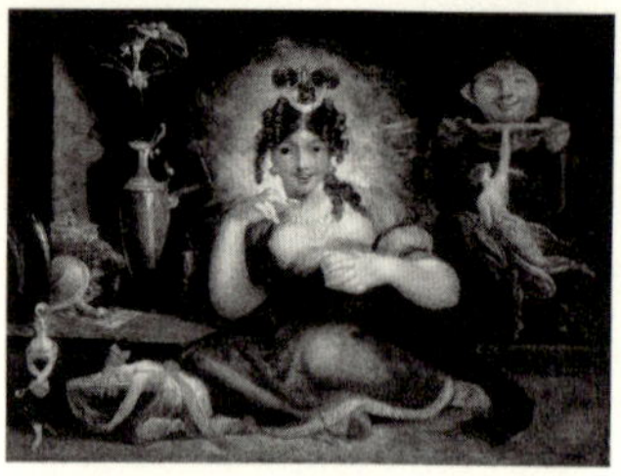

Cat. 58 *Fairy Mab**, 1815–20
oil on canvas, 102 × 127 cm
Washington, D. C., Folger Shakespeare Library,
FP a23 (Schiff 1498)

John Milton, *L'Allegro* (c. 1630), II, 97–116

...young and old com forth to play On a Sunshine Holyday, / Till the live-long day-light fail, / Then to the Spicy Nut-brown Ale, / With stories told of many a feat, / How Faery Mab the junkets eat, / She was pincht, and pull'd she sed, / And he by Friars Landthorn led / Tells how the drudging Goblin swet, / To ern his Cream-bowle duly set, / When in one night, ere glimps of morn, / His shadowy Flale hath thresh'd the Corn / That ten day-labourers could not end, / Then lies him down the Lubbar Fend. / And strech'd out all the Chimney's strength; / And Crop-full out of dores he flings / Ere the first Cock his Mattin rings. / Thus don the Tales, to bed they creep, / By whispering Winds soon lull'd asleep.

(Milton 1998, p. 71)

Fuseli first depicted Faery Mab, the generally well-disposed leader of the fairies, in 1793 (Schiff 909), a painting identified by Gert Schiff as no. 30 in the Milton Gallery. The Washington canvas is much later, different in colour and richer in composition. In a letter of 1795 to William Roscoe the artist states that the picture illustrates Milton's line 'How Faery Mab the junkets eat', a reference to the custom of leaving food out for fairies at night. The crescent moon in her hair links Faery Mab to the moon goddesses Diana and Luna and marks her out as a dream fairy. In literature she appears in Shakespeare (Queen Mab), Milton (Faery Mab) and Ben Jonson (Queen Mab), prompting various identifications of the subject of Fuseli's painting. In 1922, for example, Christie's sold it as 'Queen Mab from Romeo and Juliet' (see cat. 46). CB

References: Fuseli 1982, pp. 141–42. – Washington 1993, pp. 65–66. – London 2006, p. 162.

* Spelling of the title varies from 'Faery Mab' (Milton) and 'Fairie Mab' (Fuseli) to 'Fairy Mab' (Schiff).

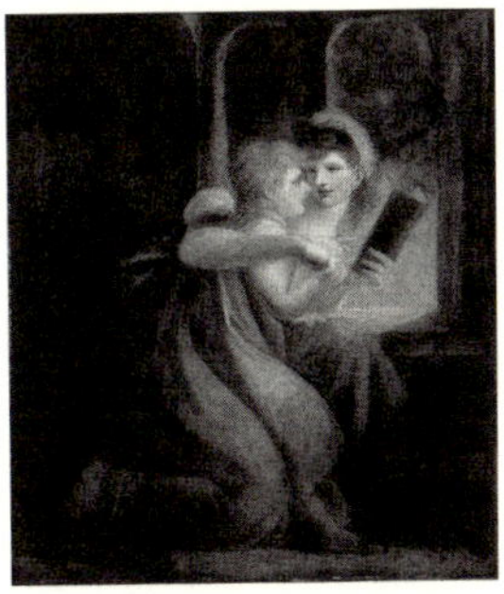

Cat. 59 *Milton when a Boy, Instructed by his Mother*, 1796–99
oil on canvas, 142 × 119 cm
Winterthur, Stiftung für Kunst, Kultur und Geschichte, 5500
(Schiff 916)

Painting no. 38 in Fuseli's Milton Gallery
Stipple engraving by John Perry, n. d. (Weinglass 303)

The last three pictures in Fuseli's Milton Gallery (nos. 38–40) address subjects from the poet's life. No biographical or other written source exists for the present strikingly emotional, genre-like image (no. 38). The 'childhood of great men' was a popular theme at the time. Fuseli derived the motif in his painting from a drawing by Raphael of a mother teaching her child (Derbyshire, Chatsworth House) that circulated widely in the form of an engraving by Marcantonio Raimondi. He enhances the intimacy of the scene by placing the faces of the mother and child close to one another. Gert Schiff draws attention to an autobiographical element, claiming that the woman in the painting possesses the idealised features of Fuseli's own mother. Certainly, his biographer John Knowles reports that the artist owed his basic education to his mother, who died at an early age.

Fuseli exhibited the painting for the first time in 1799 and subsequently produced a smaller replica for his patron William Roscoe, a Liverpudlian banker (Liverpool, Walker Art Gallery). The original remained in the artist's possession for the rest of his life and appears as no. 84 in the sale catalogue of his estate. CB

References: Knowles 1831, vol. 1, p. 6. – Schiff 1973, vol. 1, p. 219. – Stuttgart 1997, pp. 64–65.

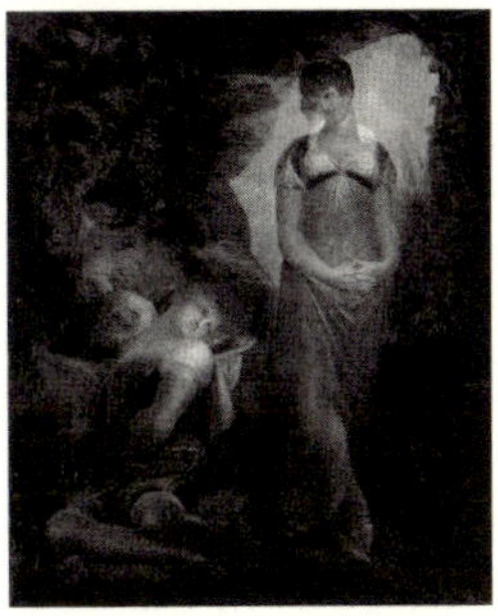

Cat. 60 *Milton when a Youth*, 1796–99
oil on canvas, 128 × 102 cm
Melbourne, National Gallery of Victoria, purchased 1981, E1–1981
(Schiff 918)

Painting no. 39 in Fuseli's Milton Gallery

Believing that the following real circumstance has been but little noticed, we submit the particulars of it, as not uninteresting, to the attention of our readers: – It is well known that, in the bloom of youth, and when he pursued his studies at Cambridge, this poet was extremely beautiful. Wandering, one day, during the summer, far beyond the precincts of the University, into the country, he became so heated and fatigued, that, reclining himself at the foot of a tree to rest, he shortly fell asleep. Before he awoke, two ladies, who were foreigners, passed by in a carriage. Agreeably astonished at the loveliness of his appearance, they alighted, and having admired him (as they thought) unperceived, for some time, the youngest, who was very handsome, drew a pencil from her pocket, and having written some lines upon a piece of paper, put it with her trembling hand into his own. Immediately afterwards they proceeded on their journey. Some of his acquaintances, who were in search of him, had observed this silent adventure, but at too great a distance to discover that the highly-favoured party in it was our illustrious bard. Approaching nearer, they saw their friend, to whom, being awakened, they mentioned what had happened. Milton opened the paper, and, with surprize, read these verses from [Giovanni Battista] Guarini: [Madrigal, xii, ed. 1598.]

'Occhi, stelle mortali,
'Ministre de miei mali, –
'Se chiusi m'uccidete,
'Aperti che farete?'

'Ye eyes! ye human stars! ye authors of my liveliest pangs! If thus, when shut, ye wound me, what must have proved the consequence had ye been open?' Eager, from this moment, to find out the fair incognita, Milton travelled, but in vain, through every part of Italy. His poetick fervour became incessantly more and more heated by the idea which he had formed of his unknown admirer ; and it is, in some degree, to her that his own times, the present times, and the latest posterity must feel themselves indebted for several of the most impassioned and charming compositions of the Paradise Lost.

(Todd 1809, pp. 26–27)

The anecdote appears in more than one idealising account of Milton's life. Henry John Todd evidently records it here as published in a newspaper, pointing out that it represents a trope familiar from other biographies of writers.

Fuseli depicted the scene as painting no. 39 in his Milton Gallery. Not sticking closely to the text, he shows the youthful poet having fallen asleep in a cave, the colours and shapes of its stone walls seemingly generating ghostly apparitions. All his life Fuseli returned to themes revolving around the role played by dreams in artistic creation and fantasy (see cats 63, 65). Peter Tomory sees in this the influence of his friend Johann Georg Sulzer, the scientist, philosopher and translator of David Hume. The two men will certainly have discussed the significance of the imagination and artistic inspiration, since Sulzer addressed them in his *Allgemeine Theorie der schönen Künste* (General Theory of the Fine Arts). Gert Schiff also relates the content of the scene to Fuseli's *Prince Arthur and the Fairy Queen* (cat. 16). CB

References: Sulzer 1792–94, vol. 1, p. 353. – Altick 1985, pp. 151–52. – Tomory 1986. – Stuttgart 1997, p. 66.

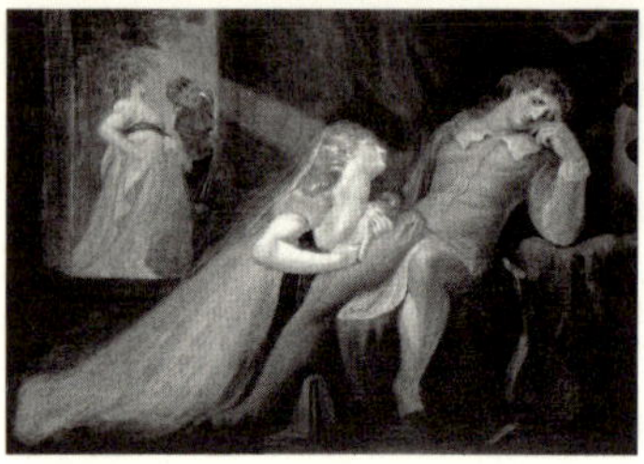

Cat. 61 *The Return of Milton's First Wife, Mary Powell*, 1799–1800
oil on canvas, 87 × 112 cm
Liverpool, Walker Art Gallery, 1539 (Schiff 919)

He [Milton] had a relation, one Blackborough, living in the lane of St. Martin's Le Grand, whom he often visited; and one day when he was visiting there, it was contrived that the wife should be ready in another room; and as he was thinking of nothing less, he was surprised to see her, whom he had expected never to have seen any more, falling down upon her knees at his feet, and imploring his forgiveness with tears. At first he showed some signs of aversion, but he continued not long inexorable; his wife's intreaties, and the intercession of friends on both sides soon wrought upon his generous nature, and procured a happy reconciliation with an act of oblivion of all that was past.
(Newton 1757, pp. XXVI–XXVII)

After little more than a month's marriage to Milton the seventeen-year-old Mary Powell returned to her parents, an act that prompted the poet to campaign for a reform of English divorce laws. The anecdote described here appears in some of the biographies of Milton frequently included in eighteenth-century editions of his works. Fuseli painted two of his five scenes from the writer's life for the second exhibition of his Milton Gallery, which took place in 1800. None of these later canvases bears a gallery number. The artist mentioned the present canvas for the first time in a letter of 18 June 1800 to his friend and patron William Roscoe.

Fuseli conveys the drama of the situation in the two figures' poses, Mary Powell kneeling beseechingly before her husband, Milton turning from her, overcome with sorrowful forgiveness. The setting enhances the effect, a ray of light falling through the doorway in the background and striking the repentant wife, for whom the poet has stopped reading the Greek text in his lap. CB

References: Altick 1985, pp. 151–52. – Stuttgart 1997, p. 66.

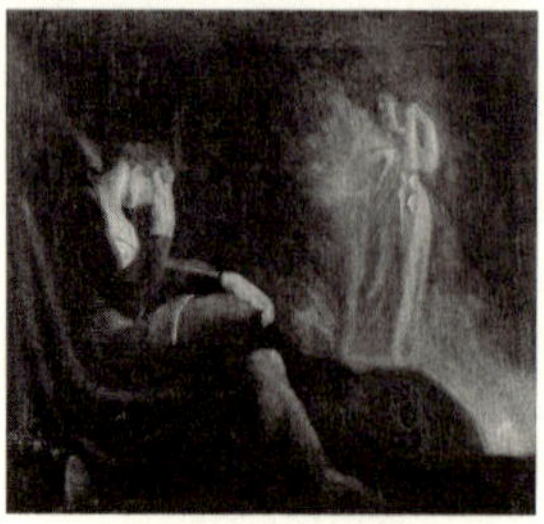

Cat. 62 *Milton's Vision of his Second Wife*, 1799–1800
oil on canvas, 95 × 100 cm
Private collection, Switzerland (Schiff 920)

John Milton, *Sonnet XXIII*

Methought I saw my late-epoused saint, / Brought to me like Alcestis from the grave, / Whom Jove's great son to her glad husband gave, / Rescued from Death by force, though pale and faint. / Mine, as whom washed from spot of childbed-taint / Purification in Old Law did save, / And such, as yet once more I trust to have / Full sight of her in heaven without restraint, Came vested all in white, pure as her mind. / Her face was veiled, yet to my fancied sight / Love, sweetness, goodness, in her person shined / So clear, as in no face with more delight. / But oh! as to embrace me she inclined, / I waked, she fled, and day brought back my night.
(Milton 1859, pp. 168–69)

Produced for the second exhibition at the artist's Milton Gallery, the painting bears no gallery number, but is easily positioned within the cycle of works on the poet's life begun earlier. Along with cat. 61, Füssli first mentions it as ready for despatch in a letter of 18 June 1800 to William Roscoe.

Gert Schiff, describing the image in notably empathetic terms, opines that in no other work did Fuseli succeed in 'rendering the character of a vision so compellingly'. The catalogue of the Hamburger Kunsthalle follows Schiff in identifying the painting as an illustration of Milton's well-known love poem *Sonnet XXIII*. This describes how the author, already completely blind, has a vision of his beloved second wife, Katherine Woodcock, whom he had never seen. He had married her in 1656, four years after the death of his first wife, Mary Powell (see cat. 61), but within a year she, too, had died of complications experienced during childbirth. Christian von Holst, writing in the catalogue of the Stuttgart Staatsgalerie, sees in the canvas not an illustration of *Sonnet XXIII*, but a depiction of Milton dictating the poem. CB

References: Schiff 1973, vol. 1, p. 221. – Hamburg 1974, p. 165. – Stuttgart 1997, p. 66.

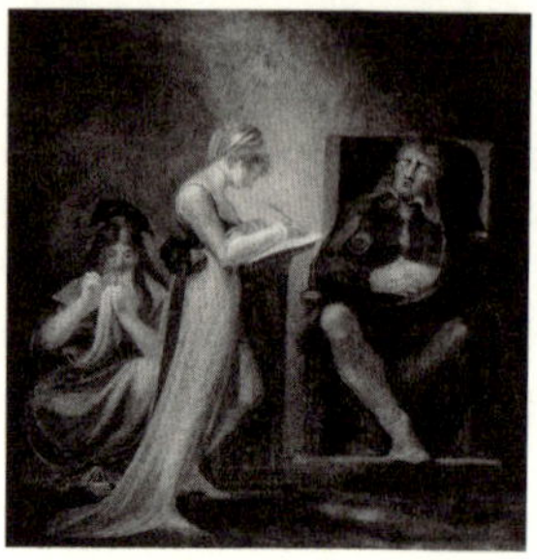

Cat. 63 *Milton Dictating to his Daughter*, 1794
oil on canvas, 121.2 × 118.7 cm
The Art Institute of Chicago, Preston O. Morton Memorial Purchase Fund for Older Paintings, 1973.303 (Schiff 921)

Painting no. 40 in Fuseli's Milton Gallery
Stipple engraving by Moses Haughton, 1806 (Weinglass 264)

The more detailed biographies of Milton (for example, Fenton 1816) indicate that his three daughters joined forces against him and that family relations were marked as much by mutual dislike as by a simultaneous interdependence. Totally blind, the poet inevitably relied on his daughters to take dictation and to read to him.

Milton's awkward personal situation accorded with Fuseli's penchant for a mixture of tragedy and pathos. The artist shows the writer, blind, impoverished and isolated following the death of his second wife, dictating his *chef-d'oeuvre*, the epic poem *Paradise Lost*, to one of his daughters. Milton's biographical circumstances also served Fuseli as a projection surface for his own years of struggle in connection with the Milton Gallery: as no. 40, the painting appeared at the end of the first exhibition there in 1799. The bare interior und the dim light underline mercilessly the oppressive atmosphere of the scene. A later, less grim version of the subject survives in the form of an engraving by Moses Haughton. CB

References: Stuttgart 1997, p. 68. – Lentzsch 2005, pp. 222–29.

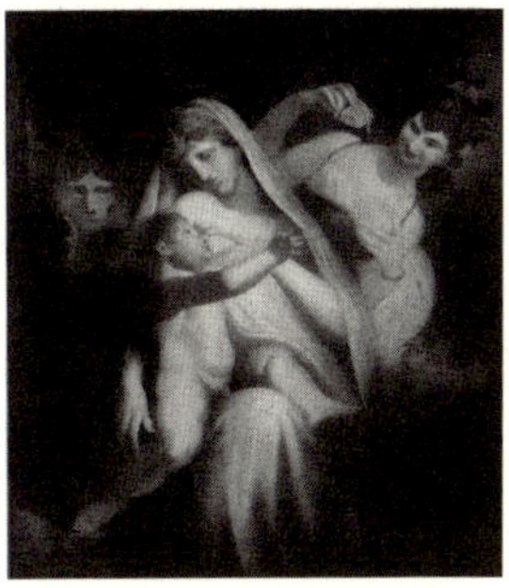

Cat. 64 *The Infant Shakespeare between Tragedy and Comedy*, 1805–06
oil on canvas, 103 × 91 cm (fragment)
London, King's College, DH/001 (Schiff 1202)

Stipple engraving by Moses Haughton after original painting, 1810 (Weinglass 288)

Fuseli was familiar with George Romney's painting *The Infant Shakespeare Attended by Nature and the Passions* (1791–92; Washington, D.C., Folger Shakespeare Library) from his work for John Boydell's Shakespeare Gallery: it formed the frontispiece of the printed version of the project. The type of image, developed by Joshua Reynolds in connection with the iconography of 'the childhood of great men', had already been adapted by Fuseli for a painting of Milton (cat. 59). In the present work he shows the boy Shakespeare being nurtured in the lap of Melpomene, the muse of tragedy. Behind her appears the joyful figure of Thalia, the muse of comedy, who likewise offers the infant her breast while inviting him to play with a butterfly. His outstretched arm signals his liking for comedy.

An engraving by Moses Haughton indicates that the painting is a fragment of a larger composition. The complete image included further characters from Shakespeare's plays on either side of the main group, beside the anxious face of Lady Constance (from *King John*) on the left and behind the figure of Caliban (from *The Tempest*), who gazes up at the boy from the lower right corner. These additional figures – Falstaff (from *Henry IV, Parts 1 and 2*, and *The Merry Wives of Windsor*), Queen Mab (from *Romeo and Juliet*), shown in the engraving in Shakespeare's cradle, Lady Macbeth and the Ghost from *Hamlet* – have either been painted over or were eliminated when the canvas was cut down.

The Jubilee, written and staged in London by the actor David Garrick to mark the anniversary of Shakespeare's birth in 1769, must have presented a similar picture. The pageant, originally planned for Stratford-upon-Avon, gathered together leading characters from the plays. In Stratford Garrick had unveiled a new statue of the playwright, and an engraving after a picture of that event painted by Robert Edge Pine may also have served as a source of inspiration for Fuseli's canvas. CB

References: Wind 1932. – Altick 1985, pp. 141–44.

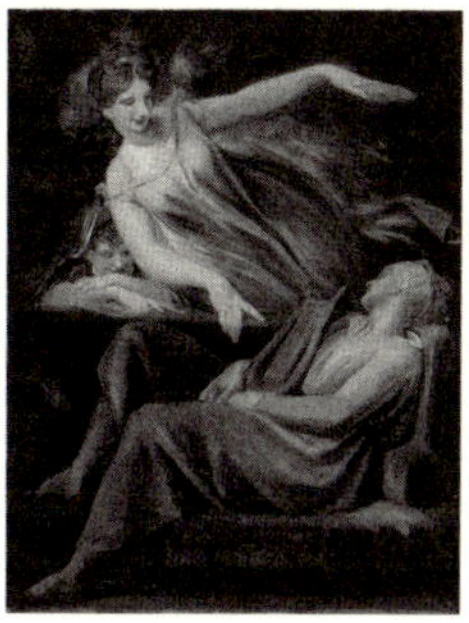

Cat. 65 *The Poet's Vision*, 1806–07
oil on canvas, 61 × 45 cm
Winterthur, Stiftung für Kunst, Kultur und Geschichte, 6581 (Schiff 1229)

Engraved by Abraham Raimbach, 1807 (Weinglass 267)

The small painting was produced in connection with the frontispiece to volume 1 of an edition of William Cowper's poems published by Joseph Johnson in 1807, seven years after the poet's death. Abraham Raimbach's engraving of it bears the title above the image and the first line of Cowper's *The Task* (see cats 27, 28) beneath it.

The poet sits asleep on a red sofa while a muse hovers over him, about to crown him with a laurel wreath and pluck the strings of the lyre lying in his right arm. Gert Schiff identifies the figure smiling mischievously behind the muse as a personification of fantasy. The letters 'MHNIN', decipherable in the open book on the left, form the ancient Greek word for 'wrath'. Schiff's idea that this is an allusion to the elements of social satire in Cowper's poem seems far-fetched. More plausible is David Weinglass's idea that the volume represents Homer's *Iliad*, which Cowper had translated and which begins with the word *mhnin*. A further reference to the *Iliad* appears in the shape of a mouse sitting in front of the book, on the arm of the sofa: Homer attaches the epithet 'smintheus' (mice-killer) to the god Apollo.

Fuseli here once more depicts sleep – or rather a dream or vision – as a creative act (see also cat. 62). The canvas belongs among his images extolling great poets (cats 59–63), which include pictures devoted to the life of Milton and an allegorical painting of Shakespeare (cat. 64). In the present work he paid homage to a poet with whom he shared a veneration for Milton and Homer. CB

References: Weinglass 1994, pp. 312–14. – Pop 2015, p. 163.

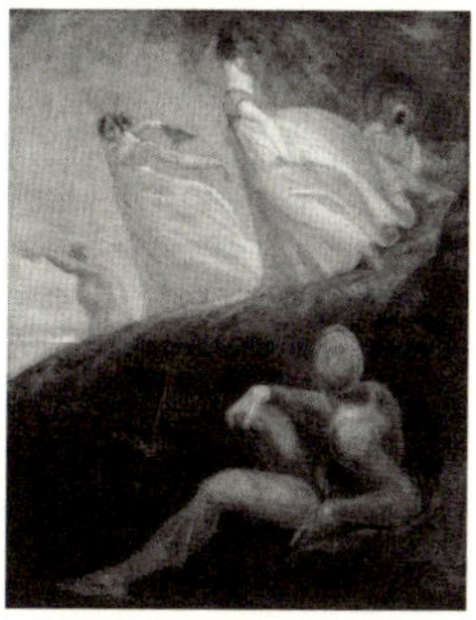

Cat. 66 *The Ladies of Hastings*, 1798–1800
oil on canvas, 111 × 86 cm
Zurich, Kunsthaus Zürich, Gift of Regine Schindler-Hürlimann, 2013, 1984/57 (Schiff 927)

No visual or verbal sources provide a clue to the painting's subject, and the title, documented as an inscription on a contemporary frame, only deepens the mystery. Lady Susan North, who once owned the picture, wrote the title 'Vision at Margate' on the stretcher. Fuseli visited Margate in 1792, yet Gert Schiff excludes that as a possible date for the canvas on the grounds that the costumes and hairstyles belong to a later time. The artist first stayed in Hastings in 1813, but Schiff, while noting that 'recourse to a previous period in his life' would not be unthinkable in the depiction of a vision, observes that the fashions shown in the painting would have been very old-fashioned indeed by then.

The subject was probably a free invention. A spade, lying beside the reclining young man, is more clearly visible in a preparatory drawing (Schiff 1081). Seeing it as an indication that the man is a treasure hunter, Schiff interprets the women in billowing garments as weather goddesses appearing to him amid a brewing storm. Popular belief had it that treasure is best discovered during thunderstorms. Citing an old German tradition of viewing artists as treasure hunters, Peter Tomory therefore suggests that the young man is the artist himself and the painting a personal allegory. CB

References: Tomory 1972, pp. 120–21. – Hamburg 1974, pp. 168–69. – Schiff 1973, vol. 1, p. 229.

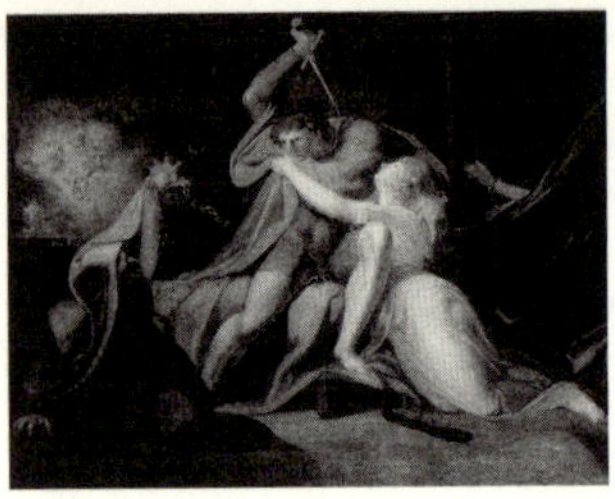

Cat. 67 *Percival Delivering Belisane from the Enchantment of Urma*, 1783
oil on canvas, 99.1 × 125.7 cm
London, Tate, presented by the Art Fund 1941, N05304
(Schiff 718)

Fuseli here indulged his penchant for dramatic and expressive actions by devising his own visual narrative, rather than taking his cue from a literary subject familiar to his public. When the painting was exhibited at the Royal Academy in 1783 he named his inspiration for the scene as the 'Provenzal Tales of Kyot'. That is the same fictitious source as that given by Wolfram von Eschenbach for his *Parzival*, a text that first appeared in printed form in 1477, and the artist asserted in a letter of 22 October 1791 to his friend the collector William Roscoe that the source was a saga of his own invention.

Percival raises his sword against the sorcerer Urma while putting his arm protectively around the frightened virgin Belisane. Fuseli fits his hero into a pyramidal composition with the shining weapon as its tip. Others are also under Urma's spell: the arm of a shackled woman hidden behind a curtain emerges on the right and, on the left, tormented faces of ghost-like beings introduce the motif of supernatural apparitions so beloved of the artist. A previous scene, showing the hero in an enchanted sleep, formed the subject of another painting, now lost, and of a mezzotint published in 1782 (Schiff 717). ER

References: Fuseli 1982, p. 74. – London 2006, p. 140.

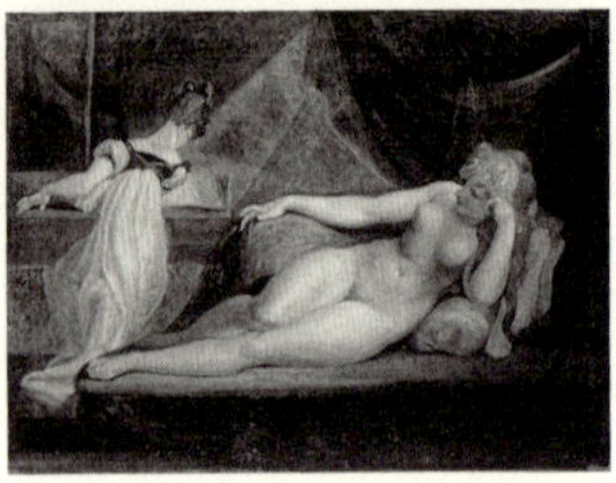

Cat. 68 *Reclining Female Nude with a Pianist*, 1799–1800
oil on canvas, 71.2 × 91 cm
Basle, Kunstmuseum Basel, G 1969.3 (Schiff 926)

The form and content of the painting, referred to by Gert Schiff as one of 'Fuseli's most attractive creations', are pictorial rather than literary in origin. They are based on Titian's *Venus with an Organist* of c. 1550, which exists in three versions (one in the Gemäldegalerie, Berlin, two in the Prado, Madrid), with a fourth, featuring a lutenist rather than an organist, in the Fitzwilliam Museum, Cambridge. A watercolour by Fuseli on the same subject, probably slightly later in date, is in the Kunsthaus Zürich (Schiff 1486).

Fuseli approaches his model freely. He replaces the background view of a landscape, for example, by an area of blue, rendering the setting indeterminate and more sheltered, intimate and otherworldly. The artist has also eliminated Venus' traditional companion, Cupid, and, with him, the mythological dimension of Titian's image. Again unlike Titian, Fuseli lends his reclining nude an almost commanding presence, along with a subtly erotic aura that Frederick Antal associates with late Mannerist ideals of beauty. Finally, the woman pianist substituting for Titain's male organist cannot be said to look over her shoulder, focusing instead on her playing and the music in front of her. Annegret Friedrich nevertheless sees a homoerotic impulse in this gender switch. On the back of the canvas Fuseli painted *Three Courtesans* (Schiff 925). Whether a connection exists between this image and that on the front, as Friedrich surmises, cannot be established beyond doubt. CB

References: Gradmann and Cetto 1944, pp. 74–75. – Antal 1956, pp. 101–02. – Friedrich 2004.

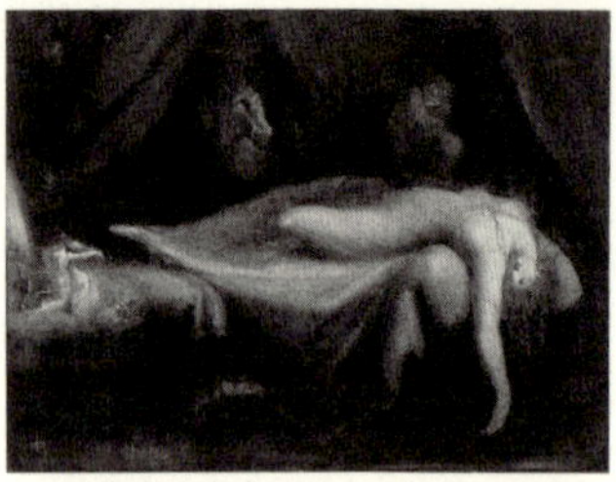

Cat. 69 *The Nightmare*, 1810
oil on canvas, 75 × 95 cm
Private collection, Switzerland
(Schiff 1502)

Engraved by W. Raddon, 1827
(Weinglass 67D)

Fuseli shot to fame overnight in London when he exhibited the first version of *The Nightmare* (The Detroit Institute of Arts, Schiff 757, see p. 25) at the Royal Academy in 1782. The painting shocked contemporaries because of its novelty and its obvious sexual undertones. It shows an incubus sitting on the stomach of a young woman lying on a bed in a pose suggestive of violation. The compelling power of the image lies in its immediacy. No single text can be adduced in support of viewing it in straightforward narrative terms as an illustration. A number of sources, ranging from a scientific didactic poem by Erasmus Darwin to the description of Queen Mab in Shakespeare's *Romeo and Juliet*, are superimposed in a pictorial invention doubtless motivated in part by the artist's desire to spark a public sensation. Petra Maisak explains how the title combines associations with the Old Norse *mara*, denoting a nocturnal demon, and the English *mare*, which Fuseli alludes to in concrete terms by including a mount for the incubus haunting the sleeping woman.

Four variations on *The Nightmare* are documented. The present version repeats on a slightly smaller scale the chief elements of the first – the white-robed woman lying on the bed with one arm dangling to the floor, the incubus and the horse staring between the bed curtains. Yet the mood of the image is more humorous than horrifying, as suggested not least by the distinctly morose look on the animal's face. In contrast to the previous variants, two small fairies appear on the dressing table on the left, a motif that links the painting to *Queen Mab* (cat. 46). ER

References: Basel 2014, pp. 108–09. – Frankfurt am Main 2017, p. 94. – Maisak 2017a, pp. 40–41.

Bibliography

Altick 1985
Richard Daniel Altick, *Painting from Books: Art and Literature in Britain, 1760–1900*, Columbus, OH, 1985.

Antal 1956
Frederick Antal, *Fuseli Studies*, London, 1956.

Basel 1988
Kunstmuseum Basel: 150 Gemälde, 12.–20. Jahrhundert, comp. Georg Schmidt, ed. Verein der Freunde des Kunstmuseums, coll. cat., 6th ed., Basel, 1988.

Basel 2014
For Your Eyes Only: Eine Privatsammlung zwischen Manierismus und Surrealismus, exh. cat., Basel, Kunstmuseum Basel; Ostfildern, 2014.

Bätschmann 1997
Oskar Bätschmann, *Ausstellungskünstler. Kult und Karriere im modernen Kunstsystem*, Cologne, 1997.

Bauer/Wertheimer 1983
Roger Bauer und Jürgen Wertheimer (eds), *Das Ende des Stegreifspiels. Die Geburt des Nationaltheaters. Ein Wendepunkt in der Geschichte des europäischen Dramas*, Munich, 1983.

Becker 2005
Christoph Becker, *Friar Puck und Fairy Shot*, exh. cat., Zürich, 2005, pp. 115–42.

Bender 1973
Wolfgang Bender, *Johann Jakob Bodmer und Johann Jakob Breitinger*, Stuttgart, 1973.

Bindman 2010
David Bindman, 'A Cosmopolitan View of the Bard: Fuseli and Shakespeare', in: *Drama and Desire. Art and Theatre from the French Revolution to the First World War*, ed. Guy Cogeval und Beatrice Avanzi, exh. cat., Marseille, Musée Cantini; Rovereto, Museo di Arte Moderna e Contemporanea die Trento e Rovereto; Toronto, Art Gallery of Ontario, Milan et al., 2010, pp. 80–85.

Blake 2011
Erin C. Blake, 'Shakespeare, Portraiture, Painting and Prints', in Mark Thornton Burnett, Adrian Street and Ramona Wray, eds, *The Edinburgh Companion to Shakespeare and the Arts*, Edinburgh, 2011, pp. 409–34.

Bodmer/Breitinger (1721–23) 1980
Johann Jakob Bodmer und Johann Jakob Breitinger, 'Die Discourse der Mahlern (1721–1723)', in: *Schriften zur Literatur*, ed. Volker Meid, Stuttgart 1980, pp. 3–19.

Bodmer/Breitinger (1727) 1980
Johann Jakob Bodmer, Johann Jakob Breitinger: Von dem Einfluß und Gebrauche Der Einbildungs-Krafft (1727). Bodmer/Breitinger: Schriften zur Literatur. ed. Volker Meid. Stuttgart 1980, pp. 28–35.

Bodmer/Breitinger (1740) 1980
Johann Jakob Bodmer und Johann Jakob Breitinger, 'Von dem Einfluß und Gebrauche Der Einbildungs-Krafft' (1727), in: *Schriften zur Literatur*, ed. Volker Meid, Stuttgart 1980, pp. 28–35.

Bown 2001
Nicola Bown, *Fairies in Nineteenth-Century Art and Literature*, Cambridge, 2001.

Bradley 1979/80
Laurel Bradley, 'Eighteenth-Century Paintings and Illustrations of Spenser's "Faerie Queene": A Study in Taste', in: *Marsyas*, 20, 1979/80, pp. 31–51.

Breitinger (1740) 1980
Johann Jakob Breitinger, 'Critische Dichtkunst' (1740), in: Johann Jakob Bodmer und Johann Jakob Breitinger, *Schriften zur Literatur*, ed. Volker Meid, Stuttgart, 1980, pp. 83–204.

Brooke 2017
Xanthe Brooke, 'Roscoe's Italian Paintings in the Walker Art Gallery, Liverpool', in: Stella Fletcher, ed., *Roscoe and Italy: The Reception of Italian Renaissance History and Culture in the Eighteenth and Nineteenth Centuries*, 2nd ed., London and New York, 2017, pp. 65–93.

Buckley 1986
B. A. Buckley, 'Sir Joshua Reynolds: The Ladies Annabel and Mary Jemima Yorke', in: *Bulletin of the Cleveland Museum of Art*, 73, 1986, 9, pp. 350–71.

Burton 1857
Robert Burton, *The Anatomy of Melancholy*, 8, exp. edition, Philadelphia, 1857.

Calè 2006
Luisa Calè, *Fuseli's Milton Gallery: 'turning readers into spectators'*, Oxford, 2006.

Carlyle 2001
Leslie Carlyle, *The Artist's Assistant: Oil Painting Instruction Manuals and Handbooks in Britain 1800–1900*, London, 2001.

Cowper 1980
William Cowper, *The Poems of William Cowper*, ed. John D. Baird and Charles Ryskamp, vol. 1, Oxford, 1980.

Cowper 1981
William Cowper, *The Letters and Prose Writings of William Cowper*, vol. 2: *Letters, 1782–1786*, ed. James King und Charles Ryskamp, Oxford, 1981.

Cowper 1995
William Cowper, *The Poems of William Cowper*, ed. John D. Baird and Charles Ryskamp, vol. 2, Oxford, 1995.

Cunningham 1859
Allan Cunningham, *The Lives of the Most Eminent British Painters and Sculptors*, vol. 2, New York, 1859.

Dallaway 1800
James Dallaway, *Anecdotes of the Arts in England*, London, 1800.

De la Motte Fouqué 1909
Friedrich de la Motte Fouqué, *Undine*, trans. W. L. Courtney, ill. Arthur Rackham, London and New York, 1909.

Debrunner 1996
Albert M. Debrunner, *Das güldene schwäbische Alter: Johann Jakob Bodmer und das Mittelalter als Vorbildzeit im 18. Jahrhundert*, Epistemata: Reihe Literaturwissenschaft, 170, Ph. D. thesis, Basel, Universität; Würzburg, 1996.

Dias 2013
Rosie Dias, *Exhibiting Englishness: John Boydell's Shakespeare Gallery and the Formation of a National Aesthetic*, New Haven, CT et al., 2013.

Dresden 1992
Gemäldegalerie Dresden: Alte Meister – Katalog der ausgestellten Werke, comp. Angelo Walther, coll. cat., Dresden, Gemäldegalerie; Leipzig, 1992.

Eichhorn 1965
Herbert Eichhorn, *Konrad Ernst Ackermann. Ein deutscher Theaterprinzipal. Ein Beitrag zur Theatergeschichte im deutschen Sprachraum*, Emsdetten, 1965.

Farington 1978–98
Joseph Farington, *The Diary of Joseph Farington*, ed. Kenneth Garlick und Angus Macintyre (vols 1–6) and Kathryn Cave (vols 7–16), New Haven, 1978–98.

Farington 1923
Joseph Farington, *The Farington Diary*, ed. James Greig, 2 vols, London, 1923.

Feingold 1982
Lawrence Feingold, 'Fuseli, Another Nightmare: "The Night-Hag Visiting Lapland Witches"', in: *Metropolitan Museum Journal*, 17, 1982, pp. 49–61.

Fenton 1816
Elijah Fenton, 'The Life of Mr. John Milton', in John Milton, *Paradise Lost: Poem in Twelve Books*, Romsey, 1816, pp. I–XVI.

Ferrara/London 2003
Shakespeare in Art, ed. Jane Martineau, exh. cat., Ferrara, Palazzo dei Diamanti; London, Dulwich Picture Gallery, London, 2003.

Frankfurt am Main 2011
Die Gemälde: '... denn was wäre die Welt ohne Kunst?', ed. Petra Maisak and Gerhard Kölsch, coll. cat., Frankfurt am Main, Frankfurter Goethe-Museum; Frankfurt am Main, 2011, pp. 62–65.

Frankfurt am Main 2017
Füsslis Nachtmahr: Traum und Wahnsinn, ed. Werner Busch and Petra Maisak, exh. cat., Frankfurt am Main, Frankfurter Goethe-Museum und Goethe-Haus: Petersberg, 2017.

Frayling 2006
Christopher Frayling, 'Fuseli's *The Nightmare*. Somewhere between the Sublime and the Ridiculous', exh. cat., London, 2006, pp. 9–20.

Friedman 1976
Winifred H. Friedman, *Boydell's Shakespeare Gallery*, New York and London, 1976.

Friedrich 2004
Annegret Friedrich, 'Variationen eines Alptraums: *The Nightmare* von Johann Heinrich Füssli', in: Volker Kapp et al., eds, *Subversive Romantik*, Berlin, 2004, pp. 118–23.

Frommert 1996
Christian Frommert, *Heros und Apokalypse. Zum Erhabenen in Werken Johann Heinrich Füsslis und William Blakes*, Aachen, 1996.

Fuseli 1789
[Henry Fuseli], 'A Catalogue of the Pictures in the Shakespeare Gallery', in: *The Analytical Review, or, History of Literature Domestic and Foreign*, 4, May–August 1789, pp. 107–112.

Fuseli 1792
[Henry Fuseli], 'Hickey's *History of Painting and Sculpture'*, in: *Analytical Review, or History of Literature*, 14, London, October 1792, pp. 161–65.

Fuseli 1982
Henry Fuseli, *The Collected English Letters of Henry Fuseli*, ed. David H. Weinglass, Millwood, NY, London and Nendeln, 1982.

Füssli 1942
Heinrich Füssli, *Briefe*, ed. Walter Muschg, Klosterberg et al., 1942.

Füssli 1944 (2012)
Johann Heinrich Füssli, *Aphorismen über die Kunst*, ed. and trans. by Eudo C. Mason, Basel, 2012.

Füssli 1973
Johann Heinrich Füssli, *Sämtliche Gedichte*, ed. Martin Bircher and Karl S. Guthke, Zürich, 1973.

Gärtner 2006
Kurt Gärtner, '*tihten/dichten*. Zur Geschichte einer Wortfamilie im älteren Deutsch', in: Gerd Dicke, Manfred Eikelmann und Burkhard Hasebrink, eds, in: *Im Wortfeld des Textes. Worthistorische Beiträge zu den Bezeichnungen von Rede und Schrift im Mittelalter*, Berlin und New York, 2006, pp. 67–81.

Gerkens 2009
Dorothee Gerkens, *Elfenbilder: Traum, Rausch und das Unbewusste – Die Erkundung des menschlichen Geistes in der Malerei des 18. und 19. Jahrhunderts*, Berlin, 2009.

Gibson/Esra 2014
Marion Gibson and Jo Ann Esra, *Shakespeare's Demonology: A Dictionary*, London et al., 2014.

Gonon 2007
Philipp Gonon, 'Erziehung zur Erhabenheit oder Erkundungen zu einer pädagogischen Trias: Bodmer, Füssli und Homer im Selbstbildnis des Wild Swiss', in: Claudia Crotti, Walter Herzog and Philipp Gonon, eds, *Pädagogik und Politik: Historische und aktuelle Perspektiven. Festschrift für Fritz Osterwalder*, Prisma, 6, Bern et al., 2007, pp. 13–30.

Gradmann/Cetto 1944
Erwin Gradmann and Anna Maria Cetto, *Schweizer Malerei und Zeichnung im 17. und 18. Jahrhundert*, Basel, 1944.

Guthke 1972/73
Karl S. Guthke, 'Johann Heinrich Füssli als Dichter', in: *Schweizer Monatshefte. Zeitschrift für Politik, Wirtschaft, Kultur*, 52, 1972/73, pp. 416–31.

Haenlein 1974
Charlotte Haenlein, 'Wiederentdeckung: Johann Heinrich Füssli, Ödipus verflucht seinen Sohn Polyneikes', in: *Du: Die Zeitschrift der Kultur*, 34, 9, 1974, p. 3.

Hall 1985
Carol Louise Hall, *Blake and Fuseli: A Study in the Transmission of Ideas*, New York and London, 1985.

Hamburg 1974
Johann Heinrich Füssli, 1741–1825, ed. Werner Hofmann, exh. cat., Hamburg, Hamburger Kunsthalle; Munich, 1974.

Harley 1982
Rosamond D. Harley, *Artists' Pigments c. 1600–1835* (2nd edition), UK, 1982.

Hattendorff 1997
Claudia Hattendorff. Die Milton-Galerie / 2. Füsslis Illustrationen für die Du Roveray-Ausgabe von *Paradise Lost* von 1802 und die Beziehung von Text und Bild bei Füssli', exh. cat., Stuttgart, 1997, pp. 82–99.

Häublein 2005
Renata Häublein, *Die Entdeckung Shakespeares auf der deutschen Bühne des 18. Jahrhunderts. Adaption und Wirkung der Vermittlung auf dem Theater* (*Theatron*, 46), Tübingen 2005.

Hausherr 1984
Reiner Haussherr, *Convenevolezza: Historische Angemessenheit in der Darstellung von Kostüm und Schauplatz seit der Spätantike bis ins 16. Jahrhundert*, Akademie der Wissenschaften und der Literatur in Mainz. Abhandlungen der Geistes- und Sozialwissenschaftlichen Klasse, 1984, 4, Wiesbaden, 1984.

Haydon 1853
Benjamin Robert Haydon, *The Life of Benjamin Robert Haydon*, ed. Tom Taylor, 3 vols, London, 1853.

Hayley 1835
William Hayley, *The Life and Letters of William Cowper*, London, 1835.

Heinz 2008
Jutta Heinz, ed., *Wieland-Handbuch. Leben – Werk – Wirkung*, Stuttgart, 2008.

Herder 1889
Johann Gottfried Herder, *Herders Briefe an Joh. Georg Hamann*, ed. Otto Hoffmann, Berlin, 1889.

Herrmann 1994
Sabine Herrmann, *Die natürliche Ursprache in der Kunst um 1800. Praxis und Theorie der Physiognomik bei Füssli und Lavater*, Frankfurt am Main, 1994.

Hochholdinger-Reiterer 2014
Beate Hochholdinger-Reiterer, *Kostümierung der Geschlechter. Schauspielkunst als Erfindung der Aufklärung* (*Das achtzehnte Jahrhundert. Supplementa*, 18), Göttingen, 2014.

Holm 2006
Christiane Holm, *Amor und Psyche: Die Erfindung eines Mythos in Kunst, Wissenschaft und Alltagskultur (1765–1840)*, Kunstwissenschaftliche Studien, 130, Munich and Berlin, 2006.

Honold 2009
Alexander Honold, 'Vom Rhein zur Donau und zurück. Die Bedeutung der deutschen Ströme in der Wiederentdeckung und Mythisierung des Nibelungenstoffs', in: Volker Gallé, ed., *Schätze der Erinnerung. Geschichte, Mythos und Literatur in der Überlieferung des Nibelungenliedes* (*Schriftenreihe der Nibelungengesellschaft Worms*, 6), Worms 2009, pp. 117–45.

Jaloux 1942
Edmond Jaloux, *Johann-Heinrich Füssli*, Montreux, 1942.

King 1983
James King, 'Fuseli as Revisor of Cowper's Homer', in: *Neophilologus. An International Journal of Modern and Mediaeval Language and Literature*, 67, 1983, pp. 468–79.

Kittler 1991
Friedrich A. Kittler, *Dichter. Mutter. Kind*, München, 1991.

Klemm 2005
Christian Klemm, 'Elementare Prinzipien der Kunst Füsslis oder die Ästhetik des Geniestreichs', exh. cat., Zürich, 2005, pp. 87–113.

Knowles 1831
John Knowles, *The Life and Writings of Henry Fuseli, Esq. M. A. R. A.*, 3 vols, London, 1831.

Lee 1967
Rensselaer W. Lee, *Ut Pictura Poesis. The Humanistic Theory of Painting*, New York, 1967.

Lentzsch 2005
Franziska Lentzsch, '*Londoner Theater: Drury Lane und Somerset House – Die Grossstadt als Bühne*', in: Zürich 2005, pp. 189–232.

Lessing 1985–2003
Gotthold Ephraim Lessing, *Werke und Briefe*, 12 vols, ed. Wilfried Barner et al., Frankfurt am Main, 1985–2003.

LIMC
Lexicon Iconographicum Mythologiae Classicae, 10 vols, Zürich et al., 1981–2009.

London 1973
Thorvaldsen: Drawings and Bozzetti – A Loan Exhibition from the Thorvaldsen Museum in Copenhagen under the Gracious Patronage of Her Majesty Queen Ingrid of Denmark, Heim Exhibition Catalogues, 18, London, Heim Gallery; London, 1973.

London 1975
Henry Fuseli, 1741–1825, comp. Gert Schiff, exh. cat., London, Tate Gallery, 1975.

London 2006
Gothic Nightmares: Fuseli, Blake and the Romantic Imagination, exh. cat., London, Tate Britain; London, 2006.

London 2018
http://collections.vam.ac.uk/item/O17298/the-fire-king-oil-painting-fuseli-henry/

Maisak 2017a
Petra Maisak, 'Füsslis Traumbilder im Wechselspiel von Kunst und Dichtung', in: Frankfurt am Main 2017, pp. 35–44.

Maisak 2017b
Petra Maisak, 'Johann Heinrich Füssli (1741–1825), *Tod der Cordelia', 1810–1820*, in: Frankfurt am Main 2017, pp. 125–26.

Mallet 1770
Paul Henri Mallet, *Northern Antiquities; or, a Description of the Manners, Customs, Religion and Laws of the Ancient Danes, and other Northern Nations, Including Those of Our Own Saxon Ancestors*, trans. Thomas Percy from the French, 2 vols, London, 1770.

Mamiano di Traversetolo 1997
Füssli pittore di Shakespeare: Pittura e teatro 1775–1825, exh. cat., Mamiano di Traversetolo, Parma, Fondazione Magnani Rocca; Milan, 1997.

Martus 2015
Steffen Martus, *Aufklärung. Das deutsche 18. Jahrhundert. Ein Epochenbild*, Berlin, 2015

Mason 1951
Eudo C. Mason, *The Mind of Henry Fuseli. Selections from His Writings with an Introductory Study*, London, 1951.

Mason 1964
Eudo C. Mason, 'Johann Heinrich Füssli und Shakespeare' in: *Shakespeare und die Schweiz*, Bern, 1964, pp. 83–103.

Matthews 2011
Susan Matthews, *Blake, Sexuality and Bourgeois Politeness* (*Cambridge Studies in Romanticism*, 88), Cambridge, 2011.

Merchant 1959
William Moelwyn Merchant, *Shakespeare and the Artist*, London, 1959.

Mielsch 1994
Hans-Ulrich Mielsch, *Die Schweizer Jahre deutscher Dichter. Christoph Martin Wieland, August Wilhelm von Schlegel, Johann Wolfgang von Goethe, Friedrich Hölderlin, Heinrich von Kleist*, Zürich, 1994.

Milton 1796
John Milton, *Paradise Lost. A poem, in twelve books. The author John Milton*, printed for J. and H. Richter, by T. Spilsbury and Son, London, 1796, p. 160.

Myrone 2006
Martin Myrone, 'Fuseli to Frankenstein. The Visual Arts in the Context of the Gothic', exh. cat., London, 2006, pp. 31–40.

Myrone 2001
Martin Myrone, 'The Sublime as Spectacle. The Transformation of Ideal Art at Somerset House', in: Solkin 2001, pp. 76–91.

New Haven 1979
The Fuseli Circle in Rome. Early Romantic Art of the 1770s, ed. Nancy L. Pressly, exh. cat., New Haven, Yale Center for British Art, 1979.

New Haven 1992
Handbook of the Collections: Yale University Art Gallery, ed. Elise K. Kenney, coll. cat., New Haven, CT, Yale University Art Gallery; New Haven, CT, 1992.

New Haven 2015
The Critique of Reason: Romantic Art 1760–1860, comp. Elisabeth Hodermarsky et al., exh. cat., New Haven, CT, Yale University Art Gallery, Yale Center for British Art; New Haven, CT, 2015.

New York 2007
Old Master Drawings, auction cat., New York, Sotheby's, 24 Jan. 2007; New York, 2007.

Newton 1757
Thomas Newton, 'The Life of Milton', in: John Milton, *Paradise Lost: A Poem in Twelve Books*, ed. Thomas Newton, London, 1757, pp. III–LXX.

Nicoll 1980
Allardyce Nicoll, *The Garrick Stage. Theatres and Audience in the Eighteenth Century*, Manchester, 1980.

Pointon 1970
Marcia R. Pointon, *Milton & English Art*, Manchester, 1970.

Pop 2015
Andrei Pop, *Antiquity, Theatre, and the Painting of Henry Fuseli*, Oxford, 2015.

Posse 1927
Hans Posse, 'Einige Neuerwerbungen', in: *Zeitschrift für Bildende Kunst*, 61, 1927, pp. 246–47.

Pressly 2008
William L. Pressly, *The Artist as Original Genius. Shakespeare's 'Fine Frenzy' in Late-Eighteenth-Century British Art*, Newark, 2008.

Rae/Young 2011
Caroline Rae and Christina Young, 'A Technical Study of Three Paintings on a Shakespearian Theme by Henry Fuseli RA', in: *The Picture Restorer*, 39, 2011, pp. 12–15.

Redgrave/Redgrave 1866
Richard Redgrave and Samuel Redgrave, *A Century of Painters of the English School*, London, 1866, vol. 2, p. 61, pp. 592–94.

Reynolds (1770) 1975
Joshua Reynolds, 'Discourse III' (1770), in: *Discourses on Art*, ed. Robert R. Wark, New Haven und London, 1975, pp. 41–53.

Richetti 2017
John J. Richetti, *A History of Eighteenth-Century British Literature*, Hoboken, 2017.
Ritchie/Sabor 2012
Fiona Ritchie und Peter Sabor, eds, *Shakespeare in the Eighteenth Century*, Cambridge, 2012.
Roselt 2014
Jens Roselt, 'David Garrick (1717–1779)', in: Peter W. Marx (ed.), *Hamlet-Handbuch. Stoffe, Aneignungen, Deutungen*, Stuttgart und Weimar, 2014, pp. 130–35.
Ruppert 1995
Rainer Ruppert, *Labor der Seele und der Emotionen. Funktionen des Theaters im 18. und frühen 19. Jahrhundert*, Berlin, 1995.
Schabert 2009
Ina Schabert, (ed.), *Shakespeare-Handbuch. Die Zeit – Der Mensch – Das Werk – Die Nachwelt*, Stuttgart, 5th ed., 2009.
Schaffhausen 1989
Katalog der Gemälde und Skulpturen, comp. Schweizerisches Institut für Kunstwissenschaft, coll. cat., Schaffhausen, Museum zu Allerheigen, 1989.
Schiff 1963
Gert Schiff, *Johann Heinrich Füsslis Milton-Galerie*, Schweizerisches Institut für Kunstwissenschaft: Schriften, 5, Zürich et al., 1963.
Schiff 1973
Gert Schiff, *Johann-Heinrich Füssli. 1741–1825*, 2 vols, Zürich und München, 1973.
Schiff 1974
Gert Schiff, 'Füssli, Luzifer und die Medusa', exh. cat., Hamburg, 1974, pp. 9–22.
Schiff 1977
Gert Schiff, *L'Opera Completa di Füssli, Milan,* 1977.
Scott 1801
Walter Scott, 'The Fire King', in *Tales of Wonder*, comp. and ed. M[atthew]. G[regory]. Lewis, 2 vols, London, 1801.
Shakespeare 1986
William Shakespeare, The Complete Works, ed. Stanley Wells & Gary Taylor, Clarendon Press, Oxford, 1986, pp. 1370.
Shakespeare 1995a
William Shakespeare, *Macbeth*, English and German, trans. Frank Günther, Munich, 1995.
Shakespeare 1995b
William Shakespeare, *Romeo and Juliet* (*Romeo und Julia*), in English and German, trans. Frank Günther, Munich, 1995.
Shakespeare 1995c
William Shakespeare, *A Midsummer Night's Dream* (*Ein Sommernachtstraum*) , in English and German, trans. Frank Günther, Munich, 1995.
Shakespeare 1995d
William Shakespeare, *Hamlet*, in English and German, trans. Frank Günther, Munich, 1995.
Shakespeare 1996
William Shakespeare, *The Tempest* (*Der Sturm*), in English and German, trans. Frank Günther, Munich, 1996.
Shakespeare 1997
William Shakespeare, *King Lear* (*König Lear*), in English and German, trans. Frank Günther, Munich, 1997.
Shakespeare 1999
King Henry V, in English and German, trans. Max Wechsler, Tübingen, 1999.
Shakespeare 2001
William Shakespeare, *Much Ado About Nothing* (*Viel Lärm um nichts*), in English and German, trans. Frank Günther, Munich, 2001.
Siegrist 1984
Christoph Siegrist, 'Poetik und Ästhetik von Gottsched bis Baumgarten', in: Rolf Grimminger (ed.), *Hansers Sozialgeschichte der deutschen Literatur vom 16. Jahrhundert bis zur Gegenwart*, vol. 3: *Deutsche Aufklärung bis zur Französischen Revolution 1680–1789*, 2nd edition, Munich, 1984, pp. 280–303.
Sillars 2006
Stuart Sillars, *Painting Shakespeare: The Artist as Critic, 1720–1820*, Cambridge, 2006.
Simon
Jacob Simon, *British Artists' Suppliers, 1650–1950,* http://www.npg.org.uk/research/programmes/directory-of-suppliers/b.php
Smith 2010
Gay Smith, *Lady Macbeth in America: From the Stage to the White House*, New York, 2010.
Solkin 2001
David H. Solkin, ed., *Art on the Line. The Royal Academy Exhibitions at Somerset House 1780–1836*, New Haven und London, 2001.
Solkin 2015
David H. Solkin, *Art in Britain. 1660–1815*, New Haven und London, 2015.
Spenser 1978
Edmund Spenser, *The Faerie Queene*, ed. by Thomas P. Roche, with assistance of C. Patrick O'Donnell, Harmondsworth, 1978.
Stähli 2009
Marlis Stähli, '"Wär es Ihnen gleichgültig ob Füßli in diesem Land oder in England den Platz fände"? Bodmer und Sulzer als Mentoren des Malers Johann Heinrich Füßli', in: Anett Lütteken und Barbara Mahlmann-Bauer (eds.), *Bodmer und Breitinger im Netzwerk der europäischen Aufklärung* (*Das achtzehnte Jahrhundert. Supplementa*, 16), Göttingen, 2009, pp. 695–734.
Stochholm 1964
Johanne M. Stochholm, *Garrick's Folly. The Shakespeare Jubilee of 1769 at Stratford and Drury Lane*, London und New York, 1964.
Sturz 1779
Helfrich Peter Sturz, *Briefe, im Jahre 1768 auf einer Reise im Gefolge des Königs von Dänemark geschrieben (1777–1779)*, Leipzig, 1779.
Stuttgart 1997
Johann Heinrich Füssli: Das verlorene Paradies, comp. Christoph Becker, exh. cat., Staatsgalerie Stuttgart; Ostfildern-Ruit, 1997.
Sulzer 1792–94
Johann Georg Sulzer, *Allgemeine Theorie der schönen Künste* (1771–1774), 4 vols, Leipzig, 1792.
Thomson 1793
James Thomson, *The Seasons*, ed. Percival Stockdale, London, 1793.
Todd 1809
Henry John Todd, *Some Account of the Life and Writings of John Milton*, London, 1809.
Tomory 1972
Peter Tomory, *The Life and Art of Henry Fuseli*, London, 1972.
Tomory 1974
Peter Tomory, *Heinrich Füssli. Leben und Werk*, Berlin, 1974.
Tomory 1986
Peter Tomory, 'Henry Fuseli's Milton when a Youth', in: *Art Bulletin of Victoria,* 27, 1986 (pages unnumbered).
Vogel 2001
Matthias Vogel, *Johann Heinrich Füssli. Darsteller der Leidenschaft* (*Zürcher Schriften zur Kunst-, Architektur- und Kulturgeschichte*, 2), Zürich, 2001.
Von Graberg 1970
Maria-Luise von Graberg, 'Die Nibelungen-Illustrationen von Johann Heinrich Füssli und Peter Cornelius', Ph. D. thesis, Berlin, Freie Universität, 1970.
Washington 1993
A Catalogue of Paintings in the Folger Shakespeare Library: 'As Imagination Bodies Forth', ed. William L. Pressly, coll. cat., Washington, D. C., Folger Shakespeare Library; New Haven and London, 1993.
Weinglass
See: Weinglass 1994.
Weinglass 1982
David H. Weinglass, ed., *The Collected English Letters of Henry Fuseli*, New York, 1982.
Weinglass 1994
David H. Weinglass, *Prints and Engraved Illustrations By and After Henry Fuseli: A Catalogue Raisonné*, Aldershot, 1994.
Weinglass 1998
David H. Weinglass, 'Johann Heinrich Füssli (1741–1825)', in: *Katalog der Erwerbungen 1992–1996*, ed. Sturzenegger-Stiftung Schaffhausen, coll. cat., Schaffhausen, Museum zu Allerheiligen; Schaffhausen 1998, pp. 44–48.
West 1991
Shearer West, *The Image of the Actor. Verbal and Visual Representation in*

the Age of Garrick and Kemble, New York 1991.

West 2012
Shearer West, 'Shakespeare and the Visual Arts', in: Fiona Ritchie and Peter Sabor, eds, *Shakespeare in the Eighteenth Century*, Cambridge, 2012, pp. 227–53.

Wieland 1805
Christoph Martin Wieland, *Oberon*, trans. William Sotheby, 2 vols, London 1805.

Wind 1932
Edgar Wind, 'Humanitätsidee und heroisiertes Porträt in der englischen Kultur des 18. Jahrhunderts', in: Fritz Saxl, ed., *England und die Antike*, Vorträge der Bibliothek Warburg, 9, Leipzig and Berlin, 1932, pp. 187–99.

Winterthur 2005
Kunstmuseum Winterthur: Katalog der Gemälde und Skulpturen, ed. Dieter Schwarz, coll. cat., Kunstmuseum Winterthur, vol. 1; Düsseldorf, 2005.

Wolf 2002
Norbert C. Wolf, '"Fruchtbarer Augenblick" – "prägnanter Moment": Zur medienspezifischen Funktion einer ästhetischen Kategorie in Aufklärung und Klassik (Lessing, Goethe)', in: Peter-André Alt et al. (eds.), *Prägnanter Moment. Studien zur deutschen Literatur der Aufklärung und Klassik. Festschrift für Hans-Jürgen Schings*, Würzburg, 2002, pps. 373–404.

Young 2002
Alan R. Young, *Hamlet and the Visual Arts, 1709–1900*, Newark and London, 2002.

Yuill 1985
William E. Yuill, '"A poem far too little known": Wieland's "Oberon" Revisited', in: *Publications of the English Goethe-Society. New Series* 54, Leeds 1985, pp. 123–47.

Zürich 1969
Johann Heinrich Füssli, 1741–1825: Gemälde und Zeichnungen, exh. cat., Zürich, Kunsthaus Zürich; Zürich 1969.

Zürich 2005
Füssli: The Wild Swiss, ed. Franziska Lentzsch, exh. cat., Kunsthaus Zürich; Zürich, 2005.

Zürich 2007a
Gesamtkatalog der Gemälde und Skulpturen, ed. Zürcher Kunstgesellschaft, coll. cat., Zürich, Kunsthaus Zürich; Ostfildern, 2007.

Zürich 2007b
Kunsthaus Zürich: Die Meisterwerke, coll. cat., ed. Zürcher Kunstgesellschaft, Zürich, Kunsthaus Zürich; Ostfildern, 2007.

Photo Credits

Aargauer Kunsthaus | Jörg Müller: p. 90
Maurice Aeschimann: p. 109 bottom
© 2018 Art Gallery of Ontario, Craig Boyko: p. 31
Dallas, The Nona and Richard Barrett 2013 Trust: p. 56
Francesco Bini @ Wikimedia Commons (cc-by-sa): p. 23
© Birmingham Museums Trust: p. 28
bpk | The Art Institute of Chicago | Art Resource, NY: p. 167
bpk | Hamburger Kunsthalle | Elke Walford: pp. 77, 153
bpk | The Metropolitan Museum of Art: p. 149
bpk | Staatsgalerie Stuttgart: pp. 146/147, 179
bpk | Staatliche Kunsthalle Karlsruhe | Wolfgang Pankoke: pp. 108, 178
bpk | Staatliche Kunstsammlungen Dresden | Elke Estel, Hans-Peter Klut: p. 127
Image courtesy Dallas Museum of Art: p. 150
Detroit Institute of Arts © Bridgeman Images: p. 28
Courtesy of Folger Shakespeare Library, Washington, D. C.: pp. 126 bottom, 134, 157, 186, 241
Freies Deutsches Hochstift, Frankfurter Goethe-Museum | David Hall: p. 131
Freies Deutsches Hochstift, Frankfurter Goethe-Museum | Ursula Edelmann: pp. 36, 107, 113
© Fylde Borough Council: pp. 128/129
Courtesy of the Garrick Club, London: pp. 68, 72
Serge Hasenböhler, Basel: pp. 132, 242
King's College London © David Tett Photography: p. 168
Kunst Museum Winterthur © Hans Humm, Zürich: pp. 124/125
Kunst Museum Winterthur © SIK-ISEA, Zürich (Lutz Hartmann): p. 154
Kunst Museum Winterthur, Stiftung Oskar Reinhart © SIK-ISEA, Zürich (Philipp Hitz): p. 40
Kunsthaus Zürich: pp. III, 1, 4, 18, 22, 31, 45, 55, 67, 80, 85, 91, 92, 99, 101, 111 top and bottom right, 121, 122, 123, 133, 170
Kunstmuseum Basel, Martin P. Bühler: pp. 78, 89, 93, 106, 137, 155, 165, 174, 175, 180
Kunstsammlung Kanton Zürich: p. 88
The Metropolitan Museum of Art: p. 75
Museum zu Allerheiligen, Schaffhausen: pp. 126 top, 136
Courtesy National Gallery of Art, Washington, D. C.: p. 46
Courtesy National Museums Liverpool: pp. 94/95
© National Portrait Gallery, London: p. 43
© National Trust Images, Derrick E. Witty: p. 26
Photo: Nationalmuseum [Stockholm]: p. 50
Reto Pedrini, Zürich: p. 151
Image by Public Catalogue Foundation (PFC): pp. 2, 164
© Caroline Rae, courtesy of King's College London: p. 192
© Caroline Rae, courtesy of Kunsthaus Zürich: p. 193
© Caroline Rae, courtesy of National Trust: pp. 190, 191
RMN – Grand Palais (Musée du Louvre) | Gérard Blot / Christian Jean: p. 54
RMN – Grand Palais (Musée du Louvre) | Hervé Lewandowski: pp. 58, 135
Royal Academy of Arts, London | John Hammond: pp. II, 98
Royal Collection Trust © Her Majesty Queen Elizabeth II 2018: p. 25
© RSC Theatre Collection, Public Catalogue Foundation (PCF): p. 130
Photo Scala, Florenz: p. 139
© Sir John Soane's Museum, London, p. 32
Garry Sommerfeld, National Gallery of Victoria, Melbourne: p. 163
© Andri Stadler, Luzern: pp. 110–11 bottom left, 177
Stiftung für Kunst, Kultur und Geschichte, Winterthur © SIK-ISEA, Zürich (Philipp Hitz): pp. 162, 169
Martin Stollenwerk, Zürich: pp. I, 109 top, 111 top left
© Tate, London: pp. 67, 148, 172/173
© The Trustees of the British Museum: pp. 24, 66
© Victoria and Albert Museum, London: pp. 3, 116/117, 243
Yale Center for British Art, Paul Mellon Collection: pp. 79, 87, 97, 114, 115, 137, 145
Yale University Art Gallery, p. 86

Front cover
Henry Fuseli, *Lady Macbeth Sleep-walking*, c. 1783 (Cat. 46)

Endpapers (front)
Endpapers (front) I: *Sherasmin and Huon Fleeing from Oberon*, 1804–05 (cat. 19)
Endpapers (front) II: *Thor Battering the Midgard Serpent*, 1790 (cat. 13)
Endpapers (front) III: *Titania Finds the Magic Ring on the Shore*, 1804–05 (Kat. 24)

Inside pages
p. 1: *Oberon Squeezing the Juice onto Titania's Eyelids*, 1793 (cat. 32)
p. 2: *The Return of Milton's First Wife, Mary Powell*, 1799/1800 (cat. 61)
p. 3: *The Fire King*, c. 1801–10 (cat. 31)
p. 4: *Amor and Psyche*, c. 1810 (cat. 1)
p. 18: *The Oath on the Rütli*, 1779–81 (cat. 15)
p. 36: *Mad Kate*, 1806/07 (cat. 27)
p. 58: *Lady Macbeth Sleepwalking*, c. 1783 (cat. 45)
p. 77: *The Creation of Eve*, 1793 (cat. 55)
p. 78: *The Nightmare*, 1810 (cat. 69)
p. 79: *Tekemessa and Eurysakes*, c. 1800–10 (cat. 3)
p. 80: *Theseus and Ariadne*, 1788 (cat. 9)
p. 177: *Amanda/Rezia Plunges into the Sea with Huon, while Fatme is Held Back*, 1804/05 (cat. 22)
p. 178: *Celadon and Amelia*, 1801 (cat. 18)
p. 179: *Satan Starting from the Touch of Ithuriel's Spear*, 1779 (cat. 50)
p. 180: *Romeo at Juliet's Bier*, 1809 (cat. 47)
p. 186: *Fairy Mab*, 1815–20 (cat. 58)

Endpapers (back)
Endpapers (back) I: *Macbeth Consulting the Vision of the Armed Head*, 1793/94 (cat. 44)
Endpapers (back) II: *The Three Witches Appearing to Macbeth and Banquo*, 1800–10 (cat. 42)
Endpapers (back) III: *The Fire King*, c. 1801–10 (cat. 31)

Colophon

Fuseli. Drama and Theatre

This catalogue has been published in conjunction with the exhibition at:
Kunstmuseum Basel
20 October 2018–10 February 2019

Exhibition

Director
Josef Helfenstein
Commercial Director
Wolfgang Giese
Curator
Eva Reifert
Assistant Curator
Claudia Blank
Intern
Lisa Gianotti
Head of Exhibitions and Collections
Charlotte Gutzwiller
Registrars
Corina Forrer, Monika Mascus
Conservation
Werner Müller, Sophie Eichner
Photography
Martin P. Bühler
Programme Curator
Daniel Kurjaković
Assistant to the Programme Curator
Tuula Rasmussen
Education
Hannah Horst, Christine Müller Stalder
Communication and Marketing
Karen N. Gerig, Vera Reinhard, Christian Selz
Exhibition Installation
Claude Bosch, Felix Böttiger, Stefano Schaller, Andreas Schweizer, Philipp Gueniat, Bruno Liechti

Catalogue

Prestel Verlag
A member of Verlagsgruppe Random House GmbH
Neumarkter Strasse 28
81673 Munich

Prestel Publishing Ltd.
14–17 Wells Street
London W1T 3PD

Prestel Publishing
900 Broadway, Suite 603
New York, NY 10003

A CIP catalogue record for this book is available from the British Library.

Kunstmuseum Basel. Edited by:
Eva Reifert with Claudia Blank

Authors of the catalogue texts: Claudia Blank (CB), Bodo Brinkmann (BB), Gabriel Dette (GD), Lisa Gianotti (LG) and Eva Reifert (ER).

Project Management Prestel
Anja Besserer
Copy editor
David Shallis, Weil der Stadt
Translation from the German
Marcel Behn, Berne (Hochholdinger-Reiterer essay, Luz text); Michael Foster, Munich (catalogue texts); Gerrit Jackson, Berlin (introduction, Reifert essay, back cover text); Katherine Whitebread, Berne (preface, biographical notes)
Design
Büro 146. Maike Hamacher, Valentin Hindermann, Madeleine Stahel, Zurich, with Fabienne Wyss
Overall production
Cilly Klotz
Reproduction
Helio Repro, München
Printing and Binding
Longo SPA | AG, Bozen
Typefaces
Rawlinson, Union
Paper
100 g/m² Salzer EOS Natural White and 170 g/m² MultiArt Gloss

FSC www.fsc.org
MIX
Paper from responsible sources
FSC® C023164

Verlagsgruppe Random House
FSC® N001967

Printed in Italy

ISBN 978-3-7913-5758-4
(English edition)
ISBN 978-3-7913-5757-7
(German edition)

www.prestel.com

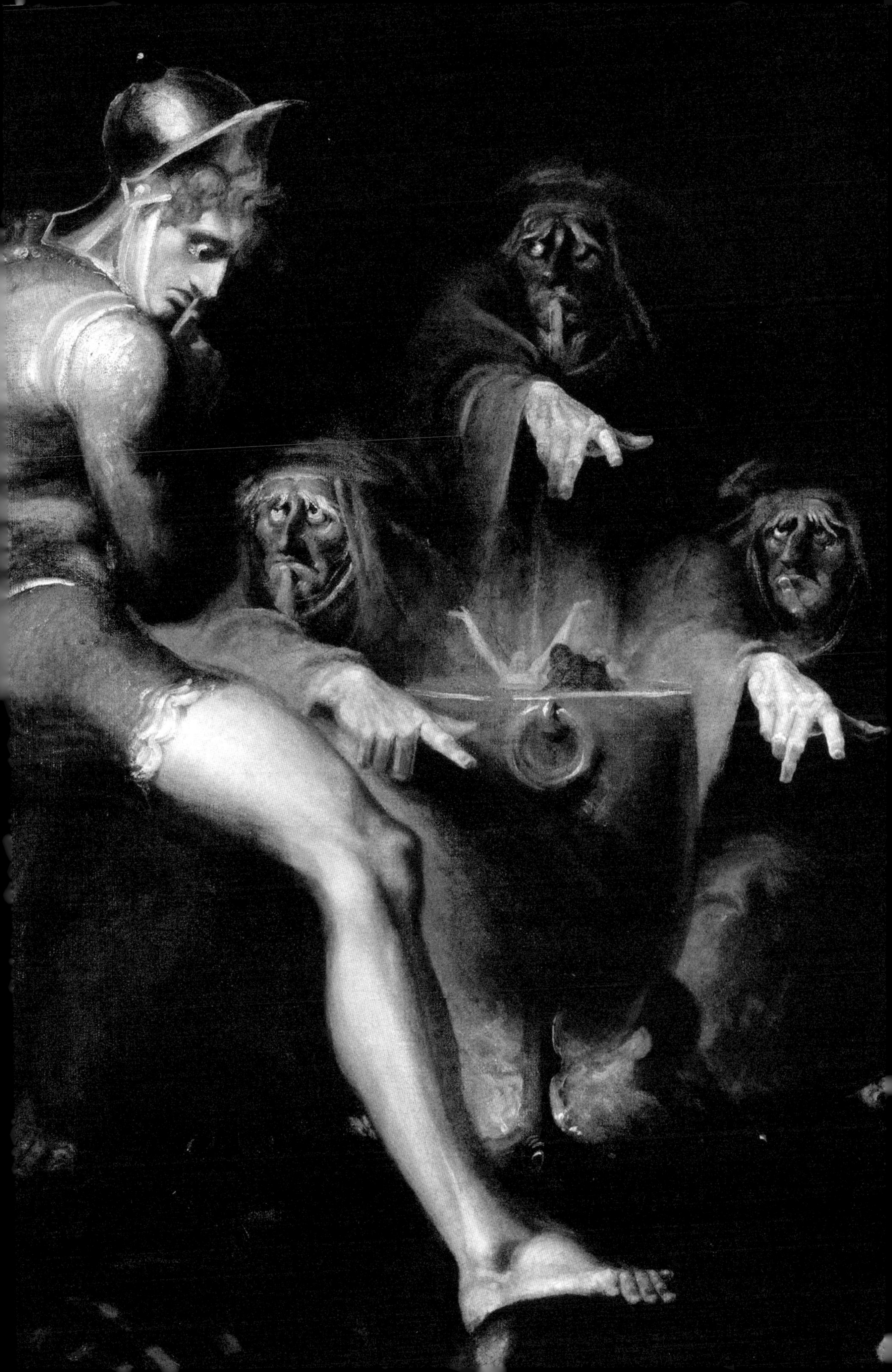

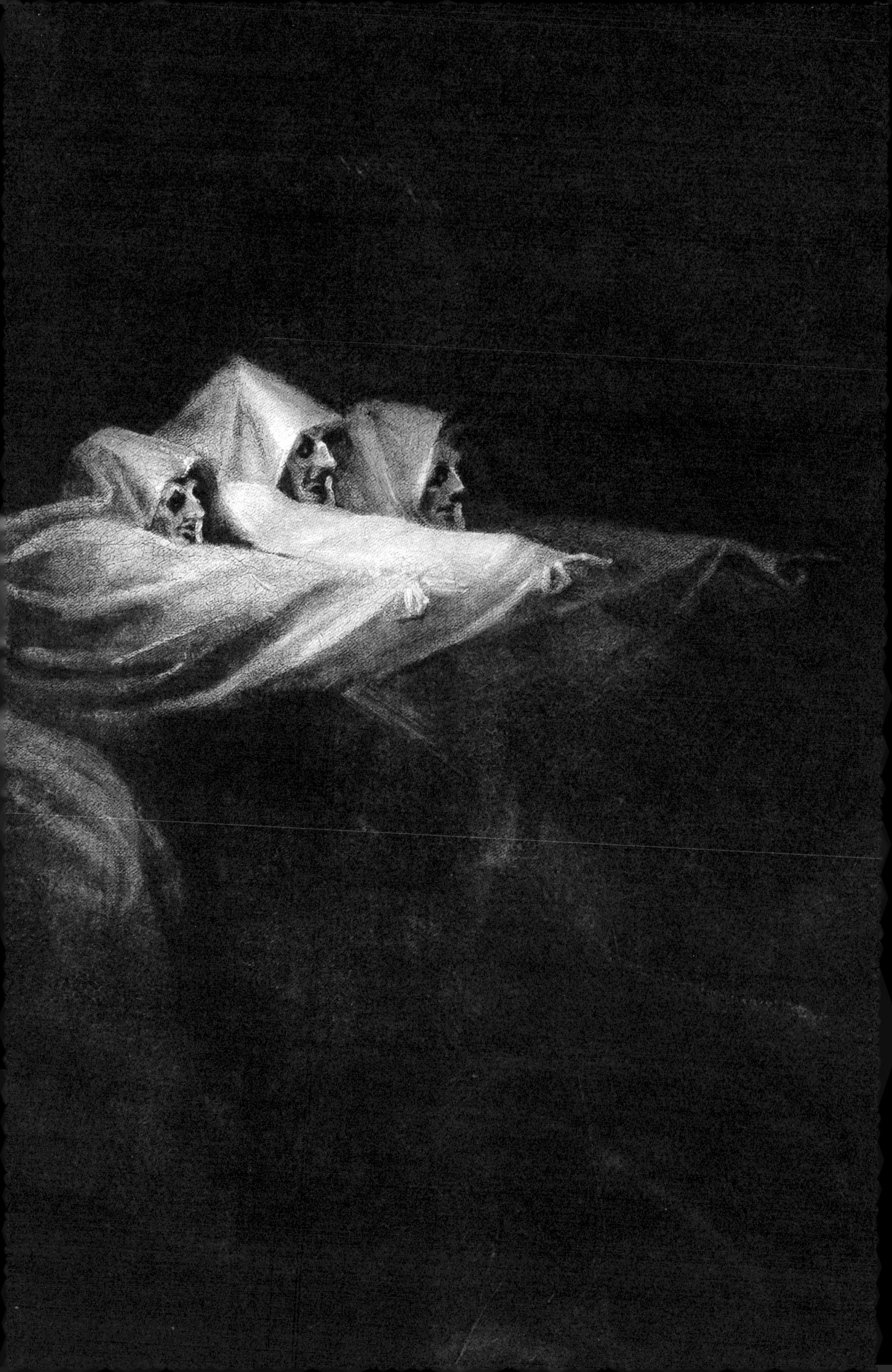